# A Servant of God

## Selected Writings of Fulton J. Sheen

# A Servant of God

## Selected Writings of Fulton J. Sheen

## Vol I

Preface to Religion
The Life of Christ
The Priest is Not His Own

Copyright © 2021 Mockingbird Press

All rights reserved. The original works are in the public domain to the best of publisher's knowledge. The publisher makes no claim to the original writings. However, the compilation, construction, cover design, trademarks, derivations, foreword, descriptions, added work, etc., of this edition are copyrighted and may not be reproduced, distributed, or transmitted in any form or by any means, including photocopying, recording, or other electronic or mechanical methods, without the prior written permission of the publisher, except in the case of brief quotations embodied in critical reviews and certain other non-commercial uses permitted by copyright law, or where content is specifically noted as being reproduced under a Creative Commons license.

Cover, "A Purple and White Tulip with Two Moths," by Dutch School, c. 1700
Cover Design by Jenny Frank, Copyright © 2021 Mockingbird Press, LLC
Foreword by Rachael Underhill, Copyright © 2021 Mockingbird Press, LLC
Interior Design by Maria Johnson

Publisher's Cataloging-In-Publication Data

Sheen, Fulton, author; Underhill, Rachael, foreword by
Servant of God : Selected Writings of Fulton J. Sheen : Volume I : Preface to Religion, The Life of Christ, and The Priest is not His Own / Fulton Sheen with Rachael Underhill

| | |
|---|---|
| Paperback | ISBN-13: 978-1-68493-000-5 |
| Hardback | ISBN-13: 978-1-68493-001-2 |
| Ebook | ISBN-13: 978-1-68493-002-9 |

1. Religion—Christianity—Catholic. 2. Philosophy & Religion—Religion & Beliefs—Christianity, I. Fulton Sheen. II. Rachael Underhill. III. Servant of God : Selected Writings of Fulton J. Sheen. IV. Title : Volume I : Preface to Religion, The Life of Christ, and The Priest is Not His Own.

REL010000 / QRM

Type Set in Schoolbook / **Franklin Gothic Demi**

Mockingbird Press, Augusta, GA
info@mockingbirdpress.com

# Contents

Foreword ............................................................................. 1

## Preface To Religion ........................................................... 3

    Chapter 1: Are You Happy ................................................... 5
    Chapter 2: What is God Like ............................................... 13
    Chapter 3: What Are You Like .............................................. 19
    Chapter 4: How You Got That Way ........................................ 25
    Chapter 5: Who Can Re-make You ........................................ 33
    Chapter 6: Is Religion Purely Individual ............................. 43
    Chapter 7: How You Are Remade .......................................... 53
    Chapter 8: Judgment ........................................................ 67
    Chapter 9: Purgatory ....................................................... 73
    Chapter 10: The Hell There Is ............................................ 79
    Chapter 11: Heaven ......................................................... 85
    Chapter 12: Faith ............................................................ 91
    Chapter 13: Hope ........................................................... 103
    Chapter 14: Charity ........................................................ 111

## The Life of Christ ........................................................... 117

    Part 1: Early Life Of Christ ............................................... 119
    Part 2: Temptations ........................................................ 129
    Part 3: The Beatitudes .................................................... 141
    Part 4: Public Life And Passion ........................................ 151
    Part 5: Death And Resurrection ........................................ 161

## The Priest Is Not His Own ................................................ 173

    Introduction ................................................................. 175
    Chapter 1: More Than a Priest .......................................... 177

Chapter 2: The Priest is Like Jacob's Ladder ......................... 193
Chapter 3: Spiritual Generation ........................................... 215
Chapter 4: The Holiness of the Priest .................................. 229
Chapter 5: The Holy Spirit and the Priest ........................... 245
Chapter 6: The Spirit and Conversion ................................. 257
Chapter 7: The Spirit of Poverty ......................................... 269
Chapter 8: The Spirit and Preaching and Praying ................. 279
Chapter 9: The Spirit and Counselling ................................ 293
Chapter 10: The Priest as Simon and Peter .......................... 305
Chapter 11: The Return to Divine Favor.............................. 323
Chapter 12: Melchisedech and Bread .................................. 335
Chapter 13: Judas and the First Crack in His Priesthood......... 347
Chapter 14: Why Make a Holy Hour? ................................... 361
Chapter 15: How to Make the Holy Hour ............................. 371
Chapter 16: The Eucharist and the Body of the Priest............ 383
Chapter 17: The Priest and His Mother................................ 395

# FOREWORD

THE selected works in this volume seek to educate both the new follower of Christ and the lifelong devotee on their place in the world and their responsibilities to God and their fellow human beings.

Archbishop Fulton J. Sheen (b. 1895–d. 1979) was a Catholic priest, writer, and presenter of several radio and television programs throughout the mid-20th century. This highly educated man of faith held two bachelor's degrees, a master's degree, a PhD in philosophy, and a Doctor of Sacred Theology. With such a thorough background in faith and philosophy, Archbishop Sheen was uniquely qualified to be an educator, both in universities and to the general public. To this end, he spent many years teaching at the Catholic University of America. He also shared what he'd learned with millions of Americans through his radio program, *The Catholic Hour*, and later through the popular television program, *Life is Worth Living*.

He also wrote prolifically, sharing many books and articles with the world. Three of those books are included in this volume. *Preface to Religion* could be considered an introductory work, intended to guide those on the periphery of religion closer to God. *The Life of Christ* explores the life, temptations, Passion, death, and resurrection of Christ—the founder of the Catholic Church. And *The Priest is Not His Own* is a unique work for the priest or seminary student to help them be a better shepherd and closer adherent to the example set by Jesus Christ.

While *Preface* and *Priest* were written for different audiences, when taken together with *The Life of Christ* they illustrate the depth of a life of faith. From the exploration of human nature and the causes of discontent to the responsibilities of the priest who has devoted his life to the Church, these three books help to illustrate the challenges of life as both a new convert and as a firm believer.

*Preface to Religion* is a work of both theology and philosophy. Beginning with the reasons for man's discontent, Archbishop Sheen proves to the reader that their unhappiness and lack of fulfillment is not because of what they have in life. For no material possession, no relationship, no achievement can ever give them the satisfaction they desire. The instinct to reach for something greater proves that there is more. For, as Archbishop Sheen writes, ". . . would there be in you a craving for unending life, perfect truth, and ecstatic love unless Perfect Life and Truth and Love existed?"

The work continues to explore the nature of God, the self, religion, judgment, and the afterlife. It discusses the role of the Catholic Church in the context of the greater world on both a micro and macro level.

*The Life of Christ* is one of Archbishop Sheen's best-loved works. Without a thorough understanding of Christ's life—His birth, actions on Earth, trials and tribulations, and ultimate sacrifice—one cannot hope to emulate His example and be a true child of God.

*The Priest is Not His Own* is written for the educated theologian who is well acquainted with scripture and the life and death of Christ. But it is unique in its call to priests to emulate Christ, not only His preaching and counselling, but his victimhood as well. Through a spirit of sacrifice in word and deed, the priest becomes closer to Christ and is better able to lead his flock. The work also includes guidance to help the priest better communicate with and instruct his followers.

When read together by the layperson, these three books can help the reader to understand the role of both the leader and the follower and get a clearer sense of where man and priest fit into God's greater plan. When read together by the priest, the books can help him to better communicate with those on the fringes of faith and guide them into the light of Christ.

# Preface To Religion

[1946]

# Chapter 1
## Are You Happy

If you saw hordes of peoples tramping the fields, with axes in their hands and pans strapped to their shoulders, you would conclude that those people had not found all the gold they wanted. If you saw armies of nurses and doctors riding ambulances, or carrying cots, you would conclude that health had not been found. When you see people crowding into theaters, charging cocktail bars, seeking new thrills in a spirit of restlessness, you would conclude that they have not yet found pleasure, otherwise they would not be looking for it.

The very fact that you can conceive of greater happiness than you possess now is a proof that you are not happy. If you were perfect, you would be happy. There is no doubt that at one time or another in your life you attained that which you believed would make you happy, but when you got what you wanted, were you happy?

Do you remember when you were a child, how ardently you looked forward to Christmas? How happy you thought you would be, with your fill of cakes, your hands glutted with toys, and your eyes dancing with the lights on the tree!

Christmas came, and after you had eaten your fill, blown out the last Christmas light, and played till your toys no longer amused, you climbed into your bed, and said in your own little heart of hearts, that somehow or other it did not quite come up to your expectations. Have you not lived that experience over a thousand times since?

You looked forward to the joys of travel, but when weary feet carried you home, you admitted that the two happiest days were the day you left home and the day you got back. Perhaps it was marriage you thought which would bring you perfect happiness. Even though it did bring a measure of happiness, you admit that you now take your companion's love for granted.

Why is it that all love songs are about "how happy we will be"; whoever hears a song about "how happy we are"? The beloved may be the sun of all delight, but sooner or later someone becomes disillusioned,

> *Observing how*
> *He had assigned to his dear mistress more*
> *Than it is proper to concede to mortals.*
>
> Lucretius

One is never thirsty at the border of the well.

Perhaps it was wealth you wanted. You got it, and now you are afraid of losing it. "A golden bit does not make the better horse." A man's happiness truly does not consist in the abundance of the things he possesses. Maybe it was a desire to be well-known that you craved. You did become well-known only to find that reputation is like a ball: as soon as it starts rolling, men begin to kick it around.

The fact is: you want to be perfectly happy, but you are not. Your life has been a series of disappointments, shocks and disillusionments. How have you reacted to your disappointments? Either you became cynical or else you became religious.

If you became cynical, you decided that, since life is a snare and a delusion, you ought to get as much fun out of it as possible. In such a case you clutched at every titillation and excitement your senses afforded, making your life an incessant quest of what you called a "good time." Or else you reacted to disappointments by becoming religious and saying: "If I want happiness, I must have been made for it. If I am disappointed here, it must be that I am seeking happiness in the wrong places. I must look for it somewhere else, namely, in God."

Here is a fallacy to the first reaction: believing that the purpose of life is to get as much pleasure out of it as possible. This would be the right attitude if you were just an animal. But you have a soul as well as a body. Hence, there are joys in life as well as pleasures.

There is a world of difference between the two. Pleasure is of the body; joy is of the mind and heart. Lobster Newburg gives pleasure to certain people, but not even the most avid lobster fans would ever say that it made them joyful. You can quickly become tired of pleasures, but you never tire of joys. A boy thinks he never could get too much ice cream, but he soon discovers there is just not enough boy.

A pleasure can be increased to a point where it ceases to be a pleasure; it may even begin to be a pain if carried beyond a certain point; for example, tickling or drinking. But the joy of a good conscience, or the joy of a First Communion, or the discovery of a truth, never turns to pain.

Man can become dizzy from the pleasure of drink, but no man ever became dizzy from the joy of prayer. A light can be so bright it will blind the eye, but no idea was ever so bright as to kill the mind; in fact, the stronger and clearer the idea, the greater its joy. If, therefore, you live for pleasure, you are missing the joys of life.

Furthermore, have you noticed that as your desire for pleasure increased, the satisfaction from the pleasure decreased? The dope-fiend, to have an equal pleasure, must increase his dose. Do you think a philosophy of life is right that is based on the law of diminishing returns? If you were made for pleasure, why should your capacity for pleasure diminish with the years instead of increasing?

Then, too, have you observed that your pleasures were always greater in anticipation than in realization? With the joys of the spirit, it is just the contrary. The cross, for example, is unattractive in prospect, but is sweet in possession. To Judas, the prospect of thirty pieces of silver was attractive, but he brought back his thirty pieces of silver. He got what he wanted and it filled him with disgust.

If your philosophy is always to have a good time, you have long ago discovered that you never really have a good time for you are always in pursuit of happiness without ever capturing it. By a twist of nature, you make your happiness consist in the quest for happiness, rather than in happiness itself, just as so many modern professors much prefer to seek the truth than to find it. You thus become most hungry where you are most satisfied.

When the first thrill of ownership is gone, and your possessions begin to cloy, your sole happiness now is in pursuit of more possessions. You turn the pages of life, but you never read the book.

That is why those who live only for pleasure become cynical in middle age. A cynic has been defined as one who knows the price of everything and the value of nothing. You blame things, rather than self. If you are married, you say: "If I had another husband, or another wife, I could be happy." Or you say, "If I had another job . . ." or, "If I visited another night-club . . .," or, "If I were in another city, I would be happy." In every instance, you make happiness extrinsic to yourself. No wonder you are never happy. You are chasing mirages until death overtakes you.

Never will you find the happiness you crave because your desires conflict. Despite the advertisements, "Eat and dance," you cannot do both at the same time. There is an exclusiveness about certain pleasures; they cannot be enjoyed in company with others. You cannot enjoy a good book and a football game at the same time. You cannot make a club sandwich of the pleasures of swimming and skiing. Even the best of pleasures, such as the enjoyment of good music or literature, cannot go on indefinitely for human resources are incapable of enjoying them without relaxation.

There may be no limit to our returning to them but there is a limit to our staying with them.

> *More! More! is the cry of a mistaken soul:*
> *Less than all cannot satisfy Man.*
>
> Blake

Your whole life is disordered and miserable if it is based on the principle of always having a good time, simply because happiness is a by-product, not a goal; it is the bridesmaid, not the bride; it flows from something else. You do not eat to be happy; you are happy because you eat. Hence, until you find out what your purpose in life is, you will never really have a good time.

Time is the greatest obstacle in the world to happiness, not only because it makes you take pleasures successively, but also because you are never really happy until you are unconscious of the passing of time! The more you look at the clock, the less happy you are! The more you enjoy yourself, the less conscious you are of the passing of time. You say, "Time passed like everything." Maybe, therefore, your happiness has something to do with the eternal! You can find happinesses in time, but what you want is Happiness that is timeless.

The other reaction to disappointment is much more reasonable. It begins by asking: "Why am I disappointed"; and then, "How can I avoid it?"

Why are you disappointed? Because of the tremendous disproportion between your desires and your realizations. Your soul has a certain infinity about it because it is spiritual; but your body and the world about you are material, limited, "cabined, cribbed, confined." You can imagine a mountain of gold, but you will never see one. You can imagine a castle of 100,000 rooms, one room studded with diamonds, another with emeralds, another with pearls, but you will never see such a castle.

In like manner, you look forward to some earthly pleasure, or position, or state of life, but, once you attain it, you begin to feel the tremendous disproportion between the ideal you imagined and the reality you possess. Disappointment follows. Every earthly ideal is lost by being possessed. The more material your ideal, the greater the disappointment; the more spiritual it is, the less the disillusionment. That is why those who dedicate themselves to spiritual interests, such as the pursuit of truth, never wake up in the morning with a dark brown taste in their mouths, or a feeling that they are run down at the heels.

Having discovered why you are disappointed, namely, because of the distance between an ideal conceived in the mind and its actualization in flesh or matter, you do not become a cynic. Rather, you take the next step of trying to avoid disappointments entirely. There is nothing abnormal about your wanting to live, not for two more years, but always; there is nothing queer about your desiring truth, not the truths of economics to the exclusion of history, but all truth; there is nothing inhuman about your craving for love, not until death do you part, not until satiety sets in or betrayal kills, but always.

Certainly you would never want this Perfect Life, Perfect Truth and Perfect Love unless it existed? The very fact that you enjoy their fractions means there must be a whole. You would never know their arc unless there were a circumference; you would never walk in their shadows unless there were light.

Would a duck have the instinct to swim if there were no water? Would a baby cry for nourishment if there were no such thing as food? Would there be an eye unless there were Beauty to see? Would there be ears unless there were harmonies to hear? And would there be in you a craving for unending life, perfect truth and ecstatic love unless Perfect Life and Truth and Love existed?

In other words, you were made for God. Nothing short of the Infinite satisfies you, and to ask you to be satisfied with less would be to destroy your nature. As great vessels, when launched, move uneasily on the shallow waters between the narrow banks of the rivers, so you are restless within the confines of space and time and at peace only on the sea of infinity.

Your mind, it would seem, should be satisfied to know one leaf, one tree, or one rose; but it never cries: "Enough." Your craving for love is never satisfied. All the poetry of love is a cry, a moan and a weeping. The more pure it is, the more it pleads; the more it is lifted above the earth, the more it laments. If a cry of joy and ravishment interrupts this plea, it is only for a moment, as it falls back again into the immensity of desires. You are right in filling the earth with the chant of your heart's great longing for you were made for love.

No earthly beauty satiates you either for, when beauty fades from your eyes, you revive it, more beautiful still in your imagination. Even when you go blind, your mind still presents its image before you, without fault, without limits, and without shadow. Where is that ideal beauty of which you dream? Is not all earthly loveliness the shadow of something infinitely greater? No wonder Virgil wished to burn his

Aeneid and Phidias cast his chisel into the fire. The closer they got to beauty, the more it seemed to fly from them, for ideal beauty is not in time but in the infinite.

Despite your every straining to find your ideals satisfied here below, the infinite torments you. The splendor of an evening sun as it sets like a "host in the golden monstrance of the west," the breath of a spring wind, the divine purity in the face of a Madonna, all fill you with a nostalgia, a yearning, for something more beautiful still.

With your feet on earth, you dream of heaven; creature of time, you despise it; flower of a day, you seek to eternalize yourself. Why do you want Life, Truth, Beauty, Goodness and Justice, unless you were made for them? Whence come they? Where is the source of light in the city street at noon? Not under autos, buses, nor the feet of trampling throngs because there light is mingled with darkness. If you are to find the source of light, you must go out to something that has no admixture of darkness or shadow, namely, to pure light, which is the sun.

In like manner, if you are to find the source of Life, Truth and Love, you must go out to a Life that is not mingled with its shadow, death, to a Truth not mingled with its shadow, error, and to a Love not mingled with its shadow, hate. You go out to something that is Pure Life, Pure Truth, Pure Love, and that is the definition of God. And the reason you have been disappointed is because you have not yet found Him!

> *If there had anywhere appeared in space*
> *Another place of refuge where to flee,*
> *Our hearts had taken refuge in that place,*
> *And not with Thee.*
> *For we against creation's bars had beat*
> *Like prisoned eagles, through great worlds had sought*
> *Though but a foot of ground to plant our feet,*
> *Where Thou wert not.*
> *And only when we found in earth and air,*
> *In heaven or hell, that such might nowhere be—*
> *That we could not flee from Thee anywhere,*
> *We fled to Thee.*
>
> — Richard Chenevix Trench

It is God for Whom we are looking. Your unhappiness is not due to your want of a fortune, or high position, or fame, or sufficient vitamins; it is due not to a want of something outside you, but to a want of something inside you. You cannot satisfy a soul with husks! If the sun could speak, it would say that it was happy when shining; if a pencil could speak, it would say that it was happy when writing—for these were the purposes for which they were made. You were made for perfect happiness. That is your purpose. No wonder everything short of God disappoints you.

But have you noticed that when you realize you were made for Perfect Happiness, how much less disappointing the pleasures of earth become? You cease expecting to get silk purses out of sows' ears. Once you realize that God is your end, you are not disappointed for you put no more hope in things than they can bear. You cease looking for first-rate joys where only tenth-rate pleasures are to be found.

You begin to see that friendship, the joys of marriage, the thrill of possession, the sunset and the evening star, masterpieces of art and music, the gold and silver of earth, the industries and the comforts of life, are all the gifts of God. He dropped them on the roadway of life, to remind you that if these are so beautiful, then what must be Beauty! He intended them to be bridges to cross over to Him. After enjoying the good things of life, you were to say: "If the spark of human love is so bright, then what must be the Flame!"

Unfortunately, many become so enamored of the gifts the great Giver of Life has dropped on the roadway of life that they build their cities around the gift, and forget the Giver; and when the gifts, out of loyalty to their Maker, fail to give them perfect happiness, they rebel against God and become cynical and disillusioned.

Change your entire point of view! Life is not a mockery. Disappointments are merely markers on the road of life, saying: "Perfect happiness is not here." Every disillusionment, every blasted earthly hope, every frustrated carnal desire, points to God. You can come to God not only by being good, but, if you only knew it, by a succession of disgusts.

The very sense of loss you feel in this world is in itself a proof that once you were possessed, and possessed by God. Though your passions may have been satisfied, you were never satisfied because while your passions can find satisfaction in this world, you cannot. If at the present time your vices have left you, do not think that you have left your vices.

Start with your own insufficiency and begin a search for perfection. Begin with your own emptiness and seek Him who can fill it. But you must be aware of your loneliness and want and disappointment before you can want Him to supply it. "Seek, and you shall find." (Matthew 7:7)

Look at your heart! It tells the story of why you were made. It is not perfect in shape and contour, like a Valentine heart. There seems to be a small piece missing out of the side of every human heart. That may be to symbolize a piece that was torn out of the Heart of Christ which embraced all humanity on the Cross.

I think the real meaning is, that when God made your human heart, He found it so good and so lovable that He kept a small sample of it in heaven. He sent the rest of it into this world to enjoy His gifts, and to use them as stepping stones back to Him, but to be ever mindful that you can never love anything in this world with your whole heart because you have not a whole heart with which to love. In order to love anyone with your whole heart, in order to be really peaceful, in order to be really whole-hearted, you must go back again to God to recover the piece He has been keeping for you from all eternity!

# Chapter 2
# What is God Like

How do you think of God? Do you think of God as Someone on a throne who sulks and pouts and becomes angry if you do not worship and glorify Him? Do you think you make Him unhappy when you do not give Him attention, or do you imagine Him as One who will punish you if you do not praise Him, or go to Church?

Or do you think of God as a benevolent grandfather who is indifferent to what you do; who likes to see you go places and do things, and does not care whether you have a good time by doing good things, or a good time by doing bad things, so long as you enjoy yourselves? Do you think of God in time of crisis as a vague ideal or a morale builder; and in time of peace as a silent partner whose name helps draw trade, but who has nothing to say about how the business shall be conducted?

If you hold either of these two views of God, you cannot understand either why you should worship God, or how God can be good if He does not let you do as you please.

Let us start with the first difficulty: Why worship God?

The word, "worship," is a contraction of "worth-ship." It is a manifestation of the worth in which we hold another person. Worship is a sign of value, the price we put on a service or a person. When you applaud an actor on the stage, or a returning hero, you are "worshipping" him in the sense of putting a value on his worth. Every time a man takes off his hat to a lady, he is "worshipping" her. Now to worship God means to acknowledge in some way His Power, His Goodness and His Truth.

If you do not worship God, you worship something, and nine times out of ten it will be yourself. If there is no God, then you are a god; and if you are a god and your own law and your own creator, then we ought never to be surprised that there are so many atheists.

The basic reason there is so little worship of God today is because man denies he is a creature. Without a sense of creatureliness, or dependence, there can be no worship. But we have not yet answered the question: "Why should you worship God?" You have a duty to worship God, not because He will pout and be imperfect and unhappy if you do not, but because if you do not worship God you will be imperfect and unhappy.

If you are a father, do you not like to receive a tiny little gift, such as a penny cigar, from your boy? Why do you value it more than a box of Corona Coronas from your insurance agent? If you are a mother, does not your heart find a greater joy in a handful of yellow dandelions from your little daughter, than in a bouquet of roses from a dinner guest?

Do these trivialities make you richer? Do you need them? Would you be imperfect without them? They are absolutely of no utility to you! Yet you love them. Why? Because your children are "worshipping" you; because they are acknowledging your love, your goodness, and by doing so they are perfecting themselves, that is, developing along the lines of love rather than hate, thankfulness rather than ingratitude, and service rather than disloyalty. They are becoming more perfect children and more happy children.

As you do not need dandelions and chocolate cigars, neither does God need your worship. If their giving is a sign of your worth in your children's eyes, then are not prayer, adoration and worship a sign of God's worth in our eyes? If you do not need your children's worship, why do you think God needs yours? If their worship is for their perfection, not yours, then may not your worship of Him be not for His perfection, but yours? Worship is your opportunity to express devotion, dependence and love, and in doing that you make yourself happy.

A lover does not give gifts to the beloved because she is poor; he gives gifts because she is already in his eyes possessed of all gifts. The more he loves, the poorer he thinks his gifts are. If he gave her a million, he would still think he had fallen short. If he gave everything, even that would not be enough. One of the reasons he takes price tags off his gifts is not because he is ashamed, but because he does not wish to establish a proportion between his gift and his love. His gifts do not make her more precious, but they make him less inadequate. By giving, he is no longer nothing. The gift is his perfection, not hers. Worship in like manner is our perfection, not God's.

To refuse to worship is to deny a dependence that makes us independent. Worship is to us what blooming is to a rose. To refuse worship would be like the rose cutting itself off from the sun and the earth, or a student denying that history can teach him anything. To withhold admiration from one who deserves it is a sign of a jealous, conceited mind.

Every man who refuses to worship God is a social climber who wants to sit on God's throne and thus become hateful and mean because of a terrible inferiority complex: he knows down deep in his creature-heart that he is not a Creator, and that he could not be godless if there were no God. The man who is irreligious is like the man who is ignorant: both are imperfect, one in relation to his intellect, the other in relation to his whole being and his happiness.

God made you to be happy. He made you for your happiness, not His. God would still be perfectly happy if you never existed. God has no need of your love for His sake for there is nothing in you, of and by yourself, which makes you lovable to God. Most of us are fortunate to have even a spark of affection from our fellow creatures.

God does not love us for the same reason that we love others. We love others because of need. Our need of love is born of our poverty. We find in someone else the supply of our lack. But God does not love us because He needs us. He loves us because He put some of His love in us. God does not love us because we are valuable; we are valuable because He loves us.

Everybody feels he is envalued by love. "Nobody loves me" is the equivalent of being valueless. It is love that confers value, and the more important the person who loves you, the more precious is your value. You are infinitely precious because you are loved by God, but God is not infinite because you love Him.

God thirsts for you, not because you are His waters of everlasting life, but because you are the thirst, He the waters. He needs you only because you need Him. Without Him you are imperfect; but without you He is Perfect. It is the echo that needs the Voice, and not the Voice that needs the echo. "In this is charity: not as though we had loved God, but because he hath first loved us, and sent his Son to be a propitiation for our sins." (1 John 4:10)

Never think that, in giving glory to God, you are giving something without which He would be unhappy, and with which He becomes a dissatisfied dictator. What is glory? Glory is clara notitia cum laude: a clear understanding of the worth of another which prompts us to praise. Glory is the result of knowledge and love.

When you are intensely interested in a subject, you love to talk about it: "Out of the abundance of the heart the mouth speaketh." Parents never tire of enthusing about their children. In like manner, a soul that knows God is his Creator, thinks about God, loves Him, and knows Him to be "so good" he cannot keep the good news to himself. The overflow of human love for Divine Love is what is meant by giving glory to God.

Notice how it differs from publicity. Publicity is artificial stimulation. It is the attribution of worth to those who have either not earned it, or who have no right to it. Film stars need publicity agents, as toothpaste needs advertising. But did you ever hear of an American hero who needed a press-agent? Praise is a by-product of his worth. The hero has worth.

Publicity tries to create worth; glory recognizes it. Publicity is the rouge on the anemic cheek of ordinariness; glory is the bloom which is the sign of health. The Church is not a publicity mill for drumming up trade for God's glory; it is a place where those who already know God's worth go to glorify Him.

Now we come to that other misunderstanding concerning God which interprets His Goodness as indifference to justice, and regards Him less as a loving father than as a doting grandfather who likes to see His children amuse themselves even when they are breaking things, including His commandments.

Too many assume that God is good only when He gives us what we want. We are like children who think our parents do not love us because they do not give us revolvers, or because they make us go to school. In order to understand goodness, we must make a distinction between getting what we want and getting what we need.

Is God good, when He fulfils our wishes, or when we fulfil His? Is God good only when He gives us what we want, or is He good when He gives us what we need even though we do not want it?

When the prodigal son left the father's house, he said: "Give me." He judged his father's goodness by the way the father satisfied his wants. But when he returned a much wiser young man, he merely asked for what he needed: a restoration of a father's love; and, hence, he said: "Make me."

The thief on the left judged the goodness of Our Lord by His power to take him down from his cross; that is what he wanted. The thief on the right judged the goodness of Our Lord by His power to take him into Paradise; that is what he needed.

The multitude in the desert were not given gold bricks or jewels or money by Our Divine Lord, and if they had been given, no one would have said that he had enough. But He gave them bread and the Scriptures added "each one had his fill." That was what they needed.

The Goodness of God means that God gives us what we need for our perfection, not what we want for our pleasure and sometimes for our destruction. As a sculptor, He sometimes applies the chisel to the marble of our imperfect selves and knocks off huge chunks of selfishness that His image may better stand revealed. Like a musician, whenever

He finds the strings too loose on the violin of our personality, He tightens them even though it hurts, that we may better reveal our hidden harmonies.

As the Supreme Lover of our soul, He does care how we act and think and speak. What father does not want to be proud of his son? If the father speaks with authority now and then to his son, it is not because he is a dictator, but because he wants him to be a worthy son. Not even progressive parents, who deny discipline and restraint, are indifferent to the progress of their children. So long as there is love, there is necessarily a desire for the perfecting of the beloved.

That is precisely the way God's goodness manifests itself to us. God really loves us and, because He loves us, He is not disinterested. He no more wants you to be unhappy than your own parents want you to be unhappy. God made you not for His happiness, but for yours, and to ask God to be satisfied with most of us as we really are, is to ask that God cease to love.

God could never let you suffer a pain, or a reversal, or experience sadness, if it could not in some way minister to your perfection. If He did not spare His own Son on the Cross for the redemption of the world, then you may be sure that He will sometimes not spare your wants, that you might be all you need to be: happy and perfect children of a loving Father. He may even permit us to wage wars as a result of our selfishness, that we may learn there is no peace except in Goodness and Truth.

Most of us creatures must be a horror to God though we delude ourselves that we are really good. We judge ourselves by our neighbor, and say we cannot be so bad because our neighbor is worse. A painting may look good under the candle light, but under the sun it is revealed as a daub. That is just what many of us must be in God's eyes. Think of the thousands you have met whom you could never love. You may even wonder how their mothers could love them, yet God loves them. He even loves them more than He loves us who look down on them with disdain and scorn.

If you want to know about God, there is only one way to do it: get down on your knees. You can make His acquaintance by investigation, but you can win His love only by loving. Arguments will tell you God exists for God's existence can be proved by reason; but only by surrender will you come to know Him intimately. A little study will tell you that your food must contain vitamins, as a little study will tell you that God created you. If, however, you do not eat vitamins once you know the necessity of vitamins, you may eventually lose your health. Likewise, if you do not love God Whom your reason proves to you, you may lose even your little knowledge.

That is one of the reasons why so many professors in secular institutions have no religion. They know about God, but they do not know God. It is one thing to know that your mother exists, it is another thing to love her. God, to these professors, is a theory, or a regulative principle of their thinking, or a final end to human aspirations, but no more. Because they do not love what they already know, because they do not act on their belief, even the little they have is taken away. They rattle the milk cans, but they never drink the milk.

As St. Paul told the Romans: "Because that, when they knew God, they have not glorified him as God, or given thanks; but became vain in their thoughts, and their foolish heart was darkened." (Romans 1:21) Most people who deny God do not do so because their reason tells them there is no God, for how could reason witness against Reason? Their denial is rather because of "wishful thinking." They feel they would be happier if there were no God, for then they could do as they pleased. Atheism, nine times out of ten, is born from the womb of a bad conscience. Disbelief is born of sin, not of reason.

Worship God because He is your perfection, more than knowledge is the perfection of the mind. Love Him because you cannot be happy without Love. Love Him quite apart from all you are, for you have the right to love Him in your heart, even though you do not always succeed in loving him in your acts. Think a little less about whether you deserve to be loved by Him; he loves you even though you are not deserving. It is His love alone that will make you deserving. Most of us are unhappy because we never give God a chance to love us; we are in love only with ourselves. Say to yourself over and over again regardless of what happens: "God loves me!" And then add: "And I will try to love Him!"

## Chapter 3

## What Are You Like

Thus far we have answered two questions: Why were you made, and what is God like? Now we ask: What are you like?

Take your heart into your hand as a kind of crucible and distil out of it its inmost nature. What do you find it to be? Are you not really a bundle of contradictions? Is there not a disparity between what you ought to do, and what you actually do? Do you not sometimes feel like a radio tuned into two separate stations, heaven and hell, getting neither but only static and confusion worse confounded.

The old Latin poet, Ovid, expressed your sentiments perfectly when he said: "I see and approve the better things of life, the worse things of life I follow." St. Paul, too, expressed your inmost moods when he cried out: "For the good which I will, I do not; but the evil which I will not, that I do." (Romans 7:19)

You feel dual, divided against yourself because you more often choose what you like, rather than what is best for you. When you do, you always feel the worse for it. Somehow, within you there is a "kink"; your human nature is disorganized. You feel frustrated; your realizations are anticlimaxes; they turn out to be the opposite of what you expected. You are a problem to yourself, not because of your more obvious faults but because the better part of you so often goes wrong.

Your soul is the battlefield of a great civil war. The law of your members is fighting against the law of your mind. Your name is "legion"—you have no unifying purpose in life; there is only a succession of choices, but there is no one over-all goal to which everything is subordinated. You are split into many worlds: eyes, ears, heart, body and soul. In your more honest moments, you cry out:

*"Within my earthly temple there's a crowd:*
*There's one of us that's humble, one that's proud;*
*There's one that's broken-hearted for his sins*
*And one who unrepentant sits and grins;*
*There's one who loves his neighbor as himself,*
*And one who cares for naught but fame and pelf.*
*From much corroding care I should be free,*
*If once I could determine which is me."*
From A Little Brother of the Rich, and Other
Verse, by Edward Sanford Martin (Charles Scribner & Sons)

How explain this basic contradiction within you? There are four false explanations: psychological, biological, intellectual and economic.

The psychological explanation attributes this tension within you to something peculiar to you as an individual, e.g., to your erotic impulses, for example, because you were frightened by a mouse in a dark closet during a thunderstorm while reading a book on sex.

This hardly fits the facts because you are not the only one who is "that way"; everyone is. There is nothing queer about you. But there is something queer about human nature. Do not think that basically you are any different from anyone else in the world, or that you have a monopoly on temptations, or that you alone find it hard to be good, or that you alone suffer remorse when you do evil. It is human nature that is queer, not you.

The second false explanation is biological: the kink in your nature is due to a fall in evolution.

No! Evil is not due to the animal in you. Your human nature is very different from the animal's. There is a great discontinuity between a beast and a human. As Chesterton says: "You never have to dig very deep to find the record of a man drawing a picture of a monkey, but no one has yet dug deep enough to find the record of a monkey drawing the picture of a man."

An animal cannot sin because it cannot rebel against its nature. He must follow it. We can sin because we merely ought to follow our nature. When you see a monkey acting crazily in a zoo, throwing banana peels at spectators, you never say: "Don't be a nut." When, however, you see a man acting unreasonably, you say: "Don't be a monkey." Man alone can be sub-human; he can sink to the level of a beast.

The peculiar thing about a man is that, though he may cease to act like a man, he never loses the imprint of human dignity. The Divine image with which he was stamped is never destroyed; it is merely defaced. Such is the essence of a man's tragedy. We did not evolve from the beast; we devolved to the beast. We did not rise from the animal; we fell to the animal. That is why unless the soul is saved, nothing is saved. Evil in us presupposes what it defaces. As we never can be godless without God, so we never could be inhuman without being human.

The third false explanation attributes the evil in you to want of education: you are perverse because you are ignorant. Once you are educated, you will be good.

No! You do not have this inner contradiction because you lack knowledge, for the educated are not all saints and the ignorant are not all devils. Enlightenment does not necessarily make you better. Never before in the history of the world was there so much education, and never before was there so little coming to the knowledge of the truth. Much of modern education is merely a rationalization of evil. It makes clever devils instead of stupid devils. The world is not in a muddle because of stupidity of the intellect, but because of perversity of the will. We know enough: it is our choices that are wrong.

Finally, the socialist explanation of this tension, namely, people are wicked because they are poor, does not explain the facts.

Never before were living standards so high. All the rich are not virtuous, and all the poor are not wicked. If you had all the money in the world, you would still have that bias toward evil. If poverty were the cause of evil, why is it that juvenile delinquency increases in periods of prosperity and why does religion prosper in the vow of poverty? If poverty were the cause of evil, then riches should be the source of virtue. If that is so, why are not the wealthy the paragons of virtue?

The world has not just made a few mistakes in bookkeeping which any expert accountant or economic advisor can correct; rather the world has swindled the treasury of faith and morality. It is not the world's arithmetic that is incorrect; it is our morals that are bad.

Since this perversion of human nature is universal, i.e., since it affects human nature (not just your personality exclusively or mine), it must be due to something that happened to human nature itself at its very origin.

Secondly, since it is not animal in its origin, but has all the earmarks of being deliberate and the result of a free choice, it must not be a part of God's original work, but must have come into being through some tendency to evil.

Thirdly, since evil is not merely a by-product of bad environment, but is endemic in the heart of man, it cannot be explained except on the basis of a universal fracture of some great moral law to which we are all bound.

Some acts of disobedience can be remedied. If I throw a stone through a window, I can put in a new one. But there are other kinds of disobedience that are irremediable, e.g., drinking poison. Since evil is so universal in the world, it must be due to a disobedience of the second kind and thus affects us in our inmost nature.

Either God created you the way you are now, or else you are fallen from the state in which God created you. The facts support the second view: the present tension and inner contradiction within us is due to some fault subsequent to the creation of human nature.

An unequivocal voice in your moral consciousness tells you that your acts of wrong-doing are abnormal facts in your nature. They ought not to be. There is something wrong inside of us. God made us one way; we made ourselves, in virtue of our freedom, another way. He wrote the drama; we changed the plot. You are not an animal that failed to evolve into a human; you are a human who rebelled against the Divine. If we are a riddle to ourselves, the blame is not to be put on God, but on us.

The fact remains: whatever you are, you are not what you ought to be. You are not a depraved criminal, but you are weak; you are not a mass of irremediable corruption for you bear within yourself the image of God. You are like a man fallen into a well. You know you ought not to be there, and you know you cannot get out by yourself.

This is a roundabout way of saying that you need religion, but not a religion with pious platitudes. You want healing; you want deliverance; you want liberation. You know very well that there are a thousand things in your life that you thank God have not been found out by man. You want to get rid of these things. You do not want a religion to cheer you up on the roadway of life regardless of which road you take.

Analyzing your soul you discover it to be like an auto that has run out of gas, and you are not quite sure of the right road. Hence, you need someone not only to give you some fuel for your tank, but also someone to point out your destination. If you have no religion at the present time, it may be because you rightly reacted against those bland assumptions that a few moral exhortations on Sunday will transform the world into the Kingdom of God.

You want a religion which starts not with how good you are, but with how confused you are. Conscious as you are of being in bondage to perverted desires, selfishness and churlish refusal to help someone in need, you cry out with the poet: "O my offense is rank; it smells to heaven."

You can love the lovable without being religious; you can respect those who respect you without religion; you can pay debts without being religious, but you cannot love those who hate you without being religious; you cannot atone for your guilty conscience without being religious.

Possibly the only reason in the world for loving the unlovely, for forgiving the enemy, is that God is love; and since as such He loves me who am so little deserving of His love, I also ought to love those who hate me.

The more you look into your soul, the more you see how false are the two modern views of human nature. Here in the liberal Western World, we hear it said that we are naturally good and progressive, and thanks to evolution, science and inevitable progress are destined to become better and better until we become a kind of God. Two world wars in twenty-one years and the fear of a third knocks that false optimism into a cocked hat.

On the other hand, you know that the totalitarian views of Nazism, Fascism and Communism are wrong for they assume that the individual man is intrinsically corrupt and can be made tame, docile and obedient only by the force of the collectivity enshrined in a dictator.

The true view of human nature lies somewhere in between the two extremes of absolute goodness and total depravity—between optimism and pessimism. Your experience tells you that you are not a saint, but it also tells you that you are not a devil. The tendency toward evil in you is not an irremediable flaw, but an accident that can be controlled.

You feel like a fish on top of the Empire State Building; somehow or other you are outside of your environment. You cannot swim back, but Someone could put you back. You feel yourself like a clock that has all the works and still will not "go," because you have broken a mainspring. You cannot supply the new mainspring. The original Watchmaker could supply it, by sending His Son. Somewhere along the line, human nature became bungled, and it has all the earmarks of having been upset by a false use of freedom.

When you buy an automobile, the manufacturer gives you a set of instructions. He tells you the pressure to which you ought to inflate your tires, the kind of oil you ought to use in the crankcase, and the proper fuel to put in the gas tank. He has nothing against you by giving you these instructions as God had nothing against you in giving you commandments. The manufacturer wants to be helpful; he is anxious that you get the maximum utility out of the car. And God is anxious that we get the maximum happiness out of life. Such is the purpose of His commandments.

We are free. We can do as we please. We ought to use gas in the tank, but if we please, we can put in Chanel Number 5. Now there is no doubt that it is nicer for our nostrils to fill the tank with perfume rather than with gasoline, but the car simply will not run on Smell Number 5. In like manner, we were made to run on the fuel of God's love and commandments, and we simply will not run on anything else. We just bog down.

## Chapter 4

## How You Got That Way

Anyone who gives freedom to another assumes great risks. A father yearns for the day when his son will be independent and able to make his own decisions. That hope is not without its fears, for freedom can be used either for weal or for woe. In a certain sense, even God took a great risk when He made man free, for the very freedom to become a son of the Eternal Father implied the possibility of becoming a rebel.

If God did not want to run that risk, there was still one other possibility. He might have made us like stones and stars, ice and hail, that is, good with the same necessity that the sun rises in the east and sets in the west.

What glory would there be in a universe wherein each element was a glittering diamond, but without the capacity to love? Is it any impeachment of God that He did not care to reign over an empire of stones? If He has deliberately set His children beyond mechanical control so that they could freely break allegiance with Him, was it not in order that there might be meaning and glory in the allegiance, when they freely choose to give it?

Instead, therefore, of making a universe wherein everything must act according to its nature, God made one in which one creature, man, merely ought to act according to his nature. In other words, He made a moral universe, a vale of character-making wherein there would be virtue, heroism, saintliness and patriotism, none of which is possible without freedom.

Fire is never praised for being hot, nor ice for being cold. But men are praised for being virtuous because they could have been vicious; they are lauded for being heroes, because they could have been cowards; and they are extolled for being saints, because they might have been devils.

God chose, therefore, to make a moral universe, but morality is impossible without freedom. Since He made us free to choose what is right, we are also free to choose the wrong. The eternal idea of Justice makes no one just, as the eternal Right makes no one righteous. In a certain sense, we are less free than freeable; we make ourselves free. Before truth and righteousness and freedom can become mature, they require training, discipline, trial and the awful possibility of failing.

The whole purpose of education is to train minds to use freedom rightly. We do not take away the freedom of youths because they might abuse it. Hence, parents offer encouragement, reward or praise to their children in order that they might choose the good rather than the evil. This is what God did at the very beginning. He did not give man the frightening responsibilities of freedom without at the same time offering him incentives to choose right rather than wrong. God would not force His happiness on anyone.

Regardless of how much you liked ice cream, you would not enjoy it if it were forced down your throat. You will never be happy doing things unless you want to do them. Hence, God gave man a free will with which he might choose the things he liked, rather than be forced to accept them. As freedom implies choice, so choice implies alternatives. So, God gave our first parents a choice.

In almost so many words, God said to Adam and Eve at the very beginning of history: As an inducement to choose what is best, I shall give you certain gifts. If you use your freedom in the direction of what is best for you, that is, for your perfection, I shall give you permanently the supernatural gift of sharing in My Nature, that is, being a child of God and an heir of Heaven. To this I add permanently some lesser gifts:—You will never die, your passions will never rebel against your reason, and your mind will be exempt from error.

What is rather difficult to understand here is the word, "supernatural." What does it mean? A stone is not constructed so as to grow. That is simply not its nature. But if the stone in your back yard suddenly began to bloom, you would say it was possessed of supernatural powers. It would have done something which belongs neither to the powers, the capacities or the nature of a stone.

In like manner, if the flower in your garden suddenly began to walk, and to get out of the rain, and to smell other flowers and to move to Florida or California in the winter, it would be something supernatural for the flower, something above and beyond its capacity and its needs. In order to do these things some new element and power would have to be added to the flower. So, too, if your dog began to quote Shakespeare, to read the market quotations and to build its own doghouse, you would conclude that something above and beyond the nature of a dog had been given to it.

By nature, that is, naturally, we are just creatures of God's handiwork. We are not, in the strict sense of the term, God's children; we are only God's creatures. But suppose God gave us the power of being His children, of sharing His Divine Life, of being a member of the family of the Trinity, of being heirs of Heaven—that would be supernatural for us, more supernatural than for a marble to sprout, and for a rose to write music, or for a dog to speak.

To preserve these gifts for themselves and posterity, one condition was imposed by God, on Adam and Eve, and it was very easy. They merely had to love God Who is their perfection. We must not think that this condition was equivalent to saying to a child: "If you eat a woolly worm, I will give you a dollar," because a woolly worm is not the perfection of a child. Rather, it was like saying to the child: "If you drink milk and eat vitamins, you will be healthy." As obeying the laws of health is the perfection of the child, so, too, obeying the will of God is our perfection.

We said that the one condition imposed was that they love God. But how could man prove his love of God? How do you know anyone loves you? Because he tells you? Not necessarily. Love proves itself less by words than by an act of choice. Human love is not love unless it is free; it is only because of the possibility of saying "No" that there is so much charm in the "Yes." Love is not only an affirmation; it is also a negation. When a husband chooses a wife, he not only accepts one woman, he excludes as wife every other woman in the world.

Our first parents were told that they must prove their love of God by an act of choice. This implied an alternative. The alternative was a choice between a fruit and a garden, the part and the whole. God said they could eat of all the fruits in the garden of Paradise, save the tree of knowledge of good and evil.

Was there anything unreasonable about the trial? Is not life filled with abundant instances of receiving rewards on the condition of love? Imagine a wealthy man going away for the summer and telling the chauffeur and his wife that they may live in his house, eat his food, drink his wine, use his cars and ride his horses, but on one condition: that they must not eat the artificial apple he has on the dining room table. The owner well knows the artificial apple will give them indigestion. He does not tell them that. They ought to trust him in the light of all he has done for them.

If the wife persuades her husband to eat the apple, she would not be a lady; and if he eats it, he would not be a gentleman. By doing the one thing forbidden, they would lose all the good things provided, and have indigestion besides and they even lose the opportunity of passing these things on to their children.

To make light of the apple in the story of the Fall is to miss the point that it was the test of love. Not to shake hands with a passerby on the street is of no importance, but not to shake hands as a sign of contempt, is very serious. Eating of the forbidden fruit was a sign of contempt: the symbol of rebellion. God was imposing a single limit to the sovereignty of man, reminding him that if he did the one thing forbidden, he would imperil all the things provided. Like Pandora, he opened the forbidden box, and lost all his treasures.

Test your own experience. Have you ever fallen? Have you ever sinned? Did anyone ever tempt you to sin against your true self? You never fell unless there was something that attracted, a whispered doubt, a lie, and a dream of being happier than you are now. Such elements were in the Fall.

Our parents were enjoying the happiness of a sinless Eden, but very soon Satan, a fallen angel, appeared and, pointing to the forbidden fruit, which was delightful to behold, whispered the first doubt. It began with a Why? "Why hath God commanded you that you should not eat of every tree of paradise?" (Genesis 3:1) The evil behind the question was: God cannot be good if He does not let you do whatever you please. Freedom to Satan is the absence of law and restraint. Satan, the father of lies, was saying: "God is a Fascist."

Have you ever noticed that the first suggestion to do wrong always comes from someone who makes you think that you would be more free if you defied your conscience? Perhaps, if you are Catholic, they said to you: "Why does the Church forbid you to marry again? After all, you have your own life to lead." The approach is diabolically clever for it makes it appear that the Church is making you do something you do not want to do and therefore, is in some way restraining your liberty Freedom, if we only knew it, is within the law of our nature, not outside it. Try to be so progressive and broadminded as to draw a giraffe with a short neck, or a triangle with four sides, and see where you end!

The second stage is ridicule. When Eve answered that it was God's command that they eat not the forbidden fruit, for, if they did, they would die, Satan ridiculed the idea: "You shall not die the death." (Genesis 3:4) God has lied to you! It is stupid to believe such silly superstitions!

If you resisted for a time the temptation to divorce and to marry again, by saying: "No! The Church is Divine"; or, "I will lose my soul if I break the law of Christ: 'What God hath joined together let no man put asunder,'" did not your tempter deny it laughingly: "Don't be silly! The

Church is only one of the sects, and you are certainly not so medieval as to believe in a soul or a hell, are you?"

Finally, comes the third stage, the false promise. Eve dwelt jealously on the one thing forbidden, rather than the many things permitted, until quite unconsciously she was ready to be convinced that Satan's promise was true. "For God doth know that in what day soever you shall eat thereof, your eyes shall be opened: and you shall be as gods, knowing good and evil." (Genesis 3:5)

The good she knows begins to pall, the evil she does not know begins to allure. More and more she turns from conscience to the imagined sweetness of the forbidden fruit. There would be but one result. They who would pluck flowers from the edge of the precipice must be prepared to fall. Swiftly the crisis is upon her, as all crises are. She eats the forbidden fruit, gives it to Adam to eat; and then the floodgates are open, and the tiny ripple of an illicit thought, ever deepening, swelling, broadening, burst into an irresistible floodwater which engulfed the world.

Have you not done exactly the same thing when you fell? When you spoke of Christ's command forbidding marriage while the other spouse was living, did not your tempter respond with a false promise: "You will be very happy with your new spouse. He is just suited for you." Or, "You always needed a husband who could appreciate you." Then came the divorce, the remarriage, and the fall.

What is unnatural or unhistorical about the Fall of man? You, too, once had your Eden of happy ignorance, of innocence unassailed. Then your self-will asserted itself; your "mine" against the Divine "Thine." You interpreted freedom as the right to rebel, or the right to do whatever you pleased, instead of the right to do whatever you ought. You were like errant steam engines, which refused to follow the tracks laid down by the Master Engineer; like golfers who refused to keep their heads down when they swung, and then blamed the clubs or the Caddy Master when they "dubbed" the shot; like copies which conspired to be originals; like adjectives which insisted on being nouns; like rays which claimed to be the sun; like printed pages which insisted you were the author.

All of these things you can do, because you are free, but when you do them, you really destroy your freedom. You are bulbs that can glow only when in contact with the Divine energy; without it you are not really yourselves. Like campaign orators you talked so much about freedom, you lost your voices, and lost your freedom of speech.

When children, we were told not to play with matches. We disobeyed and burned ourselves. Then, when mother called, we hid. We had no fear of our mother before we burned ourselves, but only after. Adam had no fear of God before he disobeyed. After his sin, God seemed to be an angry God. To the bad conscience God appears always the God of wrath. The boy who broke the vase by throwing a ball at it, says to his mother: "Now Mummy, don't get mad." Anger is not in the mother; anger is in the boy's projection to his mother of his own sense of justice. Anger is not in God; anger is in our disordered selves.

You say: "Science has proven the Fall false!" Science has nothing to say about it, because science knows man only as he is now. Because we can no longer find the core of the fruit Adam ate does not prove that Adam never ate the fruit, any more than, because we cannot find the remains of Christ, it follows that Christ never died.

"How could physical science prove that man was not depraved? You do not cut open a man to find his sins. You do not boil him until he gives forth the unmistakable green fumes of depravity. How could physical science find any traces of a moral fall? What traces does the scientist expect to find? Does he expect to find a fossil Eve with a fossil apple inside her? Did he suppose that the ages would have spared for him a complete skeleton of Adam attached to a slightly faded fig leaf?" (G. K. Chesterton, All Things Considered)

You say it is a myth? It is not! It is an historically revealed fact, verified by subsequent history and by the individual experience of man. It is an undeniable fact. You know very well that you ought to be an other-regarding creature, that your true happiness is in living for others. You also know that you are selfish, and you are weak and self-centered and sometimes hateful to yourself and others. God did not make you that way! You in some way have departed from your own true nature.

But you ask: "Well! Granted that Adam sinned! What have I to do with Adam? Why should I be punished because of him?" When Congress declared war on December 8th, 1941, you declared war without any explicit declaration on your part. What Congress did, we did. Adam is the head of the human race. "By one man, sin entered the world." (Romans 5:12)

You say: "It was very unjust of God to deprive me of friendship with Him, and of these other gifts, simply because Adam sinned." There would have been injustice if God deprived you of your due, but you are no more entitled to be a child of God than a razor has a right to bloom, or a rose has the right to bark, or a dog has the right to quote Dante. What Adam lost was gifts, not a heritage.

On Christmas Day, when you distribute gifts to your friends, would I have a right to say to you: "Why do you not give me a gift?" You would answer: "I am not doing you an injustice, because I owe you nothing. I am not obliged to give these gifts to my friends. If I had not given them gifts, I would not have deprived them of anything I owed them." So, neither did God owe us anything beyond our nature as a creature of His handiwork.

The loss of the supernatural gift of being a child of God weakened man's will and darkened his intellect without corrupting his nature. Here we must repeat; man's nature was not made intrinsically corrupt and wicked by the Fall. This is a caricature of the true doctrine. Original sin does not mean that we are born in the state we are in, but that through Adam we have fallen into that state.

The Fall disorganized man's normal human faculties, making him just as he is now, with a bias toward evil, with a will reluctant to do good, with a tendency to rationalize evil. But he is still man—not a depraved man, totally corrupt as those who ridicule the doctrine of the Fall say, but still a person able to recover part of his former gifts. The disorder in us is like getting dirt in our eyes: we still have the eye as an organ of sight, but it now sees through tears. The result is we are disorganized; suffering and pain came into life; women had to bear their children in sorrow, while men had to earn their bread by the sweat of their brow.

Because man turned his will against God, so now his passions and desires are turned against man's will. It is this fallen nature which all men have inherited. That is why the sin is called "original"—it came at the origin of human nature, and represents a loss, the soul registering a much greater loss than the body; for Man still has natural life, but he has not supernatural life.

It is right here that Christianity begins. In all other religions you have to be good to come to God. In Christianity you do not. Christianity is realistic: it begins with the fact that, whatever you are, you are not what you ought to be. If everything in the world were perfectly good, we would still need God, for all goodness comes from God. But the presence of evil makes that need more imperative. Christianity begins with the recognition that there is something in your life and in the world that ought not to be, that need not be, and that could be otherwise were it not for evil choices.

Of course you can say: "I need no religion," for, after all, if you are your own god, then you need no other God to worship; if you are perfect, then no one can make you better; if you know all Truth, then not even God can teach you anything; if you have never done wrong, then you need no Saviour. It is wonderful in these days of atheism to find so many people who believe in God—I mean themselves.

If you are dissatisfied, unhappy, feel oppressed, are weighed down with interior conflicts, neuroses, depressions and complexes; if guilt weighs upon your soul; if you need the truth other than your own, and love other than that of creatures, and life beyond that of horses; if you know you are not intrinsically corrupt; if you know that death is not a negligible incident in your life, that you cannot ignore suffering in yourself and others; if you know you cannot eliminate a self-rebuking conscience as a social illusion; if you know that you could be better than you are; if you feel like the master painting of a great artist that has become somewhat defaced and stained; if you know that you are too good for the rubbish heap, you are not too spoiled to hang in the Metropolitan Gallery; if you know that you cannot restore yourself to your pristine beauty; if you know that no one could restore you better than the Divine Artist who made you, then you have already taken the first step toward peace. Herein is the essence of Christianity. The Divine Artist did come to restore the original! That is the Good News!

## Chapter 5

## Who Can Re-make You

You remember the nursery rhyme:

*"Humpty Dumpty sat on the wall
Humpty Dumpty had a great fall
And all the Kings horses and all the Kings men
Could never put Humpty Dumpty together again."*

That rhyme expresses the condition of human nature as a result of original sin; since the Fall man is like a broken egg. The tragedy of his condition is that neither he nor any natural agent can put him together again, and that he must do so if he is to fulfil the highest purpose of his existence. Man can remedy political and economic disorders, but not the disorder inside himself. He needs God for that; hence the greater necessity of religion.

It has been said that we are like a clock whose mainspring is broken. We have the "works," but we do not "go." In order to put the clock in condition, two conditions must be fulfilled: 1) The mainspring must be supplied from the outside; 2) It must be placed inside the clock. Man cannot redeem himself any more than the clock can fix itself. If man is ever to be redeemed, redemption must 1) Come from without; 2) Be done from within.

Why must salvation come from without? Because human nature has contracted a bigger debt than it can pay. In sinning against God, we piled up an infinite debt, and we have not enough balance of merits in our finite bank to meet the burden. We barely have enough merits to meet current expenses. We cannot depend upon time to blot out our sins for time, instead of blotting out sin, adds to it.

Salvation must come from without because you can destroy life, but you cannot create it; you can blind your vision but you cannot restore it; you can destroy your communion with God by sin, but you cannot restore it. Press a rose petal between your fingers, and you can never restore its tint. Lift a dew drop from a leaf, and you can never replace it. Evil, in like manner, is too deep-seated in the world to be righted by a little kindness or reason and tolerance.

You might just as well tell a man suffering from gout that all he needed was to play six sets of tennis; or to tell a consumptive that all he needed was to take up long-distance running; or to tell a criminal that all he needed to make him a good citizen was to own a fine home with plumbing and electric lights. Man has radically failed. He cannot save himself.

The humanist experiment was tried for centuries. We need something more than the human to make us rightly human. Some intervention outside of the time-scheme is absolutely necessary. Some evil things we do are remediable, like a mistake in writing; we can turn over a new leaf. Other mistakes are irremediable, like losing a leg through carelessness.

Between God and us there is a wall. The avalanche of sin has fallen and blocked the roadway of life. He can get along without us, for He is absolutely independent of all outside causes; but we cannot get along without Him, for we are totally dependent on Him for all that we are.

Since we offended the dignity of the infinite God, our sin, in a way, becomes infinite, and calls for an infinite reparation. But we are finite. The sin does not work out. Hence, salvation must come from without. Our human will is too weak to conquer its own evil, as the sick may be too weak to cure their own disability. We need a teacher for our minds, a physician for our bodies, and a Redeemer for our souls—a Redeemer from without: outside humanity with its weakness, its sin and its rebellion.

Though salvation must come from without, it, nevertheless, must be done from within humanity. It would do no good to the clock to put the mainspring inside a radio. If salvation were not done inside humanity, it would have no relation to humanity. If I were arrested for speeding, you could not go into the court room and say: "Try me instead of the guilty one." The judge would say: "What have you to do with the case?" There is no substitution in the eyes of the law. Furthermore, any man who is conscious of his guilt does not want to be "let off." It is not human pride, but a deep sense of justice and responsibility and dignity which makes us rebel against a pardon without satisfaction.

In our relations with our fellowmen, we often say: "I want to make up for it," and there is no reason why in our relation to God we should act any differently. Surely God could condone our guilt with a single act of His will. Forgiveness without reparation by the sinner would be immoral only if it meant ignoring guilt and sin, or if it belittled the eternal necessity of righteousness. But it seems proper that offending human nature be involved in its own redemption.

In order, therefore, that fallen man may be recreated, two conditions are essential:

1) Man must be redeemed from without because no man can lift himself by his own boot straps. Since the offense of man's sin is infinite, and the reparation he can make is only finite, it follows that it can be adequately done only by God.

2) Man must be redeemed from within, otherwise the redemption would have no relation to man, and man wants to play the role in his own regeneration. He does not merely want his sins forgiven; he wants to atone for them. To answer that need God becomes man. Posit these two conditions, and you have the reason why the Redeemer should be both God and man. He should have the nature of God and the nature of man, and the two should be united in the Person of God. In that case, man could cooperate with God in his own redemption.

Imagine a pencil on a table. That pencil has a nature; and its nature is to write. Of and by itself it cannot write. In like manner, man of and by himself cannot blot out the infinite liability of his sin. Now, imagine another nature, the nature of a hand coming down to that pencil. Here we have the union of two natures in a single person which took up the pencil. The pencil is now able to write—something which it could not do before it was united with the nature of the hand.

When it does write, you do not say, the pencil writes, or my fingers write, but you say: "I write." You attribute the action of the pencil to your person. So, too, if God were to unite man to Himself, then man could do things which of and by himself he could not do. When that manhood which God assumed did anything, e.g., prayed, or breathed, or spoke or suffered, its actions would be attributed to His Person. Since He is the Person of God, it would have infinite value. This is what happened in Bethlehem: God became man and appeared in history as Jesus Christ.

Jesus Christ is both God and man. He was God before He was man. He is God who became a man, not a man who became a god. The word, "Incarnation," means "in the flesh," and signifies that Christ is born not by the conversion of the God-head into flesh, but by taking manhood into God. The Incarnation does not mean the beginning of a new Person. From all eternity He is the Person of God. All the Person of God had to do to become man was to assume a human nature. "In the beginning was the Word, and the Word was with God and the Word was God. And the Word was made flesh and dwelt among us." (John 1:1, 14)

Was His human nature like ours? Yes, in all things, save sin. He had to take His human nature from the very race that had fallen, in order that he might suffer and act as man. But his human nature could not be sinful like ours, otherwise He Himself would stand in need of Redemption, and "if the blind lead the blind, both fall into the pit." (Matthew 15:14)

The problem was how to be a man like us, without being contaminated as we were, by sin. He could be a man like us by being born of woman. He could be a sinless man, or the new Adam, by being born of a Virgin. By dispensing with the act of generation by which original sin was propagated, He escaped its infection. That is why He was born of a Virgin. The Virgin Birth broke the heritage of sin, as now for the first time since Adam there walked on earth a human nature as God meant it to be.

The Incarnation solved the problem that man ought in justice make satisfaction for his sins, but only God can. Out of pure love, therefore, God in Christ identified Himself with humanity that He might make reparation in its behalf. By becoming man, He stood on man's level. Knowing no sin, He "became sin" in order to redeem.

Just as it would be foolish to tell a wife that she need feel no shame because her husband had committed a crime, so it would be foolish to tell Christ, the Incarnate God, that He need feel no shame because He was personally guiltless.

Love means fellowship, not isolation. Human love takes on the burden of its friends; Divine Love takes on Himself the sins of the world. That is why, though sinless, He stood silent before the Judges, for the sins of the world were upon Him; that is why He who was guiltless was baptized, that He might identify Himself with the debt which all men owed. And the payment He made was not an individual payment; it was a payment on behalf of humanity whose very nature He shared.

The old human nature descended from Adam was disordered; He would not take that upon Himself. So the Holy Spirit created a perfectly new human nature in the womb of Mary, a new Adam, a new creature, a new pattern. God would not put a patch of holiness on the old garment of nature. He gave the human race a new start. Only by repeating in a way the act of creation, by making a new human out of the old, could God bring into the world a nature that could be called "a new creature."

"Behold I make all things new." (Apocalypse 21:5) With Him a new race was born out of the old race.

From the religious point of view the world is not divided into nations, races or classes, but into two humanities: the old, unregenerate humanity under the headship of Adam; and the new, regenerated humanity under the headship of Christ. How do we become incorporated into each of these humanities? By being born. Being born of the flesh makes us members of the race of Adam; being born of the baptismal waters of the Holy Spirit makes us members of the race of Christ.

The only way this continued inheritance of original sin could be broken was by a direct act of the Creator Himself. Christ achieved the re-creation of man in His Own Person; it remains for us to apply it to ourselves and through ourselves to the material universe, so that all things might be restored in Him. On the First Easter Sunday, the new humanity consisted of only one individual human being, Christ, as at Creation humanity consisted of only one individual person, Adam. By His Incarnation, Christ restored in Himself fallen Adam with his descendants.

Hence, the essence of Christianity consists not in obeying a set of commands, nor in submitting to certain laws, nor in reading Scripture, nor in following the example of Christ. Before all else, it consists in being re-created, re-made and incorporated into the risen Christ, so that we live His life, think His thoughts and will His Love.

Before studying the application of His Redemption, it is well to recall four important truths about the Person of Christ:

1) He is the only head of a religion in the world who had a pre-history. No one ever expected Buddha, or Confucius, or Mohammed or any of the more recent founders of religion. But the whole world, both Jew and Gentile, did expect Christ. The place of His birth, the city in which He would dwell, the time of His coming, the manner of His death, all were foretold by the prophets of one particular nation whom God chose as His instrument for the redemption of man.

God had been in nature as Providence; He had been in history as prophecy; now, when the fulness of time is come, God appears in history as man. At a precise moment of human history, God cut into human processes by taking upon Himself a human nature in the womb of a Jewish maiden. Time was fashioned so as to receive Christ. History worked up to Him: history worked from Him. Through Him history has meaning and purpose. That is why all history is divided into B. C. and A. D.

2) He is not primarily a teacher of humanitarian ethics, but essentially and primarily a Redeemer and a Saviour. Everyone else came into

this world to live; He came into it to die. Death was a stumbling block to Socrates; to Christ it was the goal of His life, the very gold He was seeking. So long as God remained in the heavens, He was the object of intellectual scrutiny. Once He came down into the dust of human lives, He was in the domain of historical decision. Men could no longer be indifferent to Him.

Before He came, God was either known or unknown. When He came, He would be either passionately loved or passionately hated. One can never be indifferent before the Infinite. Death in a certain sense was inevitable, for once Love and Innocence confront brute force and sin, a crucifixion follows. Suffering is always the form that love takes in an evil situation. Every mother who ever had an erring son, and every wife who ever had a drunkard husband knows that. How else could Divine Love meet sin, except by a cross? Evil breaks some human hearts. Sin broke the heart of God. "Greater love than this no man hath, that a man lay down his life for his friends." (John 15:13)

3) Jesus Christ is both true God and true man. He is not only a good man. A good man never lies, but if Christ is not what He claimed to be, the Son of God, then He is the greatest liar of all times. A good man never deceives, but if Christ cannot give what He promised, viz., peace and pardon to our hungry tired souls, then He is the arch deceiver of history. Either Christ is the Son of God, or He is anti-Christ. He is not just a good man. If He were only man, He, too, would need redemption. If He were only God, He could not redeem man; He could only forgive him.

The Redeemer of man was then both Divine and human; human that He might act in our name; Divine that His actions might have an infinite value. There are some who would say that He is the highest product of God in the whole history of the world, but that He is not God. This description does not fit Christ, God and man, though it does fit His Blessed Mother for to her was given the power in the name of all humanity to accept the Incarnation of the Son of God as in the blazing light of her innocence she answered the angel: "Be it done unto me according to thy Word."

4) He was the new Adam. The human race, it has been said, has two heads: Adam and Christ. As all men are in Adam by the flesh; men can be in Christ by the Spirit. "For as by the disobedience of one man, many were made sinners: so also by the obedience of one, many shall be made just." (Romans 5:19) The three instruments which cooperated in the Fall were: a) a disobedient man: Adam; b) a proud woman: Eve; c) a tree. These three instruments were used by God in the re-creation of man: a) for the disobedient Adam, there is the new obedient Adam, Christ;

b) for the proud woman, Eve, there is the humble Virgin Mary; c) for the tree of Eden, the new tree of the Cross on Calvary.

How did this Redemption take place?

1) By the sinless being made sin. Our Blessed Lord, though He was sinless, nevertheless willed "to be made sin for us." As a strong magnet attracts to itself iron filings, so He by an act of His Will drew unto Himself all the sins of the world that have ever been committed, sins of Jews and Gentiles, sins too awful to be mentioned, sins too terrible to be named. He permitted them all to be thrust into His Hands, as if He Himself had committed them, and the very thought of them was so terrible that, one night in the Garden, His Blood poured out from His Body in a crimson sweat. The cup was bitter, but since the Father willed it, He would drink it to its very dregs.

By coming into a world of sin, He, the Sinless One, brought the whole weight of its sin upon His Person. As doctors, who are free from disease, will sometimes accept the possibility of contagion in their eagerness to cure their patients of a disease, so He, though sinless, freely accepted the cumulative weight of human transgression that He might atone for the very punishment which our sins deserved. It was faintly like a rich man who makes himself responsible for the debts of a bankrupt, that he might start business all over again, except with Our Lord the cost was greater, namely, His life. Being God He became man that He might lay down His Life for us who were not His friends, but His enemies.

Imagine a golden chalice which has been consecrated for Divine worship and used on the altar at Mass. Suppose this chalice is stolen, mingled with alloys and beaten down to a cigarette case. Later on, it is recovered. Before the gold of that chalice can be restored to the altar, it must first of all be subjected to purging fires to burn away the dross.

It must be remolded by repeated blows of a hammer and then only may it be reconsecrated and restored to its dignity and honor.

Our human nature was like that battered and desecrated chalice, no longer serving the high purpose for which it was made. The chalice could not re-make itself. Neither could man redeem himself. So Christ took upon Himself our human nature, plunged it into the flaming furnace of Calvary's fires that the dross of sin might be burned away. Then on Easter Sunday, by rising from the dead, He reversed the Fall, and appeared as the New Man, remolded and glorified, fit for God's service and restored to God's friendship.

The Easter Resurrection was the final proof that God's love in man and for man had won the final victory over sin and death. For the worst thing that sin could do is not to bomb cities and kill a fellowman; it is to crucify God. Having done this and lost, it would never do anything as bad again. Having been conquered at its strongest point, evil must now remain eternally defeated.

Christ had achieved the re-creation of man in His own person. He did not need this Redemption for Himself, but in His Divine Love of us He took upon Himself the burden of our human nature, that He might become the life-giving Form of redeemed humanity, or the Pattern of men to whom—"as many as are willing to receive Him"—He would give the power to become the sons of God.

All that remains to be done is for all mankind to appropriate this new life to itself. He was the beginning of a new coinage to take the place of the counterfeit. He was the original, the new die; millions and millions of worthy coins can be stamped from that die. Whether we do it and thus become regenerated depends on our will. He has vindicated the Divine Justice and the honor of God's Holiness; He has become the Life in and through which we may regain the heritage of the children of God; He has in His Sacred humanity re-created the immortal life out of morality.

Upright as a Priest on the Cross, prostrate as a Victim, He has brought man to God and God to man in Himself, that "we might have life and have it more abundantly," if we in our turn, will to be made conformable to Him in His Cross and Sacrifice. Such is the mystery of Calvary. "O Happy Fault, which has merited to have such and so great a Redeemer."

The two great truths we have learned so far and which stand in opposition to much contemporary rubbish and conform so well with the facts of human experience and history are:

*Man did not come from the beast.*
*Christ did not come from humanity.*

You did not come from the dogs, but you can go to the dogs; you did not evolve from the animal, but you can devolve to the animal. You are less a risen monkey than you are a fallen angel. You were once not lower than you are now; but you were once higher. You are more a disinherited king, than you are an enthroned beast; your golden age was more in the past, rather than in the next twenty years.

The same is true of the person of Christ. As you did not come from the animal, Christ did not come from history or from man alone. History did not beget Him as it begot Lincoln and Napoleon; rather He begot history. Through Him and Him alone, the history of nation and the history of each individual man find an absolute and unalterable center. Even though you ignore Him, even though you deny His existence, you must date your denial as over 1900 years after His birth. He is the Supreme Reality of history, the cornerstone in the edifice of humanity, the keystone in the arch of time, and the measure of the world; the Lamb slain from the beginning of the world.

The title which He applied to Himself was that of the Good Shepherd who lays down His Life for His sheep. A careful study of the Gospel reveals that only through His suffering and death could the Kingdom of God be fully established and men reinstated under the authority of God. "If I be lifted up, I will draw all things to myself." Mankind had contradicted God so He would die on the sign of contradiction, which is the Cross.

The Cross makes intelligible the gravity of human sin. Some say the only reason Christ went to the Cross was to show us that He loved us. If a man were sitting safely on a pier fishing and a good neighbor came up behind him, threw himself into the river and, as he went down for the third, time, said: "This shows how much I love you," the whole ceremony would be ridiculous if it were not so tragic. But, if the fisherman had actually fallen into the river, and the good neighbor lost his life saving him, then we could say of him truly: "Greater love than this no man hath, that a man lay down his life for his friends." (John 15:13)

In like manner, the Cross is meaningful only because we are sinners and the love of the Cross is manifest because He loved us while we were sinners. Though sinners brought upon Him all manner of torture, both physical and spiritual; though they lied and vilified Him; were treacherous and malicious, He went on loving them until the end when in a last and final moment He prayed: "Father, forgive them, for they know not what they do." (Luke 23:34) Sin had caused enmity between man and God; it had produced divisions and antagonisms between man and man, class and class, nation and nation. Now, through the Cross, He reconciles the world to God, making peace through His Death and restoring us in Him to the Fatherhood of God.

The Cross of Christ forces you to make up your mind. You can be indifferent about anything else, but you cannot be indifferent about the Crucifixion. You can stand immobile before a cross as a kind of charm, but you cannot help but feel involved when you look at a Crucifix. It is the one thing in the world that either makes you feel comfortable or uncomfortable. It never leaves you detached. It challenges you to say one of two things: either to say a firm, unshakable Yes to the proposition that God is love, or else a hoarse, derisive No to the proposition that the maximal point of devotion and love is a snare and a delusion.

So compelling is the response one way or the other, that you cannot refer the Crucifixion either to history alone, or to the community alone, or to the Jews alone, or to the Romans or the Greeks. It has an individual reference as well as a cosmic reference. Each heart must answer it for himself. Try as much as you can you cannot stand before that Crucifixion and shout: "No! I will not have this man's reign over me." Like the "Amen" that stuck in the throat of Macbeth, the words will stick in your own throat. Your own heart gives the lie to your lips that say: "This is not Love!" Your flesh may be unwilling, but your spirit cries out: "Here is One to Whom I ought to commit my life." If you are willing to do that, another problem arises.

Grant that Jesus Christ is true God and true man, and Redeemer of mankind—how do I enter into relation with Him? What has He, who lived almost twenty centuries ago, to do with me? And what have I to do with Him? What possible reference could that Good Friday Cross have to my sins now? You probably often have seen planted on the rocks on the highways, signs reading: "Jesus Saves." You may have been very willing to admit this, but I am sure you must have added: "Certainly He saves, but how?"

## CHAPTER 6

## IS RELIGION PURELY INDIVIDUAL

HAVE you ever heard anyone say: "I do not want any Church standing between me and God?" Do not be too harsh on them, for this statement is due to a misunderstanding. They would never say: "I do not want the United States Government standing between me and America." To say I want no one between God and me is anti-Christian because it implies that your brother is a barrier to God's grace and not a means to it.

Did not our Blessed Lord say that before offering your gift at the altar, you should first go and reconcile yourself with the brother whom you offended, and then come and offer your gift? Did He not also make love of God absolutely inseparable from love of neighbor? Did He not teach us to pray in the context of "Our Father," not "My Father"; "our daily bread," not "my daily bread"; "our trespasses" not "my trespasses?" And if God is a Father, then the others united to Him are our brothers, and, therefore, religion must be social.

You are not allowed individual interpretation of the Constitution of the United States. A Supreme Court does that for you. Why should you insist on individual interpretation of religion and begin all religious discussions with: "Now, this is what I believe about religion" or "I feel this way about God?"

Never were the sublime and beautiful realities put so much at the mercy of a stomach. Do you have your own individual astronomy and individual mathematics? Is not the personal pronoun "I" the most indecent of all the pronouns, and do you not dislike those people whose "I's" come too close together? Why then do you think the "I" used in isolation from your fellowmen is pleasing to God?

Say not, then, "religion is a private affair" any more than your birth is a private affair. You cannot be born alone; you cannot live alone; you cannot even die alone for your death is tied up with property or at least with burial. You cannot practise religion alone any more than you can love alone.

What would happen to your patriotism if you said "Patriotism is an individual affair?" If you were the only citizen in America, could you be patriotic? If you were the only person in a town, could you be charitable? If, then, you cannot be kind alone, or sacrificing alone, or generous alone, how in the name of God do you expect to be religious alone? As generosity implies a neighbor, as patriotism implies fellow citizens, so religion implies fellowmen in relation to God.

All the best things of life come from solidarity and fellowship. God said to Hydrogen and Oxygen, say "Ours," and we have the oceans and tumbling cascades. The musician says to the scattered notes, say "Ours," and we have the symphony. The sun says to the planets, say "Ours," and we have a planetary system. Your mind says to ideas and words, say "Ours," and we have languages. America says to Americans, say "Ours," and we have democracy. Even the animals that say "Ours" survive in the struggle of existence: the bees, the ants and the birds. But those dinosaurs and ichthyosaurs who roamed in isolation and made living a private affair have perished from the earth.

Now ask yourself the important question: How do I contact Christ the Redeemer? How does He save me? How do I come to know His Truth and His Will? How do I receive His Life? Do I contact Him as an individual by reading about Him, and singing hymns to Him, or do I contact Him in fellowship and in community?

One way to answer that question is to inquire how mankind contacted God before the coming of Christ. Was religion a purely individual affair or was it corporate? Did God deal with individuals directly, or indirectly, i.e., through a race or a community?

Search the Scriptures. You will find that God always dealt with mankind through human corporations or races, or moral bodies, presided over by a divinely chosen head. The Book of Genesis reveals that the history of mankind would be a warfare not between individuals, but between two seeds, two races, two corporate wholes: the power of darkness and the power of light. "I will put enmities between thee and the woman, and thy seed and her seed; she shall crush thy head, and thou shalt lie in wait for her heel." (Genesis 3:15)

The head of the corporation of evil was Satan; the invisible head of the corporation of good was God, but God always chose a visible head of that community to act in His name. First, it was Noah, through whom and his kindred salvation would come to humanity. Later, there came the new heads of this new spiritual corporation: Abraham, Isaac and

Jacob. To this community, God promised blessing and salvation. Later on, it was Moses whom God summoned as the head of His chosen people and through whom He promised their nation: "I will take you to myself for my people: I will be your God, and you shall know that I am the Lord your God, who brought you out from the work prison of the Egyptians." (Exodus 6:7)

A covenant or contract was entered into between this community and God, in which God promised to bless them if they would obey His law and become His faithful witnesses and the bearers to the world of the Messias, the "Expected of the Nations," the Saviour of the World. After Moses, there are Josue and David and the prophets.

God always followed the same method. He never communicated His promises to individuals in the world at large, but to His chosen people through some chosen patriarch, or leader or king or prophet.

Whenever God willed to give new or special privileges to the community, He changed the name of its head, e.g., Abraham, Jacob. This corporation, or chosen body, was not always faithful; it sometimes fell into idolatry, but despite their lapses, God was with them as His instrument, guiding, controlling, directing, so that whatever they did, His purpose never failed.

It was always the chosen community or moral body, and not the individual which received God's revelation. Very likely, at the time of the flood, every individual might have liked to have his personal row boat, but God saved them in an ark under His own divinely appointed captain.

Throughout Jewish history, the community always holds first place, and the greatest punishment which could be inflicted upon any individual Jew was to be cut off from this corporate body. Even today to the Orthodox Jews, the most serious of all sanctions is in our modern language "to be put out of the synagogue," which it will be recalled was done to Spinoza.

So it came to pass that the most important word in the Old Testament was the word which expresses this corporation, or body, or congregation or society. That word was (kahal). About 200 years before Christ, the Jews translated their Scriptures into Greek because so many Jews were living away from Israel in a Greek civilization. When the translators came to the Jewish word, kahal, they translated it by the Greek word, ecclesia, which means "that which is called out," signifying that its members had been called out from the secular nations.

When finally the Messias did come in the person of Christ Jesus, true God and true man, it was only natural to expect that God would now continue to deal with mankind in much the same way that He dealt with it before, namely, through a corporation presided over by a Head whom He Himself would choose.

An "ecclesia" was already in existence when "God sent His Son, made of a woman, made under the law." (Galatians 4:4) Our Lord was born in the very heart of a divinely chosen community or ecclesia. God who in previous times spoke through the prophets, now would speak through His Son to give the fulness of revelation.

Now that the fulness of time was come, God willed to elevate His ecclesia to the fulness of truth and power and grace. As once before He had named Abraham, Moses and David as its head, so now He would name someone else as its head. Because new powers and privileges were to be given, He changed the name of that individual. As He changed Abram's name to Abraham, Jacob's name to Israel, so now He changed the name of the individual who is to be the new head, from Simon to Rock.

In English, his name is Peter. We lose the flavor of it in English because Peter and Rock are different words, but they are not in the language Our Lord spoke, nor in French, Greek, Latin and several other languages. For example, in French Pierre means Rock and it also is the name of a man. In the original Greek, Our Lord said: "Thy name is Simon: Henceforth thou shalt be called the Rock."

On that day, when the Rock confessed that Christ was the Son of the Living God, the Divine Master answered: "Thou are Peter; and upon this rock I will build my church, and the gates of hell shall not prevail against it." From now on God's ecclesia would be built upon the Rock and it would be to the whole world God's chosen community for the communication of His Divine Life, as Israel before had been the community for the communication of its promise.

No wonder the Rock, in his first Sermon on Pentecost, spoke of the continuity of God's plan, viz., that "those things which God before had shewed by the mouth of all the prophets, that his Christ should suffer, he hath so fulfilled" (Acts 3:18) "by the hands of wicked men," but none the less in accordance with His "determinate counsel and foreknowledge." (Acts 2:23)

Our Lord said this new ecclesia would start small, like a mustard seed, but it would grow into a great tree, "so that the birds of the air may dwell under the shadow thereof." (Mark 4:32) It would be a new society with other ideals, purposes and goals than the world, and, hence, would be hated by the world as He was hated. Its members would be so closely united to each other and in Him, that if anyone did any kind act to any other member, e.g., give him food, or a drink of cold water, they would be doing it for Him. The unity between Him and it, He said would be like the unity between the vine and its branches.

This new ecclesia or body was, therefore, not to be like a club which is formed by men coming together to a center for a common purpose. Rather, it was to be like a living body, from whose center life radiates until the organism is made perfect. It would not be men who would make a contribution to His organization; it would be He who would fill them with life.

If there was any human analogy for this ecclesia, it was the human body. As the body is composed of millions of tiny cells, each one living its own individual life, and yet no one able to live apart from the body, so this new ecclesia or Body would be made up of millions of individuals who were incorporated into Christ.

Just as one cell is not another, as an arm is not an ear, as an eye cannot say to the foot, "I can dispense with your services," so the teacher is not the priest, the missionary is not the family, and yet all through their different functions contribute to the order and beauty of the whole body, because it has one Invisible Head, Christ, and one visible head, the Rock, and one soul which is the Spirit of God.

The nucleus of this ecclesia or body was the Apostles, who were destined to spread out over the world, teaching all nations even to the consummation of the world. To this new ecclesia or community, He promised to communicate His Truth, His Power and His Redemption which He had exercised through His physical body.

After all, was the Truth He taught to be limited to His time, and His generation? Was His Power to be confined to those who saw His Hands? Was His sanctification to be narrowed to those who climbed to Calvary? That men of His time might have no advantage over us, He gave to this new Body or ecclesia, His Truth, His Power and His Sanctification. "I am the truth," (John 14:6) He said. But that truth He communicated to His ecclesia: "He that heareth you, heareth me; and he that despiseth you, despiseth me; and he that despiseth me, despiseth him that sent me." (Luke 10:16)

When, therefore, this new ecclesia began to teach, it would be He who was teaching through them, just as He once taught through His human nature. Since it was God's truth, it would necessarily be infallible or free from error. If the Mind is Truth itself, then the tongue that speaks it is true or infallible.

The same was true of His Power. "And Jesus coming, spoke to them, saying: All power is given to me in heaven and in earth. Going therefore, teach ye all nations; baptizing them in the name of the Father, and of the Son, and of the Holy Ghost. Teaching them to observe all things whatsoever I have commanded you: and behold I am with you all days, even to the consummation of the world." (Matthew 28:18-20) This

Divine Authority He communicated to the head of this His new ecclesia or body: "And whatsoever thou shalt bind upon earth, it shall be bound also in heaven: and whatsoever thou shalt loose on earth, it shall be loosed also in heaven." (Matthew 16:19)

If you saw Christ lift His Hand, you would know that His Will commanded it. He was now saying that His Will, His Power and His Authority would be exercised through another body, namely, His ecclesia. Disobedience to it, therefore, would be disobedience to Him, just as an insult to your body is an insult to your person.

Finally, His Sanctification and Priesthood He communicated to His new ecclesia or body. Would it not be a terrible thing if He did not? How would our sins be forgiven? Could Magdalen be forgiven and we be not forgiven? Somewhere this power to forgive sins is in the world today, and if He forgave her sins through a human nature, then, normally He will forgive our sins through other human natures in that ecclesia to whom He gave the power when He said: "Whose sins you shall forgive, they are forgiven them; and whose sins you shall retain, they are retained." (John 20:23)

These poor human natures who were given the power to forgive sins would not be holy as His nature was, but that would not spoil the absolution for the human nature is only the instrument, not the cause of the forgiveness. The sunshine is not polluted because it shines through a dirty window.

The Apostles, we said, were the nucleus of this new ecclesia or body. Through them and their successors He would still continue to teach, to govern and to sanctify. Up until the day of Pentecost, they were like chemicals in a laboratory. We know up to 100% the chemicals which enter into the constitution of a human body, but we cannot make one, because we cannot create the vivifying, unifying principle, the soul.

In like manner, the Apostles had to wait until Christ sent the Holy Spirit of God to be their unifying soul, before they could become the Body of Christ or His ecclesia. Redemption could now go on. Just as He had taken a human nature from the womb of His Blessed Mother, overshadowed by the Holy Spirit, through which He exercised the office of Teacher, King and Priest, so now He takes from the womb of humanity, overshadowed by the Pentecostal spirit, a new body, a new ecclesia, through which He still continues to teach, to govern and to sanctify.

In the days of His earthly life, Christ's life and love and power were manifested under the limited and localized form of lips, hands and feet; now, after His Resurrection and Ascension, they are manifested through other human natures, whom He has compacted and united to Himself as His New Body or ecclesia.

The Body of Christ is not only an organization; it is more like an organism. It no more stands between you and Christ than His physical body would have stood between you and His forgiveness. It was through His human body that He came to you on earth; it is through His Mystical Body or Ecclesia that He comes to you now.

Whenever, therefore, you confess your sins to a priest and hear the words: "I absolve you from your sins;" you may rightly protest: "How can man forgive sins?" The answer is: "Man cannot forgive sins, but God can forgive sins through man." The Priest is not only the representative of God, He is also the representative of the ecclesia, the Community, through which God's pardon is communicated to man.

Also, God can speak infallibly through human nature. He can speak with Divine authority through man, as He can make a child an heir of heaven through man. That is why God became man. If every contact you would have had with Our Lord Jesus Christ on earth would have been through His human nature, you may not expect now to have another contact with Him except through other human natures who represent His ecclesia.

Are you surprised to hear that Christ, who is at the right hand of the Father with the glorified human nature, is now the Head of the new body of regenerated humanity, which has been growing since the day of Pentecost, and through which His Truth is still preached, His authority is still exercised and His forgiveness still applied? Then, recall the story of the conversion of Paul, which took place a few years after the Ascension of our Lord.

This fiery Hebrew of the Hebrews grew up with an unholy hatred of Christ and things Christian, and as a young man he held the garments of those who stoned Stephen, the first Christian martyr. Paul was not just a bigot. He was a learned man, trained under Gamaliel, so powerful a disputant that the early Christians must often have wondered after the death of Stephen whom they could find to refute him.

In the Providence of God, it was reserved that Paul should refute a Paul. One day, he set out on a journey for Damascus, authorized by letters to seize the Christians of that city, bind them, and bring them back to Jerusalem. Breathing out hatred against the Lord, He departed to persecute the new infant ecclesia. Suddenly a great light shone about him and he fell to the ground, aroused by a voice like a bursting sea: "Saul, Saul, why persecutest thou me?" Nothingness dared to ask the name of Omnipotence: "Who art thou, Lord?" And He answered: "I am Jesus whom thou persecutest." (Acts 9:4, 5)

Saul was about to strike the body of believers in the city of Damascus, in exactly the same way as Christ's followers are persecuted in certain cities of the world today—and the Voice from heaven says: "Saul, Saul, why persecutest thou me?"

Christ and His Ecclesia are the same. The risen Christ, only four or five years after He had left this earth, broke open the heavens to declare to Paul and the world, that in striking His Body you strike His Head, that the branches and the vine are one; that, when the Body of the Church is persecuted, it is Christ who arises to speak. No wonder that the transformed and converted St. Paul understood Christ as well as the other apostles for he, too, had touched His Body.

Now we come to the answer of the question: How does Jesus save me? He saves me through His Body, or ecclesia, with this difference: His Body now is not physical, but mystical! It is made up of human natures infused with Divine Spirit. The only way in which we can be linked to another age is through a body of men, a body which, something in the manner of a natural body, renews itself through time.

The America of today is continuous with the America of Washington and Lincoln, through the body of government. Social clubs, baseball clubs and steel corporations do not have the same membership now as ten decades ago, but they have maintained their continuity through generations through new members.

If you are over 30 years old, you remember two world wars. Suppose you were 500 years old. You would then have known Shakespeare and Thomas More, Vincent de Paul and St. Teresa. Now suppose you were over 1900 years old. Then you would say: I knew Christ. But you could not say that, could you, if you were only 200 years old?

Now the body of Christ or the ecclesia which exists today is continuous with Him. It can say: "I was with Christ when He taught; I heard Him; I was on Calvary; I saw Him rise from the dead; I was in the upper room on Pentecost. I was with Peter and Paul when they were martyred in Rome. I pre-existed the New Testament. I was already spread throughout the entire Roman Empire before a single Gospel was written and were it not for me, the Scripture would not exist today."

It can say: "I knew Augustine and Cyprian and Ambrose, Thomas and Bonaventure. I saw enemies come from without and enemies from within, but I have chanted a requiem over their graves, and I shall live all through time, not because I am a strong organization, for my members are weak, but because my soul, which is the Spirit of God, is immortal, and because My Invisible Head has promised that the gates of hell shall never prevail against me, until time shall be no more."

How do you establish contact with Christ? As the little children did, viz., by being taken into His Arms, by being incorporated to His Body. No wonder religion is confusing when you think of yourself in New York today, and Christ way back in Galilee over 19 centuries ago. Where do you best know the spirit and the wisdom and the courage of a Lincoln? By visiting his Kentucky log cabin, or by living in America which perpetuates and enshrines his memory?

Are you among those who think of the person of Christ as you do of Caesar, or Shakespeare; of Washington, or Lincoln? Does your religion think of Christ as one who was here on this earth, and now is gone, and to whom you can have relation only by following His example, or by reading His doctrine? Have you ever adverted to the fact that, if we could get no closer to our Divine Lord than by example and by doctrine, He hardly differs from any great figure of the past?

We can know Lincoln and Washington, too, by their teachings and their example. Grant that the example and teachings of our Lord are incomparably superior, it, nevertheless, remains true, that if Christ cannot prolong Himself through space and time, then He differs but little from anyone who ever lived. If Christianity is only the memory of a Great Personage who taught, lived and suffered for an ideal in the past, and to whom we can get no closer than by our imagination flying back to Galilee, then Christianity is hardly worth preserving.

Since Christ is the true God as well as true man, He should be able to do what no man has ever been able to do, namely, to project His Life, His Truth and His Love to the very doors of our day and to the very threshold of our hearts. Then, those who lived in His times should have no advantages in love and forgiveness over those who live in our times. If He is not the Eternal Contemporary, He is not God.

No single drop of blood can exist apart from your body, but your body can exist without that single drop of blood, so the Body of Christ can live without you, but you cannot live without the Body of Christ. This is the meaning: "outside the ecclesia there is no salvation." All baptized souls, unless they guiltily refuse to, belong either in reality or in intention to this one ecclesia founded by Christ. Even unbaptized souls belong to it in intention if they live up to God's will according to the light of their conscience, and would accept Revelation if they knew about it.

You did not wait until you were 21 and then read the Constitution and American history. You were born out of the womb of America. As you were born out of the womb of political society, so as a Christian you were born out of the womb of Christ's society. You live by it, before you know it. It creates you spiritually by birth of the spirit, as your country created you by birth of the flesh.

The fact is the ecclesia is prior, both logically and chronologically, to its individual members. This ecclesia was spread throughout the entire Roman Empire before a single book of the New Testament was written. It was the Bible that grew out of the ecclesia, not the ecclesia out of the Bible.

If ever you have the happiness to visit the Central Church of all Christendom in Rome, I want you to lift your eyes above the tomb of that fisherman who was called Rock, to the greatest dome ever thrown against the vault of Heaven's blue, and read those words inscribed thereon: "Tu es Petrus et supra hanc petram, aedificabo ecclesiam meam"—"Thou art the Rock"—that is the meaning of Peter, "And upon this rock I will build my church, and the gates of hell shall not prevail against it." (Matthew 16:18) "And I will give to thee the keys of the kingdom of heaven. And whatsoever thou shalt bind upon earth, it shall be bound also in heaven: and whatsoever thou shalt loose on earth, it shall be loosed also in heaven." (Matthew 16:19)

Ecclesia!—The very word the Jews used to describe Israel as God's community; the very word the Son of God Himself used at Caesarea—Philippi. And that ecclesia was built on Peter. Peter the Rock, who has lived through these 1900 years and through 262 different personages, and whose name today is Pius XII. The word, ecclesia, means Church. The Catholic Church is the Mystical Body of Christ.

## Chapter 7

## How You Are Remade

Have you ever thought that possibly there might be a higher life than the natural life you live now? I do not mean in the next world, but in this. Did you ever advert to the fact that you could know truths beyond the power of your reason and your experience; that you could have reserves of power for crisis, temptations, sorrow and trial over and above those you now possess; that your soul could enjoy another life than the animal life you now live, and be possessed of a peace which the world cannot give?

The sinful woman, who came out at high noon to Jacob's well to draw water, was asked these questions by the One whom she later called "Saviour." Did she know that there were waters for her soul as well as for her body? "If thou didst know the gift of God, and who he is that saith to thee, Give me to drink; thou perhaps wouldst have asked of him, and he would have given thee living water." (John 4:10)

You have no right to say there is no higher life than the physical life you now live, any more than the rose has a right to say there is no life above it. When God made a tree, He owed it to His Own Truth, to give it all that was essential for its tree-ness and nothing more.

When God made you, He owed it to Himself to endow you with all that makes you a human being: a body and a soul endowed with reason and free-will. He was not obliged to make you share His nature so that you would be His child and could call Him "Father," any more than He was obliged to make a rainbow that wrote poetry. If there is a higher life above the natural, you are no more entitled to it by right, than a crystal has a right to reason, or a cow has a right to sign title-deeds, for these powers are beyond nature: they would be supernatural.

Because God created you, it does not follow that He exhausted all His love, any more than a mother exhausts all her love in giving birth to a child. In His Goodness, God could restore, if He willed it, all the privileges and gifts which were lost by our First Parents in the Fall.

Original sin, it has been said, is something like a severe illness which has upset our nature, with the result that there is a civil war going on inside us, our body rebelling against our soul, because our soul rebelled against God. Just as one country will sometimes "break off relations" with another country, so man by sin became separated from God and lost the gift by which he could attain his true supernatural end.

We have already learned that Christ by His Cross and Resurrection atoned for man's sins, and broke down the barriers which separated us from Him. By bringing Divine Life into history, He made it possible for us in some way to receive it: "I am come that they may have life, and may have it more abundantly." (John 10:10)

If you thought about religion at all, you probably asked: But how can I contact that Divine Life of Christ? What have I to do with Christ who died over 1900 years ago? Sing hymns? Listen to long sermons? Read the Scriptures? But these do not establish a vital relation with Him any more than by singing hymns to Lincoln or reading his Gettysburg Address establishes personal relations with him.

Granted that Christ did pay your debts on Calvary when you were bankrupt from sin, how does that change your nature? You may ask: What is to prevent me, once my debts are paid, from being the same kind of creature I always was?

The answer is: You could be a new creature if Christ infused into your soul in some way His Divine Life! This would not have happened if Christ remained on earth in His human nature, for then He never would have been any closer to us than an embrace, or a spoken word, or a hand lifted in blessing. That is why He said: "It is expedient to you that I go: for if I go not, the Paraclete will not come to you; but if I go, I will send him to you." (John 16:7)

His departure on the Ascension was the very condition of the Apostles receiving Him intimately on Pentecost. If He sent His Spirit, then He would not be an external voice or an example to be copied, but a veritable life to be lived: "But when he, the Spirit of truth, is come, he will teach you all truth. For he shall not speak of himself; but what things soever he shall hear, he shall speak; and the things that are to come, he shall shew you." (John 16:13) "The Spirit of truth, whom the world cannot receive, because it seeth him not, nor knoweth him; but you shall know him; because he shall abide with you, and shall be in you." (John 14:17) "Lord, how is it, that thou wilt manifest thyself to us, and not to the world?" (John 14:22)

If the glorified Christ did send His Spirit into your souls, to restore you to His Friendship, it would be purely gratuitous on His part, and being gratis, or a gift, it could appropriately be called "grace." "Every best gift, and every perfect gift, is from above, coming down from the Father of lights." (James 1:17)

If God did give this gift, He would have the same purpose you have in giving presents to your friends: to secure your happiness because He loves you. Of course, your gifts do not always make your friends happy, but God's gifts never fail to make us happy because we cannot impart a new life, while God can. These supernatural gifts which the Holy Spirit, through the merits of Jesus Christ, pours into your soul, enable you to know more than you knew before, to love more than you loved before, and to do things which you could not do by your natural powers.

As a result of sin, your engine ran out of gasoline. God made you to run on His Divine fuel, and not even the best of human fuel will ignite in the combustion of love. By God's grace, however, you are made "partakers of the Divine Nature" so that something of God's life and activity is in you. In virtue of this, you grow up to be His Children, and God is your Father. Christ is your Brother, the Holy Spirit is the Guest in your soul, and Mary is your Mother, and you are made a sharer in that ecclesia through which you share in the Truth of Christ the Teacher, the Authority of Christ the King and the sanctification of Christ the Priest.

Upon what conditions can I receive this gift of a higher life? What are the normal ways in which this Divine Life is given? What effect will it have on me? How can you contact this Divine Life which Christ merited for you?

In somewhat the same way that everything in nature received a higher life than that which it naturally possesses: a) by something higher coming down to that which is lower and b) by the lower surrendering its imperfect nature in order to be incorporated into something higher.

How can the moisture, the carbons and the phosphates in the earth ever live in the plant? First, the plant life must descend to them, take them up into its roots and branches, while the chemicals themselves must abandon the crude lifeless state they have in nature. If the plant could speak, it would say to the chemicals: "Unless you die to yourselves, you cannot live in my kingdom." Actually, the sunshine, chemicals and moisture now begin to thrill with life and vitality in the plant.

If the animal could speak, it would say to the plants: "Unless you die to your lower life of mere vegetation and submit yourself momentarily to the jaws of death, you cannot live in my kingdom. Once you live in me, you will share a life that not merely vegetates, but feels and moves and tastes and sees." Man in his turn, going down to that which is lower, says to the animals: "Unless you die to yourself by submitting to the sacrificial death, you cannot live in my kingdom. But if you die to yourself, you shall share a life that is not merely sensible, but one that thinks and loves, has ideals, laughs and is artistic."

This is precisely what Christ says to you: "Unless you die to yourself, you cannot live in My Kingdom"—but with this difference: Since we are persons, which chemicals, plants and animals are not, the sacrifice enjoined on us is not physical, but spiritual. We do not have our personality destroyed, as a plant's nature is destroyed when taken into the beast.

Otherwise the law holds good. The higher comes down to the lower; the Divine descends into the human. Such was the Incarnation: God came down to man. On the other hand, man must die to his sinful nature, his old Adam, his heritage of the Fall, and this he can do only by sacrifice and by taking up "his cross daily" and following Him. "Unless the grain of wheat falling into the ground die, itself remaineth alone. But if it die, it bringeth forth much fruit. He that loveth his life shall lose it; and he that hateth his life in this world, keepeth it unto life eternal." (John 12:24,25)

The law of transformation holds sway; chemicals are lifted into plants, plants into animals, animals into man, and since man is free, he can freely will, through the Graciousness of God, to be lifted up into Christ, so that he can say: "And I live, now not I; but Christ liveth in me." (Galatians 2:20) God came down to the level of man that He might in some way lift man to the level of God.

To be a Christian is to be born of Christ, so that our poor, weak, sinful human nature is not gilded over as so much brass, but rather is re-created, so that we become a "new creature." Our human nature inherited from Adam does not become better; it dies and is reborn as Christ died on Calvary and rose from the dead.

Even with this infusion of Divine life you must still use your will. After your car is filled with gasoline, it will not drive itself. Grace does not work like a penny in a slot machine. Grace will move you only when you want it to move you, and only when you let it move you. The supernatural order supposes the freedom of the natural order, but it does not destroy it. An alarm clock will awaken you in the morning but it will not make you get up. God's grace will aid, direct, and perfect your human actions, but only on condition that you freely cooperate with it. God breaks down no doors.

Becoming a Christian is, therefore, a regeneration; the living of a new life above the human. The life of the body is the soul; the life of the soul is Christ. Because grace or supernatural life is a regeneration, it makes no difference what your background is, nor how wicked you were, nor how many sins you committed.

Once by an act of will you make God's life your own, you live by a new Spirit, are governed by new laws, breathe a different atmosphere, and have an entirely new set of values. You are not merely made solvent after having become bankrupt by sin; you are made a new man: a new man in Christ.

Never believe those who say: "Once a thief, always a thief." Or, "You are wasting your money on that worthless creature." The Christian claim is: you are not! You can put off your old nature and put on a new. Since grace is regeneration, it makes little difference what your old nature was.

If I throw away an old coat, it makes little difference if I do so because it is torn, or because it is spotted with soup, or because it is moth-eaten, or because it is faded. The only thing that matters is: I throw it away. And when I throw it away, I get a new coat. The difference is that, by being reborn in Christ, you do not throw away something external; you bury your nature with Christ. You do it because you get a new nature, one that partakes of the very nature of God. In the strong language of St. John, "We are born of God." (John 1:13)

Though you are regenerated to share the Christ life, you are not dispensed from the necessity of preserving that life against evil, as you preserve your physical life by resistance to disease and death. Earth is not heaven, and not all the gifts we lost by original sin will be restored to us until the Final Resurrection.

What the grace of God does is to set you on the right road. Up to this time, you were on the wrong road; you were fighting against brambles, brushing thorns aside, stumbling over rocks, simply never getting anywhere. When you become a Christian, Our Divine Lord sets you on the right track. The road is marked with signs or dogmas: telling you the way to go, and which detours to avoid.

Never think that when the Church tells you: "Avoid this path—Poison Ivy," that is restricting your freedom. The Church gives you a map and marks your destination. Though you are on the right road, you still retain some of the effects of having been on the wrong road. You are still hungry, your clothes are torn, and your feet are tired.

Even on the right road, you will still have to walk, pick out a few thorns, but it will not be too difficult, for all along that road you will find places to eat the Bread of Life, First Aid Stations where your thorns can be picked out, and above all you will find divinely appointed guides whose sole business it is to bring you safely to the City of Peace.

While some people are alive in body, they may be dead in soul. When they die, they undergo what Scripture calls the "double death;" they are dead now to both the life of the body and the life of the soul. That makes clear what St. John said: "You call yourselves living and yet you are dead."

In God's eyes, there are perhaps more spiritual corpses walking around the streets today in apparent life, than there are physical corpses being carried to the graves. They can breathe, eat, think, but they are dead to the truth above reason, to love beyond the grave. Only God's grace can be to them the Resurrection and the Life.

What are the normal ways in which this Divine Life of Christ is given, if I want to receive it?

This question breaks down the time and space interval which separates us from Calvary. It asks: How is Christ's forgiveness available to me right now? How could I, if I wanted to, make my marriage a supernatural rather than a natural one? How could I develop spiritually in Christ as I develop physically? How can I contact the Divine Life?

All these questions have been answered by our Blessed Lord. Knowing that you had a body as well as a soul, He chose not to communicate His Divine Life to you invisibly. If you were an angel, you would need no sensible evidence that His Life was being poured into your soul. Being physical as well as spiritual, He willed normally to give you His supernatural life or grace under the symbol of some material sign.

Since your natural life is already full of material things which are symbols or channels for the invisible, He chose to fill your supernatural life with such external signs. For example, a handshake is more than the clasping of hands; it is the channel for the communication of something invisible and deep in the soul, namely, friendship. In other words, it is a sacrament, an outward sign of an inward reality. A letter or a spoken word is a sacrament in the broad sense of the term for it communicates more than that which meets the eye or the ear.

Our Divine Lord, not only in tribute to our physical nature, but also in order to bring the materials of a chaotic world again in the Divine order, instituted Sacraments. A Sacrament is a material sign or symbol through which God communicates His Divine Life. Through them He pours into your souls now the very Life He purchases for you on Calvary.

Since the material universe fell through man's sin, why should not the material universe by Christ's redemption minister unto justification?

Why should not the Divine Pharmacist who made minerals, roots, vegetables to minister to the physical life of man, also make use of wheat and oil and water as the medicine of His supernatural life? You would then know your sins were being washed away through the visible sign, water. You would know that your spiritual life was being nourished by the external sign of that reality, viz., bread.

Was it not Goethe who said: "The highest cannot be spoken; it can only be acted?" The Sacraments are the drama of God. He conceived them; He acts them; He elevates through them. Their efficacy does not depend on our subjective belief; they give Divine Life by the mere fact that we receive them. If we enter into them worthily, we will find ourselves lifted up into the supernatural life and perfected in it. If we enter into these Divine realities lightly, this does not mean that nothing happens.

A grain of radium might be taken by one ill with cancer, as the promise of his future health. If, however, it is handled carelessly, it may cause not restoration of health, but instead the most frightful and death dealing burns. In like manner, the very thing which should minister to eternal salvation, could by unworthiness minister unto eternal damnation.

How many Sacraments are there? Or how many ways has God chosen to communicate His Divine Life? There are seven and there can be only seven for there are seven conditions of all life either physical or spiritual. Five of these refer to the individual life of man, and two to his social life.

To live in individual physical life, five conditions must be fulfilled:
1. You must be born.
2. You must be nourished.
3. You must grow to maturity.
4. You must heal your wounds.
5. You must drive out traces of disease, for a disease is different from a wound.

Then, as a social being, two more conditions are necessary.
1. You must live under government.
2. You must propagate the human species.

You simply cannot think of physical life continuing except on these conditions.

Since there is another life above the natural, namely, the supernatural, it follows that there are seven conditions necessary for living the life of the new creature in Christ.

1. You cannot live a natural life unless you are born to it, neither can you live the Christ-life unless you are born to it. That is the Sacrament

of Baptism, by which we die to the old nature and are born to the new. As original sin is washed away, you are incorporated into the fellowship of the Kingdom of God.

2. As you cannot lead a perfect natural life unless you grow to maturity and assume responsibilities of your state in life, so you cannot lead a perfect supernatural life unless you grow into the full responsibilities of the Christian life. This is the Sacrament of Confirmation, wherein you fulfil your tasks as a soldier and apostle within the Mystical Body of Christ, through the infusion of a spirit of wisdom and counsel and other gifts which enable you to defend and understand and diffuse the Spirit of Christ.

3. As you cannot live a natural life unless you nourish yourself, so you cannot lead a supernatural life unless you nourish yourself. This is the Holy Eucharist in which you receive the Bread of Life by which you are not only united to Christ, but to all who eat of that Bread in the fellowship of the Body of Christ.

4. When you wound your natural life, you must be healed; when you wound your supernatural life by sin, you must be absolved. That is the Sacrament of Penance.

5. If your natural life suffers from a disease, the traces of that disease must be banished. Since no disease ever leaves traces comparable to the disease of sin in the supernatural life, it follows that, before meeting your God, the remains of sin must be blotted out. That is the Sacrament of Extreme Unction, which restores the harmony of organization between soul and body, that it may fulfil its vocation in time or in eternity.

You are not mere individuals in religion. You are members of the Body of Christ. In order that this spiritual corporation may perfect itself, and grow, two more conditions must be fulfilled.

6. As the natural life is perfected by propagation of the human species, so the supernatural life of the Kingdom of God is perfected by raising children of God. That is the Sacrament of Matrimony, by which husband and wife are made two in one flesh to symbolize the union of Christ and His Church: unbreakable, true and loving.

7. Finally, as your natural life must be lived under law and government, so your supernatural life must be lived under spiritual government and this is the Sacrament of Holy Orders by which Christ's priesthood is prolonged to apply the fruits of law and order to all the members of His Mystical Body.

Calvary is a great and tremendous reservoir of merit. From it flow seven channels to the human soul, and through those channels passes the same Divine Life which fills the reservoir, the only difference being the measure of the life received. While Christ is the Natural Son of God, we are only adopted sons. Two of these channels can flow into souls in the state of sin: Baptism and Penance, to beget or renew Divine Life, for both cleanse us from death: the death of original sin and the death of personal sin. All the others flow usually to a soul already vivified by the Divine Life.

Judge not the existence of those Divine outpourings by the matter you see in the Sacraments, which are but the signs of the life within; judge not baptism by the water, or the Eucharist by its bread any more than you judge the joy of friendship by a handshake or an embrace. What is the spoken word but the air put in movement? But when the soul is in it, it becomes eloquence, justice, truth, courage to do and die.

Think of what a word is when God puts His Spirit in it! What is water but a union of hydrogen and oxygen? Put the genius of man into it and it becomes vapor, commerce, power, civilization. Think of what water is when God puts Himself into it. What is bread but the mere chemical combinations of wheat, water and yeast? Unite it with the soul of man and it becomes strength, life, food, joy. Think of what bread is when God changes it into Himself.

Likewise, for the other Sacraments: That which strikes the eye in them is weak and poor, but that which strikes the soul in them is Divine. They, too, like the men who receive them, are material and spiritual, and like the Christ who instituted them, are made up of the visible and the Divine. Thanks to them, the words of our Lord are fulfilled: "I am come that they may have life, and may have it more abundantly."

In all the shocks of life, He meets us with His Life and the Redemption of His Cross—at the cradle when we are born, at the moment of our death; when we are at peace, and when we are in sin; when we share our life socially, and when we share it religiously; and in each and every instance He has used visible signs that we may know when we receive an inrush of the Life of God.

The procession of life is not upwards from the beast to man, but downwards from God to man. The source of Divine Life whence the great procession starts is in God: Father, Son and Holy Ghost. From out that Immensity the Procession of Life moved as the Father sent His Divine Son into the world of broken hearts.

Assuming a human nature from the Blessed Mother, the Procession of Divine Life moved on the earth in the Person of Jesus Christ, and finally wound its way up the hill of Calvary, and on Good Friday a soldier struck a lance into the side of that Sacred Humanity—blood and water poured forth: blood the price of our Redemption, and water the symbol of our regeneration. The Son sent by His Father now returns to the

Father, and from the Eternal Godhead the Procession of Life moves on as the Father and the Son send their Holy Spirit full of Truth and Love to the Mystical Body on the day of Pentecost.

Striking that Mystical Body as the brightness of the sun striking a prism splits up into the seven rays of the spectrum, the Procession of Divine Life broke up into the Seven Sacraments, to flood the members of that Body with Divine Life for the seven states from the cradle to the grave.

For 1900 years, Life has flowed from the Head in heaven to the Body on earth, without increase or decrease for as Creation added nothing to the Being of God, so the Church added nothing to the Life of God.

The Procession of Life moves on as Christ once more walks the earth in His Mystical Body. The River Jordan flows into every baptismal font as Christ baptizes a soul into that Body of which He is the Head; the Pentecost fires blaze again at every Confirmation as Christ sends His Spirit to make us valiant soldiers of His Body on earth.

The Cenacle table is moved to our Communion rails as Christ once more gives the Bread of Life that the members of His Body may be one as He and the Father are one. Simon's house is become a Confessional box as Christ once more raises His hands to penitent sinners bidding them go in peace and sin no more.

The cross at the right of Calvary's central Cross becomes the symbol of a million deathbeds as Christ once more purifies the soul for its last journey into Paradise, even on the very day of death. Cana's nuptials are repeated at the foot of every altar as Christ once more blesses the love which unites man and wife in an unbreakable bond, as the Holy Spirit has united Him and His Spouse, the Church, in a union of bliss through the endless eternity. The Last Supper is revivified at every ordination ceremony as Christ once more says to those whom He has chosen out of the world, "Do this for a commemoration of Me." (Luke 22:19)

Finally, when the great Procession of Life has wound its way through all nations and all peoples, infusing them with the Divine Life unto the fulness and perfection of His Mystical Body; when Christ shall have grown to His full stature, then will the Procession turn back once more to its Source in Heaven, where all nature will be subject to man as in the sacramental principle, where man will be subject to Christ as in the Incarnation, where Christ in His human nature will be subject to the Father, and where God shall be all in all.

What then, are some of the effects of this Divine Life in your soul?

The first is the Divine Presence: God begins to dwell in your soul: "If any one love me, he will keep my word, and my Father will love him, and we will come to him, and will make our abode with him." (John 14:23)

"God is charity: and he that abideth in charity, abideth in God, and God in him." (1 John 4:16)

Like Adam in the Garden, you walk in the company of God. God is nearer to you, if your soul is in the state of grace, than the air you breathe and the friends you see. This presence is not psychological, i.e., you do not achieve it by imagining yourself in His Presence; neither is it a presence through a keen memory of the scenes of our Lord's Life; it is obviously not a material presence as salt is in a box for we are in the realm of spirit. It is not the same as the universal presence of God in the world by His creative act for otherwise there would be no difference between a soul in the state of grace and a soul in the state of sin.

While God is everywhere by His Creative Power, He is not everywhere by the in-dwelling of His grace. A carpenter is in the bench he made by his power, his idea and his purpose, but the carpenter is in his son in a much more special way. In like manner, by grace, God dwells in your soul more intimately than He is by creation.

God is present by creation in the stars, and the flowers, and the sunset, without any answering presence on their part; there is no consciousness of His Presence. By grace, however, God becomes present in you a new way; He is now not only present to you by power, He is in you by love. "Try your own selves if you be in the faith; prove ye yourselves. Know you not your own selves, that Christ Jesus is in you, unless perhaps you be reprobates?" (2 Corinthians 13:5)

He is present more intimately than the truth of the multiplication table is in your mind, or the love of your mother is in your will. A new conscious relationship is established, not that of Creator and creature, but of Spouse and spouse—Bridegroom and bride. Your soul now looks on God not just as a Being who made you and to whom you are bound by justice, but as a Love who redeemed you and to whom you are united by reciprocal acts of love.

It is only when you can freely use a thing and enjoy it, that you can be said to possess it. By grace, God is in your soul. Your soul is then not a passive recipient of God's Power and Love and Truth, as a marble receives a sculptor's chisel. It may even react habitually by holding Him and possessing Him permanently.

In this you have the answer to the question: What does it mean to be a Christian? Christianity is not a system of ethics; it is a life. It is not good advice; it is Divine adoption. Being a Christian does not consist in being kind to the poor, going to Church, reading the Bible, singing hymns, being generous to relief agencies, just to employees, gentle to cripples, serving on Church committees, though it includes all of these. It is first and foremost a love relationship.

As you can never become a member of a family by doing generous deeds, but only by being born into it out of love, so you can never become a Christian by doing good things, but only by being born to it through Divine Love. Doing good things to a man does not make you his son, but being a son does make you do good things.

Christianity begins with being, not with doing, with life and not with action. If you have the life of a plant, you will bloom like a plant; if you have the life of a monkey, you will act like a monkey. If you have the life of a man, you will do the things a man does, but if you have the Life of Christ in you, you will act like a Christian. You are like your parents because you partake of their nature; you are like God if you partake of His Nature. What a man does is the externalization of what he is.

Most people have their actions governed by their background, e.g., you think a certain way in order to defend your class or your wealth or your want of it; you even build up a philosophy to suit the way you live; you do certain things because they are profitable or pleasant to you; you hate certain people because they are a reproach to your conscience or because they challenge your egotism. Your psycho-physical disposition is the center of your life and, therefore, of your actions. You are, in a word, self-determined.

To be a Christian means to discard self as the supreme determinant of actions; it means to put on the mind of Christ so as to be governed by Christ's truths; to surrender your will to His Will, and to do all things that are pleasing to Him, not to you; to control your emotional attitudes. In other words, your life instead of being self-determined is Christ-determined.

As a result of this Divine indwelling these consequences follow:

Your body by grace becomes a Temple of God. A temple is a place where God dwells and since God dwells in your soul by grace, your body is His Temple: "Know you not that you are the temple of God, and that the Spirit of God dwelleth in you?" (1 Corinthians 3:16) This is the basic reason why you as a Christian must be pure in thought and deed, not that you must avoid diseases and be hygienic but because, conscious that your body is the Temple of God, you will never pollute it by sin. You will, therefore, never have it cremated after death. A dead body, whose soul died in the state of grace, is like a church closed for repairs. Your soul will be reunited to your body after the Resurrection. As it shocks you to see a church bombed, it shocks the Church to see a body cremated.

The fact that God dwells in your soul is the foundation of what is called your interior life. Many baptized souls are ignorant of this mystery and remain unaware of it for the most part of their lives, their religion being only a memory of Jesus on earth, or else a God seated on a throne way up in the heavens. One day Louise de France, the daughter of Louis XV, said to her governess in a fit of temper: "Know you not that I am the daughter of your king?" to which the governess answered: "And know you not that I am the daughter of your God."

One of the reasons we seldom advert to the Divine Presence in our souls by grace is because we are too absorbed by creatures. That is why the Christian life is called warfare; why it demands mortification. As physical life is the sum of forces which resist death, so the spiritual life is, in a way, the sum of the forces which resist sin.

By virtue of God's grace, you become an adopted son of God and cease to be just a mere creature. Adoption means the reception of a stranger into a family. A person will adopt a child because he lacks one. God never does that for God already has a Son which exhausts the fulness of perfection.

Furthermore, though an adopted child on earth can be given the name, the title, the wealth and the influence of him who adopted, yet the adopted one could never receive his life. But God can make you share His Life. Just as your beauty, your strength, your learning, your honesty, make you pleasing to your friends, so God by the infusion of His good makes us share in His Nature, His Goodness, His Truth, and His Beauty and, therefore, makes us pleasing to Him.

Thus, you become, through Our Lord's merits, that which Adam lost by sin: God's own child.

"By this is the spirit of God known. Every spirit which confesseth that Jesus Christ is come in the flesh, is of God." (1 John 4:2)

In virtue of sharing your sonship, heaven becomes not a privilege, but a right. "And if sons, heirs also." (Romans 8:17) God the Father then will cease to be to you a grey bearded potentate who dwells far off in the heavens, but in the truest sense one Whom you now can approach as a child, a son crying, "Father." And if you ever fell into sin like the prodigal, you could say: "I will arise and go to the Father."

If you are the adopted son of the Heavenly Father, then you are also a brother of Christ, and all other sons of the Father are also His brethren. What you do to them, you will do to Him. Every time you give a drink of water to a fellow man, or bind his wounds, or wipe away his tears, or clothe his impoverished body, or feed his body, you are doing it to Christ. "As long as you did it to one of these my least brethren, you did it to me." (Matthew 25:40)

Because you are a son of the Heavenly Father, and a brother of Christ, you also have Christ's Mother as your Mother. More than that, you are made partaker of the divine nature and, as such, of the Holy Spirit of God. As the Holy Spirit is the eternal bond, which unites the Father and

Son, so the Holy Spirit now becomes the bond uniting you both to God and to all the other members of the ecclesia of God. The Holy Spirit of God thus becomes the source of your inspiration and guidance.

In moments of crisis and doubt, in worries whether to undertake this task or omit it, to go on this journey or not, listen to the voice of the Spirit within. The union of your soul and the Holy Spirit can become a kind of spiritual marriage, giving the joys of the spirit born of a unity which leaves all other joys as sorrows, and all other beauty as pain. For the first time in your life, you would begin to love not that which is lovely, but that which is Love: The Spirit of the Most High God.

Be conscious that your every word, thought and deed are enacted before a Divine Audience. As you would not break the speed laws if a policeman were around, so you will not break the Divine Laws, but not because you fear God, rather, because you love Him.

Let the Christ be the Unseen Guest at your every meal; your Divine Host in every visit; your Captain in every war; your Fellow-worker in every task; your Father in every home; your Giver of every gift; the Listener in your conversation; your Companion in every walk; your Visitor at every knock, and your Neighbor in every street; your Owner of every treasure and your Lover in every love.

When you fail to measure up to your Christian privilege, be not discouraged for discouragement is a form of pride. The reason you are sad is because you looked to yourself and not to God; to your failing, not to His Love. You will shake off your faults more readily when you love God than when you criticize yourselves. The sick person looks happily at the physician, not at his wounds. You have always the right to love Him in your heart, even though now and then you do not love Him in your acts. Keep no accounts with God or you will always be so hopelessly in debt as to be bankrupt.

Do not fear God for perfect love casteth out fear. God is biased in your favor. Would you rather be judged by the Justice of the Peace of your town on the last day, or by the King of Peace? Most certainly by God, would you not? David even chose a punishment at God's hands rather than man's for God he knew would be more lenient.

God is more lenient than you because He is perfectly good and, therefore, loves you more. Be bold enough, then, to believe that God is on your side, even when you forget to be on His. Live your life, then, not by law, but by love. As St. Augustine put it: "Love God and then do whatever you please." If you love God, you will never do anything to hurt Him, and, therefore, never make yourself unhappy.

# Chapter 8

## Judgment

If there is anything that characterizes your life, it is an intolerance of boundaries. You want the infinite. That is why you are so often disappointed: you see a tremendous disproportion between the ideal you conceived, and the reality which you attained. Still, you go on searching, simply because you have an indefinite capacity for more. You simply cannot imagine yourself as undesirous of more.

Nature sets certain limits to more for your bodies. A boy's eyes are bigger than his stomach. There is a limit to bodily pleasures. They reach a point where they become a pain, as we become sickened of their own "too much." But there are no limits to the desires of your soul. They never reach a point of satiety. There are no limits to the truth you can know, to the life you can live, and to the love you can enjoy, and to the beauty you can experience.

If this life were all, think of how much your soul would be cheated. You would be as frustrated as a woman mad about fashions, who was put into a room where there were a thousand hats but not a single mirror.

Since you have a body and a soul, you can make either one the master; you can make the body serve the soul which is the Christian way, or you can make the soul serve the body which is the miserable way. It is that choice which makes life so serious.

There would be no fun in playing games unless there were a chance to lose. There would be no zest in battle if crowns of merit rested suspended over those who do not fight. There would be no interest in drama if the characters were puppets. And there would be no point to life unless there were great and eternal destinies at stake, in which we may say Aye or Nay to our eternal salvation. "And fear ye not them that kill the body, and are not able to kill the soul: but rather fear him that can destroy both soul and body in hell." (Matthew 10:28) "For what doth it profit a man, if he gain the whole world, and suffer the loss of his own soul? Or what exchange shall a man give for his soul?" (Matthew 16:26)

There will eventually come a moment in your life when this trial will be over. I know it is a subject about which modern minds do not like to hear. The fact of death is so disguised today that morticians would, if they could, make us believe there is happiness in every box. The modern mind feels awkward in the face of death. He does not know how to extend sympathy; he scruples not at reading detective stories in which there are a dozen deaths, but that is because he concentrates on the circumstances preceding death rather than on the eternal issues involved in death. He never asks: "Saved or lost?" but only: "Who killed Cock Robin?"

St. Paul tells us, not in a harsh, stoic manner, that if we are to live to Christ, we must "die daily." A happy death is a masterpiece and no masterpiece was ever perfected in a day. Dubois spent seven years in making the wax model for his celebrated statue of Joan of Arc. One day the model was finished and the bronze was poured into it. The statue stands today as a ravishing perfection of the sculptor's art. In like manner, our death at the end of our natural existence must appear as a ravishing perfection of the many years of labor we have given over to its mould by dying daily.

The greatest reason why we fear death is because we have never prepared for it. Most of us die only once when we should have died a thousand times—aye, when we should have died daily. Death is a terrible thing for him who dies only when he dies; but it is a beautiful thing for him who dies before he dies.

There is an interesting inscription over the tomb of Duns Scotus in Cologne which reads: "Semel sepultus bis mortuus": a double death preceded his burial. There is not one traveler in a hundred who understands the mystery of love behind it.

After death there is no remedy for an evil life. But before death there is a remedy: it is by dying to ourselves, in which we follow that law of immolation which is the law of the whole universe. There is no other way of entering into a higher life except by dying to the lower; there is no possibility of man's enjoying an ennobled existence in Christ unless he is torn up from the old Adam. To him who leads a mortified life in Christ, death then never comes like a thief in the night because it is he who takes it by surprise. We die daily in order to try dying and then again in order to succeed.

Whether we like it or not, there is no escaping the truth: "It is appointed unto men once to die, and after this the judgment." (Hebrews 9:27) As your relatives and friends gather around you to ask: "How much did he leave?" the angels will ask, "How much did he take with him?"

Judgment will be two-fold. You will be judged at the moment of your death, which is the Particular Judgment, and you will be judged on the last day of the world, which is the General Judgment. The first Judgment is because you are a person and are, therefore, individually responsible for your free acts; your work will follow you. The second Judgment will be because you worked out your salvation in the context of a social order, and the mystical Body of Christ; therefore, you must be judged by your repercussions upon it.

What will the Judgment be like, and here we refer to the particular judgment? It will be an evaluation of yourself as you really are. In each of us there are several persons: there is the person others think you are; there is the person you think you are; there is the person you really are.

During life it is easy for us to believe our own press-notices, and to believe our publicity, to take ourselves very seriously, to judge ourselves by public opinion rather than by eternal truth, hence we may and do think ourselves good because our neighbor is so wicked. We may even judge our virtues by the vices from which we abstain. If we made our money under capitalists, we think labor organizations are wicked; if we made it organizing labor unions, we think capitalism is evil; if we come from the city, we look down on people from the country; we think because a person speaks with an accent, he is unimportant, that if he is black, or brown, or yellow, he is of less value.

Our very enthusiasm for the common man may be because we hate the rich; our political affiliations affect our moral judgment and make us support the party right or wrong. St. Paul describes it as going through life wearing smoked glasses: "We see now through a glass in a dark manner; but then face to face. Now I know in part; but then I shall know even as I am known." (1 Corinthians 13:12)

When the split second of judgment comes, you will take off these smoked glasses and see yourself as you really are. Now what are you really? You are what you are, not by your emotions, your feelings, your likes and dislikes, but by your choices. The decisions of your free-will will be the content of your judgment.

To change the figure: We are all on the roadway of life in this world, but we travel in different vehicles: some in trucks, some in jeeps, some in ambulances; others in twelve-cylinder cars, others in flivvers, and others in trucks. But each of us does the driving.

The judgment at death is something like being stopped by a motor-cop, except, thank heaven, the Good Lord is not as hard as the motor cops. When we are stopped, God does not say: "What kind of a car did you drive?" He is no respecter of persons. He asks: "How well did you drive? Did you obey the laws?"

At death we leave our vehicles behind, i.e., our emotions, prejudices, feelings, our state in life, our opportunities, the accidents of talent, beauty, intelligence and position. Hence, it will make no difference to God if we were crippled, over-ignorant, or hated by the world. Our judgment will be based not on our background or social position, but on the way we lived, the choices we made, and whether we obeyed the law!

Think not, then, that at the moment of Judgment you will argue a case. You will plead no extenuating circumstances; you will not ask for a change of venue, nor for a new jury, nor allege an unfair trial. You will be your own judge. You will be your own jury; you will pass your own sentence. God will merely seal your judgment.

What is judgment? From God's point of view, Judgment is a recognition. Two souls appear before the sight of God in that split second after death. One is in the state of grace, the other is not. The Judge looks into the soul in the state of grace. He sees there a resemblance of His nature, for grace is the participation in Divine Nature.

Just as a mother knows her child because of the resemblance of nature, so, too, God knows His own children by resemblance of nature. If we are born of Him, He knows it. Seeing in that soul His likeness, the Sovereign Judge, Our Lord and Saviour Jesus Christ says unto it: "Come, ye blessed of My Father. I have taught you to pray, 'Our Father.' I am the natural Son; you, the adopted son. Come into the Kingdom I have prepared for you from all eternity."

The other soul, not possessing the family traits and likeness of the Trinity, meets an entirely different reception from the Judge. As a mother knows that her neighbor's son is not her own, because there is no participation in her nature, so too, Jesus Christ, seeing in the sinful soul no participation of His nature, can only say those words which signify non-recognition, "I know you not," and it is a terrible thing not to be known by God!

Such is Judgment from the Divine point of view. From the human point of view, it is also a recognition, but a recognition of unfitness or fitness. A very distinguished visitor is announced at the door, but I am in my working clothes, my hands and face are dirty. I am in no condition to present myself before such an august personage and I refuse to see him until I can improve my appearance.

A soul stained with sin acts very much the same when it goes before the judgment seat of God. It sees on one hand His Majesty, His Purity, His Brilliance, and on the other its own baseness, its sinfulness, its unworthiness. It does not entreat nor argue, it does not plead a case—it sees; and from out the depths comes its own judgment, "Oh, Lord, I am not worthy."

The soul that is stained with venial sins casts itself into purgatory to wash its baptismal robes, but the soul irremediably stained—the soul dead to Divine Life—casts itself into hell just as naturally as a stone which is released from my hand falls to the ground.

Three possible destinies await you at death:
*Hell: Pain without Love*
*Purgatory: Pain with Love*
*Heaven: Love without Pain*

## Chapter 9

## Purgatory

THERE is one word which to modern ears probably signifies the unreal, the fictional and even the absurd in the Christian vision of life, and that is the word, "Purgatory." Although the Christian world believed in it for sixteen centuries, for the last three hundred years it has ceased to be a belief outside the Church, and has been regarded as a mere product of the imagination, rather than as the fruit of sound reason and inspiration.

It is quite true to say that the belief in Purgatory has declined in just the proportion that the modern mind forgot the two most important things in the world: the Purity of God and the heinousness of sin. Once both these vital beliefs are admitted, the doctrine of Purgatory is unescapable.

What is Purgatory but a place or condition of temporal punishment for those who depart this life in God's grace, but are not entirely free from venial faults or have not entirely paid the satisfaction due to their transgressions? Purgatory is that place in which the Love of God tempers the Justice of God, and secondly, where the love of man tempers the injustice of man.

First, Purgatory is where the Love of God tempers the Justice of God. The necessity of Purgatory is grounded upon the absolute purity of God. In the Book of the Apocalypse we read of the great beauty of His City, of the pure gold, with its walls of jasper and its spotless light which is not of the sun nor moon but the light of the Lamb slain from the beginning of the world. We also learn of the condition of entering into the gates of that Heavenly Jerusalem: "There shall not enter into it anything defiled, or that worketh abomination, or maketh a lie, but they that are written in the book of the life of the Lamb."

Justice demands that nothing unclean, but only the pure of heart shall stand before the face of a pure God. If there were no Purgatory, then the Justice of God would be too terrible for words for who are they who would dare assert themselves pure enough and spotless enough to stand before the Immaculate Lamb of God? The martyrs who sprinkled the sands of the Coliseum with their blood in testimony of their faith? Most certainly! The missionaries like Paul who spend themselves and are spent for the spread of the Gospel? Most assuredly! The cloistered saints who in the quiet calm of a voluntary Calvary become martyrs without recognition? Most truly!

But these are glorious exceptions. How many millions there are who die with their souls stained with venial sin, who have known evil, and by their strong resolve have drawn from it only to carry with them the weakness of their past as a leaden weight!

The day we were baptized, the Church laid upon us a white garment with the injunction: "Receive this white garment which mayest thou carry without stain before the judgment seat of Our Lord Jesus Christ that thou mayest have life everlasting." How many of us during life have kept that garment unspotted and unsoiled by sin so that we might enter immediately upon death into the white robed army of the King?

How many souls departing this life have the courage to say that they left it without any undue attachment to creatures and that they were never guilty of a wasted talent, a slight cupidity, an uncharitable deed, a neglect of holy inspiration or even an idle word for which every one of us must render an account? How many souls there are gathered in at the death-bed, like late season flowers, that are absolved from sins, but not from the debt of their sins?

Take any of our national heroes, whose names we venerate and whose deeds we emulate. Would any Englishman or American who knew something of the Purity of God, as much as he loves and respects the virtues of a Lord Nelson or a George Washington, really believe that either of them at death was free enough from slight faults to enter immediately into the presence of God? Why, the very nationalism of a Nelson or a Washington, which made them both heroes in war, might in a way make them suspect of being unsuited the second after death for that true internationalism of Heaven, where there is neither English nor American, Jew nor Greek, Barbarian nor Free, but all one in Christ Jesus Our Lord.

All these souls who die with some love of God possessing them are beautiful souls, but if there be no Purgatory, then because of their slight imperfections they must be rejected without pity by Divine Justice. Take away Purgatory, and God could not pardon so easily, for will an act of contrition at the edge of the tomb atone for thirty years of sinning? Take away Purgatory and the infinite Justice of God would surely reject from Heaven those who resolve to pay their debts, but have not yet paid the last farthing.

So, I say, Purgatory is where the Love of God tempers the Justice of God, for there God pardons because He has time to retouch these souls with His Cross, to recut them with the chisel of suffering, that they might fit into the great spiritual edifice of the Heavenly Jerusalem, to plunge them into that purifying place where they might wash their stained baptismal robes to be fit to enter into the spotless purity of Heaven; to resurrect them like the phoenix of old from the ashes of their own sufferings so that, like wounded eagles healed by the magic touch of God's cleansing flames, they might mount heavenward to the city of the pure, where Christ is King and Mary is Queen, for, regardless of how trivial the fault, God does not pardon without tears, and there are no tears in Heaven.

On the other hand, Purgatory is a place not only where the Love of God tempers the Justice of God, but where the love of man may temper the injustice of man. I believe that most men and women are quite unconscious of the injustice, the ingratitude and the thanklessness of their lives until the cold hand of death is laid upon one that they love. It is then, and only then, that they realize (and oh, with what regret!) the haunting poverty of their love and kindness.

One of the reasons why the bitterest of tears are shed over graves is because of words left unsaid and deeds left undone. "The child never knew how much I loved her." "He never knew how much he meant to me." "I never knew how dear he was until he was gone." Such words are the poisoned arrows which cruel death shoots at our hearts from the door of every sepulchre. Oh, then we realize how differently we would have acted if only the departed one could come back again. Tears are shed in vain before eyes which cannot see; caresses are offered without response to arms that cannot embrace; and sighs stir not a heart whose ear is deaf.

Oh, then the anguish for not offering the flowers before death had come and for not sprinkling the incense while the beloved was still alive and for not speaking the kind words that now must die on the very air they cleave. Oh, the sorrow at the thought that we cannot atone for the stinted affection we gave them, for the light answers we returned to their pleading and for the lack of reverence we showed to one who was perhaps the dearest thing that God had ever given us to know. Alas, too late! It does little good to water last year's crop, to snare the bird that has flown, or to gather the rose that has withered and died.

Purgatory is a place where the Love of God tempers the Justice of God, but also where the love of man tempers the injustice of man, for it enables hearts who are left behind to break the barriers of time and death, to convert unspoken words into prayers, unburned incense into sacrifice, unoffered flowers into alms, and undone acts of kindness into help for eternal life.

Take away Purgatory and how bitter would be our grief for our unkindnesses and how piercing our sorrow for our forgetfulness. Take away Purgatory and how meaningless are our Memorial and Armistice Days, when we venerate the memory of our dead. Take away Purgatory and how empty are our wreaths, our bowed heads, our moments of silence. But if there be a Purgatory, then immediately the bowed head gives way to a bent knee, the moment of silence to a moment of prayer, and the fading wreath to the abiding offering of the sacrifice of that great Hero of heroes, Christ.

Purgatory, then, enables us to atone for our ingratitude because through our prayers, mortifications and sacrifices, it makes it possible to bring joy and consolation to the ones we love. Love is stronger than death and hence there should be love for those who have gone before us. We are the offspring of their life, the gathered fruit of their labor, the solicitude of their hearts.

Shall death cut off our gratitude, shall the grave stop our love, shall the cold clod prevent the atoning of our ingratitude? The Church assures us that not being able to give more to them in this world, since they are not of it, we can still seek them out in the hands of Divine Justice and give them the assurance of our love, and the purchasing price of their redemption.

Just as the man who dies in debt has the maledictions of his creditors following him to the grave, but may have his good name restored and revered by the labor of his son who pays the last penny, so, too, the soul of a friend who has gone to death owing a debt of penance to God may have it remitted by us who are left behind, by minting the gold of daily actions into the spiritual coin which purchases redemption.

Into the crucibles of God these departed souls go like stained gold to have their dross burned away by the flames of love. These souls, who have not died in enmity with God, but have fallen wounded on the battlefield of life fighting for the victory of His cause, have not the strength to bind their own wounds and heal their own scars: it remains for us who are still strong and healthy, clad with the armor of faith and the shield of salvation, to heal their wounds and make them whole that they might join the ranks of the victors and march in the procession of the conquerors. We may be sure that if the penny that gives bread to the hungry body delivers a soul to the Table of Our Lord, it will never forget us when it enters into the homeland of victory.

While yet confined to that prison of purifying fire, they hear the voices of the angels and saints who call them to their true fatherland, but they are incapable of breaking their chains for their time of merit is passed.

Certainly, God cannot be unmindful of a wife who offers her merits to the captive soul of a husband waiting for his deliverance. Surely the mercy of God cannot be such that He should be deaf to the good works of a mother who offers them for the liberation of her offspring who are yet stained with the sins of the world. Surely God will not forbid such communication of the living with the dead, since the act of Redemption has guaranteed such a transferring of merits through Christ.

Responsive, then, will we be to the plea not only of our relatives and friends, but of that great mass of unarmed warriors of the Church Suffering who are yet wearing the ragged remnants of sin, but who, in their anxiety of soul to be clothed in the royal robes fit for entrance into the Palace of the King, cry out to our responsive hearts the plaintive and tender plea: "Have mercy on me, have mercy on me, at least you, my friends, for the hand of the Lord has touched me."

## Chapter 10
## The Hell There Is

WHY do moderns deny hell? Because they deny sin. If you deny human guilt, then you must deny the right of a state to judge a criminal, and the further right to sentence him to prison. Once you deny the sovereignty of law, you must necessarily deny punishment. Once you deny the sovereignty of God, you must deny hell.

The basic reason why moderns disbelieve in hell is because they really disbelieve in freedom and responsibility. To believe in hell is to assert that the consequences of good and bad acts are not indifferent. It does make a tremendous amount of difference to your body if you drink tea or TNT, and it makes a greater difference if your soul drinks virtue or vice.

It is as difficult to make a free nation without judges and prisons, as it is to make a free world without Judgment and hell. No State constitution could exist for six months on the basis of a Liberal Christianity which denies that Christ meant what He said: "Depart from me, you cursed, into everlasting fire which was prepared for the devil and his angels." (Matthew 25:41)

The modern man also denies hell because he fears his own conscience. Have you ever noticed that saints fear hell but never deny it; and that great sinners deny hell but never fear it? The modern man is accommodating a creed to the way he lives, rather than the way he lives to a creed. The Devil is never so strong as when he gets man to deny there is a devil. So long as he succeeds in getting materialists and sceptics to paint him in red tights with an arrowed tail, and carrying a long pitchfork, he has doped them to the forgetfulness of the great and overwhelming truth that he is a fallen angel.

The modern man who is not living according to his conscience wants a religion without a Cross, a Christ without a Calvary, a Kingdom without Justice, and in his church a "soft dean who never mentions hell to ears polite."

Let not those who profess to be Christian, or who limit Christianity to the Sermon on the Mount, forget that Our Lord closed that sermon with these words: "Every tree that bringeth not forth good fruit, shall be cut down, and shall be cast into the fire. Wherefore by their fruits you shall know them. Not every one that saith to me, Lord, Lord, shall enter into the kingdom of heaven: but he that doth the will of my Father who is in heaven, he shall enter into the kingdom of heaven. Many will say to me in that day: Lord, Lord, have we not prophesied in thy name, and cast out devils in thy name, and done many miracles in thy name? And then will I profess unto them, I never knew you: depart from me, you that work iniquity." (Matthew 7:19-23)

Again Our Lord said: "And if thy hand scandalize thee, cut it off: it is better for thee to enter into life, maimed, than having two hands to go into hell, into unquenchable fire: Where their worm dieth not, and the fire is not extinguished. And if thy foot scandalize thee, cut it off. It is better for thee to enter lame into life everlasting, than having two feet, to be cast into the hell of unquenchable fire: Where their worm dieth not, and the fire is not extinguished. And if thy eye scandalize thee, pluck it out. It is better for thee with one eye to enter into the kingdom of God, than having two eyes to be cast into the hell of fire: Where their worm dieth not, and the fire is not extinguished. For every one shall be salted with fire: and every victim shall be salted with salt." (Mark 9:42-48)

Why do souls go to hell? In the last analysis, they go to hell for only one reason: because they refuse to love. Souls do not go to hell just because they break the commandments; for why should the breaking of a commandment merit hell? God does not forbid lying, murder, dishonesty, adultery, to amuse Himself. They are not arbitrary commands. He forbids them because they hurt us. Their violation is a sign of our anti-love.

The Commandments of God are like a book of directions that comes with a gadget. You disobey them; you get no results. Why, then, if you are unhappy by disobeying the set of directions of One who loves you, do you say God is cruel? Hell is not a defect of God's love. Hell is a state of those who refuse to have God's love, when He offers it. Just as Heaven is the undeniable blessedness won by the wholly selfless and loving, so hell is the undeniable cursedness won by the wholly self-centered or hateful. Heaven is community; hell is loneliness.

What is the nature of the punishment of hell? It is two-fold because it corresponds to the double character of sin. Every mortal sin consists in a turning away from God and a turning to creatures. Because we turn away from God, we feel the absence of His Love, His Beauty, His Truth—and this is called the pain of loss. Because we turn to creatures and pervert them to our sinful purposes, we are punished in some way by the very creatures which we abused. Hell fire is one of the aspects of this pain of sense.

This pain of sense is an exemplification of the principle that the punishment fits the crime. If you disobey one of nature's laws, you suffer a corresponding retribution. If you become intoxicated some night and put yourself in a state of amiable incandescence, you do not necessarily wake up the next morning with an overdrawn bank account. But you do feel the effects of abusing the God given thirst by something vaguely described as a "hangover." In almost so many words the alcohol says to you: "I was made by God to be used by you as a reasonable creature. You perverted me from the purpose God intended. Now since I am on God's side, not yours, I shall abuse you, because you abused me."

For every action, there is always a contrary, an equal, reaction. "With traitorous trueness and loyal deceit. In faith to Him, their fickleness to me." Nature refuses to be our servant because we refuse to accept Our Master. Hence, there will be different kinds of punishment in hell. The fiercer the grip sinful pleasures had on a soul in this life, the more fiercely will the fires torment it in eternity. Do not try to escape this logic or blind yourself to Divine Authority by arguing that hell could not be as you have heard some preachers picture it. I am only saying: Do not reject the truth of the book because the pictures are bad.

From three distinct points of view, the pain of loss is best understood as the loss of Divine Love. Hell is a place where there is no love, for God is Love.

Hell is the hatred of the things you love. A sailor lost on a raft at sea loves water. He was made for it, and water was made for him. He knows that he ought not to drink the water from the sea, but he violates the dictates of his reason. The result is, he is now more thirsty than before, even thirsty when he is the most filled. He hates water as poison; at the same time he is mad with the thirst for it.

In like manner, the soul was made to live on the love of God, but if it perverts that love by salting it with sin, then as the sailor hates the very water he drinks, so the soul hates the perverted love it seeks. It then hates the very thing it desires, namely, the love of God. It despises the very love it craves; it abominates the very love it needs. As the insane hate most the very persons whom in their saner moments they really love the most, so the damned in hell hate God whom they were really meant to love above all things.

They become like wandering comets who every now and then approach the sun, their true center, and then swing away from the light into incredible darkness. The wicked do not want hell because they enjoy its torments; they want hell because they do not want God. They need God, but they do not want Him. Hell is eternal suicide for hating love. Hell is the hatred of the God you love.

Hell is the mind eternally mad at itself for wounding love. How often during life you have said: "I hate myself." No one who ever condemned you could add to the consciousness of your guilt. You knew it a thousand times better than they. When did you hate yourself most? Certainly not when you failed to act on a tip on the stock market. You hated yourself most when you hurt someone whom you loved. You even said: "I can never forgive myself for doing that."

The souls in hell hate themselves most for wounding Perfect Love, as you might hate yourself all your time-span for hurting one whom you loved. They can never forgive themselves for hurting Love. Hence their hell is eternal: eternal self-imposed unforgiveness. It is not that God would not forgive them. It is rather they will not forgive themselves. On earth they were selfish, not loving. In hell that selfishness is consummated and eternalized. It is the madhouse of the incurables who hate themselves for hating the Physician of their souls, the place where the mind turns against itself because it turned from God.

How often in this world the sight of moral beauty arouses indignation! The evil person incessantly wants a recasting of all values. Put one good boy in a gang of boys which spends its time in petty thievery or breaking school windows, and the chances are the gang will turn against that good boy, ridicule his moral principles, tell him he is a coward or old fashioned. Exactly that same mentality is present in adult life. Whenever a professor attacks morality and makes fun of religion before his pupils, you can be sure nine times out of ten that his life is rotten.

Goodness is a reproach to such persons: they want everyone to be like themselves, so no one can reproach their conscience. This revolt against goodness and truth is the basic cause of the persecution and mockery of religion. Now if such things are possible to corrupt souls on earth, why should they not be possible in eternity? They will still hate Love because hate has nothing in common with Love. They reject the one remedy that could have helped them, the love of Someone besides themselves.

Hell is submission to Love under Justice. We are free in this world; we can no more be forced to love God than we can be forced to love classical music, antiques, swing bands, olives, or Bach. Force and love are contraries. Love and freedom are correlative.

When you came into this world, God said: "I ask you to love me freely that you may be perfect." Suppose we freely say: "I refuse to love truth and justice and beauty or my neighbor. I shall love error, and graft, and ugliness." Later on, you die in that state. But you do not escape that Divine Love which you abused, any more than the traitor escapes the country whose love he despised.

Either you possess love, or love possesses you. In marriage a man and woman were meant to possess love, but that love can be perverted so that in the end, love possesses them. How often a husband, for example, tied to a woman by marriage is possessed by her, by her wants, her selfishness and her jealousies. Often, too, many a wife is tied to a drunkard or worthless husband until death do them part. They do not freely love one another; they are forced in virtue of the justice of their contracts to love one another until death do them part. To be forced to love anyone is hell.

The lost souls could have loved God freely, but they chose to rebel against that love and in doing so came under Divine Justice, as the criminal falls from the love of a country to its justice. They do not possess love; love possesses them. Justice forces them to love God, that is, to submit to the Divine Order; but to be forced to love is the very negation of love. It is hell! Hell is a place where Love possesses you in justice, but where you do not possess love.

Think not that hell ever ends, or that some day the damned go to Heaven. If a soul in hell went to Heaven, Heaven to it would be a hell. Suppose you hated higher mathematics; suppose your morning paper had nothing in it but logarithms; suppose everyone you met talked to you about Space-Time differentials; every broadcast you heard was on the theory of relativity; every book you read was on the subject of pointer-readings. After a while, mathematics would drive you mad. Now the souls in hell hate Perfect Life, Perfect Truth and Perfect Love—which is God—and if they had to live with that which they hated more than you hate mathematics, then God would be their great punishment, as mathematics would be yours. Heaven would be hell.

Hell must be eternal. What is one thing life can never forgive? Death, because death is the negation of life. What is the one thing that Truth can never forgive? Error, for error is its contradiction. What is the one thing that Love can never forgive? It is the refusal to love, for hate would be the destruction and annihilation of love. That is why Hell is Eternal—it is the negation of Love.

Everything does not come out right in the end for we cannot at one moment believe that we are saved by doing God's Will, and the next moment believe that it has no significance. Somehow or other, there comes to mind the final picture of mankind: The Divine Judge in the center, the sheep on the right going to Heaven, and the goats on the left going to hell. Where the tree falls, there it lies.

You ask: "How can God be so wrathful as to sentence souls to hell?" Remember that God does not sentence us to hell, as much as we sentence ourselves. When the cage is opened, the bird flies out to that which it loved; when our body dies, we fly out, either to an Eternity of love of God or to a hatred of God.

God has not a different mood for those who go to hell than for those who go to Heaven. The difference is in us, not in Him. We attribute anger and wrath to Him only because we feel His Justice as anger. Every criminal thinks that the judge has got something against him. The same justice of the judge could free him if the criminal were innocent. Then he would think the judge was kind. The sun which shines on wax softens it; the sun which shines on mud hardens it. There is no difference in the sun, but only in that upon which it shines. So there is no difference in the God of Love when He judges the wicked and the saved; the difference is in those whom He judges.

We must, therefore, get out of our heads the idea that God is mad with us when we hurt ourselves. God is never offended against us because we sin against Him, as if He were a monarch to be obeyed. We never offend God except when we do something that is contrary to our own good, or better, when we hurt ourselves. Life is important. It only takes a second for a man to lose his leg by carelessness, but he has lost it for all time. It only takes a lifetime to commit a sin, but we can lose Heaven forever. God is a loving Father indeed, and He accepts us back as He did the Prodigal, but only on condition that we are repentant.

Hell is at the foot of the Hill of Calvary; and no one of us can go down to hell without first passing over the Hill where there is a God-man enthroned with arms outstretched to embrace, head bent to kiss, and heart open to love. I do not find it hard to understand God preparing a hell for those who want to hate themselves eternally for having hated Him. But I do find it hard to understand why that same God should die upon a Cross to save unworthy me from a hell which my sins so rightly deserve.

## Chapter 11

## Heaven

It is not often nowadays that men speak of eternity; their thoughts are almost always on time. In fact, time has become one of the most important things in the world. Some years ago, before physics became the fashionable science, the human mind was wont to conceive of time as something in which things happened. Now, it is looked upon as the very fabric of the universe. Sacred Scripture tells us that a moment will come when there will be no more time. The unsacred scripture of our day tells us that time is the very essence of things.

Would we seek for evidences of this mood of temporalism, we could find them in every nook and corner of the world today. In the field of morals, for example, the current doctrine is that any action is moral, provided the time in which we live regards it as moral.

Religion, too, has drunk deep of the intoxicating draughts of temporalism, and now, reeling under its effects, it preaches a religion wholly confined to time, utterly oblivious of eternity. It no longer asks a man to save his soul for eternity; it asks him to save his body for time. It is unconcerned about citizenship in the Kingdom of God, but tremendously excited about citizenship in the Kingdom of Time. That is, incidentally, why some modern religions stress birth-control, favoring as they do the economic motive that belongs to time, rather than the religious motive which belongs to eternity.

Philosophy, likewise, has become so obsessed with that notion that it teaches with unbuttoned pride that there is no such thing as Truth with a capital "T," for truth is ambulatory: we make it as we go; it depends on the time in which we live. There are not wanting even writers who have gone to the excess of saying that God is not in eternity, but is in time, or rather He is being produced by whole cosmic floods of time, undergoing miraculous baptisms at the hands of time, and being hurled onward and forward to some goal which is not yet certain, but which time will reveal if we ever give it time enough.

The Church is not in sympathy with this mood of temporalism. It teaches that it is about time that we cease talking about time, and begin to think of the timeless. I, therefore, propose to prove the superiority of the Church's attitude over that of the modern world by showing first of all that time stands in the way of real happiness, and secondly, that only insofar as we succeed in transcending time do we ever begin to be happy.

Time is the one thing that makes real pleasure impossible, for the simple reason that it does not permit us to make a club-sandwich of pleasures. By its very nature, it forbids us to have many pleasures together under the penalty of having none of them at all. By the mere fact that I exist in time, it is impossible for me to combine the pleasures of marching with the old guard of Napoleon, and at the same time, advancing under the flying eagles of Caesar.

By the mere fact that I live in time, I cannot enjoy simultaneously the winter sports of the Alps, and the limpid waters of the Riviera. Time makes it impossible for me to be stirred by the oratory of a Demosthenes, and at the same time to listen to the melodious accents of the great Bossuet. Time does not permit me to combine the prudence that comes with age, and the buoyancy that belongs to youth. It is the one thing which prevents me from gathering around the same festive board with Aristotle, Socrates, Thomas Aquinas and Mercier in order to learn the secrets of great minds in solving the riddles of a universe.

If it were not for time, Dante and Shakespeare could have sipped tea together, and Homer even now might tell us his stories in English. It is all very nice and lovely to enjoy the mechanical perfections of this age of luxury, but there are moments when I would like to enjoy the calm and peace of the Middle Ages, but time will not permit it. If I live in the twentieth century, I must sacrifice the pleasures of the thirteenth, and if I enjoy the Athenian age of Pericles, I must be denied the Florentine age of Dante.

Thus it is that time makes it impossible to combine pleasures. I know there are advertisements which would invite us to dine and dance, but no one can do both comfortably at one and the same time. All things are good, and yet none can be enjoyed except in their season, and the enjoyment must always be tinged with the regret that time will demand their surrender. Time gives me things, but it also takes them away. When it does give, it gives but singly, and thus life becomes but just one fool thing after another.

This thought suggests the suspicion that if time makes the combination of pleasures impossible, then if I could ever transcend time, I might, in some way, increase my happiness, and this I find to be true, for every conscious desire to prolong a pleasure is a desire to make it an enduring "now." Like cats before the fire, we want to prolong the pleasure indefinitely; we want it to be permanent and not successive.

Go back in the storehouse of your memory, and you will find ample proof that it is always in those moments when you are least conscious of the passing of time that you most thoroughly enjoy its pleasures. How often it happens, for example, when listening to an absorbing conversation or the thrilling experiences of a much traveled man, that the hours pass by so quickly we are hardly conscious of them, and we say: "The time passes like everything." What is true of a delightful conversation is also true of esthetic pleasures.

I dare say that very few listening to an orchestra translate the beauty of one of Beethoven's overtures would ever notice the passing of time. In just the proportion that it pleases and thrills, the orchestra makes us unconscious of how long we were absorbed by its melodies. The contrary fact illustrates the same truth. The more we notice time, the less we are being interested.

If our friends keep looking at their watches while we tell a story, we can be very sure that they are being bored by our story. A man who keeps his eye on the clock is not the man who is interested in his work. The more we notice the passing of time, the less is our pleasure, and the less we notice the passing of time, the greater is our pleasure.

These psychological facts of experience testify that not only is time the obstacle of enjoyment, but escape from it is the essential of happiness. Suppose we could enlarge upon our experience in such a way as to imagine ourselves completely outside of time and succession, in a world where there would never be a "before" nor an "after," but only a "now."

Suppose we could go out to another existence where the great pleasures of history would not be denied us because of their historical incompatibility, but all unified in a beautiful hierarchic order, like a pyramid in that all would minister to the very unity of our personality. Suppose I say that I could reach a point of timelessness at which all the enjoyments and beauties and happinesses of time could be reduced to those three fundamental unities which constitute the perfection of our being, namely, Life, and Truth, and Love, for into these three all pleasures can be resolved.

Suppose first of all that I could reduce to a single focal point all the pleasures of life, so that in the "now" which never looked before nor after, I could enjoy the life that seems to be in the sea when its restless bosom is dimpled with calm, as well as the urge of life that seems to be in all the hill-encircling brooks that loiter to the sea; the life which provokes the dumb, dead sod to tell its thoughts in violets; the life which pulsates through a springtime blossom as the swinging cradle for the fruit.

Suppose that I could enjoy the life of the flowers as they open the chalice of their perfume to the sun; the life of the birds as the great heralds of song and messengers of joy; the life of all the children that run shouting to their mothers' arms; the life of all the parents that beget a life like unto their own; and the life of the mind that on the wings of an invisible thought strikes out to the hid battlements of eternity—to the life whence all living comes.

Suppose that, in addition to concentrating all the life of the universe in a single point, I could also concentrate in another focal point all the truths of the world, so that I could know the truth the astronomer seeks as he looks up through his telescope, and the truth the biologist seeks as he looks down through his microscope; the truth about the heavens, and who shut up the sea with doors when it did burst forth as issuing from a womb; the truth about the hiding place of darkness and the treasure house of hail, and the cave of the winds.

Suppose that I could know the truth about the common things: why fire, like a spirit, mounts to the heavens heavenly, and why gold, like clay, falls to the earth earthly; the truth the philosopher seeks as he tears apart with his mind the very wheels of the universe; the truth the theologian seeks as he uses Revelation to unravel the secrets of God, which far surpass anything the greatest minds, unaided by Revelation, can ever dream of.

Suppose that over and above all these pleasures of life and truth, there could be unified in another focal point all the delights and beauties of love that have contributed to the happiness of the universe: the love of the patriot for his country; the love of the soldier for his cause; the love of the scientist for his discovery; the love of the flowers as they smile upon the sun; the love of the earth at whose breast all creation drinks the milk of life.

Suppose you could unify at that same point the love of mothers, who swing open the great portals of life that a child may see the light of day; the love of friend for friend to whom he could reveal his heart through words; the love of spouse for spouse; the love of husband for wife; and even the love of angel for angel, and the angel for God with a fire and heat sufficient to enkindle the hearts of ten thousand times ten thousand worlds.

Suppose that all the pleasures of the world could be brought to these three focal points of life and truth and love, just as the rays of the sun are brought to unity in the sun; and suppose that all the successive pleasures of time could be enjoyed at one and the same "now"; and suppose that these points of unity on which our hearts and minds and souls would be directed, would not merely be three abstractions, but that the focal point in which all the pleasures of life were concentrated would be a life personal enough to be a Father.

Suppose that that focal point of truth in which all the pleasures of truth were concentrated, would not merely be an abstract truth, but a truth personal enough to be a Word or a Son, and that that focal point of love in which all the pleasures of love were concentrated, would be not merely an abstract love, but a love personal enough to be a Holy Spirit.

Suppose that once elevated to that supreme height, happiness would be so freed from limitations that it would include these three as one, not in succession, but with a permanence; not as in time, but as in the timeless—then we would have eternity, then we would have God! The Father, Son, and Holy Ghost: Perfect Life, Perfect Truth, Perfect Love. Then we would have happiness—and that would be Heaven.

But will the pleasures of that timelessness with God and that enjoyment of life and truth and love, which is the Trinity, be in any way comparable to the pleasures of time? Is there anyone on this earth that will tell me about Heaven? Certainly there are three faculties to which one might appeal, namely, to what one has seen, to what one has heard, and to what one can imagine.

Will Heaven surpass all the pleasures of the eye, and the ear, and the imagination? First of all, will it be as beautiful as some of the things that can be seen? I have seen the Villa d'Este of Rome with its long lanes of ilex and laurel, and its great avenues of cypress trees, all full of what might be called the vivacity of quiet and living silence; I have seen a sunset on the Mediterranean when two clouds came down like pillars to form a brilliant red tabernacle for the sun and it glowing like a golden host.

I have seen, from the harbor, the towers and the minarets of Constantinople pierce through the mist which hung over them like a silken veil; I have seen the chateau country of France and her Gothic Cathedrals aspiring heavenwards like prayers; I have seen the beauties of the castles of the Rhine, and the combination of all these visions almost makes me think of the doorkeeper of the Temple of Diana who used to cry out to those who entered: "Take heed to your eye," and so I wonder if the things of eternity will be as beautiful as the combined beauty of all the things which I have seen . . .

I have not seen all the beauties of nature, others I have heard of that I have not seen: I have heard of the beauties of the hanging gardens of Babylon, of the pomp and dignity of the palaces of the Doges, of the brilliance and glitter of the Roman Forum as its foundations rocked with the tramp of Rome's resistless legions; I have heard of the splendor of the Temple of Jerusalem as it shone like a jewel in the morning sun.

I have heard of the beauties of the garden of Paradise where fourfold rivers flowed through lands rich with the gold and onyx, a garden made beautiful as only God knows how to make a beautiful garden; I have heard of countless other beauties and joys of nature which tongue cannot describe, nor touch of brush convey, and I wonder if all the joys and pleasures of Heaven will be as great as the combined beauty of all the things of which I have heard.

Beyond what I have heard and seen, there are things which I can imagine: I can imagine a world in which there never would be pain, nor disease, nor death; I can imagine a world wherein every man would live in a castle, and in that commonwealth of castles there would be a due order of justice without complaint or anxiety.

I can imagine a world in which the winter would never come, and in which the flowers would never fade, and the sun would never set; I can imagine a world in which there would always be a peace and a quiet without idleness, a profound knowledge of things without research, a constant enjoyment without satiety; I can imagine a world which would eliminate all the evils and diseases and worries of life, and combine all its best joys and happiness, and I wonder if all the happiness of Heaven would be like the happiness of earth which I can imagine.

Will eternity be anything like what I have seen, or what I have heard, or what I can imagine? No, eternity will be nothing like anything I have seen, heard or imagined. Listen to the voice of God: "That eye hath not seen, nor ear heard, neither hath it entered into the heart of man, what things God hath prepared for them that love him." (1 Corinthians 2:9)

## Chapter 12

## Faith

REGARDLESS of your religious background, you have doubtless observed the tremendous disparity of points of view between those who possess Divine Faith through God's grace and those who have it not. Have you ever noticed when discussing important subjects, as pain, sorrow, sin, happiness, marriage, children, education, the purpose of life and the meaning of death, that the Catholic point of view is now poles apart from what is called the modern view?

You who have the faith probably have often felt a sense of inadequacy in dealing with those who have no faith, as if there were no common denominator. You and that person without faith seem to be living in different worlds. You feel powerless to penetrate the natural mentality of the modern pagan whom you meet on the street. It is like telling a blind man about color. You are not talking the same language. Like workmen on the Tower of Babel, there is no common understanding.

It was not so many years ago that those who rejected many Christian truths were considered off the reservation; e.g., the divorced who remarried, the atheists, the enemies of the family, or those who held that law was a dictate of the will, not of reason. Today, it is we who are considered off the reservation. It is they who are on it. The Christian is today on the defensive if for no other reason than because he is the exception.

The clarity of vision and certitude of those who have the gift of faith is sometimes misunderstood even by those who have faith. Hence, a Catholic is sometimes impatient with one who has not the faith, wrongly thinking that the reason he sees the truth so clearly is because of his own innate cleverness, and the reason his neighbor does not see it is due either to his stupidity or his stubbornness. Faith, it must be remembered, is not due to our wisdom, and the lack of faith is not due to their ignorance. Faith is solely a gift of God. "Flesh and blood hath not revealed it to thee, but my Father who is in heaven." (Matthew 16:17)

If you have not the faith, have you not often considered as utterly foolish, absurd and superstitious the judgments, the philosophy of life, and the outlook of those who live by faith? You think a Catholic, for instance, has surrendered both his freedom and his reason by obeying the laws of the Church and by accepting the truth of Christ in His Church.

Your judgment, then, is very much like one who looks at the windows of a church from outside, where they seem to be a meaningless confusion of leaden lines and dull colors. Once inside the church, and the leaden lines fade away as the pattern reveals itself vibrant with colors and life. In like manner, the Church may seem bewildering to those who are outside, but once you enter it, you will discover an order and harmony and a "beauty that leaves all other beauty pain."

The world today seems much more united in its negation of belief, than in its acceptance of a belief. The older generation could give you at least ten reasons for a wrong belief, such as a belief in materialism, but the modern man cannot give even one bad reason for total unbelief.

It is shockingly true that there is more in common today between a Christian in the state of grace, and a Chinaman, or Orthodox Jew, or a Mohammedan than there is between the true Christian and the average so called Christian person you are apt to meet at a night club, or even at the table in your neighbor's house.

When the Christian talks about God, the Chinaman or Orthodox Jew or Mohammedan can understand him, for they, too, believe that God is Sovereign and Judge of all men. But to the average pagan who believes man came from beast and, therefore, must act like one, all this is as so much fatuous nonsense and senile stupidity. A striking confirmation of this is that in the face of Anti-God crusades of Russia, Christians, Jews and Moslems presented a common front.

Why this difference between those who have the faith, and those who have it not? It is due to the fact that a soul in the state of grace has its intellect illumined, which enables it to perceive new truths which otherwise would be beyond its powers. Divine grace supernaturalizes that which makes us human, namely, our intellect and our will, giving them the power of higher action. The intellect still continues to know truth, but through grace operating in it as faith, it knows higher truths than those of reason. The human will in like manner, retains its love of good, but by grace, operating on it, it can now rely more on God or love Him more than by its unaided efforts:

|  | Faculty | Theological Virtues | Action | Object |
|---|---|---|---|---|
| Soul | Intellect | Faith | To believe | God |
|  | Will | Hope | To hope | God |
|  |  | Charity | To love | God |

You have exactly the same eyes at night as you have in the day, but you cannot see at night, because you lack the additional light of the sun. So, too, let two minds with identically the same education, the same mental capacities, and the same judgment, look on a Host enthroned on an altar. The one sees bread, the other sees Christ, not, of course, with the eyes of the flesh, but with the eyes of faith. Let them both look on death: one sees the end of a biological entity, the other an immortal creature being judged by God on how it used its freedom. The reason for the difference is: one has a light which the other lacks, namely, the light of faith.

This light of faith operates on human problems somewhat like an X-Ray. You look at a box with the naked eye and it appears to be of wood and tinsel and cheap wrapping paper, and, therefore, of no great value. You look at it later with an X-Ray and you see the contents of the box to be diamonds and rubies. In like manner, those who live only by the light of reason gaze upon a sick and feverish body, and see pain as valueless as a curse. But the mind endowed with the extra light of faith, sees through the pain: to him it is either a means for reparation for sins, or as a stepping stone to greater unity with His Master, whom "Life made love, and love made pain, and pain made death."

If you have not the light of faith, you may be very educated, but can you correlate your knowledge into a unified philosophy of life? Does your psychology jibe with your ethics? Does your emphasis on the dignity of man click with your denial of a soul? Rather is not your mind like a flattened Japanese lantern, a riot of colors without pattern or purpose? What you need to do is to have the candle of faith lighted on the inside of that lantern that you may see all your different lines of knowledge meet into one absorbing pattern leading to God.

Education is not the condition of receiving this additional light of faith, although an educated person can understand the faith better. Since the light of faith is from God and not from us, we cannot supply it, any more than we can restore vision if we lost our eyes. Being a true Christian, therefore, does not require an education. It is an education!

A little child who today is telling a sister in school that God made him, that he was made to know, love and serve God, and to be happy with Him in the next world, knows more, and is more profoundly educated, than all the professors throughout the length and breadth of this land, who babble about space-time deities, who prattle about new ethics to fit unethical lives, who negate all morality to suit their unmoral thinking, but who do not know, therefore, that beyond time is the timeless, beyond space is the spaceless, the Infinite Lord and Master of the Universe.

No wonder Our Lord prayed: "I confess to thee, O Father, Lord of heaven and earth, because thou hast hidden these things from the wise and prudent, and hast revealed them to little ones. Yea, Father, for so it hath seemed good in thy sight." (Luke 10:21) St. Paul later on clearly distinguished between these two kinds of wisdom: the false wisdom which uses reason to negate the God who gave reason, and the higher wisdom born of the grace of God: "For the foolishness of God is wiser than men; and the weakness of God is stronger than men." (1 Corinthians 1:25)

That is why those who live by the higher light of faith are so insistent that education be religious for, after all, if one does not know why he is living, there is not much purpose in living. There are those who would suggest that there be no religious training until the child is old enough to "decide for himself." They should also consistently suggest a child in a slum should not be removed to a better environment until he was old enough to decide for himself. Unfortunately, when that time comes he may already have contracted tuberculosis. Why not also argue that no infant should be born into the world until he is old enough to decide who his parents should be, to what economic class he will belong, and to what code he will subscribe, or even to decide whether he wants to come into the world at all.

Though faith is a gift of God, and though God will give it to those that ask it, there is one very human obstacle why more minds do not receive it, and that is Pride. Pride is the commonest sin of the modern mind, and yet the one of which the modern mind is never conscious. You have heard people say: "I like drink too much," or "I am quick tempered," but did you ever hear anyone say: "I am conceited"?

Pride is the exaltation of self as an absolute standard of truth, goodness and morality. It judges everything by itself, and for that reason everyone else is a rival, particularly God. Pride makes it impossible to know God. If I know everything, then not even God can teach me anything. If I am filled with myself, then there is no place for God. Like the inns of Bethlehem, we say to the Divine Visitor: "There is no room."

Pride is of two kinds: it is either the pride of omniscience or the pride of nescience. The pride of omniscience tries to convince your neighbor you know everything; the new pride of nescience tries to convince your neighbor that he knows nothing. The latter is the technique used by "sophomores" who pride themselves on the fact that man can know nothing. Hence, they doubt everything, and of this they are very sure. They seem to forget that the doubting of everything is impossible, for doubt is a shadow, and there can be no shadow without light.

If pride is the great human obstacle to faith, it follows that, from the human side, the essential condition of receiving faith is humility. Humility is not an underestimation of what we are, but the plain, unadulterated truth. A man who is 6 feet tall is not humble if he says: "No, really, I am only 5 feet tall."

If there ever came a moment in your life when you admitted you did not know it all, or said: "Oh! What a fool am I," you created a vacuum and a void which God's grace could fill. Before you accept the gift of faith, there may be a moment when you will think that you are giving up your reason; but that is only seeming, not real.

Your eye does not constantly look out at the light. Every few seconds it blinks, that is, it goes into temporary darkness; the blink apparently destroys vision. Really, the blink is the condition of better vision. So with your reason in relation to faith. There comes a time in conversion when you blink on your reason, that is, you doubt about its capacity to know everything, and you affirm the possibility that God could enlighten you. Then comes the gift of faith. Once that is received, you find out that instead of destroying your reason, you have perfected it. Faith now becomes to your reason what a telescope is to your eye; it opens up new fields of vision and new worlds which before were hidden and unknown.

Think not either that you lose your freedom by accepting the faith. A few years ago, I received a letter from a radio listener who said: "I imagine that you from your earliest youth were surrounded by priests and nuns who never permitted you to think for yourself. Why not throw off the yoke of Rome and begin to be free?"

I answered him thus: "In the center of a sea was an island on which children played and danced and sang. Around that island were great high walls which had stood for centuries. One day, some strange men came to the island in individual row boats, and said to the children: Who put up these walls? Can you not see that they are destroying your freedom? Tear them down!

"The children tore them down! Now if you go there, you will find all the children huddled together in the center of the island, afraid to play, afraid to sing, afraid to dance—afraid of falling into the sea."

Faith is not a dam which prevents the flow of the river of reason and thought; it is a levee which prevents unreason from flooding the countryside. Our senses were meant by God to be perfected by reason. That is why a man who loses his reason deliberately by drunkenness no longer sees as well as an animal, nor behaves as well as an animal. We say: "He has lost his senses."

Once the human senses have been deprived of reason, which is their perfection, they no longer function even as well as the sense of an animal. In like manner, once the human reason has lost faith, which is the perfection God freely intended it to have, then reason does not function as well without faith as it does with it. That is why reason alone is unable to get us out of the mess we are in today. Of and by itself, it cannot function well enough to handle the problems created by loss of faith and by misuse of reason and sin.

The following facts about faith are important:

1. Faith is not believing that something will happen, nor is it the acceptance of what is contrary to reason, nor is it an intellectual recognition which a man might give to something he does not understand or which his reason cannot prove, e.g., relativity. Faith is the acceptance of a truth on the authority of God revealing.

Faith is a supernatural virtue, whereby, inspired and assisted by the grace of God, we believe as true those things which He revealed, not because the truth of these things is clearly evident from reason alone, but because of the authority of God who cannot deceive nor be deceived.

Before faith, one makes an investigation by reason. Just as no business man would extend you credit without a reason for doing so, neither are you expected to put faith in anyone without a reason. Before you have faith, you study the motives of believing, e.g., why should I put faith in Christ?

Your reason investigates the miracles He worked, the prophecies which preannounced Him and the consonance of His teaching with your reason. These constitute the preambles of faith, from which you form a judgment of credibility: "This truth, that Christ is the Son of God, is worthy of belief." Passing to the practical order, you add: "I must believe it."

From then on, you give your assent: "I believe He is the Son of God, and this being so, whatever He reveals, I will accept as God's truth." The motive for your assent in faith is always the authority of God who tells you it is true. You would not believe unless you saw that you must believe.

You believe the truths of reason because there is intrinsic evidence; you believe in the truths of God because there is extrinsic evidence. You believe the sun is 92,000,000 miles away from the earth though you never measured it; you believe that Moscow is the capital of Russia, though you never saw it. So you accept the Truths of Christianity on the authority of God revealing in His Son Jesus Christ, Our Lord.

Faith, therefore, never is blind. Since your reason is dependent on uncreated Reason or Divine Truth, it follows that your reason should bow down to what God reveals. You believe now, not because of the arguments; they were only a necessary preliminary. You believe because God said it. The torch now burns by its own brilliance.

The nature of the act of faith was revealed by Our Lord's attitude toward the unbelieving Pharisees. They had seen miracles worked and prophecies fulfilled. They were not lacking in motives for belief. But they still refused to believe. Our Lord took a little child in His midst and said: "Amen I say to you, whosoever shall not receive the kingdom of God as a little child, shall not enter into it." (Mark 10:15)

By this He meant that the act of faith has more in common with the trusting belief of a child in his mother, than with the assent of a critic. The child believes what the mother tells him because she said it. His belief is an unaffected and trusting homage of love to his mother.

When the Christian believes, he does so, not because he has in the back of his mind the miracles of Christ, but because of the authority of one who can neither deceive nor be deceived. "If we receive the testimony of men, the testimony of God is greater. For this is the testimony of God, which is greater, because He hath testified of his Son. He that believeth in the Son of God, hath the testimony of God in himself. He that believeth not the Son, maketh him a liar; because he believeth not in the testimony which God hath testified of his Son." (1 John 5:9-10)

2. You cannot argue, or study, or reason, or hypnotize, or whip yourself, into faith. Faith is a gift of God. When anyone instructs you in Christian doctrine, he does not give you faith. He is only a spiritual agriculturist, tilling the soil of your soul, uprooting a few weeds and breaking up the clods of egotism. It is God who drops the seed. "For by grace you are saved through faith, and that not of yourselves, for it is the gift of God." (Ephesians 2:8)

If faith were a will to believe, you could produce your own faith by an act of the will. All you can do is to dispose yourself for its reception from the hands of God. As a dry stick is better disposed for burning than a wet stick, so a humble man is better disposed for faith than a know-it-all. In either case, as the fire which burns must come from outside the stick, so your faith must come from outside yourself, namely, from God.

When you try to make everything clear by reason, you somehow only succeed in making everything confusion. Once you introduce a single mystery, everything else becomes clear in the light of that one mystery.

The sun is the "mystery" in the universe; it is so bright you cannot look at it; you cannot "see" it. But in the light of it, everything else becomes clear. As Chesterton once said: "But you can see the moon and things under the moon, but the moon is the mother of lunatics."

3. Faith is unique and vital. There are not many faiths. There is only one faith: "One Lord, one faith, one baptism." (Ephesians 4:5) Out of the millions and millions of men who walked this earth, there is only One who is the Incarnate Lord; out of the millions of lights in the heaven, there is only one sun to light a world. "Upon this Rock I will build my Church"—not my churches.

Faith is like life; it must be taken in its entirety. Two mothers appeared in the court of Solomon. Both claimed a babe as their own. Solomon said that he would divide the child and give each claimant a half. One of the women protested and said: "Give the babe to her." Wise Solomon thereupon decided that the babe belonged to the one who protested, for she was the real mother. The Church is like that: it insists on the whole Truth.

Hence, you may not pick and choose among the words of the Blessed Lord and say: "I will accept the Sermon on the Mount, but not your words about hell." Or, "I believe in your doctrine of motherhood, but I cannot accept your teaching that it is unlawful for a man to divorce and marry again." The truths of God are like that babe: it is either the whole babe, or nothing.

Every religion in the world, I care not what it is, contains some reflection of one Eternal Truth. Every philosophy, every world-religion, every sect, contains an arc of the perfect round of the Natural and Revealed Truth. Confucianism has the fraction of fellowship; Indian asceticism has the fraction of self-abnegation; each human sect has an aspect of Christ's Truth.

That is why, in approaching those who have not the faith, one should not begin by pointing out their errors, but rather by indicating the fraction of truth they have in common with the fulness of Truth. Instead of saying to the Confucian: "You are wrong in ignoring the Fatherhood of God," one should say: "You are right in emphasizing brotherhood, but to make your brotherhood perfect, you need the Fatherhood of God and the Sonship of Christ, and the vivifying Unity of the Holy Spirit."

So, with every other religion and sect in the world. Today, men are starving. One should not go to them and say: "Do not eat poisons; they will kill you." We need only to give bread. In religion, in like manner, there is too much emphasis on the errors of unbelievers and not enough on the affirmation of Truth by believers. Break the bread of affirmation and teaching, and the grace of God will do the rest.

This is the great beauty of the Catholic Faith; its sense of proportion, or balance, or should we say, its humor. It does not handle the problem of death to the exclusion of sin, nor the problem of pain to the exclusion of matter; nor the problem of sin, to the exclusion of human freedom, nor the social use of property to the exclusion of personal right; nor the reality of the body and sex to the exclusion of the soul and its function, nor the reality of matter to the forgetfulness of the Spirit.

It never allows one doctrine to go to your head, like wine to an empty stomach. It keeps its balance for truth is a precarious thing. Like the great rocks in the Alps, there are a thousand angles at which they will fall, but there is only one at which they would stand.

It is easy to be a "pink" in this century, as it was easy to be a "liberal" in the 19th; it is easy to be a "materialist" today, as it was easy to be an "idealist" in the 19th century, but to keep one's head in the midst of all these changing moods and fancies, so that one is right, not when the world is right, but right when the world is wrong, is the thrill of a tight-rope walker, the thrill of the romance of orthodoxy.

4. The acceptance of the fulness of Truth will have the unfortunate quality of making you hated by the world. Forget for a moment the history of Christianity, and the fact that Christ existed. Suppose there appeared in this world today a man who claimed to be Divine Truth; and who did not say: "I will teach you Truth," but "I am the Truth." Suppose he gave evidence by his works of the truth of his statement. Knowing ourselves as we do, with our tendency to relativism, to indifference, and to the fusing of right and wrong, how do you suppose we would react to that Divine Truth? With hatred, with obloquy, with defiance; with charges of intolerance, narrow mindedness, bigotry, and crucifixion.

That is what happened to Christ. That is what Our Lord said would happen to those who accept His Truth. "If you had been of the world, the world would love its own: but because you are not of the world, but I have chosen you out of the world, therefore the world hateth you. Remember my word that I said to you: The servant is not greater than his master. If they have persecuted me, they will also persecute you: if they have kept my word, they will keep yours also." (John 15:19-20)

Hence, I believe that if the grace of God did not give me the fulness of Truth, and I were looking for it, I would begin my search by looking through the world for a Church that did not get along with the evil in the world! If that Church accused of countless lies, hated because it refused to compromise, ridiculed because it refused to fit the times and not all time, I would suspect that since it was hated by what is evil in the world, it therefore was good and holy; and if it is good and holy, it must be Divine. And I would sit down by its fountains and begin to drink the Waters of everlasting life.

*What will faith do for you?*

A. It will preserve your freedom. You still live in a world in which you are free to ask questions. Unless you build up some resistance to the organized propaganda which is more and more falling into the hands of pinks and reds, you will become the prey of their law and their authority whose very end is the extinction of your liberty.

Our Blessed Lord said the "truth will make you free." Turning His words around, they mean that if you do not know the Truth, you will be enslaved. If you do not know the truth about addition or subtraction, you will not be free to do your bookkeeping; if you do not know that zebras have stripes, you will not be free to draw them. If you do not know the truth of the nature of man, you will not be free to act as a man.

That is why as men become indifferent to right and wrong, disorder and chaos increase, and the State steps in to organize the chaos by force. Dictatorships arise in such a fashion. Such is the essence of Socialism, the compulsory organization of chaos.

That is why the Church is in full sympathy today with the multitude of people who, stirred by war, at first vaguely and then unyieldingly, believe that had there been the possibility of censuring and correcting the actions of public authority the world would not have been dragged into war.

Hence, democracy worthy of the name can have no other meaning than to place the citizen increasingly in a position to hold his own personal opinion, to express it and even to make it prevail for the common good.

B. Faith will answer the principal problems of your life: Why? Whence? Whither? If you are without faith, you are like a man who lost his memory and is locked in a dark room waiting for memory to come back. There are a hundred things you can do: scribble on the wall paper, cut your initials on the floor and paint the ceiling. But if you are ever to find out why you are there, and where you are going, you will have to enlarge your world beyond space and time. There is a door out of that room. Your reason can find it. But your reason can not create the light that floods the room, nor the new world in which you move, which is full of signs on the roadway to the City of Peace and Eternal Beatitude with God.

C. Faith will enlarge your knowledge, for there are many truths beyond the power of reason. You can look at a painting and from it learn something of the technique of the artist, his skill, and his power; but you could look on it from now until the crack of doom and you could never know the inmost thoughts of the artist. If you were to know them, he would have to reveal them to you. In like manner, you can know something of the power and wisdom of God by looking at His universe, but you could never know His thoughts and life unless He told them. His telling of His inner life is what is called Revelation.

Why should we go on saying; "I am the only judge; I am the only standard of truth." These statements remind one of the tourist who, passing through one of the galleries of Florence, remarked to the guide: "I don't think much of these pictures." To which the guide answered: "These pictures are not here for your judgment; they are your judges." So, too, your rejection of the truths beyond reason are the judge of your humility, your love of truth and your knowledge.

D. Faith will preserve your quality. Have you not noticed that as a man ceases to believe in God, he also ceases to believe in man? Have you observed that, if you have worked for or with a person of deep faith in Christ, you have always been treated with gentleness, equality and charity. You could not point to a single person who truly loves God and is mean to his fellowman.

Have you noticed that as men lose faith in God, they become selfish, immoral and cruel? On a cosmic scale, as religion decreases, tyranny increases; as men lose faith in Divinity, they lose faith in humanity. Where God is outlawed, there man is subjugated.

In vain will the world seek for equality until it has seen men through the eyes of faith. Faith teaches that all men, however poor, or ignorant, or crippled, however maimed, ugly, or degraded they may be, all bear within themselves the image of God, and have been bought by the precious blood of Jesus Christ. As this truth is forgotten, men are valued only because of what they can do, not because of what they are.

Since men cannot do things equally well, e.g., play violins, steer a plane, or teach philosophy, or stoke an engine, they are and must remain forever unequal. From the Christian point of view, all may not have the same rights to do certain jobs, because they lack the capacity, e.g., Toscanini has not a right to pitch for the New York Yankees, but all men have the right to a decent, purposeful and comfortable life in the structure of the community for which God has fitted them, and first and foremost of all, because of what they are: persons made to the image and likeness of God.

The false idea of the superiority of certain races and classes is due to the forgetfulness of the spiritual foundations of equality. We of the Western world have been rightly proud of the fact that we have a civilization superior to others. But we have given the wrong reason for that superiority. We assume that we are superior because we are white.

We are not. We are superior because we are Christians. The moment we cease to be Christian, we will revert to the barbarism from which we came.

In like manner, if the black, brown and yellow races of the world become converted to Christ, they will produce civilization and culture which will surpass ours if we forget Him who truly made us great. It is conceivable, if we could project ourselves a thousand years in the future, and then look back in retrospect over those 1000 years, that we might see in China the record of a Christian civilization which would make you forget Notre Dame and Chartres.

E. Finally, faith will enable you to possess the "Mind of Christ." "For let this mind be in you, which was also in Christ Jesus." (Philippians 2:5) Though you must meditate on the earthly life of Our Lord, you should not allow your mind to dwell exclusively on past events for by faith your minds are lifted upon the temporal and the contemporary to the eternal mind of Christ.

Everything in the universe fits into the larger rhythm of the Divine Pattern, which is denied to mortal eyes. From now on, you cease trying to find God in creatures, and begin seeing creatures in God and, therefore all of value, and worthy of your love. In the multitudinous duties of modern life, you will do nothing, which you cannot offer to God as a prayer; you will see that personal sanctity has more influence on society than social action; your sense of values will change.

You will think less of what you can store away, and more about what you can take with you when you die. Your rebellious moods will give way to resignation. Your tendency to discouragement, which was due to pride, will become an additional reason for throwing yourself like a wounded child into the Father's loving arms. You will cease to be an isolationist and begin to draw strength from the fellowship of the saints, and the Body of Christ.

You will think of God's love, not as an emotional paternalism, but as an unalterable dedication to goodness, to which you submit even when it hurts. You will be at peace, not only when things go your way, but when they go against you, because whatever happens you accept as God's will. You will rebuke within yourself all immoderate desires, all presumptious expectations, all ignoble self-indulgence because they bar the way to Him who is your Way, your Truth, and your Life.

With Paul you will say in the strength of a great faith: "I am sure that neither death, nor life, nor angels, nor principalities, nor powers, nor things present, nor things to come, nor might, nor height, nor depth, nor any other creature, shall be able to separate us from the love of God, which is in Christ Jesus our Lord." (Romans 8:38)

## Chapter 13
## Hope

It is not so much what happens in life that matters; it is rather how we react to it. You can always tell the character of a person by the size of the things that make him mad. Because modern man lives in a world which has reference to nothing but itself, it follows that when depression, war and death enter into his two dimensional world, he tumbles into the most hopeless despair.

A man can work joyfully at a picture puzzle, so long as he believes the puzzle can be put together into a composite whole. But if the puzzle is a hoax, or if it was not made by a rational mind, then one would go mad trying to work it out. It is this absence of purpose in life which has produced the fear and frustration of the modern mind.

To escape from such fear and despair, the modern man usually does one of three things:

a. He sometimes flees from existence by taking his own life. The great numerical increase in suicide, which merits to be called suicidism, is symptomatic of a spiritual disintegration, a sapping of the will to live, a plunge into the irrational and the meaningless self-destruction.

b. He sometimes develops a neurosis due to the disturbance of a godless heart. Neurosis is the common disease of every man who has no hope except in himself. Being "fed up" with life, he becomes cynical, self-centered, asserts himself in loud, boorish, boasting tones to atone for his own inner hunger, nakedness and ignorance.

Forever trying to lift himself by his own bootstraps, eternally playing the role of his own redeemer, he develops "kinks" and "psychoses" and becomes eccentric because he is out of his center, which is God. The increase of alcoholism is due to a great extent to neurosis and psychosis.

c. While not taking his physical life, he sometimes seeks to kill his psychological life, by losing it in the crowd. Cosmopolitanism, or the flight from the country, is to a great extent due to the quest of anonymity.

The modern man hates to be alone with himself; it makes him think; it reveals the awful cleavage in the depths of his soul. Hence, he seeks noise, excitement, crowds and the thousand and one other desperate hectic devices of self-conscious beings to become unconscious. The terror of a crowded tenement, and its hand-to-mouth existence is preferable to the terror of the inner depths of a soul without God. It is no wonder today we speak of the "common-man," the "mass-man" and the "man without personality."

There is another way out than suicide, frustration and anonymity, and that is the way of hope, not natural hope, but supernatural hope which settles your soul in God, and directs your will toward Him. Natural hope, because based exclusively on external circumstances, by its nature is temperamental; it fluctuates, is moody, is high when things go our way, low when things go wrong.

Supernatural hope on the contrary, is constant and invariable; it believes in the light of the sun even when the sun does not shine because it is based on a sustained collaboration with the Will of God. It may be retorted that such religion is "escapism," and "opium of the people," by creating a disinterest in the problems of this life, through concentration on pie in the sky.

This is not true! Who has done most for the world? He who serves this world only, or he who serves God first and the world through Him? Which man loves a woman more: the one who sees in her a thing of the opposite sex, or the one who loves her virtue more? Who makes the best soldier, the one who loves his life above all, or the one who loves his country more than his life? St. Francis of Assisi never produced any work of art, but who has inspired more art?

The great truth hidden behind these questions is: love of neighbor, the righting of social wrongs, zeal for political justice and equality are all byproducts of something higher. The best way to be healthy is not to spend your life trying to be healthy. There is not only sound theology, but profound human psychology in the words: "Seek ye therefore first the Kingdom of God, and his justice, and all these things shall be added unto you." (Matthew 6:33) In our modern language, aim at heaven and you will get earth thrown in!

Just as natural hope makes the will tend toward an object of its desires, e.g., it makes the farmer cultivate his crops in hope of harvest, so supernatural hope makes the will strive toward God, and incidentally its own happiness.

How do you react to the vicissitudes of life? Do you rebel because God does not answer your prayers to become rich? Do you deny God because He called away your husband, your wife, your child? In the midst of a war, do you summon God to judgment as the criminal who started it all and ask "Why does He not stop it?"

These considerations may help you to build up a firm hope in God.

1. *Everything that happens has been foreseen and known by God from all eternity, and is either willed by Him, or at least permitted.*

God's knowledge does not grow as ours does, from ignorance to wisdom. The Fall did not catch God napping. God is Science, but He is not a scientist. God knows all, but He learns nothing from experience. He does not look down on you from Heaven as you look down on an ant-hill, seeing you going in and out of your house, walking to work, and then telling an angel-secretary to record the unkind word you said to the grocer-boy.

Why is it we always think of God as watching the bad things we do, and never the good deeds? God does not keep a record of your deeds. You do your own bookkeeping. Your conscience takes your own dictation. God knows all things merely by looking into Himself, not by reading over your shoulder.

An architect can tell you how many rooms will be in your house, and the exact size of each, before the house is built because he is the cause of the becoming of that house. God is the cause of the being of all things. He knows all before they happen.

As a motion picture reel contains the whole story before it is thrown upon the screen, so God knows all. But before it is acted on the stage of history, God knows all the possible radii that can be drawn from a point in the center to the circumference. He, therefore, knows all the possible directions your human will can take.

Do not think that because God knows all that, therefore He has predetermined you to Heaven and hell independently of your merits and irrespective of your freedom.

Remember that in God there is no future. God knows all, not in the succession of time, but in the "now standing still" of eternity, i.e., all at once. His knowledge that you shall act in a particular manner is not the immediate cause of your acting, any more than your knowledge that you are sitting down caused you to sit down, or prevents you from getting up, if you willed to do it.

Our Blessed Mother could have refused the dignity of becoming the Mother of God, as Judas could have resisted the temptation to betray and repented. The fact that God knew what each would do did not make them act the way they did. Since you are free, you can act contrary to God's will. If a doctor knows that it is all for your good to undergo an operation, you must not blame him, if you refuse to have the operation and lose your health. Free-will either cooperates with or rebels against predestination; it does not "surmount" it.

Because there is no future in God, foreknowing is not forecausing. You may know the stock market very well, and in virtue of your superior wisdom foretell that such and such a stock will sell for 50 points in three months. In three months it does reach 50 points. Did you cause it to reach 50 points, or did you foreknow it?

You may be in a tower where you can see advancing a man in the distance who has never been over that terrain before. You know that before he reaches the tower he must cross that ditch, wade that pond, tramp those bushes, and climb that hill. You foresee all the possibilities, but you do not cause him to cross those obstacles. The pilot is free to drive his ship, but he is not free to drive the waves.

While God has given to each of us the power to act, He has left us free to exercise the power. Why then blame God when we abuse our freedom? God will not destroy your freedom. Hell is the eternal guarantee of our freedom to rebel, or of the power to make fools out of ourselves.

The following story illustrates the fallacy of predestination without freedom: In the Colonial days of our country, there was a wife who believed in a peculiar kind of predestination which left no room for human freedom. Her husband, who did not share her eccentricities, one day left for the market. He came back after a few minutes saying he forgot his gun. She said: "You are either predestined to be shot, or you are not predestined to be shot. If you are predestined to be shot, the gun will do you no good. If you are not predestined to be shot, you will not need it. Therefore, do not take your gun."

But he answered: "Suppose I am predestined to be shot by an Indian on condition I do not have my gun?" That was sound religion. It allowed for human freedom. We are our own creators. To those who ask: "If God knew I would lose my soul, why did He make me?" The answer is: "God did not make you as a lost soul. You made yourself." The universe is moral and, therefore, conditional: "Behold I stand at the door and knock!" God knocks! He breaks down no doors. The latch is on our side, not God's.

2. *God permits evil things for the reason of a greater good related to His Love and the salvation of our souls.*

God does permit evil. In the strong language of Scripture: "He that spared not even his own Son; but delivered Him up for us all." (Romans 8:32) Our Lord told Judas: "This is your hour." (Luke 22:53) Evil does have its hour. All that it can do within that hour is to put out the lights of the world. But God has His day.

The evil of the world is inseparable from human freedom, and hence the cost of destroying the world's evil would be the destruction of human freedom. Certainly none of us want to pay that high a price, particularly since God would never permit evil unless He could draw some good from it.

God can draw good out of evil because, while the power of doing evil is ours, the effects of our evil deeds are outside our control, and, therefore, in the hands of God. You are free to break the law of gravitation, but you have no control over the effects of throwing yourself from the top of the Washington Monument.

The brethren of Joseph were free to toss him into a well, but from that point on Joseph was in God's hands. Rightly did he say to his brethren: "You intended it for evil, but God for good." The executioners were free to nail Our Lord to the cross, Judas was free to betray, the judges were free to misjudge, but they could not prevent the effect of their evil deed, viz., Crucifixion, being used by God as the means of our redemption.

St. Peter spoke of it as an evil deed, as known and permitted by God. "Jesus of Nazareth, a man approved of God among you, by miracles, and wonders, and signs, which God did by him, in the midst of you, as you also know: The same being delivered up, by the determinate counsel and foreknowledge of God, you by the hands of wicked men have crucified and slain. Whom God hath raised up, having loosed the sorrows of hell, as it was impossible that he should be holden by it." (Acts 2:22-24)

The evil which God permits must not be judged by its immediate effects, but rather by its ultimate effects. When you go to a theatre, you do not walk out because you see a good man suffering in the first act. You give the dramatist credit for a plot. Why cannot you do that much with God?

The mouse in the piano cannot understand why anyone should disturb his gnawing at the keys by making weird sounds. Much less can our puny minds grasp the plan of God. Martha could not understand why Lazarus should die, particularly because Lazarus was the friend of Our Lord. But Our Lord told her it was in order that God's power might be revealed in the resurrection from the death. The slaughter of the Innocents probably saved many boys from growing up into men who on Good Friday would have shouted "crucify."

3. *We must do everything within our power to fulfil God's will as it is made known to us by His Mystical Body, the Commandments and our lawfully constituted superiors, and the duties flowing from our state in*

*life*. Everything that is outside our power, we must abandon and surrender to His Holy Will.

Notice the distinction between within our power, and outside our power. There is to be no fatalism. Some things are under our control. We are not to be like the man who perilously walked the railing of a ship in a storm at sea saying: "I am a fatalist! I believe that when your time comes, there is nothing you can do about it." There was much more wisdom in the colored preacher who said: "You run up against a brick wall every now and then during life. If God wants you to go through that wall, it is up to God to make the hole."

We are here concerned with those things outside your power, e.g., sickness, accident, bumps on buses, trampled toes in subways, the barbed word of a fellow-worker; rain on picnic days, death of Aunt Ellen on your wedding day, colds on vacation, the loss of your purse and moth balls in your suit.

God could have prevented any of these things. He could have stopped your headache, prevented a bullet from hitting your boy, forestalled cramps during a swim and killed the germ that laid you low. If He did not, it was for a superior reason. Therefore, say: "God's will be done."

If you tell a citizen of Erin it is a bad day, nine times out of ten he will answer: "It's a good day to save your soul." Maybe there is no such thing in God's eyes as bad weather; perhaps there are only good clothes.

I broadcast to you. There is an engineer in a glass booth who does what is technically called the "mixing." While I talk, he has his fingers on the dial. He controls the tone, the volume and the register of my voice. He does these things not to make my broadcast poor, but to make it good. God does something of that kind with our actions. We are free to perform them, but He "mixes" them with other actions and other people for the good of the universe and the salvation of souls.

We must not think that God is good because we have a fat bank account. Providence is not the Provident Loan. Sanctity consists in accepting whatever happens to us as God's will, and even thanking Him for it. "Not everyone that saith to me, Lord, Lord, shall enter into the kingdom of heaven: but he that doth the will of my Father who is in heaven, he shall enter into the kingdom of heaven." (Matthew 7:21)

Do not become impatient with God because He does not answer your prayers immediately. We are always in a hurry; God is not. Perhaps that is one of the reasons why so few Americans like Rome: they heard it was not built in a day. Evil things are generally done quickly. "What thou dost, do quickly."

In a certain sense there is no unanswered prayer. Is there a father in the world who ever refused the request of his son for a gift which would not be good for him, who did not pick him up and give him a sign of love that made him forget the request?

Every moment comes to you pregnant with a Divine Purpose; time being so precious that God deals it out only second by second. Once it leaves your hands and your power to do with it as you please, it plunges into eternity, to remain forever whatever you made it.

Does not the scientist gain more control over nature by humbly sitting down before the facts of nature and being docile to its teachings? In like manner, surrender yourself to God, and all is yours. It is one of the paradoxes of creation that we gain control by submission. You will thus learn to appreciate the advantages of disadvantages.

Your very handicaps will not be reasons for despair, but points of departure for new horizons. When caught within circumstances beyond your control, make them creative of peace by surrender to the Divine Will. From prison St. Paul wrote: "Be mindful of my bands. Grace be with you." (Colossians 4:18) Others would have said: "I am in prison. God give me grace."

Circumstances must not control you; you must control circumstances. Do something to them! Even the irritations of life can be made stepping stones to salvation. An oyster develops a pearl because a grain of sand irritated it. Cease talking about your pains and aches. Thank God for them! An act of thanksgiving when things go against our will, then a thousand acts of thanksgiving when things go according to our will.

"Giving thanks always for all things in the name of Our Lord Jesus Christ, to God and Father." (Ephesians 5:20) God does not will the sin of those who hate you, but He does will your humiliation. Things happen against your will but nothing, except sin, happens against God's will. When the messenger came to Job saying that the Sabeans had stolen his live stock and killed his sons, Job did not say: "The Lord gave me wealth; the Sabeans took it away." He did say: "The Lord gave, and the Lord hath taken away: as it hath pleased the Lord so is it done: blessed be the name of the Lord." (Job 1:21)

When anyone asks you "How are you?" remember it is not a question, but a greeting!

If you trust in God and surrender to His will, you are always happy, for "to them that love God, all things work together unto good." (Romans 8:28) "Whatsoever shall befall the just man, it shall not make him sad." (Proverbs 12:21)

Discouragement is a form of pride; sadness is often caused by our egotism. If you will whatever God wills, you always have exactly what you want. When you want anything else, you are not happy before you get it, and when you do get it, you do not want it. That is why you are "up" today and "down" tomorrow.

You will never be happy if your happiness depends on getting solely what you want. Change the focus. Get a new center. Will what God wills, and your joy no man shall take from you. "So also you now indeed have sorrow; but I will see you again, and your heart shall rejoice; and your joy no man shall take from you. And in that day you shall not ask me anything. Amen, amen I say to you: if you ask the Father any thing in my name, he will give it you. Hitherto you have not asked any thing in my name. Ask, and you shall receive; that your joy may be full." (John 16:22-24)

Be not afraid! "For this is the will of God, your sanctification." (1 Thessalonians 4:3) Think not that you could do more good if you were well, or that you could be more kind if you had more money, or that you could exercise more power for good if you had another position! What matters is not what we are, or what we are doing, but whether we are doing God's will!

Place not your trust in God because of your merits! He loves you despite your unworthiness. It is His love which will make you better rather than your betterment which will make Him love you. Often during the day say: "God loves me, and He is on my side, by my side."

Believe firmly that God's action toward you is a masterpiece of partiality and love. Be not like a child who wants to help his father fix the car before he is trained to do it! Give God a chance to love you, to show His will, to train you in His affection. Rejoice! I say again, rejoice: "Thy will be done on earth as it is in heaven."

## Chapter 14

## Charity

America's greatest enemy is not from without, but from within, and that enemy is hate: hatred of races, peoples, classes and religions. If America ever dies, it will be not through conquest but suicide.

It is heartening to know that there are many attempts to heal these wounds of hate. Principal among them are: pleas for tolerance, for the substitution of new hates, for example, Naziism, for the violent denunciation of groups as bigots. None of these remedies will eradicate hate. Tolerance pleas will not, for why should any creature on God's earth be tolerated? Substitution of other hatreds will not work, for you cannot cure small hates by big hates.

There is more tragedy than we suspect in the fact that we have become most united as a nation at a moment when we have developed a hate against certain foreign countries. Calling other people "bigots" is only a proof of our own bigotry for most generally we ascribe to others our own hidden faults.

Perhaps that is why some politicians call one another "crooked." They proclaim their own innocence by pointing to the mud on the neighbor's escutcheon. Name-calling merely rationalizes our own insincerities, and particularly those names which have never been defined, like "Fascist." Typical of its use is the case of the little girl who, on being asked why she called another little girl a Fascist, answered: "I call anyone I don't like a Fascist." That is perhaps the best definition that has yet been given.

All these remedies are ineffective because they leave our heart unchanged with all its hidden uneasiness. Hate can be eradicated only by creating a new focus and that brings us to the third of the virtues, namely, charity.

By charity we do not mean kindness, philanthropy, generosity, or big-heartedness, but a supernatural gift of God by which we are enabled to love Him above all things for His own sake alone, and, in that love, to love all that He loves. To make it clear, we here set down the three principal characteristics of charity or supernatural love: 1. It is in the will, not in the emotions. 2. It is a habit, not a spasmodic art. 3. It is a love-relationship, not a contract.

First: Supernatural love is in the will, not in the emotions or passions or senses. In human love, feelings have their places, but unless they are subordinated to reason, will, and faith, they degenerate into lust, which wills not the good of the one loved, but the pleasure of the one loving.

Because charity is in the will, you can command it, which you cannot do with natural likes or dislikes. A little boy cannot help disliking spinach, as perhaps you cannot help disliking sauerkraut, and as I cannot help disliking chicken. The same is true of your reactions to certain people. You cannot help feeling an emotional reaction against the egotistical, the sophisticated, and the loud, or those who run for first seats or snore in their sleep.

Though you cannot like everyone because you have no control over your physiological reactions, you can love everyone in the Divine sense, for that kind of love, being in the will, can be commanded or elicited. That is why love of God and neighbor can be commanded: "A new commandment I give unto you: That you love one another, as I have loved you, that you also love one another." (John 13:34)

Over and above your dislikes and your emotional reactions to certain people, there can coexist a genuine love of them, for God's sake. Charity is a consequence not of anything which affects our senses, but of Divine faith. Outwardly, your neighbor may be very unlikable; but inwardly he is one in whom the image of God can be recreated by the kiss of charity.

You can only like those who like you, but you can love those who dislike you. You can go through life liking those who like you without the love of God, but you cannot love those who hate you without the love of God. Humanism is sufficient for those of our set, or for those who like to go slumming from ivory towers, but it is not enough to make us love those who apparently are not worth loving. To will to be kind when the emotion is unkind, requires a stronger dynamic than "love of humanity."

To love them, we must recall that we who are not worth loving are loved by Love. "For if you love them that love you, what reward shall you have? Do not even the publicans this? And if you salute your brethren only, what do you more? Do not also the heathens this? Be you therefore perfect, as also your heavenly Father is perfect." (Matthew 5:46-48)

Second: Charity is not identical with kind acts. There is a tremendous amount of sentimental romanticism associated with much human kindness. Remember the great glow you got from giving your overcoat to the beggar on the street, for assisting a blind man up the stairs, for escorting an old woman through traffic, and for contributing a ten-dollar bill to relieve an indigent widow. The warmth of self-approval surged through your body, and though you never said it aloud, you did inwardly say: "Gee! I'm swell," or "Well, I've done my good deed for today." These good deeds are not to be reproved but commended.

What we wish to emphasize is that nothing has done so much harm to a healthy friendliness as the belief that we ought to do one good act a day. Why one good act? What about all the other acts? Charity is a habit, not an isolated act. A husband and a wife are out driving. They see a young blonde along the roadside changing a tire. The husband gets out to help her. Would he have done it if the blonde were fifty? He changes the tire, dirties his clothes, cuts his finger, but is all politeness, overflowing sweetness, and exuding charm. When he gets back into his own car, his heart aglow with the good deed, his wife says: "I wish you would talk that nice to me when I ask you to mow the lawn. Yesterday when I asked you to bring in the milk, you said: 'Are you a cripple?' "

See the difference between one act and a habit? Charity is a habit, not a gush, or sentiment; it is a virtue, not an ephemeral thing of moods and impulses; it is a quality of the soul, rather than an isolated good deed.

How do you judge a good piano player? By an occasional right note or by the habit or virtue of striking right notes? An habitually evil man every now and then may do a good deed. Gangsters endowed soup kitchens and the movies glorified them. But in Christian eyes, this did not prove they were good.

Occasionally, an habitually good man may fall, but evil is the exception in his life; it is the rule in the life of the gangster. Whether we know it or not, the actions of our daily life are fixing our character for good or for evil. The things you do, the thoughts you think, the words you say, are turning you either into a saint or a devil, to be placed at either the right or the left side of the Divine Judge.

If love of God and neighbor becomes a habit of our soul, we are developing Heaven within us. The difference then between earth and Heaven will be that of the acorn and the oak. Grace is the seed of glory. But if hatred and evil become the habit of our soul, then we are developing hell within us. Hell will be related to our evil life as death to poison. In Heaven there will be no faith for then we will see God; in Heaven there will be no hope for then we will possess God. But in Heaven there will be charity for "love endureth forever."

Third: Charity is a love-relationship rather than a commercial contract. There are many who think that religion is a kind of business relationship between God and the soul, and that if I give to God, He ought to give something to me; or since I owe Him worship in justice, He owes me prosperity in return.

That is exactly the attitude of the Pharisee who went up to the front of the Temple and told Our Lord that he was an honest man, the husband of one wife and gave 10% of his earnings to the Church. The assumption was that by doing these things He was putting God in His debt, as some moderns do when they say: "I can't understand why God should do this to me. I always said my prayers," or "Well, I have done my bit to religion. I send the church a check every year." In other words: "I do my part, O Lord! Now, you do yours."

If your religion is of this kind, you have no religion. Religion is a relationship; not a contract. Hence it begins not with doing good; it begins with a supernatural relation between God and your soul and your neighbor. A right relationship with God, initiated by grace, will inspire you to do good things, but doing good things does not make you a child of God.

Eric Gill once said that "a thief who loves God is a more religious man than an honest man who does not love God." This startling statement has truth in it when understood to mean that the love relationship with God can make the thief honest, but honesty in business does not establish a love relationship with God.

Religion begins with love. "Thou shalt love the Lord thy God with thy whole heart, and with thy whole soul, and with all thy strength, and with all thy mind: and thy neighbor as thyself." (Luke 10:27) The word, "neighbor," here means not the one who lives next door, but your enemy. Conceivably, it could be both simultaneously, as Our Lord implied in the parable of the Good Samaritan.

Translating Charity's commandment into the concrete, it means that you must love your enemy as you love yourself. Does that mean that you must love Hitler as you love yourself, or Kasio, or the thief who stole your tires, or the woman who said you had so many wrinkles that you had to screw on your hat? It means just that. But how can you love that kind of enemy as you love yourself?

Well, how do you love yourself? Do you like the way you look? If you did, you would not try to improve it out of a box. Did you ever want to be anyone else? Why do you lie about your age? Do you dislike your dish-pan hands, your pink toothbrush, your athlete's foot? Do you hate yourself when you miss the golf ball? Do you like yourself when you spread gossip, run down your neighbor's reputation, are irritable and moody?

You do not like yourself in these moments. At the same time, you do love yourself, and you know you do! When you come into a room you invariably pick out the softest chair; you buy yourself good clothes, treat yourself to nice presents; when anyone says you are intelligent or beautiful, you always feel that such a person is of very sound judgment. But when people say you are "catty" or selfish, you feel they have not understood your good nature, or maybe they are "Fascists."

Thus, you love yourself, and yet you do not love yourself. What you love about yourself is the person that God made; what you hate about yourself is that God-made person whom you spoiled. You like the sinner, but you hate the sin. That is why when you do wrong, you ask to be given another chance, or you promise to do better, or you find excuses. But you never deny there is hope.

That is just the way Our Lord intended that you should love your enemies: Love them as you love yourself, hating their sin, loving them as sinners; disliking that which blurs the Divine image, liking the Divine image which is beneath the blur; never arrogating to yourself a greater right to God's love than they, since deep in your own heart you know that no one could be less deserving of His love than you. And when you see them receiving the just due of their crimes, you do not gloat over them, but say: "There I go, except for the grace of God."

In this spirit, we are to understand the words of Our Lord: "Love your enemies, do good to them that hate you. Bless them that curse you, and pray for them that calumniate you. And to him that striketh thee on the one cheek, offer also the other. And him, that taketh away from thee thy cloak, forbid not to take thy coat also." (Luke 6:27-29) It is Christian to hate the evil of anti-Christians, but not without praying for these enemies that they might be saved for "God commendeth his charity towards us; because when as yet we were sinners, according to the time." (Romans 5:8)

If, then, you bear a hatred toward anyone, overcome it by doing that person a favor. You can begin to like classical music only by listening to it, and you can make friends out of your enemies only by practising charity. "If anyone strike you on the right cheek, turn your left"—for that kills hate! hate dies in the germ.

Your knowledge will get out of date; your statistics will be old next month; the theories you learned in college are already antiquated. But love never gets out of date. Love, therefore, all things, and all persons in God.

So long as there are poor; I am poor:
So long as there are prisons, I am a prisoner:
So long as there are sick, I am weak:
So long as there is ignorance, I must learn the truth:
So long as there is hate, I must love:
So long as there is hunger, I am famished.

Such is the identification Our Divine Lord would have us make with all whom He made in love and for love. Where we do not find love, we must put it. Then everyone is lovable. There is nothing in all the world more calculated to inspire love for others, than this Vision of Christ in our fellowman: "For I was hungry, and you gave me to eat; I was thirsty, and you gave me to drink: I was a stranger, and you took me in: Naked, and you covered me: sick and you visited me; I was in prison, and you came to me." (Matthew 25:35-36)

# The Life of Christ

[1954]

# PART 1

## *EARLY LIFE OF CHRIST*

Hɪsᴛᴏʀʏ is full of men who said that they came from God, or that they were gods, or that they bore a message from God. Buddha, Mohammed, Confucius, Christ, Socrates, Lao-tze and thousands of others—each has a right to be heard for his claims. There must be tests to decide whether the claims to divinity are justified. These tests, available to all men, all civilizations and all ages, are two-fold:—*reason* and *history*. *Reason*, because everyone has it, even those without faith; *history*, because everyone lives in it, and should know something about it.

Our reason tells us that if any of the claimants came from God, the least that God could do to support his claim would be to preannounce his coming. Automobile manufacturers tell us when to expect a new model. If God is sending anyone from Himself with the most important message for all men, He owes it to us to let us know *when* the Messenger is coming, *where* He will be born, *where* He will live, the *doctrine* He will teach, the *enemies* He will make, the *program* He will adopt for the future, and the manner of His *death*. By His conformity with these announcements, we could judge Him.

Reason further tells us that if God does not do this, then there is nothing to prevent any fool from appearing in history and saying: "I am from God," or "An angel appeared to me in the desert and gave me this message." In such a case there is no objective, historical test for such a messenger. We have just his word for it, and he could be suffering a delusion.

If a visitor came from a foreign country to Washington, and said he was a diplomat, we would ask to see his passport and his credentials. His papers would have to antedate his coming. If we ask for such proofs of identity from diplomats, we certainly ought to do so in the all-important subject of religion, asking: "What record is there before you were born that you were coming?"

With this test in mind, line up the claimants. Include anyone you please for, at the moment, Christ is no greater than any of them. We now address them: "Socrates, did anyone know you were coming?" "Gotama, did anyone ever preannounce you and your message, and predict that one day you would sit under the Buddha tree?" "Mohammed, was the place of your birth recorded, and given to men centuries before, so that when you did come, men would know you were a messenger from God?" "Christ, did anyone know of Your coming, the circumstances of Your life, where You would live?"

All are silent—but one. There were no predictions about Buddha, Mohammed, or anyone else—except Christ. Others just came and said: "Here I am, believe me." They were, therefore, men among men, and not the Divine in the human, which is the kind of leader we want for these hard times. Christ, alone, steps out of the line and answers: "My coming was foretold, even to the smallest detail."

He tells us to search the writings of the Jewish people and the correlated history of the Babylonians, Persians, Greeks and Romans, and for the moment, to regard their writings merely as historical documents, not as inspired writings. The Person of Christ in passing this test of reason and history speaks:

"About two thousand years before I was born, there appeared a man, Abraham, as the head of people in whom 'all the nations of the earth would be blessed.' About two thousand years before I was born, it was foretold that He Who would be born among the people of Abraham, would be also the 'expected of the nations', that is, of the Gentiles as well as the Jews. About seven hundred years before I was born, it was foretold that I would be born in Bethlehem, and that even though born in time, I already had an eternal birth.

"Not only was My birthplace foretold, but about seven hundred years before, it was foretold that I would be born of a Virgin! 'A Virgin shall conceive and bring forth a son, and His name shall be called Emmanuel.' About seven hundred years before I was born, it was foretold that the Kings of the East would bring gold and frankincense and myrrh, that I would sojourn to Egypt, and that I would live in Nazareth. About six hundred years before I was born, it was foretold that I would come within a set period after Cyrus gave out the order for rebuilding the walls of Jerusalem. About five hundred years before I was born, it was foretold that My name would be Jesus or Saviour.

"Even the details of My character were preannounced, namely, that I would be kind, console the afflicted, be rejected by My own people. The details of My death were foretold: Centuries before, it was prophesied that there would be wounds in My hands and feet, that My enemies would shake dice for My garments, and yet in putting Me to death, they would not break a bone of My body. A thousand years before, it was foretold that at My death I would be given vinegar and gall in My thirst.

"Six centuries before My birth, it was preannounced that I would ascend into heaven. So many prophecies were made concerning Me that at the time of My coming, the ancient synagogues collected 456 distinct prophecies. And it was not only the people of Israel who expected Me, but all the other peoples of the world."

We turn now to pagan testimony. Tacitus, speaking for the ancient Romans, says: "People were generally persuaded in the faith of the ancient prophecies, that the East was to prevail, and that from Judea was to come the master and ruler of the world."

Suetonius, in his life of Vespasian, recounting the Roman tradition also said: "It was an old and constant belief throughout the East, that by indubitably certain prophecies, the Jews were to attain the highest power." China had the same expectation but, because it was on the other side of the world, believed that the great Wise Man would be born in the West. The Annals of the Celestial Empire state: "In the 24th year of Tchao-Wang of the dynasty of the Chou, on the 8th day of the 4th moon, a light appeared in the southwest which illumined the king's palace. The monarch, struck by its splendor, interrogated the sages. They showed him books in which this prodigy signified the appearance of the great Saint of the West whose religion was to be introduced into their country."

The Greeks expected Him, for Aeschylus in his Prometheus, six centuries before His coming, wrote: "Look not for any end moreover to this curse until God appears, to accept upon His Head the pangs of thy own sins vicarious."

How did the Magi of the East know of His coming, if it was not from the many prophesies circulated through the world by the Jews and probably through the prophecy made to the Persians by Daniel more than 500 years before His Birth?

Cicero, after recounting the ancient oracles and Sibyls about a "King whom we must recognize to be saved," asked in expectation: "What man and of what period of time do these predictions point?" The Fourth Eclogue of Virgil recounted the same ancient tradition and spoke of a "chaste woman, smiling on her infant boy, with whom the Iron Age would pass away."

Suetonius quotes a contemporary author to the effect that the Romans were so fearful about a King who would rule the world, that they ordered all children born that year to be killed—an order that was not fulfilled, except by Herod.

Not only were the Jews expecting the birth of a Great King, a Wise Man and a Saviour, but Plato also spoke of the Logos; Socrates, of the Universal Wise Man "yet to come"; Confucius, of "the Saint"; the Sibyls, of a "Universal King"; the Greek Dramatist, of a Saviour and Redeemer to unloose the "primal eldest curse."

What separates Christ from all men is first, He was expected. Even the Gentiles had a longing for some deliverer or redeemer. This fact alone differentiates Him from all other religious leaders.

The second fact is that once He appeared, He hit history with such an impact that He split it in two, dividing all history into the period previous to His coming, and the period after His coming. Buddha did not do this, nor did any of the Indian philosophers. Even those who deny God must date their attacks upon Him as done in A.D. (*anno Domini*)—so many years after His coming.

The third fact which separates Him from all others is this: *Every other person who came into this world, came into it to live. He came into it to die.* Death was a stumbling block to Socrates—it interrupted his teaching. But to Christ, death was the goal of His life, the gold that He was seeking. Few of His words or actions are intelligible, unless we keep in mind His Cross. He presented Himself as a Saviour, rather than a Teacher. It meant nothing to teach men to be good, unless He gave them the power to be good, after rescuing them from the frustration of guilt. John gives His Eternal pre-history; Matthew His temporal prehistory in his geneology. What is significant about it is how much his ancestry is tied up with sinners and with foreigners! There are four women mentioned: Thamar, a harlot; Rahab, another; Ruth, the Moabitess, and Bathsheba. Three of them are tainted as regards womanly purity, and one, though morally good, had alien blood in her veins. These "blots on the escutcheon" of His human lineage, suggest a pity for the sinful and for the strangers of the covenant. Both such charges would later on be hurled against Him, namely "He is a friend of sinners"; "He is a Samaritan." But the shadow of a stained past beckons to the future love of the stained. Born of a woman, He was a man and could be one with mankind; born of a Virgin, overshadowed by the Spirit and "full of grace," He would be outside that current of sin which infected all humanity.

A fourth fact about Christ is that, unlike other world teachers, He does not fit into the category of a *good man*. Good men do not lie. But if Christ is not all that He said He was, namely, the Son of the Living God, the Word of God in the flesh, then He is not "just a good man"—He is a knave, a liar, a charlatan and the greatest deceiver Who ever lived. If He is not what He said He was, the Christ, the Son of God, He is the anti-Christ! But he is not just a good man.

He would have us either worship Him or despise Him—despise Him as a mere man, or worship Him as true God and true Man. That is the alternative He presents. It may very well be that the Communists, who are so anti-Christ, are closer to Him than those who see Him as a sentimentalist and a vague moral reformer. The Communists have at least decided that if He wins, they lose; others are afraid to consider Him either as winning or losing, because they are not prepared to meet the moral demands which He requires of the soul.

If He is what He claimed to be, a Saviour, a Redeemer, then we have a virile Christ for these days; someone Who will step into the breach of death and sin and gloom and despair, a Leader to Whom we can make total sacrifice and Whom we can love even unto death. We need a Christ today whose voice will be like the voice of the raging sea, and Who will not allow us to pick and choose among His words, discarding what we do not like, and accepting what pleases our fancy. We need a Christ Who will restore moral indignation, and will make us hate evil with a passionate intensity and love goodness to a point where we will drink death like water.

Even His Birth was a forecast of His Death which was the primary purpose of His coming to this earth. Caesar Augustus, the master bookkeeper of the world, sat in his palace by the Tiber. Before him was stretched a map labelled *Orbis Terarum, Imperium Romanum*. He was about to issue an order for a census of the world, for then all nations were subject to him. There was only one capital in the world: Rome; only one official language: Latin; only one ruler: Caesar. To every outpost, satrap and governor, the order went out that everyone was to be enrolled in his own city. In the fringe of the empire in a little village of Nazareth, soldiers tacked upon walls the order for every citizen to register in the town of his family's origin.

Joseph, the builder, descendent of the great King David, was obliged to register in the city of David—Bethlehem. In accordance with that edict, Mary and Joseph set out from the village of Nazareth for the village of Bethlehem, which lay about five miles on the other side of Jerusalem. Five hundred years before the prophet Micheas had prophesied concerning that little village: "Thou Bethlehem are the least of the cities of Judea and out of thee will He come forth Who is to be a ruler in Israel."

Joseph was full of expectancy as he entered the city of his family. He was confident that he would have no difficulty in finding lodgings for Mary, particularly since she was with child. From house to house, Joseph went only to find each one crowded. He sought in vain for a place where might be born the One to Whom heaven and earth belonged. Could it be that the Creator would not be at home in creation?

Up a steep hill he climbed to a faint light swinging on a rope across the doorway which signified the village inn. There he knocked, above all places else, most hopefully. There was room in that inn for the soldiers of Rome who bore on their coats Rome's screaming eagles; there was room for the daughters of the rich merchants of the East; there was room for those clothed in soft garments, who lived in the houses of the king; there was room for those who had a tip to give the inn keeper. But there was no room for Him Who came to be the Inn of every homeless heart in the world. When finally, the scrolls of history will have recorded the last words in the annals of time, the saddest line of all will be:

"There was no room in the inn."

Out to the hillside, to a stable cave, where shepherds drove their flocks in storms, Joseph and Mary went for shelter. There, in a place of peace and tranquility, in the utter abandonment and cold of a windswept cave; there, under the floor of the world, Mary, as a flesh and blood ciborium, lifted up to the gaze of all, the Host of the world. "Behold the Lamb of God Who taketh away the sins of the world." He Who was born without a mother in heaven, was born without a father on earth.

Of every other child born into the world, friends might say that it resembles its mother. This was the first instance in time that any one could say that the Mother resembled the Child. Here was the beautiful paradox of the Child Who made His Mother; therefore, the Mother was only a child. It was also the first time in the history of this earth of ours that anyone could ever think of heaven being anywhere else than "way up there," but Mary now looked down to Heaven.

In the filthiest place in the world, a stable, purity was born. He Who was to be devoured by men acting as beasts, was born amongst beasts. He Who called Himself the "living Bread descended from Heaven" was born in Bethlehem, "the house of bread," and laid in a manger, the place of food. Centuries before, the Jews had worshipped the golden calf and the Greeks had worshipped the ass. Men bowed down before them as before God. The ox and the ass now made their reparation and retribution by bowing down themselves before their God.

There was no room in the inn, but there was room in the stable. The inn is the gathering place of public opinion, the focal point of the world's moods, the rendezvous of the worldly, the rallying place of the popular. But the stable is a place of outcasts, the ignored, the forgotten, the almost impossible things. If there was any place in all the earth where the world would have expected the Son of God to be born, it would have been in an inn. The stable would be the last place in the world we would have looked for Him. *Divinity is always where we least expect to find it.*

No worldly mind would ever have suspected that He Who could make the sun warm the earth would one day have need of an ox and an ass to warm Him with their breath; that He Who, in the language of Scriptures, could stop the turning about of the Arcturus, would be subject to an imperial edict of a census; that He Who clothed the fields with grass would Himself be naked; that He from Whose finger tips tumbled planets and worlds would one day have tiny hands that were not long enough to touch the huge heads of the cattle; that feet which trod the everlasting hills would one day be too weak to walk; that the Eternal Word would be dumb; that Omnipotence would be wrapped in swaddling clothes; that Salvation would lie in a manger; that the mirth of Heaven would weep; that the bird that built the nest would be hatched therein—no one would ever have suspected that God coming to this earth would ever be so helpless. But that is just precisely why they are apt to miss Him—*Divinity is always where we least expect to find it.*

If the artist is at home in his studio, because the paintings are the creation of his own mind; if the sculptor is at home amongst his statues, for they were begotten of his brain; if a husbandman is at home among his vines, for he planted them; if the father is at home in his family, because they are his own, then surely, argues the world, He Who made the world should be at home in it; He should come into it as an artist into his studio, and as a Father into his home; but for the Creator to come amongst His creatures and be ignored, for God to come among His own and not to be received by His own, for God to be homeless at home, that to the world can only mean one thing—that that Babe could not be God. But that is just why it missed *Him. Divinity is always where we least expect to find it.*

The Son-of-God-made-man was forced to enter His own world through a back door. Exiled from the earth, He was born under the earth as the First Cave Man of Christian history. There He shook the earth to its very foundations. Being born in a cave, all who entered had to stoop. To stoop is the mark of humility. The proud refused to stoop, and missed Divinity. Those, however, who bent their ego and entered, found they were not in a cave at all, but in a new universe where sat a Babe on His Mother's lap, with the world poised on His fingers.

The manger and the cross thus stand at the two extremities of the Saviour's life: He accepted the manger because there was no room in the inn; He accepted the Cross, because men said: "We will not have this man for our king." Disowned in entrance, rejected in exit. He was laid in a stranger's stable at the beginning, and a stranger's grave at the end. An ox and an ass surrounded His crib at Bethlehem; two thieves would surround His Cross on Calvary. He was wrapped in swaddling bands in His birthplace, and would be wrapped in swaddling grave clothes in His death place—both symbols of the limitations imposed on His Divinity by taking on a human form.

The Shepherds watching their flocks nearby were told by the angels:
**"This is the sign by which you are to know him;**
**You will find a child still in swaddling clothes,**
**Lying in a manger."**

He was already bearing His Cross—the only cross a Babe could bear, that of poverty, exile and limitation. His sacrificial intent already shone forth in the message the angels were singing to the hills of Bethlehem:
**"This day, in the city of David,**
**A *Saviour* has been born for you,**
**No other than the Lord Christ."**

Covetousness was already challenged by poverty, while pride was confronted with the humiliation of a stable. The swathing of Divine Power, which otherwise knows no bounds, is often too great a tax upon minds which think only of power in terms of atomic energy. They cannot grasp the idea of divine condescension, or of the "rich becoming poor that through His poverty, we might be rich."

He Whom the angels call the "Son of the most High" descends into the red dust from which we all were born, to be one with weak, fallen man in all things, save sin. And yet it is the swaddling clouts which constitute the "sign." If He Who is Omnipotence had come with thunderbolts, there would have been no sign. There is no "sign" unless something is contrary to nature. The brightness of the sun is no "sign," but an eclipse is. He said that on the last day, His coming will be characterized by "signs in the sun" such as the sun refusing to give its light. Here the Divine Son goes into an eclipse, that only the humble of spirit may recognize Him.

Only two classes of people found the Babe: the Shepherds and the Wise Men. The simple and the learned. They who know they know nothing, and they who know they do not know everything. Never the man with one book; never the man who thinks he knows. Not even God can tell the proud anything. It takes *good will* to find God, and this truth the angels proclaimed from the heavens:
**"Peace on earth to men that are God's friends."**

As Caryll Houselander put it: "Bethlehem is the inscape of Calvary, just as the snowflake is the inscape of the universe." This is the same idea as that of the poet who said that if he knew the flower in a crannied wall in all its details, he would know "what God and man is." Scientists tell us that the atom prehends within itself the mystery of the solar system. It was not so much that His Birth cast a shadow on His Life, and thus led to His Death; it was rather that the Cross was first, and cast its shadow backward to His Birth. Ordinary mortals go from the unknown to the known and submit themselves to forces beyond their control; hence we speak of their "tragedy." But He went from the known to the known, from the reason of His Coming, namely to be "Jesus" or "Saviour," to the fulfillment of His Coming, namely the death on the Cross. Hence there was no tragedy in His life, for tragedy implies the unforeseeable, the uncontrollable and the fatalistic. Modern life is tragic when there is no belief in another life and no redemption from guilt. But for this Babe, there are no uncontrollable forces; no submission to fatalistic chains from which there is no escape; but there is an "inscape"—the microscopic manger summarizing a macrocosmis Golgothian cross.

In His First Advent Christ took the name of Jesus or "Saviour"; only in His Second Coming will He take the name of "Judge." Jesus was not a name He had before He, as the Son of God, assumed a human nature; it very properly refers to that which was united to His Divinity, not that which existed from all eternity. Some say "Jesus taught" as some might say "Plato taught," never once thinking that His Name means a "*Saviour* from Sin." Once He received this name, Calvary was more a part of Him than Washington is related to a President of the United States. The Shadow of the Cross that fell on His cradle, now fell on His naming. Either He lived up to His name, or He did not. If He did not, then He should not be called Jesus or Saviour.

Christ was not two years old when King Herod ordered the killing of the male babies of Bethlehem. It was the first attempt on Christ's life. He faced the sword when a Babe, stones when a man, the Cross at His end. Bethlehem is thus the dawn of Calvary.

The same law that would wind itself around His Apostles and around His followers for centuries, began its first circuit in fresh lives snatched from their mothers' arms—an event now commemorated in the Feast of the Holy Innocents. Upside down on a cross for Peter; a push from a steeple for James, a knife for Bartholomew, a cauldron of oil and a long waiting for John, a sword for Paul—and dashing cutthroats for the babes of Bethlehem.

"The world will hate you" is the dark eclipse that hangs over all who are signed with His seal. These Innocents died for the King Whom they never knew, at the hands of an earthly king who should have been their friend. Little lambs, they died for the sake of the Lamb, the prototype of the long procession of martyrs—children who never struggled, but were crowned.

The only acts of Christ's Childhood which are recorded are acts of obedience—to His Heavenly Father and to His earthly parents. The foundation of obedience to man is obedience to God. Delinquency in the young, is the result of delinquency in the parents. The elders who serve not God find the young serve them not. Christ's whole life was submission. He submitted to John's Baptism, though He was exempt from it; He submitted to pay the temple tax, though as the Son of the Father He was exempt from the tax; He bade His own people submit to Caesar. In being subject to creatures, though He was God, He prepared Himself for that final obedience—obedience to the humiliation of the Cross.

For the next 18 years, after the Three Days Loss, when He was 12 years of age, He Who carpentered the universe, played the role of a village carpenter, mending flat roofs and fixing the wagons of the farmers. Justin Martyr tells us that in his day—100 years after Christ's death—there were still implements to be seen which were made by His Hands.

Why this long preparation for such a brief ministry of three years?

The reason might very well have been that He waited until the human nature which He had assumed grew in age to full perfection, that He might then offer the perfect sacrifice to His Heavenly Father. The farmer waits until the wheat is ripe before cutting it and subjecting it to the mill. So He would wait until His human nature had reached its most perfect proportions and its peak of loveliness before surrendering it to the hammer of the crucifiers and the sickle of those who cut down the Living Bread of Heaven. The newly born lamb is not offered in sacrifice, nor is the first blush of the rose cut to pay tribute to a friend. Each thing has its hour of perfection. Since He is the Lamb that sets the hour for the sacrifice, and since He is the Rose that can choose the moment of His cutting, He will wait patiently, humbly and obediently, while He grows in age and grace and wisdom before God and man. Then He will say:—"This is your Hour." Thus the choicest wheat and the reddest wine will be the worthiest elements of Sacrifice—the best this world can give for its consecration and its peace.

# PART 2

## *TEMPTATIONS*

Very few today believe in the devil. This is exactly what the devil wants. He is always circulating the news of his death. The essence of God is existence, and He defines Himself as:

**"I am Who am."**

The essence of the devil is the lie, and he defines himself as: "I am who am not."

Satan never has to bother with those who do not believe in him; they are already his. But he has a lot of trouble with the saints who are constantly and literally sending him to hell. Satan keeps thousands of devils stationed on monastery walls, but only one in a large city. There are probably some places where the devil sleeps, because he has no work to do.

The devil has used many in our western world to convince us that there is no hell—a thing rather hard to believe, when there is so much evidence for hell around us. He has used the Communists to try to convince us that there is no God; they have failed to do this, but they have convinced us that there is a devil.

The temptations of man are easy enough to be understood, they always fall into one of three categories: they are either temptations of the flesh, such as lust; or of the mind, such as pride; or of things, such as avarice.

Though man is buffeted all during life by these three temptations, one or the other are more frequent during certain periods of life. It is during youth, that man is most often tempted against purity and inclined to sins of the flesh; in middle age, there is a sublimation of the flesh and the temptations begin to be those of the mind, such as pride and the lust for power; in the autumn of life, temptations very often center about avarice and the possession of material things. Seeing the end of life is near, one strives to compensate for doubts about eternal security or salvation, by piling up the goods of earth as an economic security. It is a common psychological experience, that those who have given way to lust in youth are often those who sin by avarice in their old age.

Good men are not tempted the same way as evil men, nor the Son of God Who became Man, the same way as a good man. The temptations of an alcoholic to "return to his vomit," as Scripture puts it, is not the same as the temptation of a saint to pride, though one is no less real than the other. In order to understand the temptations of Christ, it must be recalled that at the Baptism by John, when He Who had no sins identified Himself with sinners, the heavens opened, and the Heavenly Father declared Christ to be His Beloved Son. Then Our Lord goes to the mountain and fasts for 40 days, after which "He is hungry," in a typical understatement of the Gospel. Satan begins the temptations which revolve around the question: How is He to fulfill His high destiny among men? The problem is to win men. But how! Satan has an idea of how this might be accomplished, namely, by getting Him to forget His name is "Jesus" or "Saviour."

The human flesh, which He had taken upon Himself, was not for leisure, but for battle. Satan saw in Jesus, an extraordinary human being Whom he suspected to be the Messiah and the Son of God. Hence the prefacing of each of the Temptations with the conditional "If." If He were sure He was God, he would not indeed tempt Him. But if He is One Who claims to be God, then he will lead Him into other ways of treating with the sins of mankind than the way that God would choose.

Knowing Our Lord was hungry, Satan pointed down to little black stones that resembled round loaves of bread, and said to Our Lord:

"If thou are the Son of God, bid these stones turn into loaves of bread."

The first temptation of Our Blessed Lord was to become a social reformer, and to give bread to the multitudes in the wilderness who were finding nothing but stones. The path of social amelioration without spiritual regeneration, has been the one temptation to which important men of history have most succumbed. But to Him, this would not be adequate service of the Father; there are deeper needs in man than crushed wheat, and there are greater joys than the full stomach.

The evil spirit suggests: "Start with the primacy of the economic! Turn your Churches into social clubs! Forget the supernatural! Does not my Commissar go into classrooms today, and ask children to pray to God for bread? And when their prayers are not answered, my Commissar feeds them? The Dictator gives bread; God does not, because there is no God, there is no soul; there is only the body, pleasure, sex, the animal, and when we die, that is the end."

To that Temptation, Our Lord answers:
> "Not by bread alone doth man live,
> But by every word that proceedeth
> From the mouth of God."

Our Lord does not deny that men must be fed, or that social justice must be preached, but He asserts that these things are *not first*. He is saying to Satan: "You tempt Me to a religion which would relieve want; you want Me to be a Baker, instead of a Saviour; to be a social reformer, instead of a Redeemer. You are tempting Me away from My Cross, suggesting that I be a cheap leader of people, filling their bellies, instead of their souls; you would have Me begin with security instead of ending with it; you would have Me bring outer abundance, instead of inner holiness. You and your materialists say: 'Man lives by bread alone,' but I say to you: 'Not by bread alone.' Bread there must be, but remember that even bread gets all of its power to feed from Me. Bread without Me can harm man, and I refuse to hold any theory about security, apart from the Word of God, even though I must go hungry. If I give bread alone, then even dogs shall come to My Banquet. Those who believe in Me must hold that faith, even when they are hungry, starved, weak, in prison, scourged, and even rotting in your Soviet prisons.

"I am hungry! I have not eaten for forty days, but I refuse to become a mere ethical reformer by catering to the economic and to pleasure and satiety. Say not that I am disinterested in social justice, for I am feeling now the hunger of the world. My stomach groans with the starving, crawling wrecks of humanity. That is why I fasted, that they can never say God does not know what hunger is. Begone Satan! I am not like some well-fed reformer who says: 'By bread alone.' I refuse any plan which will make men richer without making them holier. Remember! I, Who say: 'Not by bread alone,' have not tasted bread in forty days!"

Satan, having failed to win Our Lord away from His Cross and Redemption by turning Him into a Communist Commissar promising bread, now turned the attack upon His Spirit and His Soul. Seeing that Our Lord refused to subscribe to the belief that man is a stomach, as he is for some economists, Satan now tempted Him to pride and egotism. As a symbol of that vanity, the devil took Him to a lofty pinnacle of the temple and said to Him:

> "Cast Thyself down from this to the earth."

Then, quoting Scripture, he continued:
> "For it is written He shall give His angels
> Charge concerning Thee, to keep Thee safe,
> And they will hold Thee up with their hands,
> Lest Thou should chance to trip on a stone."

Satan is here saying: "Why take the long and tedious way to win mankind, through the shedding of blood, the mounting of a Cross, through being despised and rejected, when you can take the short cut by a prodigy? You have affirmed Your trust in God. Very well! If You really trust, do something heroic! Prove faith, not by going to a Cross in obedience to God's Will, but by flinging Yourself down. You will never win people to Yourself with sublime truths about Your Divinity preached from church steeples and pinnacles. The masses cannot follow You; they are too far below. Clothe yourself with wonders! Throw Yourself down from the pinnacle and then stop just before you hit bottom! It is the spectacular that people want, not the Divine. People are bored! Relieve the monotony of life and their jaded spirits, but leave their guilty consciences alone!"

The devil's monologue goes on today: "How many times do you read in the press the words: 'Christ says'? Not often. But when do you not read: 'Science says'? It is the portents that people want. Science, machines, atomic fission, propaganda, publicity, anything that shows *outer power*—these our young minds crave, and not Your pinnacle truths of sacrifices, grace, forgiveness and penance! If You want to convert minds today, do a miracle: not one that requires faith, but what we call the new miracle, the miracle of science. The children of today, want not Thy miracles, O Christ; not One Who will teach their minds to be subject to God, but one who will teach them to be subject to power. My beloved Soviet Russia rightly calls religion a 'superstition,' and what do they say has killed it? Materialism! Give up Your sublime truths about the mind needing the faith, the will needing grace, the mind needing hope, the whole being needing God. Power is below! Down in the depths! Jump from your trust in God! Be a magician! Win the masses as my Communists are doing!"

The answer of Our Lord to Satan then and now is:

**"Thou shalt not tempt the Lord, thy God."**

He means: "You tempt Me, when you admire the wonders of science, and forget I am the Author of the Universe. Your scientists are proof-readers, not the authors of the Book of Nature; they can come only to the edge of the picture, but not to Me, the Artist Who painted it. You would tempt Me to prove Myself Omnipotent to your feeblest test; you would pull watches on Me and say: 'I challenge you to strike me dead within five minutes.' Know you not that I have mercy on fools? You tempt Me by making atomic bombs explode against My Will and the pleas of My Vicar on earth, and when your cities are shambles, you shriek out: 'Why does God not stop this war?' You tempt Me, saying that I have no power, unless I show it at your beck and call.

"I will never have many followers on the lofty heights of Divine Truth, I know; I will never have the intelligentsia, who are educated beyond their intelligence. I refuse to perform a stunt to win them. It is only when I am lifted on the Cross that I will draw men to Myself; it will be by My sacrifices, and not by science, that I will appeal. I will win followers not with test tubes, but with My blood; not with power, but with Love; not with celestial fireworks, but by the right use of reason and free will. No sign shall be given to this generation but the sign of Jonas, namely, the Divine rising up from below, not the Divine plunging down to hell. It is you, O Satan, who plunges to the depths below. I want men who will believe in Me, even when I do not save them; I will not open the prison doors where My brethren are locked; I will not stay the Red sickle that cuts off their heads; I will not halt the Red hammer that batters down My tabernacle doors; I want my missionaries and martyrs to love Me in prison as they go singing to their deaths. I never worked a miracle to save Myself! I will work few miracles even for My saints. Begone Satan! Thou shalt not tempt the Lord, thy God."

There is yet one area wherein man can be tempted, and that is outside his body and soul, namely in his relation to the world. "And the devil led Him up on a high mountain, and showed Him all the Kingdoms of the world in a moment of time. 'I will give thee command', the devil said to Him, 'over all these and the glory that belongs to them' . . ." Then comes the most frightening words of Scripture:

> "They have all been made over to me,
> And I may give them to whomsoever I please;
> Come then, all shall be thine, if thou wilt fall down
> Before me and worship."

Satan is saying: "You have come, O Christ, to win the world, but the world is mine; I will give it to You, if You will compromise and worship me. Forget Your Cross, Your Divinity, Your Kingdom of Heaven. If You want the world, it is at Your feet. There will be louder Hosannas than Jerusalem ever sang to its Kings; there will be no nails, Golgothas, crowns of thorns and crosses of contradiction. There is no ruler but me. Worship me and the world is Yours."

His language is more modern now, but the temptation is the same. "You will never get ahead in the world unless You accept me. If You build schools to educate children in the ways of God, I will say that You are the enemy of education; if You oppose divorce, fight against the strangulation of the fruits of love, I will say You are 'reactionary.' Your books will not be reviewed by Communist reviewers; I will flood the nation with lies, saying that You are the enemy of the State, and I will add to that the bigger lie for fools who will believe it—that You want to dominate the State, and that You are disloyal. See how my Soviet Russia advances: 37 out of every 100 people in the world are subject to it; the Soviets know that the world is mine; that is why they are getting it! Forget heaven, and grace and sacraments and God; no shedding of blood, no martyrdoms, no self-denials are necessary in my way. Just worship me *under any name*, I care not what, except do not call me 'devil.' Call me 'power,' call me 'religion,' provided you leave out Your Divinity, O Christ! Call me 'patriotism,' provided You use it to malign those who believe in the spirit; just worship me and the world is Yours."

Our Lord, knowing that those kingdoms could be won only by His suffering and death, said to Satan: "Away with thee, Satan, it is written, 'Thou shalt worship the Lord Thy God, and Him Alone shalt thou serve.' Satan, you want worship, but to worship you is to serve you, and to serve you is slavery. I do not want your world, so long as it has on it the terrible burden of guilt.

"If I had all your kingdoms, all the hearts in them would still long for something you could not give, namely, peace of soul. Even now, as you boast that Russia is yours, I tell you, there are millions behind your Iron Curtain, that are awaiting My Redemption. I do not want your world at your cheap price. I am a revolutionist too, as My Mother sang in her Magnificat. I am in revolt against you. But My revolution is not by the sword thrust outward in imperialism, but inward against sin and all the things that make war. I will first conquer evil in the hearts of men, and then I shall conquer the world. I will conquer your world by going into the hearts of your dishonest tax collectors, your false judges, your Commissars, and I will redeem them from guilt and sin, and send them back clean to their professions. I shall tell them it profits them nothing to win the whole world if they lose their immortal soul. You keep your kingdoms for the moment. Better the loss of all your kingdoms—aye, better the loss of the universe by splitting it with your bombs—than the loss of a single soul! It is the kingdoms of the world that are to be elevated to the Kingdom of God, not the Kingdom of God that is to be dragged down to the level of the kingdoms of the world.

"All I want of this earth is a place large enough to erect a Cross; there I will let you unfurl Me before the crossroads of your world! I will let you nail Me in the name of the cities of Jerusalem, Athens and Rome, but I will rise from the dead, and you will discover that you, who won the battle, lost the day, as I march with victory on the wings of the morning! Satan, you are asking Me to become anti-Christ. My Divine patience now gives way to Divine indignation. 'Get thee behind Me, Satan'."

Satan asked for a sign that He was the Son of God, and the sign was that He turn the stones into bread. At the marriage Feast of Cana, His

Mother asked Him to change the water into wine. Why was it that He refused to a kind of transubstantiation for Satan by changing stones into bread, and why, at the behest of His Mother, did He turn the water into wine?

The occasion was a Marriage Feast to which His Mother had been invited, as well as Himself. He also brought along some of His Disciples, which might have been the reason the wine gave out. In such a wine country, it was only natural that the wine steward appointed for the Feast should be the first to notice the shortage of wine. It happens, however, that the first one who did notice it was the Mother of Our Divine Lord, who went to Him. She uttered a very simple petitionary prayer: "They have no wine." Satan on the mountain top said almost the same thing: "They have no bread." The answer of Jesus to His Mother was: "Woman, what wouldst thou of me? My hour has not yet come."

The next time that He will call His Mother "Woman" will be from the Cross. Then the wine of Cana will be changed into the blood of Calvary. Here is some indication that her relationship with Him is changing. Up to this time, she has been known to the world as the Mother of Jesus; now she would begin to be known as the Mother of all that He would redeem. At the moment Redemption would be completed on the Cross, He would address her again with the title of Universal Motherhood, or "Woman."

Our Blessed Lord never used the word "hour," except in relationship to His Passion and His Death. When Judas betrayed Him, He said: "This is your hour." The night He bade farewell to His Apostles before going into the Garden of Gethsemane, He said: "Father, the hour has come." The "hour" for Him is always an hour of glory through the Cross. He was now telling His Mother that His Hour for announcing His Passion, Death and Resurrection, was not yet at hand. This was a hard decision for any Mother to make, namely, to send a Son into a battlefield with the forces of evil. In the designs of Providence, the hour of His public manifestation had not yet come. And that was why He was hesitant about taking the initiative in the miracle.

She is practically asking Him to advance the Hour in His plan. Moses' prayer stayed the arm of God, as He was about to strike the wayward people; Abraham's prayer would have saved two cities, did He find but a few just men; the plan of the Canaanite woman triumphed over the explicit refusals of Our Lord Himself. Here the plea of His own Mother, expressive of the plea of all humanity for redemption, was sufficient to induce Him to work His first public miracle, to affirm Himself as the Messias and the Saviour of men. She was so certain of her prayer, that she immediately told the wine stewards to fill the water pots, and to bring them to the master of the feast. Our Blessed Lord walked over to them, and in the beautiful language of Richard Crashaw: "The unconscious waters saw their God and blushed." No wonder the guests said to the wine steward: "It is ever the good wine that men set out first, and the worse kind only when all have drunk deep; thou hast kept the good wine till now."

Our Blessed Lord never worked a miracle in order to satisfy His own need, and for that reason He refused to work a miracle to satisfy His own hunger. In every instance when He worked a miracle, it was always as a sign or manifestation of His mission. He would not even work a miracle to save Himself from the Cross. But this miracle is called the first of the signs and wonders that He worked. The world generally gives its best first, and afterwards all its dregs and bitterness, but Christ came to reverse the order and to give the feast after the fast, the Resurrection after a Crucifixion, and the Easter Sunday after a Good Friday.

He did at a marriage feast what He would not do in a desert; He worked in the full gaze of men, what He refused to do before Satan. Satan asked Him to turn stones into bread, in order that He might be an economic Messias; His Mother asked Him to change water into wine that He might begin "His Hour" of Redemption. Satan tempted Him *from* death; Mary "tempted Him" to death. Satan would lead Him from the Cross; Mary sent Him on His way. Later on, He would take hold of the bread that Satan said men needed, and the wine which His Mother said the guests needed, and would change them both into the memorial of His Passion and His Death, then He would ask that men renew that memorial, even "unto the consummation of the world." The antiphon of His life continues to ring; everyone else came into the world to live; He came into the world to die.

In the second temptation, Satan took Him to the peak of the Temple in full view of the masses, and asked Him to be an exhibitionist, and to cast Himself down. It was an *ersatz* sacrifice and a false priesthood to which Satan summoned Him, namely, a seeming death in which He would violate the laws of nature and reason.

Our Lord in one of the incidents of His early life, met positively the second temptation of Satan by entering the Temple, and driving out the buyers and the sellers. Gradually, the vendors of articles of sacrifice had pushed themselves closer to the Temple, choking the avenues that led to it until finally, some of them, particularly the sons of Annas, gained entrance to Solomon's porch, there selling doves and cattle and changing money. Every visitor to the feast was obliged to pay half a sheckle to help defray the expenses of the Temple, and since no foreign money could be exchanged, the sons of Annas trafficked in the barter of coins.

There were men with great wicker cages filled with doves, while dealers brought into the Temple, as into the pens of a slaughter house, whole flocks of oxen and bulls and goats and sheep and lambs. The cries of the animals, mixing with the noise of the crowd, suffocated prayer and worship.

Centuries before it had been told of the Messias: "The zeal of thine house hath eaten me up." Though Satan could not make the Saviour jump from the peak of the Temple, the Saviour now moved Himself to His high mission of purifying the Temple by making war on mummeries and hypocrisies and shams.

Satan brought Him to the top of the building, but He entered into the Temple. Satan always works on the outside for show, which is the basis of hypocrisy and pride; God always works on the inside, purifying the material that the wings of the spirit may be free.

Taking ropes from the necks of the cattle, He made cords which served as a scourge, with which He drove out the traitors with their sheep and their oxen. Then, with a majestic gesture, He overthrew the tables of the money changers; to the sellers of the gentle doves, He acted gently, saying: "Take these away, do not turn My Father's House into a place of barter."

His eyes darted flames, and His face shone with Divine majesty and the polluters of the Temple, with their troubled consciences, knew in their hearts that He was right. After some time they came back to Him, and asked: "What sign canst Thou show us as Thy warrant for doing this?" They did not reproach Him for what He did, but they asked Him for His title for arrogating to Himself such a power as He claimed when He said to them: "My house shall be known among all the nations for a house of prayer. Whereas you have made it into a den of thieves." Later on He would say that one cannot serve both God and Mammon. Here, as in many other instances, He anticipated His words by divorcing the two. The very fact that He should call the Temple "My Father's House," was also an expression of His unique filial consciousness.

The answer of Our Lord was far beyond their comprehension, as He said to them: "Destroy this Temple, and in three days I will raise it up again." The Gospel immediately adds that "He spoke of the temple of His Body." These words of His would stick in their hearts, and they would repeat them at the trial: "We heard Him say, I will destroy this temple that is made by men's hands, and in three days I will build another, with no hand of man to help me." That is not what He said.

Typical of all who pervert words of truth, they wrested it from its true meaning. He spoke of the Temple of His Body which was His humanity.

They immediately asked: How could a temple that had taken 46 years to be rebuilt, be destroyed in a day or two?

What He meant was that the true Temple is the place where God lives. The God-Head was living in His human nature. If, therefore, they would destroy this human nature of His, on the third day He would rise again from the dead, and be God's temple, wherein He would be known and worshipped. The earthly temple ceases to be such, when it becomes the center of mercenary interests. He is the true shekinah, or glory of the Temple. Though men would nail Him to a Cross, He would still be raised in the hearts and minds of men, and, therefore, would be truly a "Temple not made with hands." The True Temple is the Sacred Body of the Son of God made flesh, in which He is tabernacled amongst us.

The Gospel is quick to add: "When He had risen from the dead, His disciples remembered His saying this, and learned to believe in the Scriptures, and in the words Jesus had spoken."

Though the full meaning is hidden, even from the disciples, there is still an indication that they who were driven out of the temple had a deeper insight into His meaning than they were willing to admit. They brooded over the words, and later on, when they crucified Him as the Temple, and when He lay dead and buried in a rock tomb, they came to Pilate with the remarkable story:

"Sir, we have recalled it to memory that this deceiver, while He yet lived, said, I am to rise again after three days." There was more than a passing similarity between that Temple which had destroyed itself with pollution, and the Temple of God which was now before them. Both Temples began in Bethlehem; both were destroyed and raised up again. The Chaldeans destroyed the one, and Zorababel raised it. Mankind would not have God rule over them, so they destroyed the Temple that God sent. God Himself raised it. Both were consecrated to like uses: the holocaust of obedience, the offering of the body as a reasonable service to the Heavenly Father.

Here, as elsewhere, Our Blessed Lord is proving Himself as the only man who came into this world to die. The Cross was not something that came at the end of His Life. It was something that was sealed upon Him from the very beginning. He said to them: "Destroy," and they said to him: "Crucify." The dome of the Temple, His Head, would be crowned with thorns; the foundation of it, His Sacred Feet, would be riven with nails; its transcepts, His Hands, would be laid out as a Cross, and His Holy of Holies, the Heart, would be pierced with a lance. His Crucifixion would not be a punishment inflicted upon Him for antagonizing them;

He implied that it was here ordained by His Father, because they had polluted His Father's house. He warned that they would reckon to destroy Him, but they would actually prepare Him only for a short test and the glorious Temple of a risen Body. Later on, St. Paul would say that every Christian is a Temple of the Living God, and such is the basis of his purity and his holiness. This would not have been possible were Christ not already the prototype Temple that was holy with the holiness of God. In Him, the true Temple was the altar of sacrifice and the atonement for sin.

Satan tempted Him to an apparent sacrifice, by tossing Himself from the pinnacle of the Temple, which Our Lord refused to do. But when those who had polluted His Father's House asked Him for a sign, He offered them the sign of the sacrifice on the Cross. Satan told Him to cast Himself down; Our Blessed Lord said that He will be cast down to the obloquy of death, but not because He willed to be an exhibitionist in sacrifice, but because men would demand His Death. Satan, on the peak of the Temple, would tempt Him from a true sacrifice; Our Lord in the Temple pledged Himself to a real sacrifice, but also a Resurrection.

Satan proposed exposing His Temple to possible ruin for the sake of exhibitionism, for the sake of display; Our Lord here exposes the Temple of His Body to real death for the sake of purity. Satan in the wilderness tempted Him to be a wonder worker; in the Temple, He answers that He is a Redeemer. At Cana, He said that He was going to His hour; in the Temple, He says that that Hour of the Cross will lead to His Resurrection. His Public Life will tell the same story.

# PART 3

## *THE BEATITUDES*

ONE way to make enemies and antagonize people is to challenge the spirit of the world. The world has a spirit, and each age has its peculiar outlook and set of values. One age may be described as "revolutionary," another as "capitalistic," and perhaps another as "critical." But underlying all of these, the world has certain unanalyzed assumptions which govern conduct. Anyone who challenges these worldly maxims, such as, "you live only once," or "get as much out of life as you can," is bound to make himself unpopular.

This was the first "mistake" of Our Lord, from a worldly point of view. After choosing His 12 Apostles, He delivered what is popularly called: "The Sermon on the Mount," or "The Beatitudes." So often the unthinking say: "The essence of Christianity" is the "Sermon on the Mount." The truth is that the Sermon on the Mount is inseparable from the Mount of Calvary. The day Our Lord preached His Beatitudes, He signed His death warrant. The Sermon on the Mount cannot be separated from the Crucifixion, as day cannot be separated from night.

Sitting down on a mountain top, He opened His mouth and preached:

"**Blessed are the poor in spirit;
the kingdom of heaven is theirs.
Blessed are the patient; they shall inherit the land.
Blessed are those who mourn; they shall be comforted.
Blessed are those who hunger and thirst for holiness;
they shall have their fill.
Blessed are the merciful; they shall obtain mercy.
Blessed are the clean of heart; they shall see God.
Blessed are the peace-makers; they shall be counted
the children of God.
Blessed are those who suffer persecution in the cause**

of right; the kingdom of heaven is theirs.
Blessed are you, when men revile you, and persecute
you, and speak all manner of evil against you
falsely, because of me.
Be glad and lighthearted, for a rich reward awaits you in
heaven."

To be "blessed" means to be happy.

*Poor in spirit:* "Poor" does not mean indigent. To be poor in spirit is to be conscious of one's spiritual poverty, to blush at one's own defects, to have a deep sense of nothingness before God, and to be resigned before the beneficent Hand of Providence. The foundation of all spiritual happiness is to be conscious before God of one's emptiness or one's need, like the publican smiting his breast. Poverty of spirit is the very antithesis of the worldly doctrine of self-sufficiency.

*The patient:* The patient bow to the rod of affliction, and bear injury meekly; in prosperity, they are thankful, and in adversity, they are resigned. Patience is meekness, which is opposed to anger, resentment, and retaliation. It is a consequence of the first Beatitude, for he who has learned the depth of his own weakness, will not be so ready to strike others, but will rather approach them with clemency. The land they will possess is not landed property; the Beatitude rather means that they can now enjoy the earth as a stepping stone to life eternal. The meek person is never disturbed by the fact that someone else owns something; possession to him is not an annoyance, but a pleasure which he takes as it comes; therefore, he enjoys the earth. Meek men in the Old Testament, like Caleb and Josue, inherited the Promised Land.

*Those who mourn:* Those who mourn are not the weepers from discontent, but those who feel the sorrows and the sins of the world as their own. The world regards sorrow as disaster; Our Lord looks upon it as the darkness that heralds the dawn. The sorrow here is not so much physical as spiritual, that is, for sin rather than the consequences of sin. Once the soul looks into its own past, and sees there its multiplied rejections of Divine Love, it cannot help but mourn. This contrition is the condition of moral progress and the pathway to true comfort and peace of soul.

*Those who hunger and thirst:* They are those who so yearn for holiness, which is abandonment to the Will of God in all things, that they would die rather than commit a single sin. The hunger and thirst here is not physical, but spiritual; it is not just an inner dissatisfaction with human prescriptions, but rather a yearning to attain holiness and righteousness which is conformity to the Will of God. Swine are satisfied with husks, but not the soul of immortal man. It is the desire of holiness that is blessed; the achievement and perfection of it is on

God's side. We receive it, but we do not create it. All the cups of earth of which we drink are empty, as regards the thirst of the soul. Only God can fill both the cup and him who drinks.

*The merciful:* The merciful pardon others and obtain pardon; because they need mercy, they show it; while hating the sin, they love the sinner and say: "Father, forgive." Selfishness is hell; mercy is heaven. The world gives back as a mirror what we put into it. As we show mercy, we receive it; as we forgive others, we receive forgiveness. But the Beatitudes do not assume that we will receive mercy because we show it, but rather, because we have received forgiveness of our sins from God, we will be forgiving others. Mercy is a *consequence,* not the *cause* of receiving God's Mercy. Our mercy then becomes the effort to *redeem,* but this cannot be done without sacrifice, as the Life of Christ reveals.

*The clean of heart:* The pure of heart are those who control all lusts, not as a denial of love, but as a guarding of it until the body can be used as God wills it to be used. The "seeing of God" which is the privilege of the pure, does not mean with human eyes, but with the eye of the spirit. Carnal lusts are at enmity with the spirit. Bad behaviour keeps as many from seeing God as does ignorance. Under the slavery of sex, a mind sees nothing straight. As clouds hide the sun, so habits of an unclean mind hide God. Impurity is a cataract on the eye of the soul. There is a reciprocity between sight and seeing the heavens, between a clean heart and seeing God.

*The peace-makers:* Peace is not the absence of war, but the tranquility of order. Order is the subordination of senses to reason, body to soul; reason to faith, the whole personality of God. Peace is not automatic; it is *made.* He is no peacemaker who has no scourge in his hands against evil, whose love does not hate sin, and who is incapable of righteous indignation. Peace is based not on expediency, but on justice. The peacemaker must fight without ever ceasing to be love. Such peace is first not in nations, but in souls. A peaceful world comes not by legislation, but by inner regeneration. Only he who has the peace of God in his own soul, can give it to others. God hates "peace" in those who are destined for war, and we are all destined for war against sin and evil. Those who make such peace shall be the children of God, the Prince of Peace.

The eighth beatitude about the persecuted, is the summary of the preceding seven. The persecuted are those who know that to follow Christ is to be hated; hogs will say they are dirty; goats will say they smell; wolves will accuse them of stealth. But abuse, scourges, jails, blood-martyrdoms, all these must be accepted as a blessing which bears witness to Christ. The Preacher on the Mount is not summoning men to ease and comfort, but to suffering for His Name's sake.

In these beatitudes, Our Divine Lord takes those eight flimsy catchwords of the world: 'Security,' 'Revenge,' 'Laughter,' 'Popularity,' 'Getting even,' 'Sex,' 'Armed Might,' and 'Comfort' and turns them upside down. To those who say: "Strike it rich," He says, "Blessed are the poor in spirit." To those who say: "Don't let him get away with it," He says: "Blessed are the patient." To those who say: "Laugh and the world laughs with you," He says: "Blessed are those who mourn." To those who say: "Never restrain your instincts," He says: "Blessed are the clean of heart." To those who say: "Become popular by flattery," He says: "Blessed are you when men revile you and persecute you." To those who say: "In time of peace, prepare for war," He says: "Blessed are the peace-makers."

The cheap cliches around which movies are written and novels composed, He scorns. He proposes to burn what they worship, to conquer sex instead of explaining man by it as does Freud, to tame economic lusts instead of sending minds to Adam Smith or to Karl Marx. All the modern ideas that say happiness depends on 'self-expression,' 'license,' 'having a good time,' or 'eat, drink and be merry for tomorrow you die,' He scorns because they bring mental disorders, unhappiness, false hopes, fears and anxieties. The new paganism, like its ancient masters—Seneca, Marcus Aurelius, Epictetus, give us nothing but cascading platitudes, which take man as he is. Christ talks of what man is to *become,* and through no energy of his own, but through His Grace. Nowhere do you find Him speaking those cheap platitudes posted on church lawns: "Leave the world better than you find it." But you do hear Him say: "What doth it profit a man if he gain the whole world and lose his soul?"

Those who would escape the impact of the Beatitudes say that Our Divine Saviour was a creature of His time, but not of ours, and that, therefore, His Words do not apply to us. He was not a creature of His time, or of any time, but we are; Mohammed belonged to his time: hence he said a man could have concubines in addition to four wives at one time. Mohammed belongs even to our time, because moderns say that a man can have many wives if he drives them in tandem style, one after another. But Our Lord did not belong to His days, any more than He belonged to ours. To marry one age is to be a widow in the next. Because He suited no age, He was the model for all ages. He never used a phrase that depended on the social order in which He lived; His Gospel was no easier then than it is now. As He put it: "Heaven and earth must disappear sooner than one jot, one flourish should disappear from the law; it must all be accomplished."

The key to the Sermon on the Mount is the way He used two expressions: One was: "You have heard," the other was the short emphatic word, "But." When He said: "You have heard," He reached back to what human ears heard for centuries and still hear from ethical reformers—all those rules and codes and precepts which were half measures between instinct and reason, between local customs and the highest ideals. When He said: "You have heard," He included the Mosaic Law, Buddha with his eight-fold way, Confucius with his rules for being a gentleman, Aristotle with his natural happiness, the broadness of the Hindus, John Dewey, H.G. Wells, Bertrand Russell and all the humanitarian groups of our day, who have translated some of the old codes into English and call them a new way of life. Of all these compromises, He said: "You have heard."

"You *have heard* that it was said, Thou shalt not commit adultery." Moses had said it, pagan tribes suggest it; primitive people respected it. Then came the terrible and awful BUT: "But I tell you . . ." "But I tell you that he who casts his eye on a woman so as to lust after her, has already committed adultery with her in his own heart." Our Lord went into the will, and laid hold of thought, and branded even *the desire* as a sin. If it was wrong to do a certain thing, it was wrong to think about that thing. He was saying: "Away with your hygiene which tries to keep hands clean after they have stolen, and bodies free from disease after they have ravished another." He goes into the depths of the heart and brands even the intention a sin. He does not wait for the evil tree to bear evil fruits. He would prevent the very sowing of the evil seed. Wait not until your hidden sins come out as psychoses and neuroses and compulsions. Get rid of them at their sources. Repent! Purge! Evil that can be put into statistics, or that can be locked in jails, is too late to remedy.

Looking forward to our nation, with one divorce for every four marriages, Christ affirms that when a man marries a woman, he marries both her body and her soul; he marries the whole person. If he gets tired of the body, he may not thrust her body away for another, since he is still responsible for her soul. So He thunders: "You have heard." In that expression, He summarized the jargon of every decaying civilization. "You have heard—Get a divorce; 'God does not expect you to live without happiness.' " Then came the BUT: "But I tell you, that the man who puts away his wife, makes an adulteress of her, and whoever marries her after she has been put away, commits adultery." What matters if the body is lost? The soul is still there, and that is worth more than the thrill a body can give, more even than the universe itself. He would keep men and women pure, not from contagion, but from desire; to imagine a betrayal is in itself a betrayal. So He thundered: "What God then, has joined, let not man put asunder." No man! No judge! No nation!

Next Christ laid hold of all those social theories which say that sin is due to environment, to Grade B milk, to insufficient dance halls, to not enough spending money. Of them all, He says: "You have heard." Then comes the BUT: "But I tell you." He affirms that sins, selfishness, greed, adultery, crime, theft, bribery, political corruption, come from man himself. The offenses result from our own will, and not from our glands; we cannot excuse our lust because our grandfather had an Oedipus complex, or because we inherited an Electra complex from our grandmother. Sin, He says, is conveyed to the soul sometimes through the body, and our body is moved by will. In war against all false self-expressions, He thunders out His recommendations of self-operation: "Cut it off." "Cut it out." "And if thy right eye is the occasion of falling, cut it out and cast it away from thee; better to lose one part of thy body than to have the whole cast into hell . . . And if thy right hand is the occasion of falling, cut it off and cast it away from thee; better to lose one of thy limbs than to have the whole body cast into hell." Men will cut off their legs and arms to save the body from gangrene or poisoning. But here, Our Lord transfers circumcision of the flesh to circumcision of the heart, and advocates letting out the life blood of our beloved lusts and hewing our passions to tatters, rather than be separated from the love of God which is in Him, Christ Jesus.

Next, He talks of our modern attitude of revenge, hatred, violence, expressed in those sayings of everybody: "Get even," "Sue him," "Don't be a fool," He knows them all, and all of them He says: "You have heard that it was said, 'an eye for an eye and a tooth for a tooth'." Then comes the awful BUT: "But I tell you, that you should not offer resistance to injury; if a man strikes thee on thy right cheek, turn the other cheek also towards him; if he is ready to go to the law with thee over thy coat, let him have it and cloak with it; and if he compels thee to attend him on a mile's journey, go two miles with him of thy own accord."

Why turn the other cheek? Because hate multiplies like a seed. If a Commissar preaches hate and violence to ten men in a row, and tells the first man to strike the second, and the second to strike the third, the hatred will envelop all ten. The only way to stop this hate, would be for one man, say the fifth in line, to turn his other cheek. Then the hatred ends. It is never passed on. Absorb violence for the sake of your Saviour, Who absorbs your sins and dies for them. The Christian law is that the innocent shall suffer for the guilty.

And with these sayings, He is throwing down the gauntlet to the Communists and others who try to make the innocent guilty with their mock trials. He would have us do away with adversaries, because when no resistance is offered, the adversary is conquered by a superior moral power; such love prevents the infection of the wound of hate. To endure the bore who inflicts you for a week; to write a letter of kindness to the man who calls you dirty names; to offer gifts to the man who would steal from you; never to answer back with hatred the man who lies and says you were disloyal to your country, or tells the worse lie that you are against freedom—these are the hard things which Christ came to teach, and they no more suited His time than they do ours. They suit only the heroes, the great men, the saints, the holy men and women, who will be the salt of the earth, the leaven in the mass, the elite among the mob, the kind who will transform the world. If we do not find certain people loveable, He bids us put love into them and they will be loveable. Why are we ever loveable—if it be not that God put love into us?

The Sermon on the Mount is so much at variance with all that our world holds dear, that the world will crucify anyone who tries to live up to its values; because Christ preached them, He had to die. Calvary was the price He paid for the Sermon on the Mount. Only mediocrity survives. When humanity, on the basis of intolerance, condemns to death those who say black is black and white is white, only the grays live.

Let Him Who says: "Blessed are the poor in spirit," come into the world that believes in the primacy of the economic; let Him stand in the market place where Marx and Lenin say that man lives for collective profit, or where monopolistic capitalism says man lives for individual profit. He will be so poor that during life, He will have nowhere to lay His head, and a day will come when He will die without anything of economic worth. In His last hour, He will be so impoverished, that they will strip Him of His garments, and even give Him a stranger's grave for His burial.

Let Him come into the world in which Nietzsche proclaims his gospel of the strong, advocates hating our enemies, and condemns Christian virtues as the "soft" virtues, and say to that world: "Blessed are the patient"—and He will one day feel the scourges of the strong barbarians laid across His back, as they are being laid now on the backs of our missionaries in China. He will see them take a sickle and cut the grass from a hill on Calvary, and then use a hammer to pinion Him to a Cross to test the patience of One Who awaits eternity.

Let Him come into our world with its divorce courts, its psychoanalysts ridiculing the idea of sin as morbidity, a world of progressive educators who deny discipline for the young, and preach to that world: "Blessed are they who mourn" for their sins, and they will blindfold Him and mock Him as a fool. They will take His body and scourge it until His bones can be numbered; and they will crown His head with thorns, until He begins to weep not salt tears, but crimson beads of blood, as they laugh at the weakness of Him Who will not come down from the Cross.

Let Him come into a world that believes in the philosophy of pragmatism and relativism, a world which denies Absolute Truth, which says that right and wrong are only questions of point of view, that we must be broadminded about virtue and vice, and let Him say to them: "Blessed are they who hunger and thirst after holiness," that is, after the Absolute, after the Truth which I am, and outside of which there is no other; and they will, in their broadmindedness, give the mob the choice of Him or Barrabas, will crucify Him with thieves and try to make the world believe that God is no different from a batch of robbers who are His bedfellows in death.

Let Him come into the world of Sartre, who says that my neighbor is hell, that all that is opposite me is nothing, that the ego alone matters, that my will is supreme law, that what I decide is good, that I must forget others and think only of myself, and say to them: "Blessed are the merciful," and He will find that He will receive no mercy; they will open five rivers of blood out of His body, they will pour vinegar and gall into His thirsting mouth, and even after His death, be so merciless as to lunge a spear into His Sacred Heart.

Let Him come into a world which tries to interpret man in terms of sex; which seasons the novel, movie and television show with an attack on the sanctity of marriage, which says that a marriage endures only until the glands tire; that one may unbind what God binds, and unseal what God seals, and say to them: "Blessed are the pure," and He will find Himself hanging naked on a Cross that defies their crazy affirmation that purity is abnormal, that the virgins are neurotics and that their carnality is right.

Let Him come into a world of Vishinskys and Molotovs, who believe with Lenin that one must resort to every manner of chicanery and duplicity in order to conquer the world, who carry doves of peace with stomachs full of bombs, and say to them: "Blessed are the peace-makers," or "Blessed are they who eradicate sin that there may be peace," and He will find Himself surrounded by the comrades of the Vishinskys and Molotovs, as they make the greatest war this world of ours ever saw: the war against the Son of God; after His death, they will set a guard about His grave to prevent a Resurrection, something they would not expect even from a Lenin.

Let Him come into a world that believes personality should be manipulated; that our whole life should be geared to flattering and influencing people for the sake of utility and popularity, and say to them:

"Blessed are ye when men hate you and persecute you and revile you," and He will find Himself without a friend in the world, an outcast on a hill, with mobs shouting His death and His flesh hanging from Him like purple rage.

The Beatitudes cannot be taken alone; they are not ideals; they are hard facts and realities, inseparable from the Cross of Calvary. Many men go on repeating them, but very few of us are willing to live them! It is easy to be a Communist—all one has to do is hate; it is easy to be self-expressive, all one has to do is avoid repressing the *id;* it is easy to be a liberal, all one has to do is espouse no cause as sacred, except the right to be free from discipline and the Eternal Law of God; it is easy to be a social reformer, and to take care of other people's consciences; it is easy to be a milk and water Christian who quotes the Sermon on the Mount, and forgets the Christ Who died for it. It is easy to be an intellectual and to sneer at the humble. It is easy to love those who love us.

But it is hard to love those who hate us, to pluck out one's eyes and cut off arms to prevent sinning; it is hard to be clean on the inside when the passions clamor for satisfaction on the outside; to forgive those who would put us to death; to overcome evil with good; to bless those who curse us, to stop mouthing freedom until we have justice, truth and love of God in our hearts as the condition of freedom; to live in the world and still keep oneself unpolluted from the world; to deny ourselves sometimes legitimate pleasures, like cigarettes, cocktails, movies and luxuries, in order to help missionaries feed the leprous, fill the empty rice bowls and renew hungry hearts with the grass of God; to see that all our clap-trap about the brotherhood of man is meaningless unless we all have the same God as Father! What kind of men would we be if we did not know Our Father?—a race of illegitimate children. To strive not to be like the rest of men, but to be Perfect as the Heavenly Father is perfect—this is the only new thing in the world, but there are very few who are willing to try it. Christianity has not failed; but we have failed the Christ who said: "Take up your cross and follow Me."

# PART 4

## *PUBLIC LIFE AND PASSION*

Over thirty times during His Life, Jesus Christ spoke of a *must* about His sufferings and death. Those who quarrel and bicker about who put Him to death are very much off center. Our Lord was under no outer compulsion; He was not a victim of circumstances beyond His control; He was not a devotee of the world's highest values, like a soldier dying on a battlefield; He was not a martyr for a great cause; not a moral teacher Whom the mediocre slew because they could not stand the moral lashings of His purity. He went to death not because of the plotting of evil men, nor because He was a victim of circumstances quite beyond His control, nor because of the power of the Roman Empire. True indeed, the stage was set by evil men, but Our Lord always presents Himself as One Who took charge of the plot. He went to death in obedience to His Father, with Whom He is one in nature! "The Father and I are one."

Buddha came into this world to live, so did Socrates, so did Confucius, so did Moses and the Prophets. However, there was One Person Who came into the world to die, and that was the Eternal Galilean, Jesus Christ.

The Cross came at the end of His Life, from a time point of view, but it was hovering over the crib from an intentional point of view.

There is a maxim in philosophy: "What is first in intention is last in execution." A young man decides to become a doctor. But the intention is perhaps 12 years or more before he receives his M.D. In like manner, the Cross was first in intention in the earthly life of Christ, but the last in execution. Our lives are lived forward; *His life was lived backward.* The Cross was the reason for the crib and His teaching, not His crib and His teachings the reason for His Cross.

Nothing is more beautiful in His character than the way He prepared His Apostles for that unpalatable lesson of seeming defeat as the condition of victory. How slow they were to understand the story of why He must suffer, but with what infinite patience He instructed them. He took two steps in unfolding the mystery of His death and why it was necessary:
1. An occasional reference to the need of sacrifice, until they were convinced by prophecies and miracles that He was the Son of God.
2. A bold announcement of the Cross after Peter confessed: "Thou art the Christ, the Son of the Living God."
1. Though He knew from the beginning that His Father so loved the world that He sent Him into it to redeem men from their sins, nevertheless, He could not tell this to His Apostles without arousing their prejudice or destroying their feeble faith. Instead of saying that He would sacrifice Himself, He began by telling them that they should sacrifice themselves. For example, when He was seen in the company of publicans, some of the "nice people" lifted their eyebrows, but He explained to His disciples: "I came not to save the just, but the sinners." To heal men of sin is a greater manifestation of Power than to exterminate sinners by punishment. He did not tell them at that moment, how this was to be accomplished, but only that such was His purpose.

Next, He warned them that as a result of their companionship with Him, they too would have to suffer. "The servant is not above the Master." He even tells them they are to consider themselves "blessed" when "men shall hate you . . . and cast out your name as evil." This was a strange forecast to give disciples, namely because if they followed Him they would have missiles thrown at them. Before Him and since many have preached that if you are good, you will be prosperous; Jesus tells them that if they are good, they will be persecuted: "You shall be hated by all men for My Name's sake."

He hoped they, being reasonable men, would draw inferences from such warnings as: "Fear ye not them that kill the body, and are not able to kill the soul." Why should He Who had the power to raise the dead, and lift up limbs long palsied with disease and death, now tell them not to fear those who would torture their bodies? Would His body be tortured? Was He bidding them to do something from which He would exempt Himself by His power? They knew the soul was worth more than the body, but why speak of their bodies being killed? Would they die as martyrs?

The conclusion was inevitable: He was bidding them to a life of sacrifice because He would be sacrificed. He did not yet say that He would offer Himself for the sinners of the world; rather, He said because His sacrifice was a Divine "must" laid upon Him by love, they must be prepared for the same maltreatment, because they were His servants.

Despite His patience in educating His followers, they did not grasp the lesson. The disproportion between His mind and theirs was infinitely greater than Shakespeare teaching the alphabet to a three-year-old child. Added to this was the "scandal" of the Cross, for what mysterious faith was this He was giving them which would provoke so much of the world to **hate?**

2. About the middle of His public life, the Apostles who followed Him saw the opposition against Him grow. Groups that despised one another united in one great phalanx of conspiracy, determined if possible to alienate the affections of the common people who marveled at His works.

Leaving Bethsaida, He enters the half-pagan city of Caesarea-Philippi, where there was a statue to the god Pan. While there, the culminating point of His earthly ministry occurred. When He had finished His prayer, He beckoned His Apostles to Him and asked them the most important question He ever asked: "Whom do men say that I am?" Perhaps the reason He asked about the popular judgment which men had concerning Him was to reveal to them how much in the eyes of the public He had failed. "Men," they said, "thought Him to be Elias, Jeremias, John the Baptist, or one of the Prophets."

Then He asked: "Whom do *you* say that I am?" The popular answer had been full of contradictions. Now the elect, the spiritual aristocracy was asked, but they did not answer.

One man then stepped forward, Peter, who answered: "Thou art the Christ, the Son of the Living God." Our Blessed Lord answers:

**"Blessed art thou, Simon son of Jona;**
**It is not flesh and blood,**
**It is My Father in Heaven**
**That has revealed this to thee."**

He was telling Peter that He did not know this of and by himself, but because of a revelation of His Father. It was faith that made him stand alone and apart from the world, and above all of its judgments. Our Lord, then makes Peter "the rock upon which I will build My Church."

But this is only half the story. Now that Our Lord was known to be what He is, the Messias, the Son of the Eternal Father, He prepared them for the second lesson: He is the suffering Messias spoken of by Isaias and the other prophets, "the Lamb led to slaughter," "the One on Whom are laid the transgressions of us all."

The Apostles had to learn the first lesson thoroughly before they could face boldly the second lesson, namely, that He Who is the God-Man should suffer and die. The "must" of which He spoke when He was 12 years of age, is now clearly revealed: He *must die* because He *would save*. The Divine Messias must be a rejected Messias, and a rejected Messias must be a slain Messias.

"From that time onwards Jesus began to
Make it known to His disciples
That He must go up to Jerusalem, and there,
With much ill-usage from the priests
And elders and scribes must be put to death,
And rise again on the third day."

The work of His Cross can be understood only in the light that He is the Father's Son. He told His Apostles then what He would tell them after His Resurrection, that it was "fitting that the Son of Man suffer," that the necessity of suffering comes not from rejection by elders, chief priests and scribes, nor is it due to the accumulation of popular prejudice. The web in which He is caught on Calvary's Hill will not be spun by the hands of spider men. The Divine must comes from two sides: the obedience to His Father's Will, and His love of men. The first pointed Him to the Cross, the second nailed Him there and kept Him there, despite the cries to "come down and we will believe," until the work was finished.

Peter did not understand the Divine *must*, for he "rebuked" Our Lord for suggesting that He would suffer. It was at this point that Our Blessed Lord called him "Satan." Peter had done exactly the same thing that Satan had done in the wilderness, namely, tried to turn Him away from the Cross, and make Him a political Messias Who would give belly-bread instead of soulbread. Our Lord implied that suggesting the merely human way out of a Divine Mission is identical with being diabolical. Then He told Peter that what he said savored not of the things of God, but of the things of men.

Jesus then tells them that His law should be their law: A Good Friday is the prelude to an Easter Sunday. But there is this difference. He is under a Divine Mandate of the Father to which His Will is identified perfectly. But, they are free to choose. Hence, He said He "must" suffer, but as for them: "*If* any will follow Me, let him take up his cross and follow Me." This was one of the conditions of discipleship. They knew what a cross was, for they had often seen the Romans execute criminals on the hills outside the city.

Now He says: "Whosoever does not take his cross and come after Me, cannot be My disciple." But He also consoles them by saying that the same suffering servant who mounts a Cross will one day come attended by the hosts of heaven to judge every man according to his works. The cross is only a means, not an end; it is the prelude to the crown. From now on, He spoke openly of His Death, never mentioning His Cross without His Resurrection, but they could not understand either clearly until Pentecost and the coming of the Spirit.

Another very remarkable reference to His Divine Mission of saving men from sin was manifested to His Apostles on the Mount of Transfiguration. Three major scenes of His Life took place on mountains: the Mount of the Beatitudes, the Mount of the Transfiguration and the Mount of Calvary. All three hills are related one to the other. The first was the proclamation of a message that would antagonize the world. The second was the revelation of His Glory through death; and the third, the supreme act of love, the ransom of men. The incident took place about a week after Peter had confessed that He was the Son of the Living God.

Our Lord took with Him three Apostles: Peter, James and John. Peter the "rock," James the one destined to be the first Apostle Martyr, and John the visionary of the future glory of the Apocalypse. Undoubtedly, He chose these three because they most needed strength for the hour of trial.

On the mountain top, He became transfigured, His face shining as the sun, and His garments becoming white as snow. While there, Moses and Elias conversed with Him: Moses, the publisher of the Law, and Elias, the chief of the Prophets. His Sacred Person semed to be living with the Light of Glory flashing through the threads of His earthly raiment. It was not so much a light that was shining from without, as a light coming from the essential beauty of the Godhead within. It was not a miracle, but a witness of the abiding presence of Christ's Divinity. The glory that shone around Him as the Temple of God, was not something with which He was outwardly invested, but rather a natural expression of the inherent loveliness of "Him Who came down from Heaven."

The wonder was not this momentary radiance around Him: it was rather that at all other times, it was repressed. As Moses, after communing with God, put a veil over his face to hide it from the people of Israel, so Christ had veiled His Glory in humanity. But for this brief moment, He turns it aside so that men may see it; the outgoing of these rays was the transitory proclamation to every human eye of the Son of Righteousness. In one brief moment, Heaven seemed to enshrine the earthly life, which was the Glory of God.

Peter expressed his happiness that they were there. Attempting to capture this glory which was transient, he suggested building three tents or tabernacles there: one for Moses, one for Elias, and one for Christ. Just one week before, Peter was trying to find a way to glory without the Cross. Peter now once more attempts indirectly to dissuade Our Lord from going to Jerusalem to be crucified, and thus becomes the spokesman of all those who would enter into glory without purchasing it by self-denial and sacrifice. Peter, with his impetuous character, feels that the glory which God brought down from the Heavens could be tabernacled among men, without ever purchasing it by the Cross of Calvary. But while Peter would have a glory without the Cross, Our Lord is speaking to Moses and Elias of His Death. "And they spoke of the Death which He was to achieve at Jerusalem."

His death on the Cross would not be a surprise or an accident, but a work which He came to accomplish and which would be a fulfillment of both the Law and the Prophets. In the moment of His greatest glory, He draws aside the effulgence of the Divine which is really His and shows Himself speaking of His death, of His scourging and crowning with thorns and Crucifixion. At a moment when He seemed to be least a Man of Sorrows, He converses with the Law and the Prophets of the impending tragedy. The Divine Face which was now shining so brightly with the Light of God, must be smitten and spit upon. The gossamer of light which now surrounds Him would have to be exchanged for being stripped naked on a Hill. The Sacred Brow which glistened with Heavenly Glory, would have to be studded with thorns, woven by soldiers cursing the thorns that had so lightly pricked their thumbs.

While the Apostles were standing at what seemed to be the very vestibule of Heaven, a cloud formed overshadowing them:

> "And a voice came from the cloud
> This is My Beloved Son;
> To Him, then, listen."

When God sets up a cloud, it is a manifest sign that there are bonds we cannot break. At His Baptism, the Heavens were opened and now, at the Transfiguration, they open again to install Him in His office as Mediator, and to distinguish Him from Moses and the Prophets. It was Heaven itself that was sending Him on His mission of saving men, not the perverse will of men.

The purpose of the Transfiguration was also to strengthen His Apostles for the impending blow of His death. By itself, this show of glory could have brought His earthly life to a fitting climax, if there were no sin. His own spotless life deserved the crown without the cross, the glory without the suffering. Thus thought Peter, too. But neither Peter, nor James nor John could probably have endured the shock of defeat, had they not first been strengthened by the sight of Jesus in

His glory—a forecast of what He would be after the Resurrection. It was these three to whom special revelations would be made after His Resurrection. This perfect knowledge of His future glory alone could sustain them for Calvary. Then when John at the foot of the Cross, would hear Him say: "My God! My God! Why hast Thou abandoned Me?", he could recall the assuring words from the Father in Heaven: "This is My Beloved Son."

Another interesting reference to His act of ransom was a parable that is almost autobiographical, namely, the parable of the dishonest tenants. The rulers had just been questioning Our Lord as to the authority by which He acted. The position that they took was that they were representatives and guardians of the people, and, therefore, they must prevent the people from being misled. Our Lord answers them in a parable, showing them the kind of guardians and guides they were. He points out several steps in the planting of a vineyard: it is furnished with all the necessary appliances, has a wall around it, a wine press and a tower. God had enclosed His people with His own hands, and prepared them to be a fruitful vine. The letting out of the vineyard to those who tended it, meant the commitment to His own people of responsibility. This commitment began with Abraham, who had been called out of the land of Ur, and with Moses, who gave his people commandments, and the worship of the true God by which they emerged from the wilderness of barbarism.

The next scene is one in which the owner of the vineyard claims the returns, namely, fidelity and love of God. Our Lord describes that the messengers who are the prophets were subjected to cruel treatment and often murder. The more God pleaded with them, the more bitter they became.

Under figure of speech He is saying that a special Providence which had protected and defended His people against all enemies should have prompted them to have been grateful. Then Jesus draws the last arrow from the quiver of the parable and said of the owner of the vineyard, Who is His Heavenly Father:

> "He still had one messenger left,
> His only Beloved Son,
> Him He sent to the last of all;
> They will have reverence, He said
> For My Son."

He sets Himself apart from the servants or the prophets and tells His auditors that He comes from the owner of the vineyard, God Himself. Christ here presents Himself as God's last appeal to the sinful world, a supreme gift of infinite love. The Father hopes that His Son will be counted as standing for Himself, and the gratitude and affection and reverence that is due to Him, will be shown to His Son. And Our Lord, continuing the parable, says:

"But the vine-dressers said among themselves.
This is the heir, come, let us kill Him,
And then His inheritance will be ours
So they took Him and killed Him
And cast Him out of the vineyard."

Our Blessed Lord under this symbol, reminds His hearers of the melancholy fact that He will receive but little reverence from mankind. Rebuffs and injuries and insults would be the greeting extended the Beloved Son of the Heavenly Father.

Within three days of the telling of the story, it came true. The accredited keepers of His vineyard who cast Him out of the city onto a hill that was used as a dump, contrived to put Him to death. Man can thwart God's purpose at least for a time, but as Augustine said: "They slew Him that they might possess, and because they slew, they lost."

Later, He tells His enemies that they will not come to recognize Who He is, until He has been crucified.

"When you have lifted up the Son of Man,
You will recognize that it is Myself you look for,
And that I do not do anything of My own impulse,
But speak as My Father has instructed Me to speak."

Only after the Crucifixion will they know what He spoke. The Crucifixion would not be the last in the series of failures. It would be the revelation of His glory, and would cause a reaction in men's minds concerning Him, when they finally had placarded Him outside of the city's gates. The Cross and the Crown would be the truth to the most obtuse and bigoted, "that I am that what I say I am." The forecast here is the conversion of His enemies as a result of His Death and Resurrection.

When a man is leading a great social movement, the worst thing that can happen to him is to die. But He said the cross is the condition of drawing men unto Himself. If He were merely a man, the Cross to Him would be His scaffold. But as the Eternal Son of the Father, it would be a throne. If He were a martyr, His Death would be defeat; but if He is God, it will be a victory. If He were a man, the Cross would be a repulsion; being God, it would be a world-wide attraction.

If the message that He taught had come only from a man, its chief emphasis would have been placed by His followers not on the Cross, but on the Mount of Beatitudes. It is singular that those who miss His Divine message are always the ones that insist upon the Mount of Beatitudes. If He were only a man, Christians would have drawn a veil over those hours of Calvary, and would have stressed solely the wisdom of the Teacher and the majesty of the King. Instead of this, true Christians boast of that which must have appeared as a failure to human eyes.

If Our Lord had come to this earth and had been fenced in by all the comforts of life, and after teaching the true theory of pain, had died on a soft bed, He might have been honored as a great Teacher, but He would never have drawn men to Himself. Nowhere does He say: "Obey a code," but rather, "Follow Me." Everything said about His sufferings and death revealed that He voluntarily committed Himself to some great task which His Father had given Him, and that task was first and foremost the delivery of mankind from the burden of sin. His death was as the fulfillment of Divine purpose in which His will was One with that of the Father; His words and acts are those of One who knows what He is doing and why He must do it.

Men are called to participate in the fruits of His death. Man's attitude is not to be passive toward this redemption. The obedience to His Father's Will is His own, but since He presents it as the Son of Man, it is also a representative obedience. It is the obedience which men ought to offer to God, and which they should offer, did they fulfill the obligations of sonship. Representing men, He offers that obedience in their name and for their sake, with the intention that they should identify themselves with it, and so offer themselves. He intended that men should participate in the self-offering and appropriate the power of His surrendered life. His redemptive service is not intended to be a work wrought apart from men; it is rather a work into which they are permitted to enter in such a way that what He does on their behalf becomes a very vital factor in their approach to God.

How empty and frivolous the Death of Christ would be unless human nature in some way was involved in sin. If we were sitting on a pier on a bright summer day, fishing contentedly, and suddenly saw another man jump off the pier in front of us into the river and, as he went down the third time, we heard him say: "Greater love than this no man hath, than he lay down his life for his friend," we would have found the whole proceeding quite unintelligible.

If, however, we had fallen into the waters and were drowning, and the man came in and offered his life to save us, then there would be meaning to his Death. If human nature had not fallen into sin, the Death of Christ would be meaningless. But if He had come as the Son of God to ransom us from sin in obedience to the Father's Will and restore us to a heritage which was lost, then the Cross becomes our glory.

If we were the only persons in the world who had eyes to see, would we not be staffs to the blind; if we were the only persons in the world who were healthy, would we not minister to the sick? If we seek to identify ourselves with the physical sufferings of others because we love them, why should we not be one with those who are cast down with moral suffering? If the more healthy we are, the better we serve the sick, then the more innocent we are, the more we should take on their guilt. Eventually, this would reach a point where we would sacrifice ourselves for the other's guilt. A mother loves her child! If it were possible, she would willingly take upon herself all the pains of the child. The father will take on the debts of his son, and a lover, if possible, would take on the woes of his beloved.

Picture a chalice, which only a priest may touch, stolen from the altar. It is made into a beer mug and delivered over to profane uses. Later on, the chalice is retrieved, but before it can be restored to the altar, it must be put into the flames, the dross burned away. Then it must be beaten and hammered and refashioned again from the old creature of the beer mug, into the new creature of the chalice. Only then is it fit for blessing and ready for restoration to the altar of sacrifice.

Our human nature, which once was in possession of God's grace, and which once bore resemblance to the Divine Nature, through a free act of ours lost its dignity and became delivered over to profane and unholy purposes of sin. Our Blessed Lord came to this earth and took a human nature like ours in all things except sin. He made it stand for us as the head of the new humanity, as if He Himself were guilty for all the sins of the world. Then He takes this human nature of ours, and plunges it into the fire of Calvary to have all the dross of evil and sin burned and purged away. After being beaten and hammered and put into a grave, He finally rises from the dead as the Head of the new humanity—the Pattern Man we are destined to be if we receive His Spirit.

The whole problem of Christianity, then, is how to become incorporated again to this new humanity in Christ, Who is the Son of God. That happens, as He said, through the sending of His Spirit so that He will not be an example to be copied, but a life to be lived.

# PART 5

## *DEATH AND RESURRECTION*

Some things in life are too beautiful to be forgotten, and there can also be something in death that is too beautiful to be forgotten. That is why we have a Memorial Day—to recall the sacrifices of our youth for the preservation of freedom. Freedom is not an heirloom, but a life. Once received, it does not continue to exist without effort. As life must be nourished, defended and preserved, so freedom must be repurchased in each generation. What Washington won, had to be rewon by Lincoln, then won again in World Wars I and II.

All the blood that crimsoned Valley Forge and Bunker Hill and Gettysburg, that reddened the soil of France, the Pacific Islands and Korea, cries out like Abel's blood for remembrance. Our hearts, knowing that we live because they died, answer their mute pleas by instituting a Memorial Day to recall in prayer and reverence, the sublime truth that "greater love than this no man hath, that he lay down his life for his friends."

These youths, however, were not born to die. Soldiering was an interruption to their summons to live; neither they nor their parents willed that their ship of life should be sunk so soon after launching into the sea of life. In this, all men differ from Our Blessed Lord, Who came into this world to die. Even at His Birth, His Mother was reminded that He came to *die*, as the Wise Men brought myrrh for His burial. Never before, did any mother see Death wrap its arms so quickly about a newborn Babe. Never before did the shadow of the Cross fall so quickly on a crib.

When He was still only an infant, the old man Simeon looked into the face of Him and said that He was destined to be a "sign to be contradicted"—a signal that would call out the opposition of the deliberately imperfect. The Mother, on hearing that word "contradicted," could almost see Simeon's arms fade and the arms of the Cross take their place to wrap Her Son in death. Before two years of His Life had been lived, King Herod sent out horsemen to decapitate Him.

Since, then, Our Divine Lord came to die, it was fitting that there be a Memorial of His death. If we keep a memorial of soldiers who died that we might be free from political oppression, then should not the Divine Soldier have a memorial for preserving us from the spiritual tyranny of sin? Since He is God as well as man, and since He never spoke of His Death without speaking of His Resurrection, should He not Himself institute the precise memorial of His own death and not leave it to the chance recollection of men? And that is precisely what He did the night of the Last Supper. But His Memorial was instituted — and this is important — not because He would die like a soldier and be buried, but because He would live again after the Resurrection.

In His last hours with His Apostles, He instituted not a Memorial Day, but a Memorial Action. Seated at a Passover meal which commemorated the liberation of His people from the slavery of Egypt, He prepared to fulfill it by celebrating the liberation of souls from the slavery of Satan! As the paschal lambs were being sacrificed to celebrate the deliverance from political slavery, He, the true Paschal Lamb, prepared to offer Himself to save souls from spiritual slavery. His act would be the New Testament; like the Old, it would be sealed with blood — not the blood of sheep, but the blood of Himself, the Immaculate Lamb.

At the Last Supper, Christ's eyes kindled and His whole bearing took on a majesty greater than when He spoke to Moses and Elias in the clouds. Taking in His hands a piece of unleavened bread, He lifted His eyes to Heaven, gave thanks, and over it said: "Take, eat, this is My Body Which shall be delivered for you." Then, taking the cup of wine, by another act of omnipotence, He breathed over it saying: "Drink, all of you, of this; for This is My Blood of the New Testament, Which shall be shed for many unto the remission of sins."

Note the words: "My Body Which shall be delivered for you; My Blood of the New Testament Which shall be shed." He was looking forward to the morrow, Good Friday, when He would die on the Cross — the one supreme reason for His coming to earth. It was a new Covenant, a new Testament. There had been one Covenant with Noah on leaving the ark, another Covenant with Abraham on leaving Haran, another with Moses on leading the people from Egypt. All led to this new Covenant between God and man. On God's side, it pledged remission of sins through His Death; on man's side, faith and sacrifice.

But how, it may be asked, does the changing of the Bread into His Body and the changing of the wine into His Blood, foreshadow His sacrificial Death on the Cross on the morrow? Our Lord did not consecrate the bread and wine together, but separately. This symbolic action represents the way He would be sacrificed on the Cross, namely, by the violent separation of His Blood from His Body. His Passion and His Sacrifice were beginning; on the morrow on the Cross He would be upright as a Priest, and prostrate as a Victim offering Himself for the sins of the world.

But because Our Lord's Memorial was not instituted by us, but by Him, and because He could not be conquered by death, which is a penalty for sin, but would rise again in the newness of life, He willed that as He now looked forward to His Redemptive Death on the Cross, so all the Christian ages until the consummation of the world should look back to it, the Crucifixion. In order that they would not re-enact the Memorial out of whim or fancy, He gave the command: "Do this for a commemoration of Me." That is, "Announce My redemptive Death until I come again! I will be the same Priest and Victim on both My Cross and your commemoration of My Death. But as I look forward to the Cross, you will look back to it. As this My Last Supper looks in prospect to Myself as the Victim to be immolated on Calvary, so in your commemoration you will look back to the immolation that has already taken place."

During His mortal life, Our Lord chose many varied and picturesque pulpits from which to deliver His sermons, the Words of Eternal Life. Sometimes His pulpit was Peter's bark pushed out into the sea; at other times, it was the crowded streets of Jericho, the golden gate of the Temple, Jacob's well. It seemed as if almost any pulpit pleased Him, until the day came for Him to deliver His farewell address. Then He demanded a pulpit which, like the words He was uttering, would be remembered down through the arches of the years. On Good Friday morning, as He stood on the sunlit portico of Pontius Pilate, He may have thought of making that entranceway the pulpit of His last address. There was a vast sea of faces before Him and hearts hungering for the Bread of Eternal Life—an audience like unto which anyone would have loved to open his heart.

But He, He waited a few hours for another pulpit to be given Him at the foot of the steps of Pilate's palace. That pulpit He put upon His shoulders and carried to Golgotha. That pulpit was—the Cross. Once on those heights He offered Himself to His executioners.

Hands of the Carpenter hardened by toil; hands from which the world's graces flow; feet of the Miracle Worker Who went about doing good—these now had rough nails applied to them. The first knock of the hammer was heard in silence; blow followed blow and was faintly re-echoed over the city walls beneath. Mary and John held their ears. The sound was unendurable; each echo sounded as another stroke. The cross was lifted slowly off the ground, staggered for a moment in mid-air, and then, with a thud that seemed to shake even hell itself, it sank into the pit prepared for it.

Our Lord had mounted His pulpit for the last time—and what a majestic pulpit it was! In itself the Cross was a sermon. How much more eloquently it spoke now when adorned with the Word of Eternal Life!

Like all who mount their pulpits, He o'erlooked His audience. Far off in the distance, across the Valley of Jehosaphat, He could see the gilded roof of the Temple reflecting its rays against the sun, which was soon to hide its face in shame. Here and there on Temple walls He caught glimpses of figures straining their eyes to catch the last view of Him whom the darkness knew not.

Nearer the pulpit, but off at the border of the crowd, stood some of His own timid disciples ready to flee in case of danger. Greeks and Romans were there, too, as well as Scribes and Pharisees from Jerusalem. There were those in the crowd asking Him to come down and prove His Divinity. There were the Deity-blind, mocking and spitting at Him. There were some who had followed Him for an hour, taunting Him that others He saved but Himself He could not save. There were Roman soldiers throwing dice for the garments of a God. And there at the foot of the cross stood that wounded flower, that broken thing, Magdalen, forgiven because she loved much. And there, with a face like a cast moulded out of love, was John. And there, God pity her, was His own Mother. Mary, Magdalen and John. Innocence, penitence and sacerdotal love— the three types of souls forever to be found beneath the Cross of Christ.

All was silence now. The Scribes and Pharisees had ceased their raillery, the Roman soldiers had put away their dice. The sky darkened and man grew fearful, awaiting the farewell address of the Son of God. He began to speak, and like all men who die, He thought of those whom He loved most. His first word was a word about His enemies: "Father forgive them, for they know not what they do." His second was about sinners as He spoke to a thief: "This day thou shalt be with Me in Paradise!" His third word was to His Mother and John. It was the new Annunciation: "Woman, behold thy son."

For Three Hours He suffered. Then there was a rupture of a Heart through the rapture of Love and He gave up His Life of His own Will. The Roman Centurion whose business it was to see that the crucified was dead, stayed at his post to the very end. Taking a spear, He pierced the Heart of the Christ. Blood and water poured out; water, the symbol of regeneration; and blood, the price of redemption.

Later Joseph of Arimathea went to beg Pilate for the body of Jesus, but Pilate would not release it until he had conducted his own investigation. He, therefore, called in the Centurion and inquired of him if He was really dead. Joseph showed no solicitude for the bodies of the two thieves. But he had a personal reverence for Jesus—he had refused in a council meeting earlier to consent to His death.

Nicodemus, who once came at night to consult Jesus, and other helpers wrapped Jesus according to custom in a sheet eight feet long and embalmed Him with spices. The Body was laid in the tomb, a great stone was rolled before the door of the sepulcher, and an official guard was set. It was the only time in history that a guard was set to prevent a man rising from the tomb.

In the dim dawn of the following Sunday, several women approached the tomb. The fact that they brought spices showed that they did not expect a Resurrection. It seems strange that they should have doubted, after the many references of Our Lord to His Death and His Resurrection. But whenever he predicted His Passion and Resurrection, even His disciples apparently paid more attention to His prediction of His Death than His Resurrection. It never occurred to them that His Resurrection was possible. When the stone was rolled to the door of the sepulcher, not only Christ was buried, but also all their hopes. The women thought only to annoint the body of the dead Christ, an act born of despairing and yet unbelieving love.

Two of the women at least had witnessed the burial, and their great concern was a practical one:

>"Who is to roll the stone away for us
>From the door of the tomb?"

It was the cry of a heart of little faith. Strong men had closed the entrance to the tomb by placing the huge stone against it; the women's worry was how to remove the barrier in order that they might carry out their errand of mercy. The men would not come to the tomb until they were summoned—so little did they believe. And the women came only because, in their grief, they sought consolation in embalming the dead.

When they came near, they saw that the stone, great as it was, had been rolled away. They did not immediately jump to the conclusion that His Body had risen—they concluded someone had removed the Body. But then an angel whose countenance was as lightning and whose raiment was as snow said to them:

>"No need to be dismayed;
>You have come to look for Jesus of Nazareth,
>Who was crucified; He has risen again,
>He is not here. Here is the place where they laid Him.
>Go and tell Peter and the rest of His Disciples
>That He is going before you into Galilee.
>There you shall have sight of Him as He promised you."

To an angel, the Resurrection would not be a mystery, but His Death would be. For us, the Death is not a mystery, but His Resurrection is. The angel was one keeper more than the enemies had placed about the Saviour's grave, one soldier more than Pilate had appointed.

The angel's message was the first Gospel preached after the Resurrection, and it went back again to Our Lord's Passion. When the angel spoke of Him as "Jesus of Nazareth Who was crucified," the words told: the name of His humanity, the humility of His dwelling place, and the ignominy of His Death.

All three—lowliness, ignominy and shame—were brought in comparison to His arising from the dead. Bethlehem and Nazareth and Jerusalem were all made the identifying marks of His Resurrection.

The angel's words: "Here is the place where they laid Him," confirmed the reality of His Death and the fulfillment of the ancient prophecies. We wander through a graveyard and look at tombstones almost all of which are headed with the inscription: *Hic Jacet* or "Here lies." Then follows the name of the dead, and perhaps some praise of the one departed. But here in contrast, the angel does not write, but speaks a different epitaph: "He is not here." The angel calls on the women to behold the place where their Lord's Body has laid, as though its mere desertion were evidence enough of the fact of the Resurrection. They are directed immediately to hasten and give intelligence of the Resurrection. It was to a virgin woman that the birth of the Son of God was announced. It is to a fallen woman that His Resurrection is announced.

Those who saw the empty grave were bidden to go to Peter who had tempted Our Blessed Lord once from the Cross and three times denied Him. Sin and denial cannot choke Divine Love. Paradoxical it is that the more we sin the less can we believe in His Love, and yet the more we sin and repent, the more we wonder at the marvels of His Love. It is to the lost sheep panting in the wilderness that He comes; it is the publicans and the harlots, the denying Peters and the persecuting Pauls to whom the most persuasive entreaties of love are sent. To the man who was named a Rock and who would have tempted Him from a Cross, the risen Saviour now sends through the women the message:

"Go tell Peter."

Nothing is less factual than to say the pious women were expecting Christ to rise from the dead. This was, in fact, something they never expected. The other women may have rushed back to their homes, but Magdalene raced impetuously to Peter and to John, not to announce the Resurrection, but to say: "They have carried the Lord away from the tomb and we cannot tell where they have taken Him." Just a week before, she had heard her Master say that He was the Resurrection and the Life, and now instead of believing in the Resurrection, she thought that someone had stolen away the body.

Despite the multiple predictions of His Resurrection and the comparing of Himself to Jonas, still His own disciples and followers did not believe. When finally Mary Magdalene and Joanna and Mary, the mother of James, told the Apostles of His Resurrection, they refused to believe. "To their minds, the story seemed madness and they could not believe it."

Added to the original incredulity of the women was now the incredulity of the Apostles. Their answer practically was: "You know how women are, always imagining things." In vain do we think that people before the advent of scientific psychology were not afraid of their own minds playing tricks upon them. We boast of our own incredulity in the face of the extraordinary, but our scepticism is as nothing compared to the scepticism which immediately greeted the first news of the Resurrection. What modern sceptics say about the Resurrection story, the disciples themselves were the first to say. As the original agnostics of Christianity, with one assent they dismissed the whole story as a delusion. Something very extraordinary had to happen, some concrete evidence had to be presented to all of these doubters, before they would overcome their reluctance to believe. Their scepticism was even more difficult than modern scepticism to overcome. Theirs started from a hope that was disappointed on Calvary; that was far more difficult to heal than modern scepticism, which is without hope. Nothing is further from the truth than to say that followers of Our Lord were expecting the Resurrection and therefore were ready to believe it or to console themselves for a loss that seemed irreparable. H. G. Wells wrote nothing about the Resurrection that the Apostles had not already had in their own minds.

After the Resurrection, Our Lord made many appearances; for example, to the disciples on the road to Emmaus, to the Apostles excluding Thomas, to the Apostles with Thomas, to multitudes, to small groups of Apostles, to Peter and John on the lake. Then after 40 days, He took leave of them to ascend, as He told Magdalen, back again to His Father. It took a long time to convince them, and the full meaning did not dawn in their souls until Pentecost. Then they were all ready to have their throats cut for their belief.

Less than seven weeks before, He had made His triumphal entry into Jerusalem; He had also suffered His ignominious death in Jerusalem, and now within view of it He would ascend back again to His Father. While in the city He opened their understanding, gave them the light beyond the light of reason. However excellent natural and external means may be, they still are insufficient; fullness of faith only God can give. Once that new understanding or new light comes, then everything appears differently than it was before. The difference is the same as two men walking into a room, one man being blind and the other man having eyes to see. Both have some approximation of the contents of the room, but only the man with eyes understands clearly each object and the relation of one to another. So when He opened their understanding, the words *Christ* and sin and *suffering* all had different sounds in their ears, and a different meaning in their hearts. He might have illumined their minds without any appeal to reason or history, but the practical method that He chose was the historical one. He told them all the things that had been written in the law of Moses and the Prophets and the Psalms, concerning Him, in order that they might understand the Scriptures. That these men about Him should have, in a single second, understood the full scope of history is as great a miracle as any of His healings.

Then He came back to the basic idea of His Life, namely, that He came on this earth not to live, but to suffer and die, to redeem and to be glorified. Bringing into one focal point all He had told them about the Scriptures, He said:

> **"So it was written and so it was fitting**
> **That Christ should suffer, and should rise again**
> **From the dead on the third day; and that repentance**
> **And remission of sins should be preached in**
> **His name to all nations, beginning at Jerusalem.**
> **Of this you are the witnesses."**

He said God's redemptive purpose was being revealed in the Prophets, and this redemption was to be effective by the death of the God Who became man. Once more there is a total absence of the fact that He was to leave a code or a set of rules. He emphasized the fact that His death made possible the preaching of repentance and the remission of sins to all nations and to all peoples. He said that it behooved Him to suffer. This indeed was true, because when anyone preaches absolute and Divine Truth to a world that believes in pragmatism, He will be crucified. The only way that He could show the evil of sin, was by revealing what sin could do to goodness, namely, pinion Him to a tree. If sin is a debt, that debt can be paid only by someone Who gave His life in ransom. It is very likely that He retold for them the story of God telling Abraham to sacrifice his son Isaac as a burnt offering. From the moment of that command, Isaac was a dead man, but on the third day he was released from his death sentence. He probably told them the Psalms wherein it was said of Him:

> "Thou shall not leave my soul in hell,
> Nor suffer Thy own Holy One to see corruption."

His death alone would have had no efficacy for the removal of human guilt, if He had not broken the bonds of the grave. Arising from the dead, He showed that the Redemption price paid on Calvary was sufficient, and that it was accepted by His Heavenly Father.

Now He commissioned them as His witnesses to bring repentance to all nations. When Our Blessed Lord began His public life, one of His first words was "repent." It was also the subject of His departing breath. Repentance and the remission of sins are twins; almost Siamese twins, for they cannot be separated. Repentance sees the rubbish in the temple of the body, but remission of sins drives out those buyers and sellers and makes it truly a house of prayer.

This preaching of the remission of sins was to begin at Jerusalem where He was crucified, in order that not even the place which took His life is to be exempted from His forgiveness. Those who have had great privileges and who have apparently rejected them, are not to be considered beyond the hope of forgiveness. The conversion of the world starts at home, but it only starts there. Then the Saviour said:

> "And behold, I am sending down upon you
> The Gift which was promised by My Father;
> You must wait in the city until you are
> Clothed with power from on high."

Christ told the Apostles to tarry in Jerusalem until He sent His Spirit. If He had remained on earth, they could have heard His voice, touched His hand, seen His radiant face, but if He ascended to His Father and sent His Spirit, then He would be a veritable life to be lived. This Spirit, He said, would recall to their minds all things He had told them. The Spirit would not be a code of morality written either on tablets of their minds or on tablets of stone, but would enter into their will and motivate their actions, penetrate the intellect to see truths beyond the power of reason, encourage them to love the things that He loved, and inspire them to enter into their glory as He entered into His—by dying to atone for the evil of the world.

The Spirit would not be long in coming—only 10 days hence. The Apostles were to keep their eyes in expectation upon the horizon and their hand upon the door; God in His own pleasure would endow them from a power on high. This power would not only awaken the soul of man from the deadly sleep of sin, but it would also be the comforter of the soul and above all, the source of their sanctification.

After giving them the promise of the Spirit, Our Blessed Lord led His disciples out as far as Bethany and lifted up His hands and blessed them.

> "And even as He blessed them He parted from them,
> And was carried up into heaven."

He had promised His disciples that they would follow Him and be with Him, and that He would go to Heaven to prepare a place for them. Great is the contrast between the unimaginable grandeur of the Ascension, and the sober words with which the record is set down. On the night of the Last Supper, He told His Apostles that He was soon to enter into the glory with His Father that He had before the foundations of the world were laid. He also told Pilate that He would see the Son of Man coming on the right hand of His power to judge the living and the dead. Now, He became the forerunner of Humanity in heaven.

The Apostles must have noticed, as He blessed them upon leaving, the great scars of Redemption on His hands. Peter in particular must have recalled that they were the same hands that saved him from the Galilean waves; Thomas must have lamented that it was the hand that he was bidden to touch to be cured of his doubt; all of the Apostles must have remembered that He showed them those same sacred hands to remind them that this was the mission for which He came to earth. But now that they were believing, the marks at this time were less the record of a Crucifixion than the record of a love of One Who lay down His life for His sheep.

The Ascension was necessary to equip His Apostolic Body for their universal mission. By withdrawing His bodily presence to that unseen region, which bears no special relation to any nation or people, He proclaims in the Ascension the common destiny of all the adopted sons of God. Even the best of men would not feel at home in Heaven with all of its splendor unless they would find there One Who was their brother in the Fatherhood of God. Joseph's brethren would have felt ill at ease in one of the most regal courts of the world, if their brother were not already there upon the throne. When He ascended into Heaven, He took with Himself His human nature which is like our own in all things, save sin. When He took upon Himself this human nature from His Mother Mary, He made it possible for Himself to suffer. She gave Him a body on which might be visited all the effects of sin, though He Himself was sinless. His birth and His life, therefore, made Him a victim for sacrifice and identified Him with the human race. The Ascension was necessary in order to bring Him into a state of perfect union with the Father, and in order to send the Spirit that we might be other Christs.

His continued life in Heaven, with His Glorified Humanity, is accepted by the Father on His Mercy Seat as our Intercessor. Once He offered Himself for us, the just for the unjust, whenever we identify ourselves with Him as victim, we behold in Him the expiation of our sins, and also our admission into the presence of the Father. All humanity is potentially with Him in Heaven after His Ascension, inasmuch as he is the new Adam or the Son of Man; the *actualization* of each human being as His brother or as an adopted son of the Heavenly Father, depends upon man's response to the Spirit. In Heaven, He lives to make intercession for us. In Him, all humanity will stand in such unity of love to the Father, that the Father will love all men as His sons; the Father will pour out upon all who will believe in Him the same blessings that he once poured out upon Him as the Head of humanity.

During His earthly life, He solicited us to avail ourselves of Redemption by seeing what sin cost. The evil of sin is the Crucifixion of the God-man. The worst thing that sin can do is not to bomb cities or kill children, but to crucify Goodness. No man is ever conscious of sin when he thinks of it as merely breaking a law. He never sees the full intensity of sin until he realizes what he does to a person. Many an alcoholic does not know the evil of his sin until, driving while drunk, he kills a child. So when we look not to a broken law, but at the broken Person of Christ on the Cross, we begin to see the full gravity of sin. We see it in the nails and in the crown of thorns, but we also see the love of God Who goes on loving us despite our sins.

On the Cross, Our Lord poured out His Life's Blood, not because bloodshed pleased His Father, but because the sinner deserved to die, and Christ, willing to be one with sinners, chose to bear pain as they should have borne it. He bore all of the iniquity of evil because He deigned to come into the world disorganized by evil.

If we would see the world at its worst, look at the Cross on Good Friday! The world will never do anything quite as evil as it did that day! There was darkness over the earth then, the sun refusing to shed its light on the crime that would extinguish the Light of the World! There is darkness over the world today as there was then, and for the same reason, because Christ is re-crucified in those who believe and confess His Name. Giant curtains are pulled over the Light of the World: Iron Curtains, Bamboo Curtains, and Plush Curtains. Iron curtains are pulled down in Eastern Europe where in Stygian night, hammers and sickles beat and cut. But a day will come when He will lay hold of that hammer, hold it aloft in His Resurrected, Scarred Hand, and make it look like a Cross, and the sickle will appear as the moon under Our Lady's Feet. Bamboo curtains have been pulled over China, where in the night, missionaries are ridiculed before other Pilates, slapped before other Caaphases, and beaten in other Praetoria. But as hundreds of thousands of Chinese suffer and die in His Name, and in union with His Cross, they prepare a day when the sun will rise again in the East—a sun that will be the Light of the World! Plush curtains too, of American and Western civilization have been pulled over Christ, until we work in the murky mist of self-sufficiency, of plenty, of confused idealism and deflated morality.

What do we see written across the map of the world but blood! Soldiers' blood poured out on Korean rocks; martyrs' blood crimsoning Chinese earth; Jewish blood but recently dried from Nazi persecutions in Buchenwalds and now dampened again by Christian blood in the Communist persecution; pagan blood poured charitably into blood banks to aid soldiers wounded in the bloody business of war. God never intended us to live in a world of constant hemorrhage.

We know the answer! Neither animal blood in sacrifice, nor human blood were meant to cataract and cascade over this globe. His Blood alone paid the debt of our sins! It is because we invoke not the Blood of Christ that we shed one another's blood in war. When we see His Death as Redemption, believe in Him as the Son of God Who made amends for our sins, then will this crimson scourge cease!

# The Priest Is Not His Own

[1963]

# INTRODUCTION

Most books on the priesthood may be grouped under three categories: theological, pastoral and sociological.
The theological treatises emphasize the priest as the minister and ambassador of Christ; the pastoral is concerned with the priest in the pulpit, the priest in the confessional, the priest at prayer, etc. The sociological, which is the latest type, refrains almost entirely from the spiritual, and is concerned with the statistical reaction of the study of the faithful, the unbelievers, and the general public to the priest. Is there room for another?

Such a possibility presented itself in writing our Life of Christ. In that book, we tried to show that unlike anyone else, Our Lord came on earth, not to live, but to die. Death for our redemption was the goal of His sojourn here, the gold that He was seeking. Every parable, every incident in His life, even the call of the Apostles, the temptation, the Transfiguration, the long conversation with the woman at the well, were focused upon that salutary Death. He was, therefore, not primarily a teacher, but a Savior.

The dark days in which that Life was written were hours when ink and gall did mix to reveal the mystery of the Crucifix.

More and more that vision of Christ as Savior began to illumine the priesthood, and out of it came the thoughts in this book. To save anyone from reading it through, we here state briefly the thesis.

We who have received the Sacrament of Orders, call ourselves "priests." The author does not recall any priest ever having said that "I was ordained a victim," nor did he ever say, "I am studying to be a victim." That seemed almost alien to being a priest. The seminary always told us to be "good" priests; never were we told to be willing victims.

And yet, was not Christ the Priest, a Victim? Did He not come to die? He did not offer a lamb, a bullock, or doves; He never offered anything except Himself.

> "He gave Himself up on our behalf, a sacrifice breathing out fragrance as He offered it to God."
>
> EPHESIANS 5:2

Pagan priests, Old Testament priests, medicine men, all offered a sacrifice apart from themselves. But not Our Lord. He was *Sacerdos-Victima*.

This being so, just as we miss much in the life of Christ, by not showing that the shadow of the Cross cast itself even over the crib and the carpenter shop, as well as His Public Life, so we have a mutilated concept of our priesthood, if we envisage it apart from making ourselves victims in the prolongation of His Incarnation. There is nothing else in this book, but that idea. And if the reader would like to hear that chord struck a hundred times, he may now proceed.

## Chapter 1

## More Than a Priest

THE priesthood of Christ was different from that of all pagan priests, and from the Levitical priesthood of the family of Aaron. In the Old Testament and in pagan religions, *the priest and the victim were distinct and separate. In Our Lord, they were united inseparably.*

The Jewish priests offered bullocks, goats and sheep, victims that were less a part of themselves than the robes they wore. It is easy to shed someone else's blood, as it is easy to spend someone else's money. The animal lost its life, but the priest who offered it lost nothing. Often, he did not even have to slaughter the victims. Except in the case of national offerings, when they were killed by the priest, the one who offered a victim himself slew it (LEVITICUS 1:5). This provision foreshadowed the part Israel itself would later play as the executioner of the Divine Victim. But it applies to us too; in a deeper sense, every sinner must regard himself as putting the Savior to death.

Pagan people, without knowing it explicitly, sensed the truth that "unless blood is shed, there can be no remission of sins" (HEBREWS 9:22). From the earliest times, through the kings and priests, they offered animals, and sometimes even humans, to turn away the anger of the gods. As in the Levitical priesthood, however, the victim was always separate from the priest. The sacrifice was a vicarious one, the animal representing and taking the place of the guilty humans, who thus sought to expiate their guilt in the shedding of blood.

But why, it may be asked, did the pagans, without the help of revelation, reach the conclusion expressed by St. Paul under Divine inspiration that "without the shedding of blood there was no remission of sins"? The answer is that it is not hard for anyone who ponders on sin and guilt to recognize: first, that sin is in the blood; and second, that life is in the blood, so that the shedding of blood expresses appropriately the truth that human life is unworthy to stand before the face of God.

Sin is in the blood. It can be read in the face of the libertine, the alcoholic, the criminal and the assassin. The shedding of blood, therefore, represented the emptying of sin. The Agony of the Garden and its bloody sweat were related to our sins which the Lord took upon Himself, for

> Christ never knew sin, and God made him into sin for us.
> II CORINTHIANS 5:21

That no creature is worthy to appear before the face of God was made known to man at a very early date. Adam and Eve found it out when they tried to cover their nakedness with fig leaves, after they had sinned.

> Then the eyes of both were opened, and they became aware of their nakedness; so they sewed fig-leaves together, and made themselves girdles.
> GENESIS 3:7

But fig leaves could not cover their nudity, either physical or spiritual, for the leaves soon dried up. What then was required? The sacrifice of an animal, the shedding of blood. Before they could be clothed with the skins of animals, there had to be a victim. And who made the skins which covered their shame? God did!

> And now the Lord provided garments for Adam and his wife, made out of skins, to clothe them.
> GENESIS 3:21

This is the first hint in the Scriptures of the spiritual nakedness of man being covered up through the shedding of the blood of a victim. As soon as our First Parents lost the inner grace of soul, external glory was needed to make up for it. It is ever true that the more rich a soul is on the inside, the less need it has of luxuries on the outside. Excessive adornments and an inordinate love of comforts are a proof of our inner nakedness.

The Bible contains many incidents which suggest that a vicarious sacrifice of blood was necessary for our salvation. Typical are the accounts of the healing of the leper and of the expulsion of the scapegoat in Leviticus. In both cases there is a sacrificial victim, though (as in all pre-Incarnation sacrifices) the victim is separate from the priest.

The ritual connected with the healing of a leper clearly prefigures our purification from the leprosy of sin.

> These are, two living birds.... One of the birds must have its blood shed over spring water held in an earthenware pot; the one which is left alive must be dipped (together with the cedar wood, the scarlet stuff, and the hyssop) into the dead bird's blood, and with this the priest must sprinkle the defiled man seven times, to effect his due cleansing.
> LEVITICUS 14:4-7

The living bird was let loose in the open fields to symbolize the carrying away of the leprosy; but this freedom and release seems to have been purchased by the cleansing power of blood and water of the bird that was slain. The priest offered a sacrifice, but the oblation was distinct from himself.

Here we have a hint of vicarious redemption through blood. Our Lord, on the contrary, cured the leprosy of sin by no holocaust other than His own obedient will, through which we won the glorious liberty of the children of God.

The ceremony of the scapegoat, another example of priesthood and victimhood, is described in Chapter 16 of Leviticus. The priest had to wash himself completely—and not merely his feet—before the ceremony, foretelling that the great High Priest, Christ, would be "undefiled" (HEBREWS 7:26); the priest also had to put on white linen and golden garments. As two birds were used in the former ceremony, two goats were now chosen, one to be slain and the other released. The ritual preceding release seems almost an anticipation of the Hanc Igitur at the Mass, for the priest lays his hands over the goat.

> He must put both hands on its head, confessing all the sins and transgressions and faults Israel has committed, and laying the guilt of them on its head. And there will be a man standing ready to take it into the desert for him; so the goat will carry away all their sins into a land uninhabited, set at large in the desert.
> LEVITICUS 16:21,22

As the sins of the Israelites were carried off by the scapegoat, so our sins are cleansed by no effort of our own, but only by our incorporation into Christ.

The scapegoat was driven away into a land of separation, or a wilderness, to teach us how effectively our sins have been borne into oblivion by Christ.

> I will pardon their wrongdoing; I will not remember their sins any more.
> HEBREWS 8:12

## The Incarnation

When the Son of God became man, He introduced something entirely new to the priesthood. Our Lord differed from the priests of the Old Testament, not simply because He came from a lineage other than that of Aaron, but also because, unlike all others, *He united in Himself both priesthood and victimhood.*

The consequences for all priests are tremendous, for if He did offer Himself for sins, then we must offer ourselves as victims. The conclusion is inescapable.

Scripture abounds in references to the complete identification of the offices of priest and victim in Christ.

> A victim? Yet he himself bows to the stroke; no word comes from him.
> ISAIAS 53:7

The Epistle to the Hebrews quotes Psalm 39, saying that the words of the Psalm were used by our High Priest as He entered the world.

> As Christ comes into the world, he says, No sacrifice, no offering was thy demand; thou has endowed me, instead, with a body. Thou hast not found any pleasure in burnt-sacrifices, in sacrifices for sin. See then, I said, I am coming to fulfil what is written of me, where the book lies unrolled; to do thy will, O my God. HEBREWS 10:5-7

The version of the Psalm quoted in the Epistle to the Hebrews is that of the Septuagint:

> "Thou hast endowed me, instead, with a body," as if implying the Incarnation. Similarly, David foresaw the kind of sacrifice God would eventually ask for sins when he declared: "Thou hast no mind for sacrifice, burnt-offerings." PSALM 50:18

The victimhood of our High Priest should not, however, be thought of as a tragedy in the sense that He had to submit to death, as the lambs had to submit to the knife of the Old Testament priests. Our Lord said:

> Nobody can rob me of it [my life]; I lay it down of my own accord. I am free to lay it down, free to take it up again; that is the charge which my father has given me. JOHN 10:18

Our Lord came to die. The rest of us come to live. But His death was not final. He never spoke of being our sin-oblation without speaking of His glory. His Resurrection and Ascension and His glorification at the right hand of the Father were the fruits of His voluntary offering as a Priest.

> And now, His full achievement reached, He wins eternal salvation for all those who render obedience to Him. A high priest in the line of Melchisedech, so God has called Him. HEBREWS 5:9,10

The perfection of His humanity and His eternal glory as a priest resulted from His having once been in the state of a victim. His perfection came not so much from His moral stature as from His quality of a priest-Savior. It was by His interior devotion and obedience that He acquired glory, and not just by the sacrifice considered as a shameful death.

Describing the meekness of the Lamb led to the slaughter, Scripture says

> Christ, during his earthly life, offered prayer and entreaty to the God Who could save Him from death, not without a piercing cry, not without tears; yet with such piety as won Him a hearing.
> HEBREWS 5:7

There is a Jewish saying to the effect that three kinds of prayers can be distinguished, each loftier than the preceding one: prayer, crying and tears. Prayer is made in silence; crying with a raised voice, but there is no door through which tears do not pass. The prayer of the Victim in Gethsemane was such that it rose to a poignant cry and beyond that to the sweat of tears:

> His sweat fell to the ground like thick drops of blood. LUKE 22:44

We find a symbolic representation of the union of the Priest and Victim in the very position of the cross suspended between earth and heaven, as if Jesus was rejected by man and abandoned by the Father. Yet He united God and man in Himself through obedience to the Father's Will and through a love for man so great that He would not abandon him in his sin. To His brethren He revealed the heart of a father; to His Father He revealed the heart of every son. Our Lord, therefore, is always priest and victim. No victim was worthy of priesthood save himself. Christ, moreover, was a victim not only in His body, but in His soul, which was sad unto death. No external nor internal sacrifice could be more united.

Two Scripture texts present paradoxical aspects of the priesthood and victimhood of Christ.

> He was counted among the malefactors. LUKE 22:37

> Such was the High Priest.... holy and guiltless and undefiled, not reckoned among us sinners. HEBREWS 7:26

Actually, the statements are not contradictory; they are complementary. He was reckoned with sinners, because He was the victim for their sins. But He was separated from sinners, because He was a priest without sin. He ate and mingled with sinners, shared their nature, and took on their sins. But He was separated from them by His innocence. One with sinners through sharing their nature, His sacrifice had infinite value, because He was not only man, but God.

## PRIESTS OR PRIEST-VICTIMS?

How often are we like the Galatians, bent on returning to the Old Law, in the sense that we see ourselves as priests but not victims? Do we offer Mass as if we presented a victim for sin who was totally unrelated to us, like the scapegoat or the bird? Do we ascend the altar as priests and not as victims? Do we offer the Christ-Savior to the Father, as if we were not dying with Him? Is our priesthood a two-story house to indicate our apartness, our reluctance to be a victim for others?

On the first floor is a family suffering physically, disturbed mentally, lacking food and drink. On the second floor, we live. Through intermittent acts of charity, we descend to their misery from time to time to relieve it; but do we go back right away to the relative comfort of our own lodging?

Not so with Christ, the Priest. When He went into the depths of human suffering and sin, He never went back—not until all of its misery and guilt were relieved. Once He crossed that line, there was no thought of a return until Redemption was complete.

> It is not as if our High Priest was incapable of feeling for us in our humiliations; He has been through every trial, fashioned as we are, only sinless. HEBREWS 4:15

> ... in God's gracious design He was to taste death, and taste it on behalf of all.  HEBREWS 2:9

If the priesthood and victimhood in Christ were one, how can they be dual in us? Rather,

> You, too, must think of yourselves as dead to sin, and alive with a life that looks towards God, through Christ Jesus our Lord.  ROMANS 6:11

We cannot escape reproducing in our souls the mystery enacted on the altar. Age quod agitis. As Our Lord immolated Himself, so do we immolate ourselves. We offer our repose of body, in order that others may have peace of soul; we are pure, in order to recompense for the excesses of the flesh committed by sinners.

> With Christ I hang upon the Cross.  GALATIANS 2:20

## The Eucharist Reminds Us That We Are Victims

The Eucharist commits us to both life and death, priesthood and victimhood.

As regards life, it is clear beyond question that in the Eucharist we commune with it.

> You can have no life in yourselves, unless you eat the flesh of the Son of Man, and drink His blood.  JOHN 6:54

But this is only half the picture. Is there not a catabolic as well as an anabolic process in nature, a breaking down into elements as well as a building up into organisms? In nature, death is the condition of life. The vegetables which we eat at table have to be sacrificed. They must yield life and substance before they can become the sacrament, the holy thing nourishing the body. They must be torn up from their roots and subjected to fire, before they can give the more abundant life to the flesh. Before the animal in the field can be our meat, it must be subjected to the knife, to the shedding of blood, and to fire. Only then does it become the strong sustenance of the body. Before Christ can be our life, He had to die for us. The Consecration of the Mass precedes Communion.

The ultimate heresy of the Reformation was the divorce of sacrifice and sacrament, or the transformation of the sacrifice of the Mass into a "communion service," as if there could be giving of life without death. Is there not in the Eucharist not only a communion with life but also a communion with death? Paul did not overlook this aspect:

> So it is the Lord's death that you are heralding, whenever you eat this bread and drink this cup, until He comes.
> I CORINTHIANS 11:26

If we at Mass eat and drink the Divine Life and bring no death of our own to incorporate in the death of Christ through sacrifice, we deserve to be thought of as parasites on the Mystical Body of Christ. Shall we eat bread and give no wheat to be ground? Shall we drink wine, and give no grapes to be crushed? The condition for incorporation into the Resurrection and Ascension of Christ and into His glorification is incorporation into His death.

> Those who belong to Christ have crucified nature, with all its passions, all its impulses.
> GALATIANS 5:24

As priests we offer Christ in the Mass, but as victims do we offer ourselves with Christ in the Mass? Shall we tear asunder that which God hath joined, namely, priesthood and victimhood? Does not the intimate connection between sacrifice and sacrament also tell us that we are not priests alone but victims as well? If all we do in our priestly life is to drain chalices and eat the Bread of Life, then how shall the Church

> fill up those sufferings that are wanting to the Passion of Christ.
> COLOSSIANS 1:24

Do we lift up Christ on the cross at the moment of elevation, while present as mere spectators at a drama in which we are intended to play the first role? Is the Mass an empty repetition of Calvary? If so, what do we do with the cross we were bidden to take up daily? How can Christ renew His death in our own bodies. He dies again in us.

And the people of God? Do we teach them that they must not only "receive" Communion but "give" too? They may not accept life while giving no sacrifice. The communion rail is a place of exchange. They give time and receive eternity, they give self-denial and receive life, they give nothingness, and receive all. Holy Communion commits each to a closer union not only with Christ's life but also with His death—to greater detachment from the world, to surrender of luxuries for the sake of the poor, to death of the old Adam for rebirth in Christ, the new Adam.

## First Application:
## Three Kinds Of Priest-Victims

The Canon of the Mass enumerates three kinds of victims who by prefiguring the sacrifice of Christ, became models for all priests. They were, in order, the offerings of the just son, Abel; the sacrifice of our patriarch, Abraham; and that which the High Priest Melchisedech offered. Abel offered a blood sacrifice, Abraham a voluntary sacrifice and Melchisedech a sacramental sacrifice. A priest may be victim in each of these ways.

Abel offered to God the choicest lamb of his flock, while his brother Cain offered only the fruits of the earth (GENESIS 4:3,4). God looked with favor on Abel and on his blood sacrifice, but He rejected the sacrifice of Cain, as though it implied that sin could be forgiven without the shedding of blood. The blood sacrifice of Abel is thus a model for the missionaries who are martyred for their faith, for the priests who are victims of anti-God persecution, and for all the faithful who suffer unto death rather than deny the faith.

The sacrifice of Abraham serves as a model for the sacrifice of many in our days, those who endure all the stages of martyrdom under Communist tyranny yet are denied the formal crown of the shedding of their blood. It is for such especially that the figure of Abraham's sacrifice was intended. For them was it emphasized that the sacrifice received its full reward even though the blood of the victim was not poured out (HEBREWS 11:1). This is the assurance for all who undergo a thousand martyrdoms by not being permitted to die by their persecutors, for those who are brain-washed and who spend their lives in prison or labor camps. They share in the promise and in the reward bestowed on Abraham because he was willing to sacrifice his own flesh and blood, his son, Isaac.

The third kind of priest-victimhood is that of Melchisedech. It is offered by all priests who live the mystery they enact sacramentally in the Mass. But how? By understanding the secondary meaning of the words of consecration. The primary meaning is clear and needs no elaboration. The mystery of transubstantiation takes place as we pronounce the words of consecration. There is, however, a secondary meaning, because we are priest-victims. When I say "This is My Body,"

I must also mean: "This is my body"; when I say "This is My Blood," I must also mean: "This is my blood." "Thou, O Jesus, art not alone in the Mass," the consecrating priest must pray in his soul. "On the Cross Thou wert alone; in this Mass, I am with Thee. On the Cross, Thou didst offer Thyself to the Heavenly Father; in the Mass, Thou dost still offer Thyself but now I offer myself with Thee."

The consecration is then no bare, sterile repetition of the words of the Last Supper; it is an action, a re-enactment, another Passion in me. "Here, dear Jesus, is my body, take it; here is my blood, take it. I care not if the 'species' of my life remain—my particular duties in school, parish, or office; these are only the 'appearances.' But what I am, in my intellect, my will—take, possess, divinize, so that I may die with Thee on the altar. Then the Heavenly Father looking down will say to Thee and to me in Thee:

Thou art my beloved Son; in thee I am well pleased.     MARK 1:11

When I come down from the altar I will then, more than ever, be in Mary's hands as when she took Thee down from the Cross. She was not a priest, but she could say the words of consecration in a way no priest ever said them of that Body and Blood. As she held Thee she could say, as at Bethlehem: "This is my Body; This is my Blood. No one in all the world gave Him body and blood but me."

May she who was a victim with her Son teach us never to go to Calvary without having our hearts pierced with a sword. Woe indeed to us, if we come down from Calvary with hands unscarred and white! But glorious shall we be as priests and victims, when the Lord will see in our hands the marks of His Passion, for of such He said:

Why, I have cut thy image on the palms of my hands.     ISAIAS 49:16

## SECOND APPLICATION:
## BE A VICTIM IN THE BREAKING OF THE BREAD

An unchanging ritual of the Mass is the Breaking of the Bread to remind us each time we celebrate, that the Lord was "broken" for our sins as a victim. The Old Testament already foreshadowed Christ's offering of Himself in the bread that was broken, for it was prescribed that the bread which the priest was to offer was to be "cut up into small pieces" (LEVITICUS 2:6). Even the Hebrew word for cakes of bread used in this passage is derived from a verb which meant "pierced" or "wounded." In this, the bread prefigured the condition of the victim which it symbolized:

> Nay, here is one despised, left out of all human reckoning; bowed with misery, and no stranger to weakness; how should we recognize that face? How should we take any account of Him, a Man so despised? ISAIAS 53:3

As the bread was crushed, so too would Christ be crushed:

> Ay, the Lord's will it was, overwhelmed He should be with trouble. ISAIAS 53:10

What was the sign by which the disciples on Easter Sunday afternoon knew the Risen Christ?

> They recognized Him when He broke bread. LUKE 24:35

St. Paul's account of the Eucharist stressed this victim state of Our Lord:

> ... and gave thanks, and broke it. I CORINTHIANS 11:24

Our priesthood must be like the pitchers which Gedeon's army of three hundred carried into battle. Inside of each was a lighted candle (JUDGES 7:18-20). The light was there, but it did not shine forth to confound and defeat the enemy until the pitchers were broken. Only when we are "broken" do we shed the light of Christ to defeat the forces of Satan. It is not just the soul and mind of the priest that are involved in the exercise of his ministry: it is also his body, the body broken, mortified and made a victim.

> Your bodies ... are meant for the Lord, and the Lord claims your bodies. I CORINTHIANS 6:13

Can we think that God will be any more satisfied with us, if we are only offerers and not also offered, than He was with the priests of the Old Testament? Did He not express disgust when they offered something apart and separate from themselves?

> What do I care, the Lord says, how you multiply those victims of yours? I have had enough and to spare. Burnt-offerings of rams,

and the fat of stall-fed beasts, and the blood of calves and lambs and goats are nothing to me. ISAIAS 1:11

Will He not complain that our priesthood is incomplete, unless we "break the bread" which is our body? What is it then that He wants from us? It is the offering of ourselves.

> I appeal to you by God's mercies to offer up your bodies as a living sacrifice, consecrated to God and worthy of his acceptance; this is the worship due from you as rational creatures. ROMANS 12:1

The role of the body is so often forgotten. True, the body can be the occasion and the instrument of sin, but it is also an occasion and an instrument of merit. Can it be so vile as some old spiritual writers suggested, if it is "meant for the Lord" (I CORINTHIANS 6:13), if "what is sown a natural body, rises a spiritual body" (I CORINTHIANS 15:44), and if through the Eucharist it has been endowed with immortality? It is not our soul that prays; it is the person, the composite of body and soul. In sacrifice, in particular, the body is important. It is through its exhaustion in priestly ministrations, its constant use in preaching, teaching and converting, that it becomes a "living sacrifice."

Each time that priests "break bread" during the Mass, not only will they recognize the sacrifice of Christ for them, as did the disciples at Emmaus, but also He will recognize them. No unbroken bread, no unbroken bodies, will the High Priest accept from our hands. Was not the wheat already broken to become bread? Were not the grapes already crushed to become wine? Even nature suggests victimhood as inseparable from the priesthood of offering bread and wine at table.

St. Paul was merely stressing once again the inseparability of priest and victim when he wrote to the young priest, Timothy:

> Then, like a good soldier of Christ Jesus, take thy share of hardship.... We are to share His Life, because we have shared His Death. II TIMOTHY 2:3,11

## Third Application:
## Vocations And Victimhood

Seminarians say: "I am studying for the priesthood." How often does a seminarian say or even think, "I am studying to be a priest-victim?" We insist on the dignity of our priesthood by quickly reprimanding those who show us disrespect. But do we ever insist on the indignity of our victimhood? We boast that our High Priest is Offerer and Offered. We say that we offer Mass, but do we ever think that we are offered in the Mass? Our Lord wants no more bullocks or goats; He wants those who "have crucified nature, with all its passions, all its impulses" (GALATIANS 5:24). St. Augustine said there is no need to look outside oneself for a sheep to offer to God. Each has within him that which he can crucify.

Could it be that one reason for the fewness of vocations is our failure to stress sacrifice? The young have a sense of victimhood which we underestimate. They want a mission, a challenge! When we follow the type of advertising appeal used by Madison Avenue to sell toothpaste, when we use commercial techniques in our vocation literature, do not the hearts of the young spurn our distance from the Cross? Do we not recruit fruits of propaganda rather than fruits worthy of penance?

Could it not also be that our failure to be victims discourages those who enter the seminary from persevering and becoming priests? We tell them that they cannot hope to be good priests unless they make a meditation each morning before Mass, but are there times when we ourselves jump direct from the bed to the altar? Does not this scandalize seminarians? On the other hand, how they are edified when they see their professors at early meditation with them and at their spiritual exercises! Lacking this example, they easily come to think of spirituality as something to be practiced only until the day of ordination.

A survey among 300 youths to determine what kind of priest inspired them most revealed that the first preference was for the foreign missionary; the second, for those who concerned themselves with the poor; the third, for an apostolate among the workers. The point is that the young prefer the heroic or sacrificial priest.

Vocations are more plentiful than many suspect. Of 3,500 boys under the age of fifteen questioned in a survey in one South American country, 1,800 said they felt that they had a vocation. And yet not more than forty young men are raised to the priesthood in that country each year. What happens to the others? Worldliness, the flesh? Yes. But it is proper to ask: Have we shown forth Christ Crucified to them? Those young people who feel called to a life of sacrifice, will they not draw back when they see that their ideal is not realized in us? But what encouragement is given them when they say: "That is the kind of priest I want to be." One reason why missionary societies attract the young is because their members give a living witness to their zeal for Christ. The hardships they endure, the souls they convert, the complete trust in God despite poverty and even persecution, these make the young love their priesthood through their victimhood. A survey among a group of seminarians revealed that 60 per cent of them had been inspired to enter the seminary by contact with mortified and saintly priests.

It is so easy for us to be ready, like Peter at Caesarea Philippi, to confess the Divine Christ, but far from ready to accept the suffering Christ. It was the same Peter who said, "Thou art the Christ, the Son of the Living God" (MATTHEW 16:16), and who "drawing Him to his side, began remonstrating with Him; Never, Lord, he said; no such thing shall befall Thee" (MATTHEW 16:22).

Because of this, Our Lord called him Satan, for it was Satan who at the beginning of the public ministry tempted Him to reject the way of suffering by offering him three short cuts to His Kingdom without the Cross (MATTHEW 4:1-11). The denial of His victimhood appears to Christ as something satanic.

When "Satan sits enthroned" (APOCALYPSE 2:13) at the end of time, Our Lord said that he would appear so much like Him "that if it were possible, even the elect would be deceived" (MATTHEW 24:24). But if Satan works miracles, if he lays his hands gently on children, if he appears benign and a lover of the poor, how will we know him from Christ? Satan will have no scars on hands or feet or side. He will appear as a priest but not as a victim.

We recognize fathers and sons, brothers and sisters, by family resemblances. In no other way will Our Lord know us and we Him. Our preparation for the day of His coming must accordingly consist of deepening our affinity with the Priest-Victim:

> In this mortal frame of mine, I help to pay off the debt which the afflictions of Christ still leave to be paid, for the sake of His Body, the Church.  COLOSSIANS 1:24

## Kenosis And Pleroma

Two words in Scriptures are often considered separately, when actually they are related as cause and effect. The two words, which represent another phase of the offerer-offered relationship, are kenosis and pleroma, that is to say, "emptying" and "filling." It is almost as if mountains were made by the emptying of valleys. St. Paul in a classic description of the humiliation and exaltation of Our Lord writes:

> He dispossessed Himself, and took the nature of a slave, fashioned in the likeness of men, and presenting Himself to us in human form; and then He lowered His own dignity, accepted an obedience which

brought Him to death, death on a cross. That is why God has raised Him to such a height, given Him that Name which is greater than any other Name; so that everything in heaven and on earth and under the earth must bend the knee before the name of Jesus, and every tongue must confess Jesus Christ as the Lord, dwelling in the glory of God the Father. PHILIPPIANS 2:7-11

Because He emptied Himself, He was exalted. Because there was Calvary, there was the sending of the Holy Spirit. Because His physical Body was broken, His Mystical Body grows in age and grace and wisdom before God and men.

Applying this principle to the priesthood, the emptying of self for the people of the parish produces the spiritual prosperity of the parish. The de-egotization of our lives prepares for the guidance of the Holy Spirit; the "vacancy" sign on our heart makes Christ come knocking at the entrance. He breaks down no locked doors. He will come in only if we open to Him. A box which is full of pepper cannot be filled with salt; a priest who is full of his own desires cannot be filled with the "power of the Holy Spirit" (ACTS 1:2). St. Paul singled out Timothy from among his friends as the one who was always interested in others and least concerned with self. In him, "pleroma" was complete because of the "kenosis" of egotism.

I have no one else here who shares my thoughts as he does, no one who will concern himself so unaffectedly with your affairs; one and all have their own interests at heart, not Christ's.
PHILIPPIANS 2:20-21

## Shepherd-Lamb

To change the figure, we priests are not only shepherds but also lambs. Was not Our Lord Himself both the "Good Shepherd" and the "Lamb of God" (JOHN 1:29)? As the Offerer, He is the Shepherd. As the Offered, He is the Lamb. It is this dual role of Christ which explains why He spoke at certain times during His trial and at other times was silent. He spoke as the Shepherd; He was silent as the Lamb.

The priest, too, is not only the Shepherd who cares for his sheep; he is also the Lamb who is offered in caring for them. This caring is what distinguishes Him from the hireling. One who cares for another assumes the weight of the other's condition on his own heart and bears it in love. The parishioners are not disturbers; they are our heart, our body, our blood.

The priest playing the role of a shepherd often goes to his death as a Lamb. The shepherd who would give more abundant life to the lost sheep is bound to have wolves howling about him and thus be led ultimately to his death. It was only the sight of the Shepherd crucified that made the sheep realize how much the Shepherd cared. It is interesting that St. Peter described Our Lord as "your Shepherd, who keeps watch over your souls" (I PETER 2:25).

The shepherd's primary duty is to search out the lost sheep and stay with it once found. This is what distinguishes the true shepherd from the hireling, the intellectual from the intelligentsia. Both are degreed, learned and scholarly. The difference lies in their relation to the people. The intellectual never loses that compassion for the multitude which characterized the Word Incarnate. The intelligentsia, on the contrary, live apart from tears and hunger, cancer and bereavements, poverty and ignorance. They lack the common touch. Only the cream of bookish learning and not the milk of human kindness flows through their veins.

So with the priest. Contact with people for Christ's sake is the victimhood which makes the priesthood. Only by also being a lamb offered through forgetfulness of worldly superiority does the priest become the shepherd of souls.

# Chapter 2

## The Priest is Like Jacob's Ladder

Every priest knows himself, by Divine election, to be a mediator between God and man, bringing God to man and man to God. As such the priest continues the Incarnation of Jesus Christ Who was both God and Man. Our Lord was not Priest because He was begotten eternally of the Father. He was a Priest because of the human nature He assumed and offered for our salvation. Thence derived the fullness of all priesthood, or to use the magnificent phrase of St. Thomas Aquinas, He became "fons totius sacerdotii."

St. Paul had already used an equally definitive expression to indicate our sacerdotal relationship to Christ on the one side, and to the people on the other:

> That is how we ought to be regarded, as Christ's servants, and stewards of God's mysteries.     I CORINTHIANS 4:1

As Christ's servants, we are as dependent on Him for our powers as are the rays of light dependent on the sun. But Paul insists simultaneously that we are also the stewards of God's mysteries to indicate that we remain bound to our fellow men.

Every priest is like another Jacob's ladder. Exiled from home, fleeing from a resentful brother, the wandering son of Isaac made his evening couch on the ground, a stone slab his pillow. Man is most helpless when asleep, and it was while he was in that condition that God appeared to Jacob.

He dreamed that he saw a ladder standing on the earth, with its top reaching up into heaven; a stairway for the angels of God to go up and come down. Over this ladder the Lord himself leaned down, and spoke to Jacob, I am the Lord, He said, the God of thy father Abraham, the God of Isaac. GENESIS 28:12,13

Jacob forthwith changed the name of the place where he had this vision from Luza to Bethel. The name Luza originally signified "separation," while Bethel meant the "House of God" (GENESIS 28:19). We, likewise, called to mediate between God and man, become worthy priests of the House of God only by separating ourselves from the spirit of the world. God makes up for every abnegation by a greater blessing. The condition of serving "Bethel" is "Luza," detachment from the world.

The ladder is a simple and charming picture of the priesthood of Christ:

I am the way. JOHN 14:6

It is through His Death, Resurrection and Ascension to the right hand of God that Christ has become the Mediator and re-established relations between God and Man.

Certain details of the vision are particularly noteworthy:

1. The ladder was set upon the earth. Thus was the link between earth and heaven established through Christ becoming incarnate, taking human flesh, walking our earth and being lifted up on Calvary.

2. The ladder reached up to heaven, symbolizing that Christ risen and glorified is at the right hand of the Father.

3. Angels ascending and descending represent one of the functions of the priest whose task it is to carry sacrifices and prayers to heaven and bring back graces and blessings to earth.

The cross, the ladder of mediation, was set up on the earth. It was of earthly origin, in the sense that Pilate's soldiers fashioned it; but it was not of earthly origin as a means of atonement in so far as it came forth out of history and the Divine counsels. Its top reaches to Heaven, for the divine Mediator sits at the right hand of the Father. As Our Blessed Lord said; "No one has ever gone up into heaven; but there is One who has come down from heaven" (JOHN 3:13). He is the ladder on which we ascend to God; no one goes to the Father except by Him.

Inasmuch as every priest is an alter Christus, each of us is another Jacob's ladder—having vertical relations to Christ in heaven and horizontal relations to men on earth.

## The Top Of The Ladder:
## Vertical Relationship To Christ In Heaven

Of the many ways in which we are related to Christ, our High Priest in heaven, two call for mention here:

1. Our vocation derives from Him: "His vocation (that of the priest) comes from God, as Aaron's did; nobody can take on himself such a privilege as this" (HEBREWS 5:4).

2. All the effectiveness of our priesthood comes from Him: the sacraments we administer, the truth we preach, the grace by which lost sheep are rescued, the youths whose vocations we foster, whatever supernatural work we perform.

What is the glorified Christ doing in heaven as we exercise our priesthood? "He lives on still to make intercession on our behalf" (HEBREWS 7:25). Using human words to describe Divine things, we can say that each time we offer Mass, Our Lord shows His Heavenly Father the scars in His hands, His feet and His side; for this very reason He kept them. At the Consecration of the Mass, we can imagine Our Lord as saying: "In My Hand I have engraven their hearts. Not for their worthiness, but for My love unto death, grant them graces through the Holy Spirit. My wounds healed, but My scars I kept, that I might always hold them up before Thee, O Father, as pledges of My love. If Thou couldst not strike in justice the sinful people because the uplifted hands of Abraham stood in the way, then shall not My Hands win for them that mercy I won for them on Calvary? I am not just a *Sacerdos in aeternum; I am a Victima in aeternum.*"

How did our High Priest enter into the heavenly sanctuary? Through the rending of the veil of His flesh. The Epistle to the Hebrews (9:11) compares the veil which hung before the Holy of Holies to the human flesh of Christ. Only once a year, and after the shedding of blood in sacrifice, could the High Priest pass through the veil which hid the Holy of Holies. Only after the shedding of His Blood on Calvary could Christ the High Priest enter the Holy of Holies of heaven.

The earthly life of Our Lord might be thought of as being led outside the veil, as many of the ceremonies of atonement in the Old Testament were enacted in the sanctuary outside the Holy of Holies. In yet another sense, Our Lord's preaching and miracles were restricted to a very small part of the world. His mission on earth was confined to Galilee and Judea. But after His Ascension and the coming of the Spirit, His priesthood was exercised even to the ends of the earth. His human nature was a veil, which kept Him for a time from manifesting His full glory. That veil of the flesh had to be rent on Calvary before He could enter into the full exercise of His priesthood.

Good Friday saw a double rending of the veil: One was the rending of the veil of the Temple which was torn from top to bottom. It signified that the Holy of Holies would now be open to all men:

> And all at once, the veil of the temple was torn this way and that from the top to the bottom. MATTHEW 27:51

But when Our Lord said "It is achieved" (JOHN 19:30), the human flesh which had been a veil hiding the Unseen from man was rent asunder by the piercing of His flesh by the centurion's lance, and the Heart of Eternal Love was revealed,

> bidding us cling to the hope we have in view, the anchorage of our souls. Sure and immovable, it reaches that inner sanctuary beyond the veil, which Jesus Christ, our escort, has entered already, a high priest, now, eternally with the priesthood of Melchisedech.
> HEBREWS 6:18-20

So long as that veil of the flesh was in place, it shut out man from the full vision of the Holy God, revealing Him only as "a confused reflection in a mirror" (I CORINTHIANS 13:12). But the mediation and intercession became heavenly after the shedding of blood.

The high priest in the Old Testament might stand amazed at the beauty of the veil, but he could not pass through it, except by blood. So with Christ:

> It is His own blood, not the blood of goats and calves, that has enabled Him to enter, once for all, into the sanctuary; the ransom He has won lasts for ever. HEBREWS 9:12

And again:

> We can enter the sanctuary with confidence through the Blood of Christ. HEBREWS 10:19

The rending of the veil of the Temple from top to bottom was not the work of man but the act of God. So our Redemption is the work not of man but of God become Man.

## Christ Our Only Mediator

The only intercession is that of our High Priest in heaven, for there is no other name given to men whereby they may be saved (ACTS 4:12). The sand of the Moslem, the penances of the Hindu, the quietism of the Buddhist cannot avail for salvation. If proof of this affirmation were necessary, one need cite only the example of Moses.

The reason Moses was not permitted to enter the Promised Land was that he disobeyed the Divine Command and struck the rock when directed merely to speak to it. Two incidents involving a rock are recorded in the Bible story of Moses. One was at Raphidim in the second year after he had led them from Egyptian bondage. The other was at Cades in the 38th year of the wandering. In both instances the people were suffering from great thirst and the rock saved them, the rock which, as St. Paul says was Christ (I CORINTHIANS 10:4).

The first time the people needed water, God said to Moses, "Thou hast but to smite that rock" (EXODUS 17:6); and immediately there flowed from it water. Some thirty-six years later, when there again was an acute drought, God told Moses to "lay thy command upon the rock here" (NUMBERS 20:8), that is, "speak." Instead, speaking in an egotistic way, Moses addressed the people:

> Listen to me, he said, faithless rebels; are we to get you water out of this rock? NUMBERS 20:10

Then Moses struck the rock instead of addressing it. Despite his pride, God gave Moses the water, but He told him that as punishment he would not enter the Promised Land.

> Why did you not trust in Me, and vindicate My Holiness in the sight of Israel? It will not be yours to lead this multitude into the land I mean to give them. NUMBERS 20:12

The Hebrew text uses a different word for "rock" in the two accounts. In the earlier incident, it is Tsur, so named to indicate its sharpness; in the later, seta, stressing its elevation. From St. Paul we know that the rock was Christ. We may, accordingly, surmise that the sharp rock directed by God to be struck was the symbol of Christ smitten in the sharpness of the Cross from Whom would come the waters of Redemption and the Spirit (JOHN 7:39).

The second elevated rock which was not to be smitten but spoken to or interceded with, is it not a symbol of Christ risen and glorified in Heaven, to whom we need only speak in order to receive the living waters (JOHN 7:37)? Redemption is already complete. No more Calvaries are needed.

> The death He died was a death, once for all, to sin; the life He now lives is a life that looks toward God. ROMANS 6:10

Never again will there be a Rock which, when struck, will yield the waters of everlasting life. Redemption is only in Christ. Yet His role has not terminated. He continues to be our Advocate with the Father, and to apply the fruits of Redemption. In this, also, he differs from the priests of the Old Testament.

> One who has no need to do as those other priests did.... What He has done He has done once for all; and the offering was Himself.
> HEBREWS 7:27

How else can our sins be forgiven except through His abiding forgiveness? There is no doubt that civil tribunals are of great use in adjudicating disputes. But what about the great sins against God, not only in the Church, but outside of it? For this we need Divine Redemption.

The two sons of Heli abused their office by oppression and debauchery. They, as priests, had a right to a certain part of the animal sacrifices that were offered; instead of being content with the parts God allotted them, they stole meat which God had ordered to be burned. To such disobedience the young priests added impurity and scandal which discouraged people from coming to the house of the Lord. Their father said to them:

> If man does wrong to man, God's justice may yet be satisfied; if man sins against the Lord, who shall plead his cause for him?
> I KINGS 2:25

To that question they could have no answer.

But God in His appointed time Himself answered it, and the answer is the Blood of the High Priest whose eternal act of love the priest has the power to renew in the Sacrifice of the Mass. If He is not invoked, or if He is rejected, then there is no forgiveness.

> If we go on sinning wilfully, when once the full knowledge of the truth has been granted to us, we have no further sacrifice for sin to look forward to. HEBREWS 10:26

> Who can be our adversary, if God is on our side? He did not even spare His own Son, but gave Him up for us all; and must not that gift be accompanied by the gift of all else? Who will come forward to accuse God's elect, when God acquits us? Who will pass sentence against us, when Jesus Christ, who died, nay, has risen again, and sits at the right hand of God, is pleading for us? Who will separate us from the love of Christ?  ROMANS 8:31-35

Our specific relation as priests is to the top of the ladder. It falls to us to contact the Eternal Lover in heaven Who "lives on still to make intercession on our behalf" (HEBREWS 7:25).

The priesthood of Christ in heaven is an abiding and continuing one. Whatever man may need as man in each circumstance of effort, of conflict or of sin, he has an effective advocacy through Christ Who pleads our cause with the Father:

> ... if any of us does fall into sin, we have an Advocate to plead our cause before the Father in the Just One, Jesus Christ. He, in his own person, is the atonement made for our sins, and not only for ours, but for the sins of the whole world.  I JOHN 2:1,2

This is the vertical side of our priesthood, whereby we contact the Holy of Holies, and whereby we are entitled to be called "ministros Christi." At every moment of our priesthood we are or should be in contact with the Divine Intercessor. Too often, when someone appeals for help in trouble and exposes to the priest his depressed soul, we tell him to pray. Certainly! But do we intercede? We have direct communication with the Divine Advocate; we have the privileges of an ambassador. To tell the one whom it is our office to help that he should pray while we intercede not, is to be unfaithful to our high office. To offer Mass from time to time for all who "labour and are burdened" (MATTHEW 11:28) is the mark of a holy priest who knows the way to the Holy of Holies.

## THE BOTTOM OF THE LADDER:
## HORIZONTAL RELATIONS WITH THE PEOPLE

In order to be our priest, Christ assumed a human nature. We likewise continue His Priesthood not alone by having contact with Him in Heaven, but also by remaining human and speaking to Him in the name of all humanity. Vertically we are related to Christ in Heaven; horizontally, we are related to men on earth. As Christ took upon Himself our infirmities, and bore our ills, so also we are representative of sinful humanity:

> The purpose for which any high priest is chosen from among his fellow-men, and made a representative of men in their dealings with God, is to offer gifts and sacrifices in expiation of their sins. He is qualified for this by being able to feel for them when they are ignorant and make mistakes, since he, too, is all beset with humiliations.
> HEBREWS 5:1,2

Why is it that Our Lord chose us who are so weak? Each of us knows many who would surely have been more responsive to the grace of ordination. It would be an insult to Divine Wisdom to imagine ourselves the best material available. Why did God not choose angels to mediate between sinners and God? Because sympathy, the compassion, the suffering together which only one who has suffered knows, would be lacking experimentally to the angel. Our Lord Himself assumed the "nature of a slave" (PHILIPPIANS 2:7), in order the more specifically to share our woes and our wounds. No one can ever say that God does not know what it is like to suffer as he does. Even the one thing absent from His human nature, the quality of femininity, He compensated for to the greatest extent possible by calling "the Woman" to share (as much as Mary could) His Passion with Him.

Even outside His Passion, whatever He did for man in His compassion for his ills "cost" Him something. He never immunized Himself from our infirmities. He even seemed to lose something when He healed: "a power has gone out from Me" (LUKE 8:46). He groaned when He raised Lazarus from the dead. "And Jesus ... sighed deeply, and distressed Himself over it" (JOHN 11:33).

We never offer Mass or say our Breviary as individuals. That is one reason why a server or other should assist at Mass. And though the Mass is offered to the Heavenly Father by the Church, its intercession is not for the Church alone but for those also who are not yet of the house of Israel, to whom also we are sent. Such is the meaning of those words which we recite at the Offertory when we offer in the four directions of the earth the chalice of Salvation *"pro nostra et totius mundi salute."*

The priest in the Old Testament was given detailed instructions which emphasized his bond to his people.

> And whenever Aaron goes into the sanctuary, he will carry on his breast, on the burse that gives counsel, the names of Israel's sons,

> putting the Lord in mind of them eternally. And within the burse that gives counsel thou wilt put the touchstones of wisdom and of truth. These shall be on Aaron's breast, when he enters the Lord's presence; as long as he is there, he will be carrying on his breast the arbitrament of the sons of Israel.  EXODUS 28:29,30

The names on the shoulder stones can be understood as the burden his people represented for him, as the cross would be our burden. But the breastplate, placed over the heart indicated that he still bore them affection and love.

Because of our horizontal relations to the world, we must bear the name of Everyman in our hearts, and that not only in our private prayer, but whenever we offer the sacrifice of reparation and tearful intercession to the great High Priest in Heaven. The intentions of our Masses are wider than those who requested them. They embrace the faithful and the world.

> Hark how the priests, that wait upon the Lord, make lament between porch and altar, crying aloud: Spare thy people, Lord, spare them; thy chosen people, do not put them to the shame of obeying heathen masters!  JOEL 2:17

Always touched with sympathy for human infirmities, we bear the burden of nations in our hearts. Between the sanctuary and the tabernacle, clad in the vestments which identify us as the representatives of Christ, we speak for the dumb, atone for the sinful, plead for the Judases and intercede for those "who do not know what they are doing" (LUKE 23:34).

The intercession of the priest before the throne of God must be a tearful one. In this our High Priest has given us an example of human sympathy, for He wept three times: once for human grief, misery, desolation and death, at the tomb of Lazarus; once for a city, a civilization, a decaying culture, a rotting government, corrupt priests, at Jerusalem; finally, for human sin, pride, greed, egotism, and all that catalogue of capital evils, at Gethsemane. If we start (as we must) at the bottom of the ladder, having compassion on all men, nothing that happens to others is foreign to us. Their grief is our grief, their poverty our poverty. No matter whose the souls that wax weary, no matter whose the hands that hard burdens bear, our reaction is always the same. "My woe," we cry in the deep of our own afflicted co-suffering spirit, "my grief, my cross!"

## How Intercession Affects Our Mass

Granted our identification with those who are ignorant and make mistakes (HEBREWS 5:2), our thoughts will be their thoughts as we offer the Holy Sacrifice of the Mass.

At the Offertory, for example, we will see all humanity on the paten and in the chalice. As Our Lord obtained the first elements of His own human Body from a woman, so for the Eucharist He takes bread and wine from the earth. The bread and wine are thus representative of mankind. Two of the substances which have most widely nourished man are bread and wine. Bread has been called the marrow of the earth; wine, its very blood. In giving what has traditionally made our flesh and blood, we are equivalently offering all mankind on the paten.

The people no longer bring bread and wine as they did in the early church, but their contributions to the Offertory collection permit the purchase of the bread and wine. There would be less resistance to the collection basket if we made more effort to present it as a symbol of the incorporation of the entire congregation into the Sacrifice of the Mass. Similarly, we could simultaneously edify and win the Lord's blessing if we ourselves gave generously to every collection to which we ask the people to contribute. Why should we be exempt from a sacrifice for the Propagation of the Faith on Mission Sunday? "Be as generous as possible" is idle talk, if the generosity of the pastor has not preceded the generosity of his flock.

Before the bread could be placed on the paten and wine poured into the chalice, how many elements of the economic, financial and technical world had to be brought into play! The wheat needed farmers, fields, sacks, trucks, mills, commerce, finance, buying and selling. The grapes required vineyards, bottles, winepresses, time, space, chemistry, a thousand years of accumulated skills.

At the Offertory, therefore, we gather up the whole world into the narrow compass of a plate and a cup. Every drop of sweat, every day of labor, the decisions of the economist, the financier, the draughtsman and the engineer, every exertion and invention that went into the preparation of the elements of the Offertory are symbolically redeemed, justified and sanctified by our act. We bring not only redeemed man, but unredeemed creation to the steps of Calvary and the threshold of Redemption.

As the wheat Mary ate and the wine she drank became a kind of natural Eucharist to prepare for the Lamb of God Who would sacrifice Himself for the world, so are all material things sanctified through the Offertory of the Mass.

In the Consecration, Christ renews His sacrifice in an un-bloody manner. The act of love that prompted that sacrifice is eternal, for He is the Lamb "slain in sacrifice ever since the world was made" (APOCALYPSE 13:8). What the priest does each time he speaks the words of Consecration, is to apply Calvary and its fruits to a particular place and a particular time. Localized at one point in space and one moment in time, Calvary is now universalized in space and time. The priest takes the Cross of Calvary with Christ still hanging on it, and he plants it in New York, Paris, Cairo and Tokyo, and in the poorest mission of the world. We are not alone at the altar; we are in horizontal relations with Africa, Asia, our own parish, our city—everyone.

Clinging to the chasuble of every priest, for example, are 600 million souls in China who as yet know not Christ. When the priest takes the host in his hand, he is looking at fingers gnarled from slavery in the salt mines of Siberia. As he stands before the altar, his feet are the bleeding feet of refugees tramping westward toward barbed wire beyond which lies freedom. The flame of the candles reflects the flow of blast furnaces tended by gaunt men who for their labors are denied economic justice. The eyes gazing on the host are wet with the tears of the widow, the suffering and the orphan. The stole is a sling in which the priest carries on his shoulder living stones, the burden of the churches, the missions of the entire world. He drags the whole of humanity to the altar, where he joins heaven and earth together. For his hands raised at the Consecration merge into the Hands of Christ in heaven, who "lives on still to make intercession on our behalf" (HEBREWS 7:25).

In the Offertory, the priest is like a lamb led to the slaughter. In the Consecration, he is the lamb slaughtered as the sacrificial victim. In the Communion, he finds that he has not died at all, that he has on the contrary really come to the abundant life which is union with Christ. The one who surrenders himself to the material and allows himself to be possessed by it, is like a drowning man weighed down by the water that has entered and taken possession of his lungs. Such a one can never recover himself. But where the surrender is to God, we get ourselves back ennobled and enriched. We find that our death was after all no more permanent in the Consecration than was the death of Calvary, for Holy Communion is a kind of Easter. We give up our time, and get His eternity; we give up our sin, and receive His grace; we give up petty loves, and receive the Flame of Love.

In this union with Christ we are not alone, for Communion is not merely the union of the individual soul and Christ; it unites Christ to all the members of the Mystical Body and in an extended way through prayer to all humanity.

> The one Bread makes us one Body, though we are many in number; the same Bread is shared by all.     I CORINTHIANS 10:17

Sharing the Body of Christ in Holy Communion wipes out all accidental distinctions of race, class or condition. Here we are one with the whole of redeemed humanity, and indirectly with the earth, of which Christ described His true followers as the salt.

But we who offer this Chalice and eat of this Bread must constantly remind ourselves that this priestly office imposes spiritual obligations. The Israelites in the desert were fed with manna on their journey and drank water from the rock, and yet

> for all that, God was ill pleased with most of them; see how they were laid low in the wilderness.     I CORINTHIANS 10:5

Not everyone who receives Communion is saved. It avails us not to be priests unless we are victims, for only those who die with Him will live with Him.

Our need to die in Christ before we can live to Christ reflects one of the great differences between the High Priest and his human priests; He was without sin, but we are not. Hence, the priest must offer Mass, not only for the people but also—and this is often forgotten—for himself:

> And, for that reason, must needs present sin-offerings for himself, just as he does for the people.     HEBREWS 5:3

On the cross Our Lord, as priest, begged forgiveness for sinners: "Father, forgive them" (LUKE 23:34); sinless, He asked no pardon for Himself. With us, on the contrary, it is not so. We must offer the Holy Sacrifice for our own failings and sins.

The Old Testament priest was obligated to offer for himself a greater sacrifice, a more expensive animal. Since his blessings were greater, his sins also were greater.

> He will offer the bullock to make intercession for himself.
>     LEVITICUS 16:6

The analysis of this text developed in the Epistle to the Hebrews so impressed the author as a seminarian that he resolved to let no week of his priestly life go by without offering a Mass in honor of Our Blessed Lady and to the Great High Priest in reparation for his failings and sins. This resolve he has kept for decades and hopes with God's grace to keep until the divine Mercy finally calls him to eternal union with the Tremendous Lover.

## Conclusion

No priest should ever so act that Jacob's remark about himself could be applied to his meditations on the priesthood. When Jacob arose from his vision at Bethel, he said:

> Why, this is the Lord's dwelling-place, and I slept here unaware of it!
> GENESIS 28:16

As Jacob failed to recognize the nearness of God, the priest often fails to recognize the greatness of his calling. How often we sleep, unmindful of the Eucharist, His dwelling place! Only in rare moments do we come to the frightening realization of our vocation. We are more conscious of the bottom of the ladder than the top. Humanity is nearer to us; we can feel it. But the top is seen only by faith. It takes a kind of Luza, of separation from the world to make us see Bethel, the House of God. Our priesthood is best illumined in the fires of victimhood. We become significant to our fellow men not by being a "regular guy" but by being "another Christ." Our effectiveness at the bottom of the ladder depends on our communication with the top. Popularity is not necessarily influence. "Woe upon you," said Our Lord, "when all men speak well of you" (LUKE 6:26). Greatest is our compassion for others and our ability to elevate them when we have come down from heaven (JOHN 3:13). The bottom of the ladder is best discovered from the top.

## First Application: Separation From The World

Though as priests we are taken from among men and must therefore never be unsympathetic to their afflictions, though we are in the world, we are never of it, for our High Priest has called us out of this world. The Epistle to the Hebrews presents a profound reason why this must be so:

> Let us, too, go out to Him away from the camp, bearing the ignominy He bore.
> HEBREWS 13:13

What did "away from the camp" mean? It meant to be the rejected one of the world. The "camp" in Scripture was the city of Jerusalem, the religious center of the world. The Temple had expelled Him, the priests had delivered Him over to the Gentiles; they denied Him a place to die in the city, as they denied Him an inn at His birth. Outside the camp was always the place of reproach. It was there the refuse and the trash were dumped.

> And now, to make amends for his fault,... the skin and all the flesh... he will carry away from the camp... and burn them over a wood fire.
> LEVITICUS 4:8,11,12

Unless the world sees a difference in the places we frequent, in our activities and in the pleasures in which we indulge, in the language we use, in our dress, it will not respect our testimony. Separated from the world, separated unto God—these are the negative and positive sides of our priesthood.

In fact, the more success and prestige we enjoy in the world, the more honors laid on us, the more we must refuse to avail ourselves of worldly rewards and consolations. The temptation to be "of the world" becomes great when a priest has popularity thrust on him because his work calls on him to utilize the mass media, the press, television or radio. Then more than ever must he impress on himself that it is one thing to be popular, another to be influential. Pope John XXIII once gave thanks to God because a well-known cleric, who had great success among all classes of people, had suffered. This is what keeps him humble, he said. In the proportion in which we seek what the world can give, we become unable to give what the world needs. Great inspirations come in the desert, or away from the world.

> The word of God came upon John, the son of Zachary, in the desert.
> LUKE 3:2

Silence constitutes an integral part of this isolation. It is not always proper to speak all that we know.

> Do not cast your pearls before swine.     MATTHEW 7:6

Some like to talk about religion endlessly, as Herod did until John the Baptist introduced Herod's own moral problem. Religion is less a subject for discussion than for decision.

> Be sure thou dost not tell any man of it. MATTHEW 8:4

> Be sure nobody hears of this. MATTHEW 9:30

Our High Priest stands between us and displays of popular applause, of surface approbation. Like Jacob's ladder, though we are rooted in the earth, we must be supported by heaven, else is there no ascending or descending of the angels. At each moment of our apostolate, the world must say of us what the Sanhedrin said of Peter and John after the Resurrection, that they "recognized them now as having been in Jesus' company" (ACTS 4:13). If the fires which enkindle our activity are other than the flame of the Holy Spirit, we are but "echoing bronze, or the clash of cymbals" (I CORINTHIANS 13:1).

Every priest should meditate frequently on the two newly ordained priests, the sons of Aaron. Aaron and Moses had offered their sacrifices and God had shown approval by consuming them with miraculous fire. The new priests, Nadab and Abiu, without waiting for instructions, prepared to make a return to God for His gift by the offering of incense, which was symbolic of prayer. But they ignited their thuribles, not with the sacred fire of the altar (LEVITICUS 16:12) but with a strange fire which God had forbidden.

> There were two of Aaron's sons, Nadab and Abiu, who took up their censers and put coals and incense into them, to burn unhallowed fire in the Lord's presence, not in accordance with His command; whereupon the Lord sent down fire which devoured them, and they died there in the Lord's presence. LEVITICUS 10:1,2

What this strange fire which they offered was, we do not know. All we do know is that as they reached the door of the tabernacle where Moses and Aaron were standing, they were met by a consuming blast of fire. They had used some fire of the world, not the fire of God symbolic of the Holy Spirit.

The scene recalls a similar one described in the Acts of the Apostles (5:1-10), the destruction of Ananias and Sapphira, who used not the spirit of Pentecost in their giving, as Nadab and Abiu did not use the fire of God in their priesthood. Fire that is of our own kindling does not make a pleasing sacrifice to God. Only the Spirit of God can provide an acceptable fire.

> Those who follow the leading of God's Spirit are all God's sons. ROMANS 8:14

The nearer men are to God, the more exposed they are to the touch of His chastening hands. What might pass unnoted in others will be punished in them.

The priest who does not depend upon the Holy Spirit but seeks to furnish a fire or a spirit of himself, provokes the Lord by presumption. God accepts only what His Spirit inspires. We must bring back to God what He has given. He rejects all counterfeit. He will have Divine fire or none. Otherwise the fire of Divine approval becomes the fire of Divine wrath. Strange fire was punished with hallowed fire. God's fire quenched their censers together with the light of their life.

Twice we are reminded that Nadab and Abiu had no children (NUMBERS 3:4 and I PARALIPOMENA 24:2). Priests whose ministry is not inspired by the Holy Spirit have a sterile priesthood. It is not continued through vocations. If they lack the Spirit of Christ, so will they lack spiritual progeny. The priestly life enkindled by the ignis alienus of the world cannot grow old with the comfort of young priests whose vocations it fostered. But the priest on fire with the Holy Spirit will never be barren. His parish, his school will flower with vocations. Thus has every priest a measure of the fire which blazes in his soul. The Nadabs and the Abius cannot enkindle love of Christ, but was there ever a Paul without a Timothy?

## SECOND APPLICATION:
## LOSS OF OUR EGO

Christ our High Priest, the Ladder of Jacob, was not a human Person, though He had a human nature. His manhood was not the center of personality; the human nature had no conceivable existence apart from the Eternal Word who called it into being and made it His own.

The human nature was a garment with which He clothed His Divine Person, or rather an instrumentum conjunctum Divinitatis by which He acted on humanity. It was not a separable instrument, in the way in which a pencil is separable from the hand of the writer, but one eternally united to the Word, even now in heaven, as the pledge, pattern and model of our resurrection and glory.

Through the instrumentality of this human nature, Our Blessed Lord exercised three offices. He was Teacher, King and Priest; these three offices which He communicated to His Church to be exercized by the human instruments He chose to be His ministers. Consequently, in His Mystical Body, He still continues to teach, to govern and to sanctify. What He did through the Body He took from Mary, He does now through the Body He took from humanity and filled with His Spirit at Pentecost.

Now if our Mediator brought together God and man, heaven and earth, eternity and time, in the unity of His Divine Person, what does that mean for us priests? How does it affect the ideal of the priesthood in the Church? What it specifically does is to submerge the human personality of the priest so that he can say: "I am no longer my own." Human personality answers the question, "Who is it?" Our human nature answers the question, "What is it?" The priest who continues the Life of Christ seeks to be one with Him so completely that the personality which governs his every thought, word and deed is the Personality of Christ Himself. As the human nature of Christ had no human person, so the priest seeks to have no source of responsibility other than Christ Himself. We strive to eliminate the "Ego" and substitute the "Christus-Sacerdos-Victima."

Though the Hypostatic Union can never be repeated, every priest must try in a distant and imperfect way to reproduce it in his priesthood. We too seek to have "two natures in one person." One nature we have inherited from Adam; the other "nature" is grace, by which we are made "partakers of the Divine Nature." While, in no strict sense, are these like the two natures in Christ, they help to point up the problem of our "ego." The ideal is so to submerge our personality in the Person of Christ as to think with Him, will what He wills, make Him the source of our responsibility and our power.

If a painter felt the urge to create a beautiful picture, but had available only a canvas that did not belong to him, he might decide that it would not be worth the effort. The analogy is one that can be applied to the great High Priest; if He does not own us, if He is not the directing Personality of all our actions, He will not work through us as He works through those who belong to Him. We operate too much through our power, not His.

I, as a person, use a pencil as an instrument. If the pencil were endowed with its own personality, it might say: "I will not write," or "I will go up when you want me to go down," or "I will blunt my point." There would be little I could do with that instrument. So it is with us, if our personality is in conflict with His; or if it has a little secret garden of some petty love or secret sin, which He cannot enter. In such a case, the fault of our priesthood is not in Him, but in us. Our ego "frustrates" Divinity. He wills one thing; we will another. We become but broken rungs on the ladder to heaven.

Maybe the Nestorian heresy is alive today—and in us? Nestorius taught that there were two persons in Christ. Do not we sometimes live as if there were two persons in us; the person who wishes to be rich and the Person of Christ Who had nowhere to lay His Head? The person who seeks to escape work, and the Person of Christ Whose greatest conversions were made when He was tired? The person who never makes a convert, and the Person of Christ Who is always in search of the lost sheep.

He called us as persons to the priesthood bidding us to crucify ourselves, to de-egotize and to make ourselves empty vessels for the heavenly treasure. That is why we are bidden to live a life "hidden with Christ in God." Only in self-forgetfulness does Christ reign in us.

## To Christ Crucified

I am not moved to love Thee, O my Lord,
By any longing for Thy Promised Land;
Nor by the fear of hell am I unmanned
To cease from my transgressing deed or word.
Tis Thou Thyself dost move me—Thy blood poured
Upon the cross from nailed foot and hand;
And all the wounds that did Thy body brand;
And all Thy shame and bitter death's award.
Yea, to Thy heart am I so deeply stirred
That I would love Thee were no heaven on high—
That I would fear, were hell a tale absurd!
Such my desire, all questioning grows vain;
Though hope deny me hope I still would sigh,
And as my love is now, it should remain.
                    Translated By Thomas Walsh[1]

As the scientist learns the secrets of nature by being passive before it, so we learn the mysteries of our High Priest by being passive before Him. Nature would never unfold the pages of its laws, if the scientist imposed his mind upon it; so neither will the High Priest confer that fullness of power upon us, unless we are like empty vessels before Him. St. Paul says that he kept down his self-will and was made weak in everything that involved his personality, in order that he might increase within himself in the power of God.

But He told me, My grace is enough for thee; My strength finds its full scope in thy weakness. More than ever, then, I delight to boast

---

[1] From the book An Introduction to Spanish Literature, by George Tyler Northup, University of Chicago.

of the weaknesses that humiliate me, so that the strength of Christ may enshrine itself in me.
I CORINTHIANS 12:9

There is nothing that God could not do without me. But there are many things that He has elected to do through me, provided I am a supple instrument in His Hand. The true continuation of the Priesthood is, therefore, the giving of ourselves so completely to the great High Priest that we have no other feelings, or emotions, or desires than Christ Himself:

Yours is to be the same mind which Christ Jesus shewed.
PHILIPPIANS 2:5

Why when land was about to be divided among the twelve tribes did the tribe of Levi receive none? Because it was the tribe of the priesthood. What did they need since they possessed the Lord? What a lesson!

That is why the Levites have no lands assigned to them like their brethren, the Lord thy God has promised them that He himself will be their portion.
DEUTERONOMY 10:9

## THIRD APPLICATION:
## THE IMPORTANCE OF EX OPERE OPERANTIS

When we act in the Church's name in dispensing the sacraments, we are instruments of God by which grace is conferred by the simple performance of the action, or as the Scholastics said, ex opere operato. Sunlight is not polluted by passing through a dirty window. God can write straight with crooked lines. A person could be as validly baptized by a Judas as by a Peter.

This is true of the sacraments. But the priest is bound to perform many other duties, to console the sick, to preach the Gospel, to convert sinners, to stir souls to penance, to foster vocations, and all these duties require our own sacrifice, our detachment and the laborious fashioning of ourselves to the image of Christ. The effectiveness of such actions ex opere operantis requires the surrender of our personality to Christ.

Speaking of the actions of Christ, the theologians say that everything He did was a Divine act because He was a Divine Person, a principle they express by the statement that actiones sunt suppositorum. This principle can by analogy be applied to the priest. All of the actions of his nature are to be attributed to the Person Christ:

> Whatever you are about, in word and action alike, invoke always the name of the Lord Jesus Christ, offering your thanks to God the Father through Him.
> COLOSSIANS 3:17

We act, live, think, preach not in our name or personality, but in His. We are only branches. He is the Vine (JOHN 15:1-10). The vine and the branches have the same life, are nourished by the same sap, and work together in the production of the same fruit. They form but one being, they have one and the same action. Our oneness in Him is so total, that we cry out with Paul:

> I hang upon the Cross, and yet I am alive; or rather, not I; it is Christ that lives in me.
> GALATIANS 2:20

Our sublime dignity does not consist exclusively in the priestly character given in Holy Orders, but in what this character also demands as its complement, namely, Christ taking the place of our personality. Then we grow in Christ as Mary did. Certainly, Our Blessed Mother was richer spiritually on Christmas Day than on the day of the Annunciation; richer at Cana than at Bethlehem, richer at Calvary than at Cana, and richer in the Upper Room at Pentecost than on Golgotha.

The ideal is accordingly to have the Person of Christ as the single source of our responsibility both in acts which produce their effect ex opere operato and in those which are fruitful ex opere operantis. Our sinful life does not destroy the essential value of the former kind. When in the confessional the priest says, "I absolve," it is Christ Who absolves; when at Mass he says, "This is My Body," it is Christ Who offers His Body to the Father. And so on for all the sacraments. But in the priest's other acts, it should be Christ Who is again visiting the sick and instructing those who seek truth. This kind of union with Christ, however, does not come simply from ordination. It demands mortification.

The faithful see Christ in us at the altar and in the confessional and at the font. Do they see Christ in us at the table, in the school, on the golf course, or in the hospital? Are these places for our ego to assert itself, or are they occasions for others to see Christ in the dining room of a Simon or a Lazarus? Christ does not come off with the chasuble, nor is our ordination folded in a pocket as easily as a stole. Unbelievers do not see us in vestments; they see us in shops, in theatres, at meetings. Whether they see Christ in us depends on whether we act like Christ.

An electric wire attached to the generator will give no light if the bulb is burned out. One of the reasons why Christianity does not influence the world more is that few Christians shine more brightly than those who lack the faith. Is this not true also of many priests, in spite of the fact that the priest should be a different person from all others, because he is the Person of Christ?

St. Francis de Sales saw a young priest on his ordination day about to enter the church for his first Mass. The young priest stopped as if he was talking to someone invisible; the problem seemed to be who should pass first. The priest explained to St. Francis de Sales: "I just had the happiness of seeing my Guardian Angel. Previously, he always walked before me; now that I am a priest, he insists on walking behind me."

By the surrender of our ego to the Person of the High Priest we exercise an influence like that of the eighteenth century French court preacher, Bishop Jean Baptiste Massillon on Louis XIV. "Father," the king complimented him one day, "I have heard many orators in this chapel and I was always very satisfied; but every time I hear you, I am dissatisfied with myself."

Holy priests always make sinners say what the Samaritan woman said to the menfolk of her city:

> Come and have sight of a man who has told me all the story of my life; can this be the Christ?         JOHN 4:29

## Chapter 3

## Spiritual Generation

"Increase and multiply" is a law of sacerdotal no less than of biological life. The production of new life is generation, a function that does not pertain exclusively or even primarily to the flesh. God is the source of all generation.

Begetting is not an impulse from below but a gift from above; rather than an evolution from animals, it is a descent from Deity.

> What, says the Lord thy God, shall I, that bring children to the birth, want power to bring them forth? ISAIAS 66:9

Every mother who begets a child, every hen which hatches its young, every mind which conceives a new idea, every bishop who ordains a priest, every priest who fosters a vocation, all reflect that eternal act of generation in which the Father says to his Son:

> Thou art my son; I have begotten thee this day. PSALM 2:7

The understanding of the eternal generation of the Second Person of the Trinity provided by such carnal generation is, however, very remote and obscure. Somewhat more precise—though still of course analogical—is the operation of the human intellect when it "conceives" ideas. Where do we get the idea of "fortitude," "relationship" or "spirituality?" We have never seen these concepts in the pedestrian world of oranges, sidewalks and coins. Whence came they? The mind generated them; once begotten, they remain distinct from the mind, but not separate from it. The fruits of thinking, namely, ideas, do not drop from the mind like apples from a tree, or the newborn from parents. They exist in the mind and yet with characters of their own.

In like manner, does God as the Eternal Thinker have a Thought, a Word. Because this Wisdom was "generated," we call God Who Thinks the Father, and the Word or Idea Who is "generated" the Son. The Father was not first and then the Son. An unbelieving father said to his son who asserted that the Father and Son were equal: "I existed before you did, and therefore the Father existed before the Son." The boy answered: "Oh no! You did not begin to be a father until I began to be a son."

## THE BLESSED VIRGIN MARY AND GENERATION

Was not the Blessed Mother herself generated in the Mind of God? Before she was immaculately conceived in the womb of her mother, St. Anne, she was "immaculately conceived" in the Mind of God. That is why the words of Proverbs (8:22-30) are applied to her:

> The Lord made me His when first He went about His work, at the birth of time, before His creation began. Long, long ago, before earth was fashioned, I held my course. Already I lay in the womb, when the depths were not yet in being, when no springs of water had yet broken; when I was born, the mountains had not yet sunk on their firm foundations, and there were no hills; not yet had He made the earth, or the rivers, or the solid framework of the world. I was there when He built the heavens, when He fenced in the waters with a vault inviolable, when He fixed the sky overhead, and levelled the fountain springs of the deep. I was there when He enclosed the sea within its confines, forbidding the waters to transgress their assigned limits, when He poised the foundations of the world. I was at His side, a master-workman, my delight increasing with each day, as I made play before Him all the while.

## THE APOSTLES AND GENERATION

Just as God the Father has a Divine Son and countless millions of adopted sons by grace, so Mary had not only Jesus as her Son, but all those other children who were, in the person of John, commended to her on Calvary.

Fecundity, generation and fruitfulness mark the teachings of the faith, beginning with the command to "increase and multiply" (GENESIS 1:22). So it is to the end, for the final book of the Bible declares that the

Tree of Life itself is fecund, "the tree that gives life, bearing its fruit twelvefold" (APOCALYPSE 22:2). In the same vein, the Apostle Paul describes his converts as the fruits of his generation: "It was I that begot you in Jesus Christ, when I preached the gospel to you" (I CORINTHIANS 4:15). Timothy he addressed as "my own son in the faith" (I TIMOTHY 1:2), and again as "his well-beloved son" (II TIMOTHY 1:2).

So too does James assure us that God has begotten us in Truth:

> It was His will to give us birth, through His true word, meaning us to be the first-fruits, as it were, of all His creation.      JAMES 1:18

And John stresses the theme of our Redemption by reminding us that carnal generation is as nothing compared to the spiritual generation by grace:

> Their birth came, not from human stock, not from nature's will or man's, but from God.      JOHN 1:13

God hates sterility. He punishes disobedience with barrenness. When He promises His people a blessing, it is expressed in terms of fecundity:

> There shall be no unfruitfulness in thy land.      EXODUS 23:26

But the one who has no spiritual children is under a curse. Only those who walk with the Lord and yield to the Spirit are gifted with fruitfulness:

> Thou shalt be blessed as no other people is blessed; man and woman, sire and dam shall breed.      DEUTERONOMY 7:14

## THE SPIRITUAL GENERATION OF PRIESTS

The priest is pledged to celibacy, not because human generation is wrong, but because it must yield so that he can devote himself wholly to a higher form of generation: the begetting of children in Christ by bringing to Him those who never knew Him, by restoring to Him those lost in sin, and by arousing in those who already love Christ the inspiration to serve Him more fully as religious or priests. The energy which otherwise would be used for the service of the flesh is not buried in a napkin. It is transformed so that it serves chaste generation in the Spirit.

Too often the vow of chastity is presented negatively as the avoiding of carnal and sinful pleasures. But is pure water only the absence of dirt, a white diamond merely the negation of carbon? Chastity is sometimes mistakenly called cold, but not by Francis Thompson, who proclaims it a "passionless passion, a wild tranquility." Chastity is fire. No life is produced without fire. Even the virginal conception of Our Lady had its fire—not human indeed, but the Fire of the Holy Spirit. At that moment, she undoubtedly had an ecstasy of soul surpassing the flesh ecstasy of all humans combined. Such is the joy of begetting through the Pine Love of the Spirit.

## "Father"

No form of address is so widely used for a priest, and none so appropriate as "Father." It stresses precisely the priest's close relationship to God,

> The Father of Our Lord Jesus Christ, that Father from whom all fatherhood in heaven and on earth takes its title.
> EPHESIANS 3:14,15

But if the priest is thus a father, then God may properly inquire of him where are his offspring. The bishop alone, of course, has the power to beget a priest in ordination, but every priest has the power and duty to foster the vocation. When we go before the judgment seat of God, each of us will be asked: "Whom have you begotten in Christ?" Woe to those who are barren! When Our Lord comes to us looking for the fruit of our Fatherhood, we must not be as the barren fig tree which merits only a curse.

Physical maternity is not without its labor, and to a mother in labor, Our Lord likened His Passion: "... because now her time has come" (JOHN 16:21). But spiritual parenthood, our mission, is not without its labor too, as Paul said of Onesimus:

> And I am appealing to thee on behalf of Onesimus, the child of my imprisonment.
> PHILEMON 1:10

The mother of Samuel the Prophet was, after many years of sterility, blessed with a son who was to prove mighty in Israel because her heart was right with God. Those who desire the glory of God, she proclaimed in thanksgiving, will find that the life which has been barren can become unusually fruitful:

> See how at last the barren womb bears many.  I KINGS 2:5

And what above all things will assure us of begetting children in Christ, if it be not our oneness with the Christ-Victim? Having enumerated seven miracles or signs which Our Lord worked to prove His divinity, St. John observed that few who had witnessed the signs had been convinced by them (JOHN 12:37). But Christ had yet another way to win souls:

> Yes, if only I am lifted up from the earth, I will attract all men to Myself.  JOHN 12:32

Miracles are not a cure for unbelief. On being informed that Lazarus had been raised from the dead, some of the Pharisees sought to kill him and thus destroy the evidence. But the spiritual harvest which Our Lord assured us would come from His Cross cannot be denied. The means He proclaimed to draw souls to Himself constitute an infallible source of spiritual fecundity for those who live in its shadow.

## CONVERT MAKING

Has administration taken precedence in the life of many pastors over evangelization? Has organization swallowed up shepherding? Are souls to be reckoned only on index cards? Are the sheep in the fold to be used only for shearing, or is each member of the laity to be encouraged and helped to develop his own specific apostolic vocation? The question is one that each pastor can answer for himself only by searching the depths of his own conscience. What he has to remember is that he is the father not only of the sheep who are in the fold:

> I have other sheep too, which do not belong to this fold;
> I must bring them in too.  JOHN 10:16

Does not Canon Law make the pastor responsible for all souls in his parish? Yet how many pastors devote themselves seriously to trying to incorporate those not of the fold into the Mystical Body of Christ? Every priest should ask himself how many adults he baptized in the past year as the fruit of his zeal; how many fallen-away Catholics he brought back to the Father's House. Why do some priests never make a convert while others make hundreds? Can it be because one takes his title of "Father" seriously while the other does not?

> When I preach the gospel, I take no credit for that; I act under constraint; it would go hard with me indeed if I did not preach the Gospel.
>
> I CORINTHIANS 9:16

Administration is absolutely essential; to ignore it would be to overlook the fact that each member has a specific function in the Mystical Body. But the Holy Spirit has not called us to be mere bankers, real estate men or blueprint experts. Such activities are at best incidental to a primary function which the Apostles understood. The Spirit was not given them to sit at counting tables:

> It is too much that we should have to forego preaching God's word, and bestow our care upon tables.
>
> ACTS 6:2

On the other hand, it is not enough to be "sacristy" priests devoutly beseeching the Lord to send souls to us, while ignoring His command:

> You must go out to the street-comers, and invite all whom you find there.
>
> MATTHEW 22:9

All around us potential converts abound. The tragedy is not only that they lack faith, but that we seldom ask them to embrace it. A non-Catholic lawyer was asked on his death-bed by his Catholic partner of twenty years, "Now, that you are nearing your end, how about coming into the Church?" The dying man raised his eyebrows. "If your faith meant so little to you during the twenty years you have known me," he replied, "it cannot make that much difference now."

Conversions are not more difficult in our times than before; but the approach must be different. Today, people are looking for God, not because of the order they find in the universe, but because of the disorder they find in themselves. They are coming to God through an inner disgust, a despair that may be called creative.

> Out of the depths I cry to Thee, O Lord,
>
> PSALM 129:1

Religion is sometimes said to be losing its influence in the world. To the extent that such is the case, part of the reason undoubtedly is that we do not appear to the unbeliever as different from anyone else. The missionary, the priest who lives in the slums, the saintly priest who spends himself with souls—these always inspire, and they inspire because they reveal Christ and Him Crucified.

Doubting Thomas must not be judged too harshly for the conditions he laid down before he would believe. All he asked for was fair evidence.

> Until I have seen the mark of the nails on His hands, until I have put my finger into the mark of the nails, and put my hand into His side, you will never make me believe. JOHN 20:25

No deep conviction is aroused in the incredulous until they see the scarred hands and the broken heart of the priest who is a victim with Christ. The mortified priest, the priest who is detached from the world—these inspire, edify and Christify souls.

Being a father of many children requires work. Our Lord made His two greatest converts when He was tired. The eight-hour day, five-day week is not prescribed in the Scriptures. God gave Moses hundreds of details about the tabernacle, but one piece of furniture was not mentioned. The tabernacle lacked a chair. Altar, laver, table, lamp, censers and drapes are all listed, but there was no place for the priest to sit down. When are we meant to sit down in the sense of resting from our priest-victimhood? Our Lord "sat" after He had spent Himself for our Redemption:

> whereas He sits for ever at the right hand of God, offering for our sins a sacrifice. HEBREWS 10:12

We also read of Him "standing" in heaven. When Stephen was stoned, he saw "Jesus standing at God's right hand" (ACTS 7:55), suggesting that when His Church is persecuted, Our Lord stands in heaven. If such is the symbolic meaning, the High Priest surely stands today to strengthen the third of the people of the earth who groan interiorly under the beating of the hammer and the cutting of the sickle of Communism!

Certainly for the priest, work is his lot while on earth: "Finish your journey while you have the light" (JOHN 12:35). It was no oversight on God's part to omit a chair when furnishing the tabernacle. The priest was not ordained to be a sitter. Christ's promise is that those who overcome will "sit" with Him at the Heavenly Banquet.

The earthly father must work for and be with his family; the spiritual father in like manner, must work for and be with souls. Our Lord gave us the example:

> There they crucified Him, and with Him two others, one on each side with Jesus in the midst. JOHN 19:18

In the great moment of redemptive love, He is found in the midst of saved and sinners, among good thieves and bad thieves. His mediators and ambassadors can no more isolate themselves from sinners than He did. We are separated from them as holy priests, but one with them as victims for their sins. Nor do we go amongst them to convince them of their error so much as to break bread for their starving souls.

The spirit of the true father is less canonical than evangelical. Canon Law concerns the relations of the Church and its members. The Gospel concerns the mission of the Church to the world. The parish or the diocese is not the limit of our fatherliness. As Our Lord got closer to the cross, He had more and more dealings with those who were not Jews. After the cross, His message was to the world. Two things always seem to go together in a bishop or a priest: love of conversions and love of the foreign missions. The Catholics close to us we must indeed sanctify, but souls in distant lands who have never heard the good tidings, must also be redeemed.

### Conversion Is Victimhood

Can it be that the Communists excel us in their zeal to spread their beliefs? Zeal unfortunately is not always in direct proportion to truth. Fire has two qualities: light and heat. Light is truth. Heat is love. We have the truth, but sometimes not the zeal or love; we have the light, but not always the heat. But the Communists have the heat and not the light, the zeal and not the truth.

There is a dangerous tendency among many in modern times who call themselves Christians to divorce Christ and the cross.

And what would Christ be without the cross? Another teacher like Buddha or Lao-tse; a sociologist spreading whipped cream on socially disapproved behavior; a psychoanalyst reducing guilt to a complex and banishing sin as a "hangover" from savagery; a preacher too polite to mention hell or divorce; a reformer for whom all discipline is masochistic and who proclaims self-restraint and moderation as unnatural and in conflict with the biological urge to self-expression.

And who picks up the cross without Christ? The Communists! Into a disordered and falsely liberal world, they introduce order, law, obedience, discipline, study, conformity to the all-holy will of the Party, detachment from Western excesses, and above all, a crushing of the ego for the sake of the kingdom of earth. But as the Christ without the cross would be a weak, effeminate Christ unable to save us from sin, so the cross without Christ is tyranny, dictatorship, concentration camps, slavery and Sovietism.

Are we living in a world distinguished by an abundant outpouring of the anti-Pentecostal spirit? Has part of the earth caught fire with the flames of hell, while the fires of Pentecost sputter in our hands like little candles incapable of setting the world ablaze?

To suggest that the fires of Pentecost are dying would be not only blasphemy but a denial of proud facts; for the hope and glory of our age are to be found in the endurance of the Church of Silence and the unveiling of new fires by our missionaries. Yet is there not many an individual priest who should sadly contrast his own smugness with the zeal of the Communists, and ask himself why some who want to be good and who profess the truth, still lack a passionate conviction for Christ. The Lord said to Moses:

> The fire on the altar must burn continually. Never must the altar be empty of this perpetual fire. LEVITICUS 6:12,13

Under the Law of Moses the priest had each morning to feed the fire with fresh logs and carry the ashes away from the camp (LEVITICUS 6:10,12). The morning fires of meditation, the self-denial which carries from the heart the dead things of the world—these are the conditions of the perpetual fire which burned in St. Paul for the conversion of the entire human race:

> Thus nobody has any claim on me, and yet I have made myself everybody's slave, to win more souls.... I have been everything by turns to everybody, to bring everybody salvation. I CORINTHIANS 9:19,22

## FOSTERING VOCATIONS

Another aspect of the role of the father in begetting spiritual children in Christ is the fostering of vocations. It is accordingly appropriate for the priest to ask himself what contribution he is making. It is often said that there is a decline in vocations, but it is necessary here to distinguish between vocation and response. God calls. That is the Divine side. We respond. That is the human side. Pius XII in the Encyclical Menti Nostrae said:

> The Church will never lack priests sufficient for its mission.

Every study of vocations reveals that many youths under fifteen feel the call. One survey indicated that 40 per cent of students in secular schools and 50 per cent of students in Catholic schools thought of a vocation after they were twelve. In another survey, 60 per cent of boys in normal school, 23 per cent in professional schools, 37 per cent in technical schools and 66 per cent in classics affirmed that at some time in their life they hoped to become priests or religious.

Many who have felt the call just wander away. Rather than a deliberate turning aside, there is compromise or straying. Youths with vocations, like sheep in a field, look around the world instead of up to heaven; and before they know it, they have lost sight of the Good Shepherd. The reasons are many, but often one of them is the failure of the priest to talk to an altar boy about the priesthood, to neglect to thank him when he gets up to serve the early Mass. A cutting reprimand for a trivial misdemeanor may alter a young man's plans—for such a cause Tito left the Church.

> Now, son of man, prophesy doom to ... the shepherds of my flock. This be thy message from the Lord God: Out upon Israel's shepherds, that had a flock to feed, and fed none but themselves.
>
> EZEKIEL 34:2

We must surely hope that we do not fall under this Divine Judgment. Nevertheless, as God's word, it must urge us to greater care of the young:

> The milk drank, the wool wore, the fat lambs slaughtered, but pastured these sheep of mine never at all! The wasted frame went unnourished, the sick unhealed; nor bound they the broken limb, nor brought strayed sheep home, nor lost sheep found; force and constraint were all the governance they knew. So my sheep fell a-wandering, that shepherd had none; every wild beast fell a-preying on them, and they scattered far and wide.
>
> EZEKIEL 34:3-5

When we appear before the Lord to be judged by the use to which we put the chrism with which our hands were anointed, He will ask us if we have continued our priesthood?

> I will hold them answerable for the flock entrusted to them, and they shall have charge of it no more, feed themselves out of its revenues no more. From their greedy power I will rescue it; no longer shall it be their prey.
>
> EZEKIEL 34:10

What young priest and religious will then proclaim our fruitfulness? What aid that we gave the Society for the Propagation of the Faith, or the Opus Sancti Petri for educating native seminarians will be recorded in the Book of Life? In how many Catholic homes will we have encouraged the vocations of worthy youths by our visits? What spiritual exercises will be noted as conducted by us for young men and women who felt drawn to the priesthood or the religious life?

How fruitful a vineyard of vocations is the sacristy! To see a priest making his meditation before Mass does more for an altar boy's vocation than a thousand pieces of inspirational literature.

Being a spiritual father to future priests requires dedication. Aaron and the priests of the Old Testament were anointed in three places: the right ear, the right thumb and the big toe of the right foot (LEVITICUS 14:14-28). The threefold anointing suggests a three-fold dedication: to be attentive to the hearing of the Word of God, for the ear signifies obedience (EXODUS 21:6), as Our Lord was obedient unto the death of the Cross (PHILIPPIANS 2:8); to use his hands constantly in performing good deeds, as Christ finished the work given to Him by the Father (JOHN 4:34; 9:4; 18:4; HEBREWS 10:5,7); and to walk always in the ways of God, for sweet are the feet of those who spread the news of the Gospel.

> See where they bring good news on the mountain heights, proclaiming that all is well.   NAHUM 1:15

The secret of fostering vocations may be summed up in this Old Testament ceremony, namely, the encouraging of spiritual sensitivity, of good works and of flight from evil.

1. The young must first hear the call of God. It is then the priest's role to keep his soul sensitive to God's voice. As in Baptism, we touch both ears saying, "Ephphetha" ("Be opened"), so in preparation for Orders, we keep the soul alert to God's whisper, for He does not shout a vocation.

2. The ear needs the hands to translate into good works the pious inspiration of God. Aspirants to the priesthood therefore serve the altar, instruct children in the faith, act as counselors to the young, thus fitting their hands to be anointed one day by the bishop.

3. Vocations prosper through discipline, too, for the priest must walk the narrow path to salvation, not the broad way to destruction (LUKE 13:24). The world and the flesh have strong solicitation for youth. They must be protected from sin as God protected the Jews in going out of Egypt:

> Thus the people had Pharao's leave to go on their way; but God did not lead them by the nearest road, the road through Philistia. Here they would have found themselves met by armed resistance, and perhaps, in despair of their enterprise, returned to Egypt.
>
> EXODUS 13:17

Canon Law places an obligation on every priest, especially pastors, to foster the signs of vocation observed in youths with whom they come in contact.

Dent operam sacerdotes, praesertim parochi, ut pueros, qui indicia praebeant ecclesiasticae vocationis, peculiari-bus curis a saeculi contagiis arceant, ad pietatem informent, primis litterarum studiis imbuant divinaeque in eis vocationis germen foveant (CANON 1353).

One parish in the United States had no vocations in forty years. A new pastor in a single year developed ten vocations. The difference was due to his spirituality. His ear heard the call of the Lord of the Harvest for vocations, his hands were busy in promoting devotions to the Sacred Heart, and his feet visited every family in his parish.

Some years ago I was eating in a hotel restaurant when a boy about twelve, who shined shoes for a living, began to swing on a velvet curtain at the entrance. The headwaiter yelled at him and ordered him out of the hotel.

I followed the boy into the street. He told me he had been expelled from a Catholic school by a pastor and a nun who assured him that he could never again attend a Catholic school. I took him to the pastor and the nun involved and reminded them of three other "bad" boys expelled from religious schools: one for drawing pictures during geography class, another for fighting too much, the third for keeping bad books under his mattress. They were respectively Hitler, Mussolini and Stalin. How different, under God, might world history have been if their leaders had taken more pains to reform them!

The pastor and the nun agreed to re-admit the boy. In due course he was ordained a priest and today he is a missionary in the Arctic.

What a blessed life is ours! What a beautiful role celibacy plays when it facilitates a higher kind of generation, when it inspires the priest to imitate the Father in begetting the Word, to imitate the Christ Who begot us in the Spirit as an *alter Christus!*

Our days are blessed by a deepening of liturgical devotion and an upsurge of participation in the Eucharistic mysteries on the part of the laity. Such developments are a tribute but also a warning to the clergy, for as the laity become more spiritual, so must they. The Church is in danger when the laity are more spiritual than the clergy:

> You are the salt of the earth; if salt loses its taste, what is there left to give taste to it? MATTHEW 5:13

Much earlier the prophet Osee had issued the same warning:

> Priest, now, shall fare no better than people. OSEE 4:9

It is not possible to create esteem for the priesthood except through an admiration for the priest's victimhood. No mother brings a child into the world without labor. No priest begets a vocation or makes a convert or sanctifies a soul except under the shadow of the cross. And as an alter Christus, every priest must realize his ability to beget in the spirit. We are usually conscious of our sacramental power at Mass and in the confessional, but do we have confidence in our power to excite vocations? When we place our hand on a boy who gives spiritual promise and say, "Some day you will be a priest," do we believe Our Lord will support our judgment and our blessing? Many a priest can look back on the blessing he gave a youth who is now an ordained priest. He did not confer the vocation on the young man. God did that. But there is such a thing as a priestly strengthening of the vocation in the soul. As Our Lord prayed to His Father, so must we pray confidently to the Lord:

> And He will bring honour to Me, because it is from Me that He will derive what He makes plain to you. JOHN 16:14

How happy the death of the priest who knows that he has passed on the torch of life which Christ ignited in his soul. And until that hour, without the benefit of sitting down in the tabernacle of the Lord, each of us will say with Paul to those whose vocation we have fostered:

> My little children, I am in travail over you afresh, until I can see Christ's image formed in you! GALATIANS 4:19

# Chapter 4

# The Holiness of the Priest

The moral and spiritual life of the priest is related in two ways to the Mystical Body of Christ. His holiness helps to make the faithful holy. The sanctity of the Christian community, in turn, helps to make him holy.

At the Last Supper, Our Lord gave His priests a compelling reason why they had to be holy, holding Himself up as the example:

> I dedicate Myself for their sakes, that they too may be dedicated through the truth. It is not only for them that I pray; I pray for those who are to find faith in Me through their words.  JOHN 17:19,20

He sanctified Himself not for Himself alone, but for them too. They in turn were to sanctify themselves for the Church and all future believers. Spirituality begins at the top, not at the bottom. The mirror reflects the light of the sun, but does not create it. Sanctity is a pyramid:

> Gracious as balm poured on the head till it flows down on to the beard; balm that flowed down Aaron's beard, and reached the very skirts of his robe.  PSALM 132:2

God is holy; that holiness comes to earth in Christ. He bestows it on His priests with their cooperation; they, in the measure in which they accept, contribute to making the people holy. The people do not give the priest the special powers to sanctify which he possesses. It is Our Lord who gave these powers, and He gave them to enable the priest to make the people holy. From the mountain, where one communes with God, sanctity descends:

So Moses went down again to the people, and rid them of defilement.
EXODUS 19:14

For the sake of the Church, Our Lord came into the world and (as He said) He sanctified Himself. But what precisely does this expression mean? How can one consecrate himself? Could Aaron consecrate himself? Could I consecrate myself? But He could consecrate Himself, because He is a "high priest, now, eternally with the priesthood of Melchisedech" (HEBREWS 6:20). He could sanctify Himself, because He was both priest and victim:

Order your lives in charity, upon the model of that charity which Christ shewed to us, when He gave himself up on our behalf, a sacrifice breathing out fragrance as He offered it to God.
EPHESIANS 5:2

In Biblical usage, to dedicate or sanctify meant to set apart as an offering to God, a sacrifice.

Thou shalt set apart for the Lord thy God all the firstborn of thy cattle and sheep. DEUTERONOMY 15:19

There is no ransoming the first-born of ox or sheep or goat; they are set apart for the Lord. NUMBERS 18:17

All Old Testament sacrifices were holy to the Lord as types of the "first-born" (LUKE 2:7) who, in a special way became sanctified, that is, was set apart as a sacrifice for our salvation, on Good Friday. His own official sanctification, as He affirmed the previous night, was the meritorious cause of His priests and people being sanctified. St. Paul understood this clearly:

Christ shewed love to the Church when He gave Himself up on its behalf. He would hallow it. EPHESIANS 5:25,26

## The High Priest's "Our Father"

From the foregoing it is clear that Our Lord made Himself "holy" or "priestly" or "saintly" for our sakes. To reproduce this holiness in us priests, the help of heaven is needed. The night of the Last Supper He spoke to the Heavenly Father in our behalf, saying His own "Pater

Noster." Previously, He had said to the apostles, when they asked how they were to pray:

> And He told them, When you pray, you are to say, Father.
> LUKE 11:2

Our Lord never said "Our Father" of Himself and us together, but "My Father" and "Your Father," because He is the Natural Son; we, the adopted sons. His sacerdotal prayer of Holy Thursday night, like the prayer He had given the apostles on the earlier occasion, contained seven petitions. The first "Our Father" was for everyone, but this "Our Father" is for priests alone. It sums up the virtues that distinguish the priest.

1. Perseverance: "Holy Father, keep them true to Thy name" (JOHN 17:11).
2. Joy: "That My joy may be theirs, and reach its full measure in them" (JOHN 17:13).
3. Deliverance from evil: "That Thou shouldst keep them clear of what is evil" (JOHN 17:15).
4. Holiness through sacrifices: "Keep them holy, then, through the truth" (JOHN 17:17).
5. Unity: "That they may all be one; that they too may be one in Us, as Thou Father, art in Me, and I in Thee" (JOHN 17:21).
6. His Constant Companions: "This, Father, is my desire, that all those whom thou hast entrusted to Me may be with Me where I am" (JOHN 17:24).
7. Enjoy His glory in heaven: "So as to see My glory" (JOHN 17:24).

How often the note of joy and glory and happiness is struck! And everything is conditioned on being "with Him"; this was His purpose in choosing them as His priests. But before He offered that prayer, He told us that we would never be immune from trial. The "joy" set before us is similar to that with which He embraced the Cross. But the victory is certain. We have already won! Only the news has not yet leaked out!

> In the world, you will only find tribulation; but take courage, I have overcome the world.
> JOHN 16:33

## What Holiness Involves

Our Lord sanctified Himself for our sakes, and that—as has been indicated—involved sacrifice. He immolated Himself, just as whatever was dedicated to the Lord under the Old Testament was immolated.

As the shepherd, so the sheep; as the priest, so the people. Priest-victim leadership begets a holy Church. What the priests are in the parish, the diocese and the nation, that likewise will the faithful be. As multitudes got the bread at Capharnaum through the disciples, so the faithful get the sanctification of Christ through our sanctification. Seeing this goal reached, the last outburst of Our Lord's sacerdotal soul was: "It is achieved" (JOHN 19:30). The tens of thousands of lambs who shed their blood as types were no longer needed. The Lamb of God had immolated Himself. Every priest must perform a like act of self-oblation, and then pass on its fruits to the whole people: "Do this for a commemoration of me" (LUKE 22:19).

The specific thing Christ directed every priest to repeat and renew was the sacramental symbol of His death. The living out of this death is sanctification.

But why must the Cross be taken up daily? Because there is a ransom price on every soul. Some of them cost much. They require a great sacrifice. It is not that Christ withholds His Mercy, but that He has willed to dispense it through our hands. And unless the hands of the priest are scarred hands, Christ's mercies do not so readily pass through them. Blessings, power, healing, influence get clogged by worldliness.

The Church makes no impression in the world so long as those outside see it only as a "sect" or an "organization" or "one of the great religions." Our Lord made His impact through His Cross (JOHN 12:32). The wounded Christ redeemed; and only a wounded Church can effectively apply that Redemption. When the Church is making progress, where conversions are numerous, there Christ is poor again, tired again from missionary journeys, a victim once again in His saintly priests.

Every worldly priest hinders the growth of the Church; every saintly priest promotes it. If only all priests realized how their holiness makes the Church holy, and how the Church begins to decline when the level of holiness among priests falls below that of the people! God still thunders to His priests:

> I have set watchmen, Jerusalem, upon thy walls, that shall never cease crying aloud, day or night; you that keep the Lord in remembrance, take no rest, nor let Him rest neither, till He has restored Jerusalem, spread her fame over all the earth. ISAIAS 62:6,7

Watchmen are we, who have been put on the walls of the Church by the High Priest. Day and night we must pray and preach without ceasing so as to merit the description given by St. Augustine: *"aut precantes aut praedicantes."*

Our dedication to the people is not only on Sundays, or at Mass once a day, or hearing confessions on Saturdays. We are told to do two things: (1) "Take no rest"—strange as it may seem. No chairs! Remember? (2) "Give God no rest." Did we ever tell a beggar who wanted money, "Ask me for it when I cross the street; if I do not give it to you, follow me and seize my coat; if that does not get you what you want, throw a stone at my window at midnight." But God does say: "Wrestle with me, as Jacob did. Give me no rest." Like the importunate widow who aroused the judge, so we are to cry to the Priest-Victim in the face of the enemies of the Church:

> Give me redress against one who wrongs me. LUKE 18:3

> I tell you, even if he will not bestir himself to grant it out of friendship, shameless asking will make him rise and give his friend all that he needs. LUKE 11:8

What we are, the Church is; what the Church is, the world is. The world and all it contains is finally a highway on which the Bride, the Church, goes to meet the Bridegroom for the heavenly nuptials. Politics does not ultimately determine war and peace. What is decisive is the spiritual state of the Church living in and leavening the world. To read the Old Testament is to recognize that history is the hand of the Lord who blesses and punishes nations according to their deserts. What we do to sanctify ourselves sanctifies the world. When the shepherd is lazy, the sheep are hungry; when he sleeps, they are lost; when he is corrupt, they grow sick; when he is unfaithful, they lose their judgment. If the shepherd is not willing to be a victim for his sheep, the wolves come and devour them.

Each morning we priests hold in our hands the Christ Who shed blood from His veins, tears from His eyes, sweat from His Body to sanctify us. How we should be on fire with that love, that we may enkindle it in others!

Do we suffer for the wandering sheep? Do we warm ourselves by a fire talking to maidservants as Peter did, while the Lord is crucified again in the souls of sinners? Do we adopt an intransigent position with the enemies of the Church, forgetting that a Saul was made a Paul? We dress in black; but it is not to mourn Christ, for He has conquered. We are in mourning for those who bar their doors against our knock, for those still unwilling to believe though one should rise daily from the dead, for those who reach us vinegar as we cry "Sitio!" (JOHN 19:28). Night and day, giving God no rest, we will utter over and over again:

> I dedicate Myself for their sakes, that they too may be dedicated through the truth.
> JOHN 17:19

## HOLY CHRISTIANS GUARANTEE HOLY PRIESTS

Holiness descends in the Church from the all Holy God through Christ, His bishops and His priests, to the entire community which is the Mystical Body. But there is simultaneously an ascending movement of holiness from the Christian community to the all Holy God. Particularly is this true of vocations to the priesthood and the religious life.

There is no priest who does not go through the motions of urging the faithful to pray for vocations. But too often, the phrases are formal. They are what is expected of one. In the priest's mind, they are a part of the announcements, on a level with the card party for the Ladies Auxiliary or the CYO skating meet.

These other activities are, of course, not to be sneered at. They, too, foster a Christian life and therefore stimulate vocations. But can we put them in the same category as prayer? Out of hundreds of possible ways of fostering vocations, prayer was the single one Our Lord specified:

> The harvest, He told them, is plentiful enough, but the laborers are few; you must ask the Lord to Whom the harvest belongs to send laborers out for the harvesting.
> LUKE 10:2

What prompted these words? Luke says that Christ spoke them on the occasion of choosing seventy-two disciples (LUKE 10:1). Matthew sketches the background in more detail. It was after a long journey, he noted, and the Lord's heart was touched by compassion for the masses who hungered for knowledge of heaven but did not know where to search for what they lacked:

> Yet still, when He looked at the multitudes, He was moved with pity for them, seeing them harried and abject, like sheep that have no shepherd. Thereupon He said to His disciples, The harvest is plentiful enough, but the laborers are few; you must ask the Lord to Whom the harvest belongs to send laborers out for the harvesting.
> MATTHEW 9:36,37,38

Not only those already in the Church but equally those outside it make Him yearn for laborers, lest the plentiful wheat rot in the fields.

His compassion for the multitude was twofold. Because they were hungry, He miraculously fed the five thousand. Because their souls suffered, sheep without a shepherd, He was moved with pity.

Every true priest has the same heart-tearing pity as he flies over a great city, Paris, New York or London. Down below he sees with Christ's eyes millions of souls unfed by the Eucharist, unhealed by penance, living in houses built on sand because they know not the Rock. He sees in them what Our Lord saw when He looked at the multitudes—danger of eternal loss! Here are countless acres ripe for harvesting, but how few the laborers to gather!

Our Lord indicates that this harvest of souls is convertible. He is enthusiastic about the prospects of winning souls, and His words are intended to project that enthusiasm to His priests. He made a similar expression of confident anticipation when the crowds streamed out of Samaria to hear His words:

> Why, lift up your eyes, I tell you, and look at the fields, they are white with the promise of harvest already.  JOHN 4:35

As wheat does not oppose the sickle, so the masses will not oppose us. One wonders if we do not underestimate the possibility of conversions. The failure may simply be in our defective preparation and approach. The unbelievers will not go to hear philosophers, but they will go to hear saints. Priests who work in the slums amid the outcasts report that they rarely meet with an insult. Like the wheat, the masses will bend only before a certain kind of harvester. Not finding us as we should be, they turn their backs on us. But when they encounter a priest whose life expresses the message he brings, they are ready to be harvested.

What Our Lord asked us to pray for was laborers. He did not say: "My Father is Almighty; He can make the few accomplish much." He knew the extent of His Father's power, but He was also one with His Father in the divine plan to sanctify man with the aid of human means. In the Incarnation, His human nature was instrumentum conjunctum divinitatis. In the prolongation of His Incarnation, He uses us as instruments. Though He could reap the harvest without men, He will not.

But only laborers and not idlers are acceptable instruments. The priest must study to perfect his mind, not wearying the people with stale repetitions. It is true that "words will be given you when the time comes" (MATTHEW 10:19); but what Our Lord here promised was not inspiration for those who do not prepare their message, but the help of the Spirit for those persecuted beyond human resource. In the designs of Providence, the gift of final perseverance may depend for a priest not only on the amount of evil he has done, but on the good he has left undone.

The laborers must go into the harvest fields, to the masses, to the unbelievers, to the abandoned, the rudderless. Is it not possible that the Lord withholds many vocations from dioceses and mission societies because of the growing use of priests in strictly secular activities? Why specifically does God call a man to the priesthood? It is not easy to justify the placing of a priest in insurance, building, accountancy, banking, publicity and promotion, when the need is so grave for convert-makers, for missioners to search out the lost sheep and lead them gently to the fold of Christ. Do we lack dedicated and reliable laymen able to do such tasks as well or better? If the Lord was so particular about the fragments of bread, which He ordered gathered up, then will He not insist jealously that His priests do precisely that for which He called them?

Why did Our Lord, when He spoke of vocations, single out precisely the word, "Pray!"? Because prayer is the expression of the Christian community and the yearning of the Church. As the Church gets the kind of Pope she deserves, so she gets the kind and number of priests she deserves. Why do Ireland and Holland have so many vocations? Because the Catholic people of these small but intense countries, rich in their faith, want priests, and they pray to be given the priests they want. Why do some countries have so few? Because few people, even few parents, pray for priests. "Ask, and the gift will come" (LUKE 11:9). Can we hope to receive, if we do not ask? There are probably hundreds of thousands of vocations hanging from heaven on silken cords; prayer is the sword that cuts them. The laborers are available potentially in the Heart of Christ; it is our petitions that actualize them. "... And I was never consulted?" (ISAIAS 30:2).

Are there prayers in Church for vocations? Do mothers pray for vocations for their children? Do the faithful pray the Lord "to send laborers out for the harvesting" (MATTHEW 9:38)? Do school children pray for the call of God?

What the Christian community wants ardently, the Lord of the Harvest will grant. That is why Our Lord told us to pray. The command was intended for all, but it was given directly and specifically to the apostles and the disciples, as His ambassadors and co-workers among the people. Prayer in the Church is alone primary; publicity and its methods are secondary. The search for vocations begins on our knees. One bishop had no candidates for the priesthood in two years. He began a campaign of prayer in the schools of his diocese, and without any other publicity he had activated forty vocations at the end of one year.

The original Greek word (ἐκβάλλω) for "sending" laborers into the fields is stronger than the Latin (MATTHEW 9:38). It means that the Lord of the harvest would thrust them out, or propel them forward. The same Greek word is used by MATTHEW (8:31) for the expulsion of a devil out of a man (though different words are used in describing the incident in MARK 5:8 and LUKE 8:29); it takes a great power to drive the priesthood into a man. This power Our Lord said He would exercise, if we prayed. It even suggests that from totally unexpected and impossible places, He would inspire vocations.

## Effect On Community On Saintliness Or Sinfulness

Every slightest failing on our part brings the community under the judgment of God. Every least increase of priestly virtue brings it blessing.

When the Israelites took Jericho (JOSUE 6:1-21), God ordered that the city be destroyed and its wealth given to Him as the fruit of victory. But one Israelite disobeyed. Yielding to temptation, Achan appropriated to himself a garment and some precious ornaments, violating the Divine command (JOSUE 7:1). Later, when Josue was routed in battle, the Lord revealed that the reason for his defeat was the secret sin of Achan. The evil of one brought destruction and death on his entire community.

Personal sins, even the most secret, have repercussions on all the Church. A cut finger pains the whole man. The ripple caused by a stone thrown into a pond touches every point on the shore. A hidden violation of Christ's law by any of His members reverberates through and disturbs the equilibrium of the entire Mystical Body.

Josue, under the inspiration of God ordered the destruction of Achan and the stolen goods:

> And there Josue said, Thou hast brought trouble on us, and now it is the Lord's turn to bring trouble on thee. JOSUE 7:25

Now, if the sin of one layman so affected the ecclesia of Israel, how much more must the failings of one priest affect the ecclesia Dei! But the influence of one good soul, one saint, works to the good of the whole community. God was willing to spare Sodom and Gomorrah for the sake of a few just men. Abraham stopped at ten and the cities were destroyed (GENESIS 18:16-19528). But God does not necessarily stop at ten. Blessings, vocations and conversions abound, and judgments are averted, because of the few who are good. For Jacob's sake, God multiplied the flocks of Laban (GENESIS 30:27). Out of respect for Joseph, God prospered the house of Potiphar (GENESIS 39:5). The wicked city of Segor was saved because of the prayer of Lot:

> Once again, said he, I yield to Thy entreaty; I will not overthrow the city Thou pleadest for. GENESIS 19:21

Because of Paul, 276 souls were saved in a violent storm at sea (ACTS 27:24,34).

Before God sent Jerusalem into captivity as a punishment, He told Jeremias that one good man would save it:

> Go the rounds of Jerusalem, search the streets of it with hue and cry; and if you find one man there that faithfully does his duty, and keeps troth, then the city shall be pardoned. JEREMIAS 5:1

After He had inflicted judgment on Jerusalem, He gave the reason:

> Who would close the breach, intercede with Me to spare the land from ruin? Never a man was found! What wonder if I have poured out My vengeance, burnt them up in My anger? It was but their deserts I gave them, says the Lord God. EZECHIEL 22:30,31

Finally, when the Last Judgment comes, the days of vengeance,

> there would have been no human creature, if the number of those days had not been cut short; but those days will be cut short, for the sake of the elect. MATTHEW 24:22

It could well be that God's wrath—and let us not forget that the Apocalypse (6:16) speaks of ira Agni—is withheld from cities because of saintly souls among the clergy and the religious and the laity. God could not strike as long as Moses stood between Him and the people.

> So the Lord relented, and spared His people the punishment He had threatened. EXODUS 32:14

What converts could prayer win in Mission lands! The materialism of Japan would fragment, like the shell of an egg, to reveal the life within, did we but pray for Japan.

How slight would be the sacrifice, yet how much would it mean to the Vicar of Christ, if every priest who lives in comfort sent even a few of his Mass stipends to the Holy Father through his Society for the Propagation of the Faith!

O blessed intercessors are we! The salt of the earth! The lights of the world! Without good men, the world would be corrupted and in darkness. We sanctify ourselves not for us as individuals but for all as God's people. We do not save our soul alone; either we save it in the context of our neighbors and of the Mystical Body, or we lose it. No cell of my body can live normally outside my body, but my body can live without any given individual cell. In toto Christo we live and work.

To neglect intercession is to sin against God.

> Never may I offend the Lord by ceasing to pray for you, and pointing you to the good paths, the right paths. I KINGS 12:23

If we priests lack a heart to sigh and cry for the abominations and miseries of others, great is our reason to fear for ourselves. We cannot speak of unbroken fellowship with Our Lord without unbroken fellowship with the Church and the world.

> God has proved His love to us by laying down His life for our sakes; we too must be ready to lay down our lives for the sake of our brethren.
> I JOHN 3:16

## Choosing Candidates For The Priesthood

Since the holiness of the priest in God's designs makes the Church holy, those who seek the priesthood but are wanting in holiness must be purged.

> Have you never been told that a little leaven is enough to leaven the whole batch? Rid yourselves of the leaven which remains over, so that you may be a new mixture, still uncontaminated as you are.
> I CORINTHIANS 5:6,7

When public relations techniques are used to promote vocations, with advertising in religious publications and direct mailings designed to encourage young people to join a given society or community, the danger is always present that stress will be placed on numbers to the neglect of quality. St. Thomas insists that the weeding out of the unfit is an obligation of those charged with the selection of candidates.

Deus numquam ita deserit Ecclesiam suam quin inveni-antur idonei ministri sufficienter ad necessitatem plebis, si digni promoverentur et indigni repellerentur. Et sic non posset tot ministros inveniri, quot modo sunt, melius est habere paucos ministros bonos quam multos malos (Supp. q. 36, art. 4, ad I).

One cannot fail to be struck by the symbolic significance of the instructions God gave Gideon to identify the shock troops of his army:

> Separate those who lap the water like dogs, and those who go down on their knees to drink. JUDGES 7:5

And who were marked for elimination? Those who made themselves comfortable by lying flat on the ground and drinking leisurely. And who were taken?

> But the Lord said to Gideon, These three hundred men who lapped the water shall win you deliverance. JUDGES 7:7

Great truths are revealed to and placed in the custody of the few who are dedicated to the battle of faith. The imposing appearance of great numbers may blind us to the need for God's help, may make us overlook the necessity of training seminarians to be priest-victims. Hence the advice of St. Paul to Timothy:

> As for the imposition of hands, do not bestow it inconsiderately, and so share the blame for the sins of others. I TIMOTHY 5:22

To present candidates for ordination without due judgment, is to risk being held responsible for the subsequent defaults of those who fail the great High Priest. The priest must, therefore, avoid the methods of the world in promoting vocations. It is possible to win customers in business by publicity techniques, but vocations require a different approach. We may never be many, we may never be wise in the eyes of the world, but whatever we do must be done through the foolishness of the Cross.

> Consider, brethren, the circumstances of your own calling; not many of you are wise, in the world's fashion, not many powerful, not many well born.... no human creature was to have any ground for boasting, in the presence of God. I CORINTHIANS 1:26,29

## Value Of Prayers For Vocations In The Family

Every family is a church within a church. "Greet the brethren at Laodicea, and Nymphas, with the church that is in his household" (COLOSSIANS 4:15).

The classic example of the prayers of a mother for a vocation is Anna. Anna was barren. "Why had the Lord denied her motherhood?" (I KINGS 1:5). She promised God that if He would send her a son, she would consecrate him to God as a priest. In prayer, three times she humbly called herself the handmaid of the Lord, addressing Him as the "Lord of hosts" (I KINGS 1:11). The Magnificat hearkens back to the prayer of Anna. So fervently did she pray, that Heli the high priest thought she was drunk saying: "Wilt thou always be at thy cups? Give thy stomach a rest from the wine that so bemuses thee" (I KINGS 1:14).

Anna, however, was not drunk. She was only pouring out her soul to the Lord (I KINGS 1:15). In due time, her prayer was answered and she called the son Samuel, "in token that he was a gift she had won from the Lord" (I KINGS 1:20).

Anna had not just asked for a son, but a son whom she might dedicate to God. She puts him at the service of the temple where "as he grew he advanced in favour both with God and with men" (I KINGS 2:26). Later, there was a formal unfolding of Samuel's vocation, when three times "the Lord's call came to Samuel" (I KINGS 3:4). Each time Samuel thought it was Heli who called, running to him each time saying:

> I am coming, he answered; then ran to find Heli, and said, I am here at thy summons.... Till then, Samuel was a stranger to the Divine voice; the Lord had not made any revelation to him.   I KINGS 3:5,7

Samuel mistook God's voice for Heli's, but Heli told him the next time he heard the voice to say: "Speak on, Lord; thy servant is listening" (I KINGS 3:9).

God calls His servants to tasks which are manifested only by degrees. Too often we say: "Tell me first what you want me to do, and I will see whether I want to." But the advice of the old priest to Samuel was "Put yourself in God's hands. He will show you your work." St. Paul was told to go to Damascus and his vocation would be revealed. When we open our ears, God opens His lips. We know God's truth when we do His will. Later on Samuel was called to re-create Israel as Moses had created it.

The point of the story is that a vocation comes through prayer, often that of a mother, even when all seems hopeless. In a survey of a group of seminarians, three out of four indicated that their mothers were a major inspiration in the development of their vocation. St. Paul had already noted the influence of a mother and a grandmother in fostering the vocation of Timothy.

> That faith dwelt in thy grandmother Lois, and in thy mother Eunice, before thee; I am fully persuaded that it dwells in thee too.
> II TIMOTHY 1:5

St. Paul praises the faith of this young priest and finds the instrumental cause in a pious family background. It was the third generation of this faithful family which bore the fruit of a vocation. Origen conjectured that they were relatives of St. Paul. Like the celebrated mothers of Augustine, Chrysostom and Basil, and like the mother of many a priest today, their sincerity and unfeigned faith produced a heritage for the Church. Lord Shaftesbury once said: "Give me a generation of Christian mothers and I will change the face of the earth in twelve months."

The decay of the home is often blamed for the fewness of vocations in our times. While this is true, forget not Christian homes! We can too easily become like Elias bemoaning the corruption of Israel.

> See how the sons of Israel have forgotten Thy covenant, thrown down Thy altars, and put Thy prophets to the sword! Of these, I only am left, and now my life, too, is forfeit.
> III KINGS 19:14

The Lord told him, nevertheless, that he had been more faithful than he suspected:

> Yet I mean to leave Myself seven thousand men out of all Israel; knees that have never bowed to Baal.
> III KINGS 19:18

There is much good, did we but seek it out. What Pascal said applies equally to vocations and to converts: "There are only two classes of men who can be called rational—those who serve God with all their hearts because they know Him, and those who seek Him wholeheartedly because they know Him not."[2] We can easily be too severe on others. When

---

[2] Pascal's pensees, "Apology," No. 2106, translated by H. F. Steward, D.D., Pantheon Books, Inc., 1950

James and John suggested to Christ that He punish the Samaritans who would not receive Him, they drew this rebuke:

> You do not understand, He said, what spirit it is you share. The Son of Man has come to save men's lives, not to destroy them.
>
> LUKE 9:55

Few are the priests whose level of service to their flocks is such as to merit the tribute paid by the Galatians to St. Paul, when they described him "as God's angel, as Christ Jesus" (GALATIANS 4:14); but the opportunity is at every moment present for every priest to feel his greatness and his littleness, his power and his nothingness.

> O sacerdosl Tu quis es?
> Non es a te, quia de nihilo.
> Non es ad te, quia es mediator ad Deum.
> Non es tibi, quia soli Deo vivere debes.
> Non es tui, quia es omnium servus.
> Non es tu, quia alter Christus es.
> Quid ergo es? Nihil et omnia,
> o sacerdosl.

# CHAPTER 5

# THE HOLY SPIRIT AND THE PRIEST

SINCE the priest is an alter Christus, he must know the role the Spirit played in Christ's life.

At every moment of His life on earth, the Savior was completely under the guidance of the Spirit. Even as the breath of God stirred over the waters in the first dawn of creation and the Lord said, "Let there be light" (GENESIS 1:3), so did the Spirit inspire Mary in the very moment of the Incarnation.

> The Holy Spirit will come upon thee, and the power of the most High will overshadow thee. Thus this holy offspring of thine shall be known for the Son of God.   LUKE 1:35

At His Baptism, there was seen:

> The Spirit like a dove, coming down and resting upon Him.
>    MARK 1:10

> He returned from the Jordan full of the Holy Spirit and by the Spirit He was led on into the wilderness, where He remained forty days, tempted by the devil.   LUKE 4:1,2

While the chords of His Heart are still vibrating in response to a voice from heaven, He is summoned by the Spirit into the wilderness. Was not Saul, in the morning of his life in Christ, sent for three years to Arabia? Is not character compacted through struggle direct and personal, with the forces of both good and evil? No one shall be crowned unless he has struggled. He was led, by the Spirit's direction, into a wilderness for a trial. As Moses in Median, as David around Bethlehem, as Elias around Horeb, so the Spirit draws the Savior into retreat. David must meet Goliath alone before he can meet the hosts of the Philistines. Each priest must first win the spiritual victory alone and within himself, before he can repeat that victory in the lives of others.

Next, the endowments for His mission on earth were communicated to Him from the same source. As Isaias foretold:

> One shall be born, on whom the Spirit of the Lord will rest; a Spirit wise and discerning, a Spirit prudent and strong, a Spirit of knowledge and of piety, and ever fear of the Lord shall fill His heart.
> ISAIAS 11:2,3

After He had put the tempter to flight, He returned to His home town of Nazareth and in the synagogue He read the appointed lesson of the day, paraphrasing ISAIAS (61:1,2), and showing by His first words that His every action, especially His preaching, was the work of the Spirit. He had emerged from the conflict, not weakened but strengthened.

> The Spirit of the Lord is upon Me; He has anointed Me, and sent Me out to preach the gospel to the poor, to restore the broken-hearted; to bid the prisoners go free, and the blind have sight; to set the oppressed at liberty, to proclaim a year when men may find acceptance with the Lord, a day of retribution.
> LUKE 4:18,19

Later on, it is by the Spirit that He vanquishes the mightiest of foes:

> When I cast out devils, I do it through the Spirit of God.
> MATTHEW 12:28

Evil is conquered by the Spirit, not by complaining and ranting. And to attribute such victory to any other power is blasphemy against the Spirit. Then comes the role of the Spirit in the Crucifixion—a sublime truth often forgotten.

> ... the blood of Christ, who offered Himself, through the Holy Spirit, as a victim.
> HEBREWS 9:14

He is both Priest and Sacrifice, through the Spirit, Who alone makes that unity, either in Him or in us. It is also the Spirit which gives the sacrifice an eternal efficacy. The Spirit helps us over the difficulty created by the fact that Our Lord's sacrifice took place on a hill, and yet belongs to a heavenly sanctuary. It is the Spirit, independent of time and place, which makes our daily renewal of Calvary possible.

The Spirit too played a role in His Resurrection and descent into Limbo.

> In His mortal nature He was done to death, but endowed with fresh life in His Spirit, and it was in His Spirit that He went and preached to the spirits who lay in prison.         I PETER 3:18,19

The same Holy Spirit is operative in communicating the merits of Redemption to mankind, and particularly through the priesthood. Even the pre-announcement of our salvation was effected through the Spirit. St. Peter looking back on all of the prophecies says that they looked forward to Christ through the Spirit:

> Salvation was the aim and quest of the prophets, and the grace of which they prophesied has been reserved for you. The Spirit of Christ was in them, making known to them the sufferings which Christ's cause brings with it, and the glory that crowns them; when was it to be, and how was the time of it to be recognized?
>         I PETER 1:10,11

Thanks to the Spirit, the prophets pre-announced Christ; thanks to the Spirit, the Apostles reported Him. Those who have the Spirit know Christ to be the center of the universe; that all history up to the moment of the Incarnation looked to Him, and that all history since the moment of the Ascension is a preparation for His second coming. Some modern scholars find only a "myth" in the Scriptures; Peter bids us recognize in them the Spirit. As the Spirit functioned in announcing Christ, so the Spirit functions in continuing Christ. The night of the Last Supper, Our Lord told His priests that the Father would send the Spirit in His name (JOHN 14:26). After the Resurrection, He breathed on them saying:

> Receive the Holy Spirit.         JOHN 20:22

It almost seems that in the mystery of Redemption, each Person of the Blessed Trinity hides behind the other. The Son hides behind the Father, for it is the Son Who reveals the Father. Similarly, we would never know the Love of the Father, if He had not sent His Spirit. The Son in turn, hides behind the Holy Spirit, for it is through the Holy Spirit that we understand that Jesus is the Lord. Jesus Himself insisted on this aspect. He stressed that it was the Holy Spirit who would reveal Him.

At the Last Supper, Our Lord explained the role of the Holy Spirit in the lives of His priests. He had just been telling His disciples that they would be persecuted as He was persecuted. Now He tells them that though the Spirit would not manifest Himself visibly in a human form, as He had done, the Spirit would make them understand what He, Jesus, had said to them:

> Well, when the truth-giving Spirit, who proceeds from the Father, has come to befriend you, He whom I will send to you from the Father's side, He will bear witness of what I was. JOHN 15:26

It is the Spirit who tells the priest the whole scope of his work as days roll on, as new problems arise, and as new enemies hate. New dimensions of meaning in Christ's life, of which we never dreamed before, will become clear. This inner witness of Christ's depth and worth will be our support in a hostile world. Our grasp of the Life of Christ will not be confined within the narrow limits of Bethlehem and Jerusalem.

> And He will bring honor to Me, because it is from Me that He will derive what He makes plain to you. JOHN 16:14

To glorify or honor Christ means to manifest His hidden excellence when His human nature was admitted into the full participation of the power and glory of the Father. This the human mind cannot conceive or apprehend; to enter into this mystery is the work of the Spirit of the Glorified Christ.

Those who say they want only the "Jesus of the Gospels" forget that the Gospels speak of the full revelation of Our Lord through His Spirit. He proclaimed the very incompleteness of His words, insisting that fuller knowledge would come later.

Had Our Lord remained on earth, He would have been just an example to be copied. By abandoning the earth for heaven, He becomes a life to be lived. That is why it was better that He should go.

## The Spirit Reveals Christ

A priest often meets a man, a good man, but one to whom God has not given the priceless gift of faith. That man will evaluate Jesus Christ.

He will be fair to Him within the limitations of his own human judgment. Christ was a great thinker and a holy man, he will say, equating Him with Buddha, Confucius, Socrates and Plato. St. Paul, however, tells us:

> It is only through the Holy Spirit that anyone can say, Jesus is the Lord.  I CORINTHIANS 12:3

They who have not the Spirit call him "a great man," "a teacher," "a master"; but to see Him as the Lord of heaven and earth, as the Son of the Living God, comes only through the Holy Spirit.

This being so, may it not be that our failure to read the Scriptures, to preach redemption, to inspire converts, to give better spiritual direction, to convert sinners, is because we have not sufficiently pondered and absorbed the counsels given us by the Lord at the Last Supper?

Why do some feel uncomfortable in the Presence of God? Is it because of an excessive love of comfort, a spirit of envy and jealousy, a pleasure in their status as clerics, a kind of sword-activism in place of prayer and watching? May this want of the Spirit of Christ not explain a reluctance to appear more often and more joyously in His Eucharistic Presence? Would not a person who hated mathematics be unhappy at a convention of mathematicians? The soul that hated truth (to speak in inadequate human terms) would suffer more in heaven than in hell; analogically speaking, the want of the Spirit of Christ makes us shrink from His companionship.

> Tryst there must be, if friends will meet and journey together.
> AMOS 3:3

The priest must not postpone this union with the Holy Spirit to a more convenient season (ACTS 24:25). If he neglects growth, decay sets in. There comes a time when it is too late to repent, even to ask for a drop of water to "cool my tongue" (LUKE 16:24).

Baptism makes every Christian a new creature and an ambassador of Heaven. Ordination intensifies these spiritual attributes in the priest. But though we dispense holiness, we are not automatically holy. It is the Spirit who makes us more priestly day by day, because He takes the things of Christ and reveals them to us, bringing to remembrance all the words of Christ (JOHN 16:14; 14:26). Becoming a holy priest is not completed the day of ordination, nor do the blessings of the Spirit flow to us without great effort on our part. We are "workers together with God." We stand in need of knowledge if we are to communicate it to others, if we are to bring our bodily appetites into subjection (I CORINTHIANS 7:29-31), and if we are to be patient under the pressure of work, loving every human being with that charity which flows from the consciousness that Our Lord died for them too. All these qualities are progressive, and it was one who himself had made that uphill fight who best expressed what it means:

> And you too have to contribute every effort on your own part, crowning your faith with virtue, and virtue with enlightenment, and enlightenment with continence, and continence with endurance, and endurance with holiness, and holiness with brotherly love, and brotherly love with charity. Such gifts, when they are yours in full measure, will make you quick and successful pupils, reaching ever closer knowledge of our Lord Jesus Christ; he who lacks them is no better than a blind man feeling his way about; his old sins have been purged away, and he has forgotten it. Bestir yourselves then, brethren, ever more eagerly, to ratify God's calling and choice of you by a life well lived. II PETER 1:5-10

## THE ROLE OF THE HOLY SPIRIT IN INTENSIFYING CONFLICT

Every priest, though ordained to be a Peter, retains within him the frailty of the Simon-nature. St. Paul describes the resulting civil war between Peter and Simon.

> Inwardly, I applaud God's disposition, but I observe another disposition in my lower self, which raises war against the disposition of my conscience, and so I am handed over as a captive to that disposition towards sin which my lower self contains. Pitiable creature that I am, who is to set me free from a nature thus doomed to death? Nothing else than the grace of God, through Jesus Christ our Lord. If I am left to myself, my conscience is at God's disposition, but my natural powers are at the disposition of sin. ROMANS 7:22-25

Even before Paul, Plato had observed that there is a war in each of us against himself. Anyone who does not take up the sword against that lower nature is destroyed by it. Sin first takes possession of the flesh; and once entrenched there, it attacks the mind and finally displaces it from its position of authority.

A man may have priestly powers and yet be governed by nature, for the grace of ordination does not destroy the flesh:

> To live the life of nature is to think the thoughts of nature; to live the life of the Spirit is to think the thoughts of the Spirit; and natural wisdom brings only death, whereas the wisdom of the Spirit brings life and peace.
>
> ROMANS 8:5,6

The priest is like a mountain climber. The Holy Spirit bids him go higher, but below him are the abysses. What the Holy Spirit does in the soul of a priest is not only to make him more aware of the conflict within himself, but also to make him more conscious of sin. Divine grace does not so act as to prevent a man absolutely from sinning, but the Spirit takes the fun out of it. It is not possible for a priest to love a human being with the full powers of his soul, precisely because he has already fallen in love with the Perfect, namely, Christ through His Spirit. All other love is dissatisfying and bitter.

A sin committed by a priest, consequently, pains him more intensely than does the same sin to one not a priest. This is because of the greater gift of the Spirit. Imagine two men marrying two shrews who were identical in their disgruntled nature. One had enjoyed the love of a beautiful and devoted wife who died; the other was married for the first time.

Which of the two suffers the more? Obviously the one who knew before the better love. So with the priest. Having enjoyed the ecstasy of the Spirit of Love, he can never be satisfied with human substitutes.

At the Last Supper Our Lord told those He had chosen as His first priests how the Spirit would intensify the conflict.

> He will come, and it will be for Him to prove the world wrong, about sin ...
>
> JOHN 16:8

No man really understands sin who thinks of it merely as the breaking of the law. This is a defect which results from basing moral theology exclusively upon the Commandments. To do so is to develop in the young an attitude which makes them ask, "Is this a mortal or a venial sin? How far can I go without committing grievous sin?" The full understanding of sin comes only through the Holy Spirit, and until He enlightens the soul, it is blind to our sinfulness. No matter how great our powers of reasoning, we can produce real conviction of sin only through the Spirit.

But what does the Spirit do in the soul? Our Lord said the Holy Spirit would convict men of sin because "they have not found belief in Me" (JOHN 16:9). By not believing in Him, men crucified Him. Hence, it is the crucifix that brings to the soul the profound consciousness of guilt. It becomes for each his autobiography. The skin of Christ is the parchment, His Blood the ink, the nails the pen. There we see written the story of our life. This close relationship between the sense of sin and the crucifix enabled St. Peter to win three thousand souls for the Lord on the day of Pentecost. He reminded his hearers that they had crucified Christ (ACTS 2:36). To sin against faith thus means to refuse to believe in Christ to the point of rejecting and crucifying Him.

> Unless the Spirit has mastery in this war of Simon and Peter, the priest remains but a child in the nursery, not an ambassador in the sanctuary. The Lord gives him milk, as St. Paul gave the Corinthians not meat; you were not strong enough for it.... Nature still lives in you.                                                I CORINTHIANS 3:2

As some acorns sprout, yet never become great oaks, so some ordinations make only spiritual saplings, not trees planted by the waters of life. The spiritually undeveloped priest has two characteristics:

1. A protracted infancy. There is a full assent to the Creed, but there is wanting the beauty of priestly holiness through the indwelling of God's Spirit. Because of this long infancy, there is a continual oscillation of sin and amendment, of failure and re-establishment in grace, of pettiness and the domination of the priest-state. There is a confession of individual sins, but no facing up to the fact that he is presuming on God's mercy and that he is living in a worldly state. The flesh is the rule of life and not the Spirit.

2. The second mark of this carnal life is that it renders the priest unfit for receiving more spiritual truths; never being won away completely from the flesh, he never has that emptiness which is essential for receiving the Spirit. A man can be empty in soul like the Grand Canyon, but such emptiness is unprofitable. The fruitful kind of emptiness is that of a nest, which the dove of the Holy Spirit can fill, or the emptiness of a flute, through which the breath of the Holy Spirit can pipe the joyful tunes of being one with Christ.

## The Spirit
## And Reparation For Sins

Because the Holy Spirit deepens our sense of sin in relation to the Crucifixion, the practical result should be to engage the priest in constant reparation for his sins. The Epistle to the HEBREWS (5:3) bids the priest do precisely this; in our language, it tells him to offer Mass sometimes for himself. Our sins are more serious than the same sins in the laity, which is why God ordered greater sacrifices for priests. The ordinary people could offer a kid for their sins (LEVITICUS 4:28). Even a ruler of a nation could do the same. But the priest had to offer a bullock.

> Such a transgression, if it be committed by the high priest then in office, brings guilt upon the whole people, and he must make amends for it by offering to the Lord a young bullock without blemish.
> LEVITICUS 4:3

Responsibility is in proportion to privilege. The priest represents the people, and therefore his sin affects the whole Church. He is the embodiment of the people's sanctity as a community of worshippers.

It would be quite wrong to imagine that those who do not live by the Spirit do not experience remorse, or that conflict is absent from their lives. Sin which does not come out properly in confession to be washed away by contrition and absolution, often comes out abnormally in complexes, such as imputing evil motives to others, hypercriticism, or a love of distracting pleasures. Such a condition can easily lead to despair. The devil then pounces gleefully on his prey. The APOCALYPSE (12:10) calls the devil, "the accuser of our brethren." Before the sin, Satan assures us that it is of no consequence; after the sin, he persuades us that it is unforgivable. Before the sin, he represents himself as the friend of man urging him on to revolt; after the sin, he smothers the soul in a false belief that deliverance is impossible.

To doubt forgivness is the beginning of hell. Scripture tells us that Cain found no place for repentance, though with tears he sought it (GENESIS 4:13). Remorse, not contrition, brings unavailing tears, as it did to Saul over the loss of his kingship, Judas over the loss of his apostleship, and Cain over the loss of his apostleship. But the Holy Spirit sees guilt in relation to Calvary to give us urgent hope and then pardon, for on that hill we hear the cry:

> Father, forgive them; they do not know what it is they are doing.
> LUKE 23:34

This awakening of a sense of sin through the Spirit applies not only to the priest but to the faithful whom he shepherds. Sermons on hell fire awaken fear, but unless the Spirit is with the preacher, the fear is servile, not filial. Souls are led to repentance only through "the Sword of the Spirit, God's Word" (EPHESIANS 6:17). Now what does this Sword of the Spirit do in souls? It heightens the conflict between the body and soul, between the spirit of the world and the spirit of Christ.

> God's Word to us is something alive, full of energy; it can penetrate deeper than any two-edged sword, reaching the very division between soul and spirit, between joints and marrow, quick to distinguish every thought and design in our hearts. HEBREWS 4:12

Sinners are melted into contrition through the Spirit; they see the civil war in their own souls through the Spirit; the Spirit reveals the hidden sins which they hoped no one could detect; the Spirit shows that man is a fallen creature and needs power from on high. The Spirit will convince atheists of their unbelief. No evil can be crucified until it is recognized and diagnosed, and brought into the light. Self clothes itself in so many disguises that nothing but the Spirit can compel it to reveal its true sinful character. A priest with the Spirit of Christ will get a sinner to confession in circumstances in which the priest without the Spirit will fail. Scolding a sinner in the confessional may drive him away, but fitting him up in the Spirit of Christ will make of him a true penitent. Even a priest who is naturally a poor speaker can through the Spirit of Christ make his words effective beyond his orative talents:

> Human indeed we are, but it is in no human strength that we fight our battles. The weapons we fight with are not human weapons; they are divinely powerful, ready to pull down strongholds. Yes, we can pull down the conceits of men, every barrier of pride which sets itself up against the true knowledge of God; we make every mind surrender to Christ's service.... I CORINTHIANS 10:3-6

### THE SPIRIT AND LOVE OF SOULS

Every priest, when he goes before the Lord for judgment, will be asked: "Where are your children?" The vocation of the priest is primarily to beget souls in Christ. Shall we mount the pulpit and denounce unnatural birth control in the flesh, while we practice it in the spirit? Shall mothers be blamed for not having more children when our baptismal records show no souls begotten in Christ in years? The limits of our parish and the boundary of our duty are not the faithful alone, but "other sheep too, which do not belong to this fold" (JOHN 10:16). Every soul is our responsibility and many would enter the Church, did we but ask them. The error of many priests is that they are concerned more with the administrative than with the evangelical.

Do we organize for soul-saving with the same zeal as we organize for "drives"? When money is needed, a priest thinks nothing of organizing a door-to-door canvas; but how often does he make a door-to-door canvas for converts? Are we having our parish continually replenished by souls that come to tell what God has done for them? Where the Holy Spirit is, there are conversions:

> And each day the Lord added to their fellowship others that were to be saved.                                      ACTS 2:47

Our conversions per priest per year in the United States are fewer than three. But who among us does not know many who have left the One Fold and One Shepherd, because of broken vows, lust for a second or third marriage, sophomoric pride, or any one of the seven pallbearers of a soul, commonly called the seven capital sins? Do we have catechetical centers and use them to train the laity to be apostles and to live out the full responsibilities of the Sacrament of Confirmation? Every parish should be a nursery of souls that are not of the fold; every priest, a shepherd in search of lost sheep; every Mass, a proclamation that redemption must be spread to the world:

> What, cry they of Jacob, is the Lord so easily offended?
> MICHAEAS 2:7

Is the Holy Spirit less bountiful to save souls now than at Pentecost? Is the tenor of our priestly life holding in check those fires and mighty winds of conversion? Why do the Pentecostal fires burn so brightly in the mission lands and so feebly in our parish? Has the tide of the Spirit run out of our harbors? The fault is not in the Spirit, for "God does not repent of the gifts He makes" (ROMANS 11:29). The rushing of the mighty winds has not calmed and stilled itself into stagnancy or sterility. The Holy Spirit is still ready to overshadow our priesthood, so that we may bring forth those who are holy.

The priest acts from without, the Holy Spirit from within. We wish one another blessings; He gives blessings. He alone can plant in a heart, by His divine husbandry, the seed that will blossom into a "new creature in Christ" (II CORINTHIANS 5:17). The selfishness and sloth which make us shrink from searching for souls can be consumed by His Spirit. All round about us, in our parishes, in our daily contacts with men, are countless masses of souls that are like gold ingots covered with dross. And we, if we but had the fire of the Spirit, would burnish them into jewels of the Kingdom of God!

## Chapter 6

## The Spirit and Conversion

As the Spirit does not fail, but is given to those who ask, souls are no more difficult to convert now than at any other time. The approach must be different, as the approach to the Roman was different from that to the Jew. In psychological terms, every conversion starts with a crisis, moral or spiritual. The moral crisis begins with a moment or a situation involving some kind of suffering, physical, emotional or spiritual; with a dialectic, a tension, a pull, a duality, or a conflict. The crisis is accompanied, on the one hand, by a profound sense of one's own helplessness, and on the other hand, by an equally certain conviction that God alone can supply what the individual lacks.

If there were only a sense of helplessness, there would be despair, pessimism, eventual suicide. This is, indeed, the condition of the post-Christian pagan: he feels the total inadequacy of his own inner resources against the overwhelming odds of a cruel universe and falls into despair. He has one-half of the necessary condition for conversion— namely, a sense of crisis—but he fails to link up his powerlessness with the Divine Power which sustains and nourishes the soul. In such a situation, paganism gives place to what might be called creative despair: "despair," because the man recognizes his spiritual disease; "creative," because he knows that only a Divine Physician can bring healing.

The crisis of conversion is sometimes spiritual rather than moral. This is frequent among those who have been seeking perfection, but are not yet possessed of the fullness of the faith and sacraments. Some such souls have led a good life on the natural plane; they have been generous to the poor and kind to their neighbors and have furthered at least a vague fellowship with all peoples. Others have had a smattering of the supernatural life; they have led as Christ-like a life as they knew how, living up to faith in Him as they saw His light. The crisis in their souls begins at the moment when they either recognize that they have tremendous potentialities not yet exercised or begin to yearn for a religious life which will make greater demands on them.

Up to that moment of crisis, they have lived on the surface of their souls. The tension deepens as they realize that, like a plant, they have roots which need greater spiritual depths and branches meant for communion with the heavens above. The growing sense of dissatisfaction with their own ordinariness is accompanied by a passionate craving for surrender, sacrifice, and abandonment to God's will. The shift from mediocrity to love may be occasioned through the example of a saint, the inspiration of a spiritual book, the desire to escape from mere symbols to divine reality. However it comes, there is a duality present from the moment the soul hears Christ saying:

> But you are to be perfect, as your heavenly Father is perfect.
> MATTHEW 5:48

Conversion is the introduction of a new Spirit. The unconverted man has an incompatible spiritual Rh factor in his human nature, which is corruptive; it is overcome by making him "share the Divine Nature" (II PETER 1:4) through a blood infusion of Calvary and Pentecost. Conversion, therefore, is totally different from proselytism, which is only a change in group membership, or the putting on of a new label. But conversion is a μετάνοια, a change of character, the becoming a new man.

## THE SPIRIT MAKES CONVERTS, NOT US

The work of conversion is accomplished by the Holy Spirit, through the use of human means. The Spirit may place a rod in the hands of a shepherd. His action may induce an awareness of the absence of God in the soul, or it may create a sense of God's presence and of His actual grace working in the soul. In all instances, the Holy Spirit illumines the mind to see a truth not visible before, and strengthens the will to do things never before attempted. Job speaks of one way in which the Spirit touches the soul in suffering:

> Sometimes in visions of the night, when deep sleep falls upon men as they lie abed, He speaks words of revelation, to teach them the lesson

they need. This is one means by which He will turn a man away from his designs, purge him of his pride; and so the grave is disappointed, the sword misses its prey. Or else He will use the pains of the sickbed for a man's correction, and leave his whole frame wasted with disease.  JOB 33:15-19

The priest must never think that his preaching and zeal won the convert. Lydia listened to Paul, but the Scripture says,

and the Lord opened her heart so that she was attentive to Paul's preaching.  ACTS 16:15

Here was a woman already religious, described as a woman of prayer; yet her mind needed the tuition of the Holy Spirit in order to understand what she had heard. Incidentally, Lydia was the first convert in Europe and it was from her house that the evangelization of Europe began.

Sometimes the revelation of the Spirit is gradual, as with the woman at the well. She first called Our Lord a "Jew" (JOHN 4:9), then a "man" (JOHN 4:12), then a gentleman when she addressed Him as "Sir" (JOHN 4:15), then "a prophet" (JOHN 4:19), then the "Messias" (JOHN 4:25), and finally "Saviour of the world" (JOHN 4:42).

The jailer at Philippi was the second convert in Europe (ACTS 16:27-34), and he was moved by the Spirit through fear and through the word of Paul. The Ethiopian treasurer illustrates how the Holy Spirit directs a priest to one whose conversion is divinely willed:

The Spirit said to Philip, Go up to that chariot and keep close by it.  ACTS 8:29

The Ethiopian already had some concept of religion, for he was reading the fifty-third chapter of Isaias. The Holy Spirit moves even souls dedicated to sorcery and magic. Such souls in their darkness may be searching for the truth. A sorcerer named Elymas had tried to turn the Proconsul, Sergius Paulus, from the faith, the rudiments of which he had received through the preaching of Paul. "Then Saul, whose other name is Paul, filled with the Holy Spirit,..." (ACTS 13:8) blasted the sorcerer. Incidentally, this is the first time that the Scriptures give Saul the Roman name of Paul. Denouncing Elymas as a son of the devil, Paul struck him blind—his first miracle. One wonders if Paul recalled that he himself was struck blind at the time of his conversion. Was it in order that the temporary blindness might give light, as did his own?

Venerable Bede says, "The Apostle remembering his own case, knew that by the darkening of the eye, the mind's darkness might be restored to light." Sergius Paulus then became strengthened in his faith. It was the first appearance of Christianity before a Roman aristocrat and official.

No soul is beyond conversion. The Lord assures us through the prophet Joel that He will make good the bad years.

> Profitless years, when the locust ravaged you, Gnaw-all and Ruin-all and Spoiler, that great army of mine I let loose among you, they shall be made good. JOEL 2:25

Converting souls in keeping with our vocation to be "fishers of men" is not easy, because each catch takes its toll of effort. But losing is the condition of gaining in the realm of the Spirit. We never profit another without being "inwardly aware of the power" that has proceeded from us, as Our Lord was when He healed the woman with the issue of blood (MARK 5:30). But who are the energetic priests? Are they not the zealous priests? Nothing is as fatiguing as boredom. Filled with the Spirit of Christ, a priest working with souls is like the burning bush which was aflame, but did not burn out (EXODUS 3:2). Every exhaustion of spiritual energy by a priest creates a vacuum for a richer endowment of the Spirit, until souls become his passion:

> It is He Who gives the weary fresh Spirit, Who fosters strength and vigour where strength and vigour is none. ISAIAS 40:29

Every pastor should from time to time go through the baptismal record and see how many sheep have been brought to the Shepherd in the course of his ministry. How often does he find a name inscribed in the Book of Life with his own name listed in the column which reads: "Baptized by-------"? A parish can wither without converts for years, as for fifteen years the House of God lay unfinished, until God spoke to the people saying:

> The Lord of hosts bids you put heart into the work; is not He, the Lord of hosts, at your side? AGGAEUS 2:5

So in a parish without spiritual stone being added to spiritual stone, the Lord bids us work. There can be no work apart from strength. We supply the work, God the power. It is comfort that makes us shirk the work of conversion. We are clothed, but are we warmed by the fire of Pentecost? The wages we earn—are they put into a bag with holes, or are we laying up the richer treasury of souls and covering up the mountain of our own failings? Saving souls is the assurance of our salvation.

> My brethren, if one of you strays from the truth, and a man succeeds in bringing him back, let him be sure of this; to bring back erring feet into the right path means saving a soul from death, means throwing a veil over a multitude of sins. JAMES 5:19,20

We priests are only spiritual farmers; we till the soil, God drops the seed. We make no converts. We must never count up our converts or we will one day begin to think that we, not the Lord, made them. The same divine energy that wrought Creation and Redemption saves souls.

## THE SPIRIT AND INSTRUCTION

Instructing is not arguing. One can win an argument and lose a soul. The priest must be patient with bigots. If we believed the lies they believe about the Church, we would hate it a thousand times more than they.

The priest must try to discover if the objections against the faith expressed by an enquirer are in fact intellectual, or if instead they are basically moral, that is, if they are rooted in some improper behavior. So-called "reasons" are sometimes rationalizations to justify the way people live. It is important to find out not only what people say about Christ and His Church but why they say it. This was the technique used by Our Lord with the woman at the well. She introduced a theological problem when her real problem was a moral one, namely, her five husbands. He, nevertheless, did not cast her aside even though He saw through her presence. Instead, He showed her what her real problem was, and she was converted.

The priest's best approach to enquirers is neither to prove they are wrong, nor to prove that he is right, but simply to offer bread to the hungry and drink to the thirsty. Our Faith is the satisfaction of the soul's desire, not the didactic presentation of a syllogism. The priest must prepare himself carefully for every discussion with an enquirer. Before starting to instruct, he should spend an hour in thinking up analogies, examples, and answers to possible objections.

To save souls we must be holy. The Lord does not use dirty tools. How can we go to sinners if they say: "Physician, heal thyself" (LUKE 4:23)? Nor can we bid fallen-aways to return to the obedience they owe the Church if they are able to question our own way of living and acting:

> An errand these prophets ran, but none of Mine; a message they gave, but not of My sending. Privy to My design had they been, ah, then they should have uttered My own warnings, and so I might have turned My people aside from false paths, and erring thoughts!
>
> JEREMIAS 23:21,22

Instruction to the enquirer should be so formulated as to prove that we love what we believe. If we show little enthusiasm for the sublime truth we communicate, how shall the convert learn to love that truth?

## THE SPIRIT AND LOST SHEEP

Our love of souls must be persistent. We get used to reading the Parable of the Good Shepherd, but do we understand that for us priests it is a spelling out of our obligation to seek the lost sheep. Leaving a dinner, breaking an evening's entertainment, interrupting a siesta, all such efforts are summed up in leaving

> those ninety-nine others on the mountain-side, and go out to look for the one that is straying,
>
> MATTHEW 18:12

Nothing unspiritual is sacred in the face of a spiritual need.

Even the "banished" ones, those outside the Church through bad marriages, those who spurned the Sacred Heart though He spurned them not—are not these part of our ministry?

> Never a soul will God suffer to be lost in the reckoning; still He busies Himself with remedies to save the life of him who is banished.
>
> II KINGS 14:14

The banished son of the Church remains a son and the true priest grieves as long as he is away from his home. How many are the couples in invalid marriages who are ready to live as brother and sister, if only this possibility were properly presented to them? God's love is active on behalf of even the worst and the unworthiest of souls. Grace is given to many who were written off by priests of little faith, for God has said, "the sinner's death is none of My contriving!" (EZECHIEL 33:11). Is not God a Father and is not the priest a "father"? We must never imitate the elder brother who would not receive back the prodigal. Here were two sons who lost the Father's love: one because he was "too good" and the other because he was "too bad"; but the latter it was who found that love again (LUKE 15:11-32).

As His servants, we have confidence in His power:

There is a stronger power at work in you, than in the world.
I JOHN 4:4

Our zeal for conversions will go through three stages: a heavenly prayer, exhausting identification with others, and finally, the healing of the soul. St. Mark tells us (7:34) that Our Lord, when confronted with a deaf and dumb man, likewise performed the miracle of curing him in three steps. "... He looked up to heaven, and sighed; He said, Ephpheta, (that is, Be opened)."

The condition of all apostolate is a realization that Heaven grants it. To look in the first instance anywhere else, for example, to publicity or organization, is to miss the source of power. If we make this mistake, we can next anticipate that costly pity and compassion in which we are one with the ignorant, the dull and the deaf. Only then is the eye opened to faith, the ear to the sound of the word of God. No one can give sight to the spiritually blind unless he gazes into heaven. What we give depends on what we receive.

How often Our Lord's sighs are mentioned in Scripture, for example, at the sight of the hardness of hearts and unbelief, at the sight of a leper, a hungry multitude, in the face of hostility and over the dead body of Lazarus! All the ills and evil of man's fate and conduct weighed on His priestly Heart. So the worth of our efforts is in proportion to the expanse of sympathy and feeling we have for unconverted souls. The depth of a priest's compassion is the measure of his apostolic success.

Here, too, it is pertinent to meditate on the relation between the love of the Holy Spirit and the Eucharistic Presence on the one hand, and our sympathy for souls on the other. The gaze and the sigh went together in Our Lord. Likewise, the look at the tabernacle and the sympathy for the sick are twins. He who prays, sympathizes; he who has the Spirit has a body that takes up a cross daily for his people; he whose eyes sweep the heavens for the Spirit, has the keener gaze for the lost sheep of earth. The habitual communion with God is the root of the priest's compassion. Pity is second; Our Lord is first.

When the Spirit seeks to work in us for souls, our nature shrinks from the task. But it is something like swimming: it becomes a joy after the shock of the first plunge. We grow weary, of course, but God is unwearied in giving us new strength. Age is not the determining factor. The young who lack the Spirit tire more quickly than the old who have it.

> Youth itself may weaken, the warrior faint and flag, but those who trust in the Lord will renew their strength, like eagles new-fledged; hasten, and never grow weary of hastening, march on, and never weaken on the march. ISAIAS 40:30,31

The natural man steadily tends to exhaustion. All life lived on the creature level digs its own grave. But the man who trusts in the Unwearied God does not follow the earthly law of fatigue. Unzealous priests are tired in mind before they are tired in body. Their exhaustion is ennui due to the loss of the Spirit. But the true apostle, though he may sit like his Master, "tired after His journey, by the well" (JOHN 4:6), can nevertheless account a converted soul as "food to eat of which you know nothing" (JOHN 4:32). Grace abhors a vacuum, as nature does. The empty house of the Gospel that was not filled by the Spirit was occupied by seven devils.

Thanks to the Spirit, though the priest grows older in years, he becomes younger through ascent to the altar of God where youth is renewed. Exertion without the Spirit is impatience; impatience, touched by the Spirit, is zeal for souls. As the diamond cutter works diamonds and the sculptor stone, so the priest works souls.

> Like a shepherd He tends them, gathers up the lambs and carries them in His bosom. ISAIAS 40:11

In the parish, in the school, the priest will watch that not one such soul is plucked out of his hands (JOHN 10:11-28). Authority over the Church and its souls was not given to Peter until he had made a triple promise to love. Any authority the priest exercises has the same foundation. The priest will be as tender in love to his people as Jacob was to his flock:

> I may lose a whole herd if I overdrive them. GENESIS 33:13

## THE SPIRIT AND THE SCRIPTURE

It has been said that a characteristic gesture of many priests, when they take the Bible from a shelf (after looking for it for several minutes), is to tap it with the hand to knock the dust off. This may explain why pulpit orators are so fond of a few routine texts, such as: "Come you that have received a blessing from My Father" (MATTHEW 25:34), or "Come to me, all you that labored and are burdened" (MATTHEW 11:28); and on Mission Sunday: "Go out, making disciples of all nations" (MATTHEW 28:19). Why is it that the less prepared the preacher is, the more he is inclined to find fault with his parishioners? And the less he examines his own conscience in meditation, the more he resorts to moralistic nagging.

The saintly priest, on the contrary, tells his flock: "We are Christ's ambassadors, then, and God appeals to you through us" (II CORINTHIANS 5:20). But if God appeals, He does so through His Word: "I preached God's Gospel to you" (II CORINTHIANS 11:7).

The preacher will do well to ponder on the technique used by St. Paul at Thessalonica:

> Over a space of three sabbaths he reasoned with them out of the scriptures, expounding these and bringing proofs from them that the sufferings of Christ and His rising from the dead were fore-ordained; the Christ, he said, is none other than the Jesus whom I am preaching to you. ACTS 17:2,3

When he spoke to King Agrippa, Paul used exactly the same method of preaching:

> Yet there is nothing in my message which goes beyond what the prophets spoke of, and Moses spoke of, as things to come; a suffering Christ, and One Who should shew light to His people and to the Gentiles by being the first to rise from the dead. ACTS 26:22

St. Peter uses the Scriptures in exactly the same way to develop the truths of the faith:

> Salvation was the aim and quest of the prophets, and the grace of which they prophesied has been reserved for you. The Spirit of Christ was in them, making known to them the sufferings which Christ's cause brings with it, and the glory that crowns them; when was it to be, and how was the time of it to be recognized?
> I PETER 1:10,11

Can the preacher today do better than Peter and Paul? Regardless of how many times people hear the Scriptures, they can always find something new in them. St. Paul has set out the reason why this is so:

> Everything in the scripture has been divinely inspired, and has its uses; to instruct us, to expose our errors, to correct our faults, to educate us in holy living; so God's servant will become a master of his craft, and each noble task that comes will find him ready for it.
> 
> II TIMOTHY 3:16,17

The Scriptures are not merely a record of historical events that have passed. They constitute for every age a revelation of God's mind and will to each individual. Many of the incidents recorded in the Old Testament provide a perspective to give us a fuller understanding of events that occurred later and are described in the New Testament. GENESIS 21:10-12, for example, recounts a quarrel in Abraham's family. Ishmael, his child by Agar, mocked and insulted his younger child Isaac, the son of promise, whose mother was Sara. Sara sided with Isaac and decided that Agar and Ishmael should be driven out of Abraham's house. Such family quarrels and maternal revenge may not seem to have much pertinence until we read GALATIANS 4:30, where St. Paul explains that the casting out of the bondwoman and her son was to show that they were yet in bondage to the Law, and were consequently not entitled to share in the inheritance of the Gospel.

Not only does Scripture derive its inspiration from the Spirit, but the Spirit alone makes its meaning clear. Before his conversion Paul was versed in the Scriptures, yet could not see in them that the Lord was the Christ. Our Blessed Lord told the Pharisees that they poured over the Scriptures but did not realize that they referred to Him (JOHN 5:39). Whatever beneficial effect was produced on the listener always came through the Holy Spirit.

> Our preaching to you did not depend upon mere argument; power was there, and the influence of the Holy Spirit, and an effect of full conviction.
> 
> I THESSALONIANS 1:5

When St. Paul recalled the effect of his preaching on the Corinthians, he probably had in mind his lack of success in Athens. St. Paul had given a very learned talk at Athens, quoting several of the Greek poets, but the effect was limited to one or two conversions. St. Paul thereupon left Athens for Corinth. During the forty-mile trip, he must have meditated on his want of success and tried to determine why he had failed. Later on, when he wrote to the Corinthians, he contrasted preaching by philosophy and eloquence, and preaching by the power of the Spirit.

So it was, brethren, that when I came to you and preached Christ's message to you, I did so without any high pretensions to eloquence, or to philosophy. I had no thought of bringing you any other knowledge than that of Jesus Christ, and of Him as Crucified.

I CORINTHIANS 2:1-3

There are two kinds of knowledge about Christ: the speculative and the practical. The former is obtained by study, the latter only through the Holy Spirit who leads us to accept Jesus as Lord and Savior.

## CHAPTER 7

## THE SPIRIT OF POVERTY

POVERTY is not an economic but a spiritual condition. The vow of poverty not only allows for what is necessary to provide for one's material needs, but permits a man to live according to his state of life. Poverty, in relation to the priesthood, is a spirit. That is why Christ said:

> Blessed are the poor in spirit. MATTHEW 5:3

All men are poor in the sense that they have no natural claim to what is essential for the Kingdom of Heaven. Of themselves, they do not even know what they lack. Only when the Spirit takes possession of them, so that they become poor in spirit, do they recognize that they are destitute and blind and naked. That is why the beatitude referring to poverty in spirit is followed closely by one designed to console those who mourn. As poverty implies helplessness, so mourning implies a sense of guilt and corruption. The two are related like humility and patience, as ISAIAS (66:2) points out:

> Nothing you see about you but I fashioned it, the Lord says; My Hand gave it being. From whom, then, shall I accept an offering? Patient he must be and humbled, one who stands in dread of My warnings.

The priest who is poor in spirit is a mendicus rather than a pauper. His most conscious moments testify to his emptiness, his dependence on God and his unworthiness. Only they will enter the Kingdom of Heaven who have cast off self-will, self-reliance, economic security as a substitute for Divine trust. The two attitudes are set out in sharp contrast in the message to the angel of the church of Laodicea recorded in the APOCALYPSE (3:17), a message which we, in the richest nation in the world, can well take to heart. To those in the church of Laodicea who glory in their own success, saying

> "I have come into my own; nothing, now, is wanting to me," the angel is directed to say: "And all the while, if thou didst but know it, it is thou who art wretched, thou who art to be pitied. Thou art a beggar, blind and naked; and my counsel to thee is, to come and buy from me what thou needest; gold, proved in the fire, to make thee rich, and white garments, to clothe thee, and cover up the nakedness which dishonors thee; rub salve, too, upon thy eyes, to restore them sight. It is those I love that I correct and chasten; kindle thy generosity and repent."

Poverty of spirit is based on the example of Our Blessed Lord.

> You do not need to be reminded how gracious our Lord Jesus Christ was; how He impoverished Himself for your sakes, when He was so rich, so that you might become rich through His poverty.
> II CORINTHIANS 8:9

He was a child of a poor mother born on a journey, first cradled among animals. His poverty was voluntary. He who had made the waters, asked for a drink; He who had made the beasts, borrowed one for a procession; He who had made the trees, borrowed a Cross. Satan offered Him all the riches of the world—the short cut to popularity—and He refused them, even though worn out by a forty-day fast. Joseph found Him a cave in which to be born; and another Joseph, a cave in which to lay His broken Body—for birth and death were equally alien to Him as God.

If such was the poverty of spirit of Christ, it is obvious that the priest, the alter Christus, has no choice but to cultivate a like spirit. The priest is already rich—rich with the grace of vocation, the grace of ambassadorship, the grace of Orders. Being rich in Christ, he has no need of being rich in Mammon. The Bible records that the tribe of Levi received no land, because the Lord was the riches of those chosen to be His priests:

> This, too, the Lord said to Aaron: You are to hold no lands, no portion is to be assigned to you, among your fellow-Israelites. I am all thy portion; these others have their several possessions, thou hast Me.
> NUMBERS 18:20

## The Riches Of The Priest

Far greater is the wealth of the priests of the New Testament who enjoy the familiarity of the Incarnate Lord and the riches of the Spirit: "... how rich is the glory He bestows" (ROMANS 9:23); "So rich is God's grace, that has overflowed upon us in a full stream" (EPHESIANS 1:8).

> The Catholic priest ought to be remarkable for his detachment from worldly things just as much as for his love of chastity.... avarice which the Holy Spirit calls the root of all evils, can lead a man to any crime. The priest who allows this vice to get hold of him, even though he may stop short of crime, is making common cause, whether he knows it or not, with the enemies of the Church, aiding them in their evil designs.
>
> PIUS XI,
> Encyclical on the Catholic Priesthood, December 20, 1935

What abundance the priest possesses! He dispenses the pardon of Christ to those who repent of their sins. He has at his disposal the richness of the wisdom of Christ! Sitting at His Feet, the priest hears what Plato could not teach and what Socrates never learned.

Why do the few who are rich rarely support the missions? Why does the Church so often have to struggle against poverty, and why do conversions multiply more rapidly in poor countries, like Vietnam, than in prosperous countries? The reason is that there is a kind of balance struck beneath the wealth of heaven and the wealth of earth.

> Thou didst receive thy good fortune in thy life-time, and Lazarus, no less, his ill fortune; now he is in comfort, thou in torment.
>
> LUKE 16:25

Heaven, too, has its economics. The crudest words in Scripture will be pronounced on the last day against those who got all the worldly things they wanted:

> They have their reward already.    MATTHEW 6:16

Appealing to his brethren everywhere, St. James confirms that rich pockets often have poor hearts, that poor pockets have hearts full of the riches of faith:

Listen to me, my dear brethren; has not God chosen the men who are poor in the world's eyes to be rich in faith, to be heirs of that kingdom which he has promised to those who love him?  JAMES 2:5

Our Blessed Lord insisted that His love of the poor and His efforts to save them were evidence of the truth of His claim to be the Messias:

The poor have the gospel preached to them.  MATTHEW 11:5

But woe upon you who are rich; you have your comfort already. Woe upon you who are filled full; you shall be hungry. Woe upon you who laugh now; you shall mourn and weep. Woe upon you, when all men speak well of you; their fathers treated the false prophets no worse.  LUKE 6:24-26

Poverty of spirit draws the priest to a closer union with the Person of Christ. A function of all ownership is to extend personality. A man is free on the inside because he has a soul; he is free on the outside, or economically, because he owns property. The human personality becomes enriched through things.

The priest, however, has another way to extend his personality: not by acquiring stocks and bonds, but by a greater reproduction in himself of the Hypostatic Union. He crushes his ego and its desires, so that in him there are two "natures" in one person: on the one hand, his human nature; on the other, his "participation in the Divine Nature" through grace and the losing of his human personality in the Person of Christ. Being less dependent on things, he becomes more and more an instrumentum Divinitatis.

It is Christ that lives in me.  GALATIANS 2:20

Crucified to the external extension of personality, the priest grows internally and becomes the extension of the Person of Christ. The less staffs the priest has to lean on—and staffs which pierce his hands—the more the Lord leans on him. Poor in himself, he is rich in Christ. The parishioners then do not see the human person in him: they see Christ, living, teaching, visiting, consoling, renewing Calvary. The instinct of parishioners is infallible: they know in whom Christ lives. Of one priest, they say: "He's a good Joe"; of another, "He is another Christ."

To the extent to which the wealth of a priest consists in the things of the Spirit, to the same extent the need for an outside complement to perfect his personality is reduced. The priest's confidence, as he confronts life, is derived less from the power of what he holds in reserve, than from his total reliance on Providence and on the Goodness of the Heavenly Father.

## Prosperity Unfavorable To Priestliness

Yet another reason for being poor in spirit is that temporal prosperity is unfavorable to spiritual advancement. Take the case of Solomon. He stepped downward, Scripture informs us, through multiplication. First, he multiplied gold and silver for himself; then he multiplied horses which he bought from Egypt; next, he multiplied wives. There is here a definite hint that carnality followed a love of wealth. Finally, he adored the false gods of his concubines. Confucius says that lust is the sin of youth, power the sin of middle age, and avarice the sin of old age. Avarice in the old can even represent the sublimation of the lusts of their youth.

> So the Lord was angry with Solomon for playing Him false.
> III KINGS 11:9

The suggestion is that God was angry precisely because of the great blessings He conferred on Solomon, for every sin is aggravated by the mercies we have received. How much more, therefore, is sin aggravated after the gift of a vocation? Our Lord said that if He had not come and spoken to His people, they would have been comparatively without sin (JOHN 15:22).

Hoarding, on one occasion recorded in the Bible, received a terrible punishment. After the Jews had crossed over the Jordan, Josue won a victory and then set out for Hai where he was ignominiously routed. The defeat threw Josue and his people into despondency, and Josue complained to the Lord:

> Better had we remained at our old post beyond the Jordan. O Lord my God, that I should see Israel turn their backs before their enemies!
> JOSUE 7:7,8

Thereupon the Lord explained the reason for the reverse. They were being punished because of the violation of a Divine command that no Jewish soldier should take for his own use any of the spoils of Jericho. One man, however, had violated the command; tempted by the sight of a costly Babylonian garment, some silver, and a bit of gold, he secreted them for his own use.

Though only one man in the entire army was guilty, the whole army was punished with defeat. The sin was imputed to and visited upon the entire nation:

> But the Lord said to Josue, Rise up; why dost thou lie there, face to ground? Guilt rests on Israel; they have transgressed My Covenant, by taking forfeited plunder for their own use; it has been stolen away secretly, and hidden among private goods.    JOSUE 7:10,11

If the sin of one, who was not even a priest, affected all of Israel, will not the greed of a priest affect the parish? If the army was defeated at Hai because of such avarice, will not building projects and social organization suffer defeat because of the material aggressiveness of a servant of God? The guilt of one, even personal and hidden, can bring down Divine judgments on the whole parish. Did not Saul's violation of the agreement he made with the Gabaonites occasion much later a famine that lasted three years (II KINGS 21:1)? Did not David's obstinacy in taking a census which he had been warned not to take, occasion a pestilence to the destruction of seventy thousand of his subjects (II KINGS 24:10-15)?

The greed of Josue's soldier, Achan, was hidden; but God had witnessed the sacrilegious robbing of gold and silver He had ordered appropriated to His own use in the sanctuary. The crime had, moreover, been committed immediately after the celebration of the Passover, relating it even more closely to the altar and cult. To appropriate what belongs to the altar of God is more serious in God's eyes than the sinner always realizes.

Without naming the person, God revealed the fact and left it to the church of Israel to discover the offender. Justice took its course, and the sentence was executed. Achan with his children and his cattle were stoned to death; afterwards his tent, the stolen property and all his belongings were consumed by fire.

## THE PRIEST NOT ONLY BEGS BUT ALSO GIVES

When the priest in the pulpit asks the people to contribute to a diocesan expansion plan, does he first reach into his own pocket? When on Mission Sunday he urges the parishioners to make a sacrifice to spread the Church in Africa, Asia or elsewhere, does he play his primary role in sacrifice? It is not fitting to ask others to give to a cause without setting the example. Can the Lord look on us with more favor than He looked on Achan, if we hide our bank accounts when the needs of the world are so pressing? And what blessings does He bestow on priests who give until it hurts, and then a little more? Fortunately, such priests are more numerous than is sometimes recognized. The Achans make the headlines, the scandalous hoarders become notorious; but there is a great army of priest-victims whose identity will become public only on the day of the great revealing.

Poverty of spirit does not begin with an act of the will to do with less; it begins with the Spirit of Christ in us. External poverty follows the internal. Indifference to the accumulation of possessions follows zeal for Christ. The greater the concern with material things, the lesser is the dedication to the spirit. Some priests may exhibit the externals of poverty, or what passes for such. They may be careless about the way they dress and act, soup on the vest, torn cassock, unswept aisles in the church—but these things have no relation to poverty of spirit. They may reflect simply a lack of dignity and culture, a lust for saving, or a general carelessness about the dignity of one's person. To be unconcerned about being dirty impairs personality; poverty of spirit exalts it.

Three aspects of priestly poverty can be distinguished. In his personal life, poverty directs the priest to limit himself to the strictly necessary. In his apostolate, poverty of spirit inspires him to use spiritual means to attain his apostolic goals. In his use of resources, poverty obliges him to count only on God. As St. Augustine said, the poor in spirit are those who have hope only in God.

The priest can convince an incredulous, perverse and luxurious generation only by the acts of virtue opposed to those vices. That is why of all the virtues, the virtue of poverty seems the one most needed in our days. Pius XI stated that its practice was essential to defeat Communism.

The American priest lives at a level of material comfort higher than that of his brother priests anywhere in the world, but it does not necessarily follow that every American priest is attached to his comforts. Many would leave them tomorrow, if circumstances made it necessary. The growth of the missionary spirit among priests in the United States demonstrates this fact. But the temptation is always present, and the priest who allows his soul to become possessed of a desire for wealth, can cause the gravest scandal. The danger of giving scandal is particularly great in the case of the diocesan priest. He cannot hide his lust behind a corporation, a society, or a group. Violations of the individual vow of poverty can sometimes be hidden behind a corporate selfishness. But the diocesan priest has no such facade. If he loves luxury, it shows, it shocks, and it scandalizes. On the other hand, his example is all the greater when he shows the detachment demanded by his station and office.

## POVERTY OF TIME AND TALENT

But the spirit of poverty is not to be understood merely in terms of material things. The Spirit beckons us to seek other, not less important goals. The priest must seek in particular a spirit of poverty in regard to time and in regard to self-satisfaction.

Time can become an object of hoarding, just like stocks and bonds. The priest may set up a schedule for rest, siesta, sleep and recreation, and routine can become a habit to the extent that anyone who disturbs it is in danger of judgment. But the neighbor has claims; hunger has claims; bereavement has claims. Our Lord had His rest disturbed, for He could not be hid. Two of His outstanding converts were made when He was tired, another conversion resulted from an interruption. Siesta time is not sacred; the "day off" is not sacred. These legitimate recreations are expendable, if a soul can be saved. As St. Paul said, we are to redeem the time,

> ... hoarding the opportunity that is given you, in evil times like these.
> EPHESIANS 5:16

Many priests have taken a resolution never to waste a minute of time, particularly when the welfare of a soul is concerned. Keeping visitors waiting in the parlor, delaying a sick call, complaining because a penitent is late—these are all forms of avarice.

> Let us practice generosity to all, while the opportunity is ours, and above all, to those who are of one family with us in the faith.
> GALATIANS 6:10

The pastor who believes that being made a shepherd of souls dispenses him from hearing confessions or administering the Sacrament of the Sick, shows that greed of time which St. Peter felt came on with age, and against which he warned:

> Look anxiously, then, to the ordering of your lives while your stay on earth lasts.
> I PETER 1:17

God insists on "Today" (HEBREWS 3:13). The devil says: "No more of this for the present" (ACTS 24:25), as Felix put off listening to Paul.

The lazy priest always has less time than the zealous priest, because the former is thinking in terms of the interruptions to his leisure, while the latter seeks the opportunity to be another Christ. The priest's time is not his own; it is Our Lord's. The more we enrich ourselves with time, the more we impoverish the Kingdom of God.

The virtue of poverty is too rich in content to be limited to money. The saying that time is money takes on a new meaning when we understand what is meant by poverty of time. No priest was ordained for an eight-hour day or for five days a week. He is ordained for the Kingdom of God, which is "opened to force" (MATTHEW 11:12). Time is for pardon.

> We are careful not to give offence to anybody, lest we should bring discredit on our ministry; as God's ministers, we must do everything to make ourselves acceptable. We have to shew great patience, in times of affliction, of need, of difficulty; under the lash, in prison, in the midst of tumult; when we are tired out, sleepless, and fasting. We have to be pure-minded, enlightened, forgiving and gracious to others; we have to rely on the Holy Spirit, on unaffected love, on the truth of our message, on the power of God.   II CORINTHIANS 6:3-7

## POVERTY OF SELF-SATISFACTION

Not less important for the priest than poverty of time is poverty of self-satisfaction. There is no such thing in priestly spirituality as being satisfied because we have done our duty. It is not enough to perform the most essential activities, to work in the chancery, to administer cemeteries, to make converts, to fulfill one's hours "on duty." On one occasion (MATTHEW 25:30; LUKE 17:10) the Apostles were looking for a crown of merit before their work was done, seeking applause before their orchestration was finished. Our Lord had to remind them that they were not entitled to sit down at the banquet of life simply because they had fulfilled their duties. Even when they had done all they were supposed to do, they had still to regard themselves as "unprofitable servants." A special reward requires more than merely to do one's duty.

> If any one of you had a servant following the plough, or herding the sheep, would he say to him, when he came back from the farm, Go and fall to at once? Would he not say to him, Prepare my supper, and then gird thyself and wait upon me while I eat and drink; thou

shalt eat and drink thyself afterwards? Does he hold himself bound in gratitude to such a servant, for obeying his commands? I do not think it of him; and you, in the same way, when you have done all that was commanded you, are to say, We are servants, and worthless; it was our duty to do what we have done. LUKE 17:7-10

Our service is an arduous one; it involves not only labor in the fields in the day-time, but serving tables at night. It is the mere duty of the priest to work both morning and evening. When he is exhausted, he cannot say: "Well, I already did my Boy Scout duty today." Rather must he tell himself: "I am worthless, an unprofitable servant." The less there is of self-satisfaction, the more zeal there is in His service. Counting the converts we have made may eventually make us believe that we, rather than the grace of God, made them. "I built three rectories; now I can retire; I heard confessions three hours today, I have done my duty." Labor union rules might regard that as sufficient; but we belong to a different union, where love, not hours, is the standard. When we think of all the Lord has done for us, we can never do enough. The word 'enough' does not exist in love's vocabulary. It is like telling the mother tending her sick child that she has done her duty and should take it easy.

In the parable about the unprofitable servant (MATTHEW 25:14-30), Our Lord describes a frequently ignored element of the priesthood. The priest is used to hearing himself being called an ambassador. He is reminded that he is an unprofitable servant as seldom as he is reminded that he is a victim. But the servitude which Christ describes is one of love, not one of duty. Our Lord refuses to distinguish between "work" and "extra work," between "on duty" and "standing by," between eight hours and eighteen hours. No airs of self-complacency are Divinely permitted to the priest. No self-pity, no pluming ourselves on our administrative talent, no such thing as saying: "I built a high school; now the bishop should make me a monsignor." The moment we become self-complacent about our achievements, the work spoils in our hands.

We are worthless servants when we have done our best. What are we then when we fail to do our best? We become unworthy even to be His servants, His priests. To our Redeemer alone belongs the merit and glory of our services; to us belongs nothing but the gratitude and humility of being pardoned rebels.

# CHAPTER 8

# THE SPIRIT
## AND PREACHING AND PRAYING

PREACHING is not the act of giving a sermon; it is the art of making a preacher. The preacher then becomes the sermon.

It is from the heart's overflow that the mouth speaks.
LUKE 6:45

The preacher without the Spirit of Christ is like Giezi whom Elias sent to revive a dead man. Although he brought with him the prophet's staff, no miracle happened, for the virtue of the staff was negated by the hands that held it (IV KINGS 4:25-38). One may hold the Scriptures of the Lord in the pulpit, as Giezi held the staff in his hand, but no souls are saved. The absence of an inner spiritual life makes sermonizing dull, stale, flat and unprofitable.

It is possible for the priest to experience a hardening as a result of his intimate contact with the spiritual, without becoming spiritual. Sacristans are privileged to work close to the Eucharistic Lord, but that does not prevent some sacristans from being perfunctory in their genuflections. Jewelers become used to jewels. Husbands grow bored with beautiful wives, if there is no "stirring up of the first zeal." Contact with the Divine is a privilege that can similarly turn into indifference, unless each day one tries to get a step closer to the Lord. Trafficking with the Word of God one Sunday after another, without prayer and preparation, does not leave a priest the same; it leaves him worse. Failure to climb means to slide backward. There is no defense against acedia, against the tragic loss of Divine reality, except a daily renewal of faith in Christ. The priest who has not kept near the fires of the tabernacle can strike no sparks from the pulpit.

What answer to judgment shall the priest give who squanders hours a day on newspapers, television and magazines, yet cannot spare half an hour of the Lord's time to prepare his soul for the pulpit? No wonder if he produces shoddy, cheap moralizings and ulcerous scoldings which do damage to his espousal with the Spirit and dishonor the Christ Whose ambassador he is. Is he not rather like the hireling who "takes to flight because ... he has no concern over the sheep" (JOHN 10:13)? What right have we to preach to others who "labour and are burdened" (MATTHEW 11:28), if we ourselves shirk the burden of our calling? Is being caught up in the whirling machinery of "busy-ness" an adequate excuse for what is in reality laziness?

> But what if sentry, when he sees the invader coming, sounds no alarm to warn his neighbours? EZECHIEL 33:6

And yet to each priest the Lord has said:

> Thou are My watchmen; the warning thou hearest from My lips, to them pass on. Sinner if I threaten with death, and word thou give him none to leave off his sinning, die he shall, as he deserves to die, but thou for his death shalt answer to Me. EZECHIEL 33:7,8

The priest at ordination was told to preach. The office is to be taken so seriously as to make every priest cry out with Paul:

> It would go hard indeed with me if I did not preach the Gospel. I CORINTHIANS 9:16

If a pastor fails to feed his parishioners with the Word of God, they may well be the first on the day of judgment, to demand his punishment for having left them spiritually starved. Do we repay our redemption, our vocation and our other blessings from the Lord by such disregard for His commands? How shall we call on the rocks and mountains to cover us from His merited indignation!

How much more our words would burn as we preach, if we prepared our sermons before the Eucharistic Lord; if our meditation each morning was on the subject of next Sunday's sermon; if before preaching, we prayed for five minutes to the Holy Spirit for Pentecostal fire; if we kept the Scriptures ever open near us, that we might gird ourselves with their truth when mounting the pulpit? Every person to whom we preach we shall meet again on the judgment day. How great our joy then, if we have rectified their consciences and elevated them to the embrace of the Sacred Heart. No wonder that Moses, Elias and Jeremias all tried to run away from the crushing burden of delivering the Word of the Lord.

And shall we substitute the ledger for the Bible, the begging sermon for the penitential summons, tawdry platitudes for the scandal of the Cross? In the Old Testament, God ordered that the fire on the altar should never go out. Are not we ministers of the High Priest Who cast fire on the earth and willed that it be enkindled?

## THE SCRIPTURES
## OUR INSPIRATION

What inexhaustible subjects for sermons the Spirit gives us in the Scriptures. There is no occasion for which the Bible lacks a fitting theme, a pertinent application. There is, for example, the judgment on men who defy God, such as Balaam (NUMBERS 23:7-24:25; 31:8), Goliath (I KINGS 17:10-55), Sennacherib (II PARALIPOMENA 32:1-21).

Then there are the parables of the Old Testament, for example, Balaam's seven parables (NUMBERS 23:7,18; 24:3; 15:20-23); Samson's (JUDGES 14:12); the ewe Lamb (II KINGS 12:3); the wise woman of Thecua (II KINGS 14:6); the trees choosing a king (III KINGS 20:39); the parable of old age (ECCLESIASTES 12:1-7); the poor wise man in a little city (ECCLESIASTES 9:14).

Wonderful indeed would be the preacher who could improve on the five cries for mercy in the Gospel: Blind Bartimaeus (MARK 10:46,47); ten lepers (LUKE 17:11-13); the woman of Canaan (MATTHEW 15:21,22); the father of a demon-possessed boy (MATTHEW 17:14,15); and the rich man in hell (LUKE 16:23,24).

What more applicable today than the story of Rahab (JOSUE 2:21 and HEBREWS 12:27), whose red string typified the long current of blood clamoring for Redemption; the woman full of good deeds—the only person Peter ever raised from the dead (ACTS 9:36-42); or Naaman the Leper (IV KINGS 5:1-14) who ridiculed the idea that God should use "sacraments" to manifest His saving power?

The lesson of the seven great intercessors is similarly pertinent to our times: Abraham for Sodom (GENESIS 18), Juda for Benjamin (GENESIS 44:18), Moses for Israel (EXODUS 32:11), Jonathan for David

(I KINGS 20:32), Joas for Absalom (IV KINGS 14), Esther for the Jews (ESTHER 5), and Christ for His priests (JOHN 17).

## Preaching Repentance

But of all possible subjects for sermons, study of the Bible inevitably leads to the conclusion that the most important is repentance. It was the subject of John the Baptist's preaching (MATTHEW 3:8). Our Lord's first sermon was on repentance (MATTHEW 4:17). Our Lord gave it as the reason of His coming (LUKE 5:32). It was the subject of Peter's first sermon to his fellow Jews (ACTS 2:38) and of his first sermon to the Gentiles (ACTS 11:28). It was the subject Paul said he never failed to preach before Jew and Gentile (ACTS 20:21); it was the theme of Peter's last message (II PETER 3:9) in which he asserted that the only reason God gave us more time to live was to repent. It was the subject both of Our Lord's first sermon and of His last. "Repentance and remission of sins should be preached to all nations" (LUKE 24:47).

The message of Our Lady at Lourdes was "Do penance"; the same words were repeated at Fatima: "Do penance." But how often is penance preached? The current tendency is rather to downgrade the need for penance, to reduce the severity of the fast and the number of days of obligatory fasting. To make religion comfortable, however, is enough to make the Angel cry out again to any church like Ephesus:

> Repent, and go back to the old ways. APOCALYPSE 2:5

To the church of Pergamum, the same warning was sounded:

> Do thou ... repent; or I will come quickly to visit thee.
> APOCALYPSE 2:16

Why repentance? Because it is the first act of a soul which turns back to God, the first stroke that severs sin from the heart. The Scriptures contain no expressions of vengeance against other sinners as terrifying as those directed by the Spirit of God in DEUTERONOMY (29:20,21) against those who obstinately delay repentance.

But the preaching of terror is not essential for repentance. Souls need not be like Dante, who went through Hell before he reached Paradise. The lighting of sulfurous coals in the pulpit is not Our Lord's path to repentance. St. Paul told Timothy how to woo souls from an evil life, and meekness was the approach he urged.

A servant of the Lord has no business with quarrelling; he must be kindly towards all men, persuasive and tolerant, with a gentle hand for correcting those who are obstinate in their errors.

II TIMOTHY 2:24,25

Before the thunder, we see the light. But to thunder against souls without bringing to them the light of God's truth and the love revealed through the Sacred Heart may bring a smile to their lips. It will not, however, bring them to their knees in repentance.

## The Priest At Prayer

Three kinds of prayer in the Spirit should be of special concern to every priest: his unsaid prayers; his prayers made up of crosses; and his Breviary.

*1. The Priest's Unsaid Prayers.*

Because the priest is never free from the infirmities of a fallen nature, despite his sublime calling, Scripture often bids him to pray. But little help is found in weak human nature or in spiritual books, or even in the will itself, to inspire the necessary prayer. For one of the most neglected aspects of priestly prayer is the role which alone the Holy Spirit can play in its fructification.

Bad habits, acedia and lukewarmness may all conspire to prevent an increase in the level of prayer, but the Divine Spirit can enlighten the darkest soul and cleanse the foulest heart. The Holy Spirit is not indifferent to the obstacles created by man's carnal nature. As a nurse gently lifts a patient in his bed, so does the Holy Spirit sustain the priest in his weakness.

> ... when we do not know what prayer to offer, to pray as we ought, the Spirit Himself intercedes for us, with groans beyond all utterance: and God, who can read our hearts, knows well what the Spirit's intent is; for indeed it is according to the mind of God that He makes intercession for the saints.       ROMANS 8:26,27

Often, we do not even know what we should pray for. St. Paul himself was in this condition, when he asked for the removal of the thorn in the flesh. When James and John asked for the right and left places alongside the Savior, Our Lord told them that they knew not what they asked. But to recognize that we do not know what to pray for, is already an indication that we are on the path to be guided by the Spirit. Too often our prayers tend to be mere blueprints which we bring to God to rubberstamp. But when the Holy Spirit guides, prayer immediately rises above the level of petition.

## Our Two Intercessors

We have two intercessors: one is Christ Himself; the Other is the Spirit. Christ speaks on our behalf. The Spirit intercedes in us that we may pray. He puts our hearts in a praying mood. He increases our boldness to draw nigh to the throne of grace. He suggests the things that we should pray for, multiplies our prayers, and gives us His Power.

What is meant by the groans of the Holy Spirit (ROMANS 8:26)? Very likely the secret workings of the heart toward God in a prayer that is without speech or vocal utterance. Very often, in deep affliction and distress, the human heart speaks not, but rather groans. As Christ intercedes for us in Heaven, so does the Holy Spirit, in afflictions and trial intercede in us on earth, revealing to us our need, creating holy aspirations, searching our hearts to expose what is wanting to our priesthood.

The Holy Spirit turns the dissatisfaction which each priest contains within himself into an inarticulate prayer. While creation longs for development, the priest—feeling his weakness—sighs for salvation. His very groaning proves a longing for the Infinite. With Augustine he knows that he was made for the Divine High Priest and is restless until he rests in Him. Very often we pray with the illusion that we know best what we should pray for. St. Paul suggests that, on the contrary, we often are ignorant of what we should pray for; hence the need of the illumination and guidance of the Spirit.

Pythogoras forbade his disciples to pray for themselves, because they did not know what was expedient for them. Socrates more wisely taught his disciples to pray simply for good things, for God knows best what sort of things are good. Our ignorance and our feebleness are alike grounds for asking the illumination of the Spirit to bring us into harmony with God's Will, whether in peace or in trial. The showers of Heaven are not less fertilizing because they fall at night; neither are the promptings of the Spirit less real and beneficial, when they reach the soul during seasons of spiritual gloom and ignorance. How consoling it is to know that Christ deputes the Spirit to intercede in us on earth, while He Himself intercedes for us in Heaven!

There is no priest in the world who does not at some time experience in an unutterable form this longing for greater communion with Christ.

It defies all petition. In the unutterable cry, the Spirit reads a desire for communion with Him fuller than that which has yet been satisfied. When He makes intercession for us, it is not by direct supplication from Himself to the Father; it is by becoming the Spirit of supplication in us. When the Breviary becomes hard, when we struggle in prayer and the soul seems to lose touch with God, we have reached the point where we must pray for the Spirit of prayer. Finally, the Spirit makes us so intimate with God that we scarcely pass through any experience before we speak to Him about it, whether we visit the sick, preach, hear confessions, begin the office, or listen to the woes of a caller in the parlor.

## The Undertones Of Priestly Prayer

Priests are often reluctant to reveal their inner spiritual life even to their brother-priests. They tend to hide it from others and perhaps even from themselves, with the result that few know what goes on in their hearts. Yet even the weakest have aspirations toward goodness unsuspected by their critics. And many of the best hesitate to be seen in prayer by their brethren. But all the while, thoughts of holiness, or a sadness for not being more holy, flood their hearts. These undertones need articulation, these burdens need a wing, these mumblings need utterance; and that is the work of the Holy Spirit.

The effort to hide saintliness from others may often arise from an awareness of one's imperfections, so that we leave them to the Holy Spirit to define in our solitude. Few priests like verbal or vocal prayers. This is a fact. This is not because good priests are unprayerful. But because their prayers are sighs, their aspirations are inspirations. They have no sense of shouting to God across an abyss. Always conscious of their mission, they feel the deep silent work of the Spirit within them. They have few petitions. They rarely make a novena for something they want; they set the people to make the novenas. Their best prayers are unspoken; their prayers are within their prayers—the talking to the Father, as does the Son through the Spirit Who inspires them what to say.

Thus we have the Father to Whom we pray and Who hears prayer. We have the Son through Whom we pray, per Christum Dominum Nostrum, and we have the Holy Spirit in Whom we pray, Who prays in us according to the Will of God with such deep, unutterable sighings. The intercession of the Holy Spirit within us is as Divine as the intercession of Christ above. Our very weakness, our humiliation and the grossness of our flesh provide the sphere of operation for the Holy Spirit, Who awakens the soul to come out and meet its Lord. As we grow in the knowledge of the Spirit dwelling within us, in the reality of His breathing within us, we begin to recognize how much beyond all our theology is that divine hunger by which He draws us heavenward.

How different the priesthood becomes when we start with the principle that we do not know what we want! Then we pray to the Spirit that we may properly understand our needs. Before a school or convent is built, before the parish makes plans for a social affair, the first prayer is to ask the Holy Spirit if the project is in conformity with God's Will. We often lose the benefit of prayers by proposing to ourselves improper ends. As St. James said:

> What you ask for is denied you, because you ask for it with ill intent.
> JAMES 4:3

Scripture assures us that the true mark of participation in the divine Nature is the following of the Spirit:

> Those who follow the leading of God's Spirit are all God's sons.
> ROMANS 8:14

As Christ carries on His intercessory work in Heaven, He applies it through the Spirit Who could not come until He was glorified (JOHN 7:39). The work that the Blood of Our Lord effected in Heaven when He entered beyond the veil, now continues to be applied through His Spirit, so that Christ's prayers become ours and ours are made His. But His Spirit is ours not only in time of prayer but in every moment of life.

*2. Our Crosses*

The priest devoted to the Spirit has an answer when trials, injustices, betrayals, disappointments, broken health or temptations assail him: he knows that the Spirit has prepared them. He immediately recalls that

> by the Spirit, He was led on into the wilderness, where He remained forty days, tempted by the devil.
> LUKE 4:1

The grouchy old pastor to whom an assistant has been assigned, the indolent television-viewer whom the zealous pastor has no choice but to accept—these and other such apparently diabolical trials are permitted by the Spirit, just as the Spirit led Our Lord to the devil. Under the guidance of the Spirit every trial enriches the soul of the priest. He best heals wounds who has felt a similar wound.

The priest never complains against either his bishop, his brother-priests, or his people, if he sees that the Spirit is the author of his trials. Look at poor Jonas, and yet see how much God had to do with his mission to preach penance! His trials seemed to arise from purely natural causes, and yet the Lord had decreed each and every one of them: "But now the Lord sent out a boisterous wind over the sea...." (JONAS 1:4); "At the Lord's bidding, a great sea-beast had swallowed him up...." (JONAS 2:1); "And now, at the Lord's bidding, the sea-beast cast Jonas up again...." (JONAS 2:11); "...at God's bidding a worm ... struck at the plant's root and killed it" (JONAS 4:7); "...at the Lord's bidding the sirocco came ..." (JONAS 4:8).

Once we understand that all trials come from the Lord, they lose their bitterness and our heart is at peace. When such trials arise, we must beg the faithful to fight with us through their prayers. A measure of the value we set on prayer is the insistence with which we ask the flock entrusted to our care to pray for us. St. Paul in prison wrote the Philippians that he will have no further worry over his soul's health if he has them "to pray for me, and Jesus Christ to supply my needs with his Spirit" (PHILIPPIANS 1:19). He knew he could not work without the intercession of his converts. He valued Lydia's prayers and those of her household; he valued the jailer's prayers; he desired the prayers of Euodias, Syntche and Clement; and to the Ephesians he wrote:

> Pray for me too, that I may be given words to speak my mind boldly, in making known the Gospel Revelation, for which I am an ambassador in chains. EPHESIANS 6:19,20

The priest may claim the prayers of his people, for through their prayers he receives from the Spirit whatever he needs. Yet how few are the parishes which place primary stress on prayer when a high school is being built or a mission being preached! Fund-raising campaigns are organized to get the money and telephone canvassers are enlisted; but are prayers presented as the first priority in order to draw down the blessing of God? The priest can save souls without eloquence, but he cannot move them without prayer and the Holy Spirit. To build a church we need "stones that live and breathe" (I PETER 2:5), but what are the "living stones compacted in charity" if not the Christian community united in prayer? To build a church we need holiness, but whence comes holiness save from the Spirit? How many parishioners ever pray for the pastor or his assistants? If some do not, may not the reason be that from our prison cells of spiritual need, we priests have not urged them to pray for us, as did Paul the Philippians?

*3. The Breviary*

Few like to admit that they are bored by something they are expected to enjoy. The Breviary belongs in this category. Priests are expected to rave about their love of it, but many of us are like those affected people who pretend to love the opera, when they neither enjoy nor understand it. Why not admit the truth about the Breviary: many of us find it "strange talk" (JOHN 6:61). But when asked if we will go away, we have the courage to refuse, and to repeat with Peter: "Lord, to whom should we go?" (JOHN 6:69).

Maybe the Breviary was meant to be difficult for the average priest. Could it not be a wrestling with God like that of Jacob (GENESIS 33:24)? If we learn to see it in this light, it may still be a constant struggle, but it will fall into the category of incessant and prolonged intercession. We pray it then as Our Lord prayed in the Garden, with drops of blood crimsoning the earth, as the friend who kept knocking at the door in the night for a loaf of bread, as the widow who was resistless in her pleading to the judge, as the Syro-Phoenician woman who would settle for the crumbs that fell from the Master's table. Importunity means not dreaminess, but sustained work. If laborare est orare, then is it not sometimes true of the Breviary that orare est laborare?

Our faith clings to the Breviary as the poor woman from the land of Tyre and Sidon clung to the Lord (MATTHEW 15:21-28). She had three handicaps to overcome: Christ's silence; the resistance of the disciples; and finally Christ's seeming rejection of her as unworthy to share His glory. Are not these our three common difficulties with the Breviary? Our High Priest seems to be silent; the Church makes us use a tongue which is hard; and all too often we let ourselves become convinced that Our Lord is not very pleased with us. Yet we struggle along, day by day, inspired by a sense of duty and faith. And if we do, will not Our Lord say to us in the end, as He said to that woman:

For this great faith of thine, let thy will be granted. MATTHEW 15:28

## THE BREVIARY IS WEIGHTED

May not the Breviary also be difficult because in it we gather up not only all the intentions of the Church, but also the un-praying, the sinners, those who turn their backs on God, those who delay repentance? It is not easy for us to do this any more than it was easy for Our Lord, Who was sinless, to be "made ... into sin" (II CORINTHIANS 5:21). Everyone would like to have a feeling of devotion when he prays, but what if we pray for those who have only sensibility and no devotion?

Whenever we pick up that book, we pick up Japan and Africa, two billion unbelievers, fallen-aways, the burden of the churches throughout the world. If millions are reluctant to pray, do we not feel their reluctance? If the unconverted drag their feet, how can we take wings and fly? Three times during His Agony Our Lord came back to His three Apostles seeking consolation. The Breviary is not a personal prayer; it is an official prayer and therefore is weighted down "with the burden of the Churches." And until we realize that we are vocalizing the prayer of the Church, will we understand both its beauty and its burden?

Our Lord poured forth His personal prayers to His Father on the mountain top, but when He prayed for His enemies, He was bleeding on a gibbet (LUKE 23:34). The more His prayer was related to redemption, the more He suffered. Easy indeed it is for us to love God solitary and alone, but suppose we have to pray for those who do not love? Do we not take on their lovelessness? And is this not good for us, for if all our prayers were personal, would they not be selfish? Then we might try to bargain with God as Jacob did:

> If God will be with me, he said, and watch over me on this journey of mine, and give me bread to eat and clothes to cover my back, till at last I return safe to my father's house, then the Lord shall be my God.
> GENESIS 28:20,21

Jacob loved God while loving himself. But in the Breviary we are making an act of love, not only for the Church but also for her enemies. The Breviary, like the angel, is the test of our strength; as the angel shook Jacob and made him reel and roll, so the Breviary tests our endurance. If the Breviary be approached as a work, as a wrestling with God, as an intercession on the cross, as something intended to bring us not consolation but struggle, we shall eventually learn to enjoy the battle and turn it to the glory of God.

Despite all our complaining, we love the Breviary. Our life has two principal "gripes": one, the food in the seminary before we are ordained; two, the Breviary after we are ordained. But we grow fat on the meals, and we advance in holiness with the Breviary. We expect too much from it, at first, as does a bride of her groom. But once we realize that when we pick up the "book," we are not mockingbirds singing for ourselves alone, that our melody is rather the song of the angels rising to the throne of God on behalf of the Mystical Body and the world, it becomes easier. We may not understand every word, but God understands what we do not.

While it is true that it is only the Spirit who can make our reading of the Breviary fruitful, there are many things we can do to prepare ourselves for the soft caress of His breath.

## Aids To The Breviary

1. Read the office of the day in the presence of Our Lord in the Blessed Sacrament, a practice for which a plenary indulgence is granted. Furthermore, since the Breviary is the Body of Christ praying, it is read with more faith when closely united with the Head Who "lives on still to make intercession on our behalf" (HEBREWS 7:25).

2. Advert to the fact that most of the Psalms confront us with two figures: one is the Sufferer; the other is the King. It helps us to interpret the suffering psalms as the Church, and the kingly psalms as Christ. That long Psalm 118 would thus become the Church pleading its love for Christ, the New Law. And when we come across "cursing psalms," it may be well to remind ourselves that of all bad men, religious bad men are the worst, and that the Judge takes sin seriously.

3. Often appeal to the Holy Spirit during the recitation. As a mother first prays for her child even before he can know what she is doing, then teaches him to pray so that later she may pray with him, so does the Spirit pray in the Breviary first in us and then through us.

> Go on praying in the power of the Holy Spirit; to maintain yourselves in the love of God, and wait for the mercy of Our Lord Jesus Christ, with eternal life for your goal. JUDE 20,21

4. Offer certain hours of the office for specific intentions. How often is a priest not asked to pray for someone: a boy taking an examination, a mother before childbirth, a father going on a trip, or a young couple about to be married? The Breviary, the Church's prayer, gathers up all these intentions of the parish, the diocese, the nation, the world. It helps to offer a particular psalm for a determined person.

5. The Breviary can never be properly read while listening to the radio or watching television, or with one ear and half the mind concentrated on a baseball game. Magna abusio est habere os in Brevario, cor in foro, oculus in televisifico.

> No need for Me to prove thee a guilty man, thy words prove it; thy own lips arraign thee.  JOB 15:6

> This people does Me honour with its lips, but its heart is far from Me.  MATTHEW 15:8

Moments of mental soaring may occasionally accompany the recital of the Breviary, but in general the vision of the Mount of the Transfiguration is followed by the descent to the plain. Moments of exaltation are few and far between. We must be content to go on like pilgrims, usually on foot, sometimes with broken boots.

The Breviary is, however, not only a yoke and a burden; it is also a duty—a duty of love. The two aspects seem almost contradictory, but the test of love is self-sacrifice, not emotion. Besides, the duty itself is a good. When we lose faith, we lose a sense of duty. How this duty is performed will depend upon the level of behavior. If a priest is egotistic, the Breviary will be said out of duty alone; if he is conscious that it is the prayer of the Church, the duty will have love in it; if he is a priest-victim, love will fan duty into an ardor which feels no obligation. Jacob had to toil seven years for Rachel, yet "they seemed to him only a few days, because of the greatness of his love" (GENESIS 29:20).

# CHAPTER 9

# THE SPIRIT AND COUNSELLING

Not all who visit a psychiatrist have need of his services, as some who come to the priest have need of a psychiatrist. Catholics who are not emotionally disturbed will sometimes consult a psychiatrist because the pastor and the clergy have given up counselling. It used to be that the two regular advisers, each with his own area of action, were the family physician and the pastor. Today the doctor is often more interested in diseases than in sick people, while too many priests rely more on their index cards than on the Gift of Counsel. Psychiatrists occasionally fill the void created by the want of genuine concern for the ills and woes of people on the part of the clergy. The state has largely taken over education; now psychology would take the soul away from the priest.

To permit this to happen would be a failure in respect to a major duty. Yet how preserve this side of our ministry except by the Holy Spirit? Abundant treatises on psychological counselling are of course available; but while much assistance is to be gleaned from them, in the same way that a loudspeaker aids the preacher, they still remain in the natural order. Unless they are used under the guidance of the Spirit, they will avail naught.

Not every person who is disturbed emotionally or spiritually, falls within the province of the priest-counsellor, but the number whom he could help is greater than generally suspected. Two major causes of mental unhappiness are a want of purpose in life and an unrequited sense of guilt. The Holy Spirit alone can reveal the full purpose of life in Christ, and the Holy Spirit alone can convict us of sin. It is surprising how few Catholic books on counselling have references to the supernatural order, to grace, faith, mortification and prayer. The stress on such aids as "keeping your chin up," "self-confidence," "lifting yourself by your bootstraps," tends to make the Christian overlook the unseen influences which alone are ultimately capable of giving lasting rest to weary souls.

The concern of the priest as counsellor is solely with those souls who do not belong in the domain of medicine and psychiatry. However, this does not restrict him to the care of normal souls, for those who are abnormal because of a denial of guilt, fall equally under his jurisdiction. It is the task of the priest, and he enjoys the power of the Spirit, to regenerate and progressively remould all such souls into the Divine Image. And once restored to the heavenly inheritance, they can say with Paul:

> We, after all, were once like the rest of them, reckless, rebellious, the dupes of error; enslaved to a strange medley of desires and appetites, our lives full of meanness and of envy, hateful, and hating one another. Then the kindness of God, our Savior, dawned on us, His great love for man. He saved us; and it was not thanks to anything we had done for our own justification.     TITUS 3:3-5

## No Carnal Wisdom In Counselling

The aim of all counselling is to move the person from the realm of flesh to that of the Spirit:

> To live the life of nature is to think the thoughts of nature; to live the life of the Spirit is to think the thoughts of the Spirit.
> ROMANS 8:5

The therapy of the Spirit seeks "a renewal in the inner life of your minds" (EPHESIANS 4:23).

Where does the priest get the gifts of counsel, the discernment of spirits, the wisdom to understand human hearts? Partly from study, but principally from prayer to the Holy Spirit:

> Is there one of you who still lacks wisdom? God gives to all, freely and ungrudgingly; so let him ask God for it, and the gift will come.
> JAMES 1:5

> the Spirit comes to the aid of our weakness.
> ROMANS 8:26

The attitudes, judgments and values of people are determined by the spirit that moves them. Their spirit is either of Christ or of the world (I CORINTHIANS 2:12). What spirit is it that leads the young into lust, a slavery to pleasure and rebellion against authority, that causes the middle-aged to be immersed in cares, and the old to grow avaricious?

Our century may well witness a phenomenon of alarming proportions: a growth in diabolical possession and a renewed interest in Satan. Plays, novels, books and movies can be expected to use his name more and more, not as something evil, but as something fascinating, to play with the flames of hell as children will play with fire.

## THE GOAL OF THE PRIEST COUNSELLOR

Priestly counsel based on natural knowledge alone cannot deal with such an enemy. Diabolical possession must be met by Christ-possession in the priest, so that he is restless to open to hearts the treasures of God's goodness; to disclose sin that it may be redeemed; to leave the ninety-nine just to seek the one that is lost; to ferret out leaders and train them in the apostolate and the making of conversions; to wrap about them the mantle of the Sacred Heart; to listen without interruption to the distressed, recognizing the dignity of the person who speaks; to reconcile husband with wife by revealing to them how they can sanctify one other, as St. Paul did for the unhappy couples of Corinth (I CORINTHIANS 7:14); to act in such a way that two tides meet in his priestly heart as they met at Bethlehem: the tide of human need and the tide of Divine fulfillment; to look at the fallen-aways as Our Lord looked on Peter and drove him to tears (LUKE 22:61); to have the same Pauline patience which restored Mark to usefulness; to oppose himself everywhere to the awful waste and wear and tear of sin; to pray for those who seek him out (for prayerlessness is the insomnia of the soul); to make people think as they leave the parlor, that they have been with Christ; to understand that the Holy Spirit gives strength to those who spend it; to realize that as there is no beauty in the slothful animal, so there is no power in the slothful priest; to pray daily to the Holy Spirit to teach him to find enjoyment only in souls; to be convinced that he cannot reach a sinner with the fingertip of parochial organization, or raise one soul to sanctity with a lavish expenditure of cheap advice; never to hesitate to receive a visitor for the sake of his own comfort, knowing that God gives him no reward without the dust of toil; in a word, to be "another Christ" and not just "another Joe."

It is all very well to tell the poor and the hungry of the parish to register with Catholic Charities, but the priest will be held personally responsible before God for his compassion for the poor. One may never use a social agency to escape a priestly duty. One wonders what was in the mind of the Jewish priest who passed by the wounded man on the road from Jerusalem to Jericho (LUKE 10:31). As he continued on his way, did he tell himself, to use modern equivalents, that he would tell the social center in the next town to send an ambulance? But he is eternally recorded in the Gospel as the one who failed his fellow man in his hour of need. In neglecting our neighbor, we turn away our "own flesh and blood" (ISAIAS 58:7). It is not only the purse that must be drawn out to help the poor; the purse means nothing without the heart.

> The merciless will be judged mercilessly. JAMES 2:13

## SAINTLY PRIESTS ARE SOUGHT OUT BY THE DISTRESSED

The best counsellors are not the worldly wise with tape-recorders, or those who know all the psychological tricks of interviewing, more concerned with congenial surroundings than the presence of the Spirit. The best guides of souls are saintly priests and priests who have suffered in union with Christ. Through such does the Holy Spirit pour His seven gifts. Those who live close to Christ impart Christ. As St. Augustine said: "What I live by, I impart." Suffering brings wisdom, but books bring only natural understanding. The priest who has been crucified and endured his passion with patience will always be found to be the merciful priest. If there is a long line outside one confessional on Saturday and only one or two outside another, it is time for a priest to ask himself some questions. Holiness draws penitents to holy priests. The attraction of such priests is the attraction of Christ Himself.

> If only I am lifted up from the earth, I will attract all men to Myself. JOHN 12:32

No priest sees problems so sympathetically as the priest who is standing on the watch tower of Calvary. Like the sun, it cannot be seen, and yet it illumines all else.

How many souls say of that great army of saintly priests: "He showed me my heart," or "He showed me the loveliness of Christ," or "It was like talking to Our Lord." It is not possible for a priest, at one and the same time, to be clever and to show that Our Lord is mighty to save. With noble iteration, no less than thirty-three times does St. Paul use the expression "in Christ." To him it is the secret of "encouragement, loving sympathy, common fellowship in the Spirit" (PHILIPPIANS 2:1). The priest imbued with this concept, because he has "crucified nature with all its passions and all its impulses" (GALATIANS 5:24), always directs others in the shadow of the Cross and the light of the Spirit.

## COUNSELLING AND THE CONSCIENCE

Priestly counselling is basically the application of the Redemption to the individual. It is not just preaching to one person instead of preaching to a crowd; for in counselling, the individual presents his problem as does a patient to a doctor. The priest establishes the facts, as the doctor does; then he presents his diagnosis and treatment, always mindful of the words of Our Lord:

> Only the Spirit gives life; the flesh is of no avail; and the words that I have been speaking to you are Spirit and Life. JOHN 6:64

The Spirit is particularly important when the priest is dealing with a problem of behavior rather than an intellectual one. In almost nine cases out of ten, those who have once had the Faith but now reject it, or claim that it does not make sense, are driven not by reasoning but by the way they are living. Catholics usually fall away not from any difficulty with the Creed, but from some difficulty with the Commandments. When this happens, the priest's task is to arouse the conscience through the Spirit. There is not much reference to the conscience alone in Scripture, but there is abundant testimony that the conscience is aroused by the Holy Spirit. St. Paul tells us that it was his conscience that was illumed by the Holy Spirit, making him ready to be doomed in order to save his brethren:

> I am telling you the truth in Christ's name, with the full assurance of a conscience enlightened by the Holy Spirit. ROMANS 9:1

It is the work of conscience to witness to our fulfillment of our duty toward God; but it is the work of the Spirit to witness to God's acceptance of our faith in Christ and our obedience to Him. Thanks to the Spirit, the testimony of conscience and the declaring of Christ, in our life become identical. Conscience alone in a person may be likened to a room that is very poorly lighted, and in which the Commandments are printed on the wall in small characters. When the Holy Spirit illumines the conscience, a brilliant light is shed upon those characters. The Holy Spirit restores consciences, so that they accept the guidance of the law of Christ. The Holy Spirit also shows the conscience the relationship between sin and its purging by the Blood of Christ, so that there is no more a consciousness of sin (HEBREWS 9:14; HEBREWS 10:2-22).

It is never enough for a priest to tell his people that they must follow their conscience; he must constantly seek the illumination of their conscience by the Spirit.

> The end at which our warning aims is charity, based on purity of heart, on a good conscience, and a sincere faith.     I TIMOTHY 1:5

One never understands the enormity of sin except through the Spirit, a truth which Our Lord explained to His priests the night of the Last Supper. Sin is best treated and overcome, not solely in relation to the breaking of a commandment, but in terms of the breaking of our bonds with the Father, Son and Holy Spirit. Sin disrupts our ties with the Heavenly Father because it alienates us as sons. Such is the message of the parable of the prodigal son (LUKE 15:11-32). Sin also re-enacts Calvary:

> Would they crucify the Son of God a second time, hold Him up to mockery a second time, for their own ends?     HEBREWS 6:6

A personal equation must be established between the soul and the crucifix. Sins of pride are understood through the crown of thorns; sins of lust through the torn flesh; sins of avarice through the poverty of nakedness; and sins of alcoholism through thirst. Moreover, sin must be seen as resisting the Spirit of Love (ACTS 7:51); as stifling the Spirit of Love (I THESSALONIANS 5:19); and as distressing the Spirit of Love (EPHESIANS 4:30).

Conscience is always enlightened when sin is seen as hurting someone we love. No sin can touch one of God's stars or silence one of His words, but it can cruelly wound His Heart. Once the penitent understands this truth, he can see why he has such emptiness and desolation in his soul: he has hurt one he loves.

Many who approach a priest still try to conceal their conscience. They offer spurious reasons to explain their actions. The priest who remains on a purely psychological level cannot always see through such deceits, and in consequence he cannot help the one who has come to him. It takes a spiritual X-ray to penetrate such a mind:

Who else can know a man's thoughts, except the man's own spirit that is within him? So no one else can know God's thoughts; but the Spirit of God. And what we have received is no spirit of worldly wisdom; it is the Spirit that comes from God, to make us understand God's gifts to us; gifts which we make known, not in such words as human wisdom teaches, but in words taught us by the Spirit, matching what is spiritual with what is spiritual. Mere man with his natural gifts cannot take in the thoughts of God's Spirit; they seem mere folly to him, and he cannot grasp them, because they demand a scrutiny which is spiritual. Whereas the man who has spiritual gifts can scrutinize everything, without being subject, himself, to any other man's scrutiny. Who has entered into the mind of the Lord, so as to be able to instruct him? And Christ's mind is ours.
I CORINTHIANS 2:11-16

Thousands would flock to us every year, mail from frustrated souls would reach our doors, the young would seek us out, hearts unnumbered would seek comfort in our confessional, did we but realize the extraordinary powers of direction, counselling and guidance that come from living in the Spirit of Christ.

## Counselling Through Sympathy

Compassion is identification with others, whether they be laughing or weeping:

Rejoice with those who rejoice, mourn with the mourner.
ROMANS 12:15

Such heart-unity with the woes of others, as the parable of the Good Samaritan teaches, is independent of our natural feelings. The Psalms also inspire us to a like sympathy for everyone we meet.

Time was, when these were sick; what did I then? Sackcloth was my wear; rigorously I kept fast, prayed from my heart's depths. I went my way sadly, as one that mourns for brother or friend, bowed with grief, as one that bewails a mother's loss. PSALM 34:13,14

When Elizabeth, after being long childless, finally brought forth John the Baptist, her neighbors and her kinsfolk, hearing how wonderfully God had shewed His mercy to her, came to rejoice with her. LUKE 1:58

Did not the woman who had lost her piece of money and found it, call in her neighbors to rejoice, as did the shepherd who found the lost sheep? Did not Our Blessed Lord weep over His enemies whom He knew were about to stain their hands with His Blood (LUKE 19:41)? Did He not say also that the angels in heaven are not indifferent spectators at the conversion of sinners (LUKE 15:7-10)? When Our Blessed Lord saw the tomb of His friend, Lazarus, did He not weep so that the Jews exclaimed: "How he loved him" (JOHN 11:37)?

The weddings and the funerals in the parish, the converts and the fallen-aways, the faithful youths and the juvenile delinquents, the bigots and the men of good will—to all of these the sympathy of Christ goes out in the priest as he fulfills the words of Paul:

Bear the burden of one another's failings; then you will be fulfilling the law of Christ. GALATIANS 6:2

Everywhere in the Bible, the priest is pictured as binding up the broken, bringing back those that have been driven away, carrying lambs in his bosom, and gently leading those that are with young (EZECHIEL 34:2, 4; ISAIAS 40:11). This is a great worry to a good priest, and he may feel the burden so much as to cry out as Moses did:

Lord, he said, why dost Thou treat me thus? Must I carry a whole people like a weight on my back? I did not bring this multitude of men into the world; I did not beget them; and Thou wouldst have me nurse them in my bosom like a child.... I cannot bear, alone, the charge of so many; it is too great a burden for me.
NUMBERS 11:11-14

At other times, the spiritual priest full of anxiety for his converts, will compare his feelings with the pangs of a woman in childbirth:

My little children, I am in travail over you afresh, until I can see Christ's image formed in you. GALATIANS 4:19

Such a priest will express a special sympathy on sick calls to those who suffer. No priest can sympathize who is "outside" the suffering of others. "Crucifixion with Christ" through zeal and work and self-denial, will enlighten others by reminding them that Our Lord carried His scars with Him to heaven. When therefore, He lays His hand affectionately on any heart, He leaves the impression of His nails. The sick will be assured that their sufferings are not a punishment for their own sins so much as an opportunity to join in reparation for the sins of the world.

The priest will show such souls that there are no accidents in life, that the Providence of God rules the fall of a sparrow or the loss of a hair, that He made the wind that caused Jonas to be caught, that He made the sea-beast which swallowed him, that all sufferings that come to us even from our friends are to be seen as coming from His hand. In the Garden did He not say to Peter:

> Am I not to drink that cup which my Father Himself has appointed for Me? JOHN 18:11

Even the cup of sorrow which comes from those who should reach us the wine of friendship, must be seen as God's gifts bitter though it be.

The priest's own life may be full of a peculiar kind of suffering "from false brethren" (II CORINTHIANS 11:26) who ridicule his zeal, criticizing him if he interrupts a deserved rest in order to help a tortured soul, or if he pays two visits in one week to a dying mother of seven children. But none such barbs will make him bitter. His patient bearing of those who break bread with him will arm him with sympathy for others. His attitude will be like that of David when Semei took up stones to throw at David and cursed him. One of David's generals asked if he should cut off his head. David replied:

> Let him curse as he will; the Lord has bidden him curse David, and who shall call him to question for doing it? II KINGS 16:10

All things, all people, even our own brother priests, are sometimes used for our chastening, that we may better be able to console others. Thus will be verified in us, as in another Christ, the words of Simeon:

> ... to be a sign which men will refuse to acknowledge; and so the thoughts of many hearts shall be made manifest.... LUKE 2:34,35

## COUNSELLING THE SINNER

A woman is said to have gone to confession after an absence of thirty years. The confessor, a priest who in thirty years had never made a meditation before Mass, barked a bitter question at her: "Why have you stayed away from the Church for thirty years?" Her reply was a logical one. "Because, Father, thirty years ago I met a priest just like you."

A Spanish story has it that a priest who showed little mercy to a penitent heard a voice from the crucifix: "I, not you, died for her sins."

So jealous is God of His mercy that sometimes He permits priests to fall into the very sins they unjustly and inordinately condemn. If there is anything devotion to the Sacred Heart brings home to the priest, it is His mercy and His love of sinners.

No matter how strong the grip of vice, the penitent must still be assured that no mountain of guilt is so great as not to be removable by the Blood of Christ. Ever mindful of the treasures of mercies he has received from the Sacred Heart, the confessor will assure every sinner that "even lame folk shall carry plunder away" (ISAIAS 33:23), as the people of Jerusalem were told when victory seemed impossible.

Many sinners, particularly those guilty of sins which cause excessive introversion, are prone to adopt the language of Cain:

Guilt like mine is too great to find forgiveness.          GENESIS 4:14

They may even curse the day of their birth, as did Job (3:1; 27:2) and Jeremias (20:1-18), or even ask God to take away life as did Elias (III KINGS 19:4). But did not Our Lord Himself on the Cross, shutting out the consolations of Divinity, cry out (as He suffered for the darkness of atheists and agnostics):

My God, my God, why hast Thou forsaken Me?
         MATTHEW 27:46; MARK 15:34; PSALM 21:2

Such souls must be assured:

Was there ever such a God, so ready to forgive sins, to overlook faults? ... He loves to pardon.          MICHAEAS 7:18,19

And after all, if they had never sinned, or we had never sinned, how could we all call Jesus "Savior"?

We come from a world where God is ever working in love, where His sympathy never grows cold, where His mercy never tires, where His tenderness never wearies.

My Father has never ceased working, and I too must be at work.
         JOHN 5:17

He makes use of every faintest hope, waterpots at a marriage feast, loaves and fishes in a boy's basket, a Matthew at a desk, a man sitting under a tree, a student with Isaias in his hands—He notes them all in compassion. The key to his apostolate is not "the human touch," but the Christ-touch.

He held out His Hand and touched him.    MARK 1:41

Close, intimate, personal contact with affliction and grief is the key to counselling in the Spirit. The spontaneous impulse of pity breaking through the barriers of disease and disgust is the Christ-touch continued in the priest. He touches the leper and is unpolluted, as He took on sin and was without sin; so the priest, like a sunbeam, passes through a fouled humanity without stain.

Counselling is touching where there is disease or misfortune; it is not the simple giving of advice. A shake of the hand could be more of an occasion of grace than a meal sent superciliously from an agency. The priest takes the hand of the diseased whom he wishes to help; he goes down to their level, sees the old with their eyes, and the cancerous with their thoughts, knowing all the while that he can make them holy only to the extent to which Christ has already touched him.

## CHAPTER 10

## THE PRIEST AS SIMON AND PETER

No other Apostle arouses as much sympathy as Peter in the priest's heart. He seems very close to each of us in his conflicts and emotions, his strength and his weakness, his resolve to be heroic and his disastrous failure to live up to his aspiration. At one moment he is humble, at another proud. He affirms fidelity to his Lord, then denies. He is so supernatural, yet so very weak and natural. He extols as Divine the Master he loves, only to be frightened by a servant girl into saying that he does not know "the man." No chain is stronger than its weakest link, and the weakest link in the entire apostolic chain was the first link, Peter—and the Son of God holds on to that. Hence the "gates of hell shall not prevail."

### TWO "NATURES" OF EVERY PRIEST

Like Peter, every priest has two "natures": a "human nature" which makes him another man, and a "priestly nature" which makes him another Christ. The Epistle to the Hebrews identifies these two aspects. The priest is different from ordinary men as the one who offers sacrifice in their name.

> The purpose for which any high priest is chosen from among his fellow men, and made a representative of men in their dealings with God, is to offer gifts and sacrifices in expiation of their sins.
> HEBREWS 5:1

Nevertheless, the priest is like every man in his weakness.

He is qualified for this by being able to feel for them when they are ignorant and make mistakes, since he, too, is all beset with humiliations, and, for that reason, must needs present sin-offerings for himself, just as he does for the people. HEBREWS 5:2-4

An angel would not make a fitting priest to act on behalf of men. He does not possess a body subject to temptations, nor has he experimental acquaintance with human suffering. He would lack the weakness which makes for sympathetic understanding. But though a priest is like men, he must also be unlike them. He is withdrawn from among men, so that he may act in Christ's name and appear as Christ to men.

It is significant that the first one chosen by Jesus to be a Christian priest was given a new name to represent his new character. He did not, however, lose his old name. Instead, he now had two names. He was at one and the same time, Simon and Peter. Simon was his natural name; Peter was his vocation. As Simon, he was the son of Jona. As Peter, he was the priest of the Son of God. Peter never entirely got rid of Simon. But once called, Simon never ceased to be Peter. Sometimes it is Simon that rules; at other times it is Peter.

It might parenthetically be noted that Peter's brother, Andrew, was the one who was constantly making introductions. He introduced his brother Simon to Our Lord (JOHN 1:41). When a group of Gentiles approached Philip and asked to meet Jesus, Philip consulted Andrew and together they went to Jesus (JOHN 12:20-22). Andrew also introduced the lad who had the loaves and fishes (JOHN 6:8). Andrew began his work of witnessing within the family circle.

He, first of all, found his own brother Simon, and told him, we have discovered the Messias (which means, the Christ), and brought him to Jesus. Jesus looked at him closely, and said, Thou art Simon the son of Jona; thou shalt be called Cephas (which means the same as Peter). JOHN 1:41-42

Maybe someone in our family circle, a parent or a teacher, brought us to Christ, who by vocation changed our name. However great the dignity of our Christ-like office, we still bear with us the human nature descended from our own Jona. Even as Our Lord made Peter the rock on which He built His Church, He reminded him that he was taken from among weak men:

> Blessed art thou, Simon son of Jona.  MATTHEW 16:17

We drag our physical inheritance, our congenital weaknesses, our temperament and our body to the altar. The Simon element never leaves us, even when we take on the role of Peter. The sinful and the sinless, the human and the divine, the old Adam and the new, our bond to an earthly mother and our filiation to a heavenly Mother—under both of these aspects we ascend the altar steps, carry the Eucharistic Lord to a bedside, and sit long tedious hours dispensing mercy and hope to sinners.

On ordination day, we wrongly imagined that the Simon-nature had disappeared. But reality soon reasserted itself. The Simon-Peter conflict reappeared.

> The impulses of nature and the impulses of the Spirit are at war with one another; either is clean contrary to the other, and that is why you cannot do all that your will approves.  GALATIANS 5:17

> Of this I am certain, that no principle of good dwells in me, that is, in my natural self; praiseworthy intentions are always ready to hand, but I cannot find my way to the performance of them.
> ROMANS 7:18

The passage of the years and the growth in spiritual maturity cause certain kinds of temptations to decline, but others take their place. The demon of the noonday gives way to the demon of night. When Peter toward the close of his apostolate wrote his first epistle, he suggested by the opening words that he believed the Simon in him to be dead, for he identified himself as "Peter, an apostle of Jesus Christ" (I PETER 1:1). However, in his second and last epistle, shortly before his martyrdom, he acknowledged the continuing struggle of the man of the flesh against the man of God: "Simon Peter a servant and apostle of Jesus Christ" (II PETER 1:1).

In every priest either Simon has the mastery or Peter. In the prototype, in Simon Peter himself, Peter gradually achieved dominion over Simon thanks to the Holy Spirit. After Pentecost, one hears less of Simon, and when the name is mentioned, there is a reason for it. Thus, Cornelius is directed to send for "Simon, who is surnamed Peter" (ACTS 10:5), because outsiders would know him best by the one name, Christians by the other. James, at the Council of Jerusalem, uses the name Simon out of an old and familiar friendship. Elsewhere, the word is Peter. The impulsive daring that was Simon's is changed into steadfast, bridled courage. In that last Epistle, nevertheless, he himself repeats the name so long unused, that it must have vanished from all but the most retentive memories. But if he reverted to it, he did so with a purpose, to recall humbly from out the mist of years his old unsanctified self.

The turning point in the spiritual life of a priest is not only his vocation, his calling. It is also that moment when he becomes obedient to the Spirit. This is a kind of second ordination, a crisis which carries him from being a priest merely by office, into the possession and manifestation of the Spirit of Christ.

Before Peter possessed the Spirit of Christ, the tug of war between his earthly and his priestly nature was revealed at Caesarea Philippi, when he confessed the Divine Christ but denied the suffering Christ. The Father had illumined his mind to recognize and proclaim that

> Thou art the Christ, the Son of the living God.   MATTHEW 16:16

But when Our Lord announced that He would be crucified, Peter, drawing Him to his side,

> ... began remonstrating with Him; Never, Lord, he said; no such thing shall befall Thee.   MATHEW 16:22

Here in a vignette we have the entire paradox, which has proved for many a stumbling stone, a scandal, of infallibility and peccability. We have Christ's vicar Divinely guided in his office as key-bearer to the gates of heaven and earth. We have also this same Peter, the rock, the bearer of the keys, left to himself and without guidance, stigmatized as Satan. Paradox it is, but also fact. What Simon-Peter is there in all the priesthood who has not seen this scene re-enacted a thousand times in his own person; at this moment, another Christ; at that, another Satan?

Peter was willing to confess Christ the priest, but not Christ the victim. Men called to be rocks can become stones of stumbling. The Lord himself, however, defined His terms of service in clear language. The priesthood means imitation of Christ, and imitation means self-crucifixion. An unwillingness on the part of a priest to follow Him to Calvary, can sound to Our Blessed Lord only like the voice of the devil himself, that is to say, the voice of Simon repeating the sentiments with which Satan at the very start of His public life had tried to tempt Him away from the Cross. Our Lord did not take away Peter's vocation. He contented Himself with warning him that the flesh was with him and that in a moment of overconfidence he would fall. Peter is thus set forth by

Our Blessed Lord as a constant reminder that it is in their strongest qualities, unless they are periodically renewed by Divine grace, that men are most liable to fail.

## THE COMPROMISING PRIEST

No man can serve two masters. The priest nevertheless, will sometimes try to make the best of both the Simon and the Peter in him. Christ does not want it that way. In His priest there is no place for calculated less or more. Our Lord requires unmeasured love, but sometimes our nature asks for a compromise. It was such a spirit Our Blessed Lord had in mind when He urged His followers not to be satisfied with merely doing what they are obligated to do.

> If a man ... compels thee to attend him on a mile's journey, go two miles with him of thy own accord. MATTHEW 5:41

Our Lord may have been referring here to the forced transport of military baggage, not just to forced attendance on or company of someone. The supreme example would be Simon of Cyrene, who was compelled to carry the Cross (MARK 15:21).

St. Luke gives a vivid picture of the priest who is unwilling to do all the Lord requires of him, of the attempt at compromise and the half-obedience to the Divine Will. It is noteworthy that in the opening presentation, the protagonist is described by the sole name of Simon. Here is the passage (LUKE 5:1-6):

> It happened that He was standing by the lake of Genesareth, at a time when the multitude was pressing close about Him to hear the Word of God; and He saw two boats moored at the edge of the lake; the fishermen had gone ashore, and were washing their nets. And He went on board one of the boats, which belonged to Simon, and asked him to stand off a little from the land; and so, sitting down, He began to teach the multitudes from the boat. When He had finished speaking, He said to Simon, Stand out into the deep water, and let down your nets for a catch. Simon answered Him, Master, we have toiled all the night and caught nothing; but at Thy Word I will let down the net. And when they had done this, they took a great quantity of fish.

After being rejected in His own home town of Nazareth, Our Blessed Lord directed His steps to Capharnaum, which would henceforth be His base of operations. He found Himself so pressed by the crowds that He took refuge in a boat belonging to Simon. Floating off a little from the land, He began to teach the people. Then, when He had finished speaking, He turned to Simon and told him to launch out into the deep. "Let down your nets for a catch," He directed him.

Simon, however, was far from convinced. He was not prepared to challenge Him, but neither would he obey wholeheartedly. Even the word he used in answering Jesus reflected the ambivalence of his attitude. "Master," he said. It was the same word that Judas would use when betraying Him, a word without hint of recognition of the Divine, at most an admission of His status as a teacher, a rabbi. Simon's words reveal his thoughts. "What does He, coming from Nazareth, know about the way to fish at Capharnaum," he was surely thinking. "At this time of day who would dream of catching fish? The professional fisherman knows that night is the time to fish, and we have worked all night yet found nothing."

Peter knew all about fishing on the lake of Genesareth. It was accordingly as a mark of respect to the Master, as one might say, to humor Him, that he agreed to go part way: "but at Thy word I will let down the net." Our Lord had asked for nets; Peter compromised with a net. Our Lord asks for complete obedience; the servant gives a begrudging response. The flesh is not spirit; reason is not faith. Peter, relying on reason, let down a net. He flung into the Lord's face the bitter cry of life's unfruitful hours. But when the net caught a quantity of fishes so great that it was near breaking, suddenly there appeared from behind the bulk of Simon the priestly form of Peter:

> Simon Peter fell down and caught Jesus by the knees; Leave me to myself, Lord,... I am a sinner. LUKE 5:8

Notice the double changes of name. Christ is no longer "Master"; He is "Lord." Simon is no longer Simon; he is Simon Peter. The priest's nature asserts itself over that of the man under the impact of the miracle wrought by the High Priest for the benefit of Simon's unworthy self. It was more than fish that Simon caught; it was the Lord. As Coventry Patmore puts it:

> In strenuous hope I wrought,
> and hope seem'd still betray'd
> Lastly I said,
> "I have labor'd through the night, nor yet
> have taken aught;

But at Thy word I will cast forth the net!"
And lo, I caught
(Oh, quite unlike and quite beyond my thought,)
Not the quick, shining harvest of the sea
For food my wish,
But Thee.

So long as we think of Our Lord as "Master," we feel that what we are doing is enough, that we can settle for a net when He calls for nets. The moment, however, the Holy Spirit makes us realize His Lordship, makes us understand we are His priests through the Spirit, there comes over us the terrifying awareness of sin. The more we recognize the holiness of the High Priest, the more conscious we are of our own failings. The condition of all our priestly success is not in us the workers, nor in the nets of our schools and clubs. The worker failed, the net was near breaking. Our sufficiency is from God. The failure to catch souls must not be ascribed to God. We fail rather because we look upon Him only as Master, and not as Lord, or because we render less than complete obedience to His will.

The moment that Simon Peter was struck by his unworthiness, it is likely that Our Lord took him by the hand. So at least the last words of the account suggest.

> But Jesus said to Simon, Do not be afraid; henceforth thou shalt be a fisher of men.     LUKE 5:10

Our Blessed Lord seems paradoxically to draw priests closest to Him, when they are most conscious of the distance which separates them from Him. We preach the Word of God effectively only when we have trembled at the Word. The priests and the missionaries who make the most converts are those with the deepest and most overwhelming sense of personal unworthiness.

If a priest complains that he cannot make converts in his parish, his city or his mission, it is time to ask if he is relying on his own resources. There is always a reason if the Divine guarantee, "Thou shalt be a fisher of men" (LUKE 5:10), is not effective. I recall a parish in South America in which only eight of the eight thousand faithful attended Sunday Mass. A new pastor in six years raised to eighteen hundred the number of Holy Communions on week days. He preached eighty closed retreats a year, and he had the joy of seeing over 98 per cent of his people fulfill their religious duties. Our Lord did not say that we would be fishers for men, but fishers of men. Success comes through our union with Him.

## Peter And Judas

Every bad priest is close to being a good one; every good priest is in danger of being a bad one. The line between sanctity and sin is a fine one. It is easy to cross, and the one who crosses can quickly gain momentum in either direction. St. Thomas said that everything increases its motion as it nears its proper place or home. Saints grow rapidly in charity; wicked men rot quickly. We can see the truth of the point if we compare Peter and Judas. There seemed to be little difference in them for a long time, and then suddenly all the difference between being a saint and a devil.

The two of them were called to be priests, but that was only the first of the many points of similarity between them. Our Lord called them both devils. He called Peter "Satan" (MATTHEW 16:23; MARK 8:33) for tempting the Priest not to be a Victim on the Cross. Judas he called a "devil" one day at Caphamaum (JOHN 6:71), referring to the future betrayal, when "Satan entered into him" (JOHN 13:27) at the Last Supper.

Our Lord warned both Peter and Judas that they would fall. Peter rejected the warning. Though others might deny the Master, he asserted with bravado that he never would. Judas was similarly warned.

> The man who has put his hand into the dish with Me will betray Me.
> MATTHEW 26:23

Putting this into terms meaningful to us, it means that Judas would accept a "toast" from Our Lord and still "lift up his heel against Him." Judas also knew enough Scripture to understand that his act of betrayal was being likened to the betrayal of David by Ahitophel (II KINGS 15:31).

Both Peter and Judas carried out the betrayals which Christ had foretold. Peter fell when challenged by a maid-servant during the night of Christ's trial. Judas performed the nefarious deed in the Garden when he delivered Our Lord to the soldiers.

Our Lord made a positive effort to save both from their own weakness. He gave Peter a look.

> The Lord turned, and looked at Peter.   LUKE 22:61

He addressed Judas as "friend" and accepted his kiss.

> Wouldst thou betray the Son of Man with a kiss?   LUKE 22:48

The Lord only looked at Peter, but he spoke to Judas. Eyes for Peter, lips for Judas. There is nothing that Jesus will not do to save His priests. Both Peter and Judas repented, though in a crucially different sense.

And Peter went out, and wept bitterly.            LUKE 22:62

And now Judas, His betrayer, was full of remorse at seeing Him condemned, so that he brought back to the chief priests and elders their thirty pieces of silver; I have sinned, he told them, in betraying the blood of an innocent man.            MATTHEW 27:3,4

Why is one at the head of the list and the other at the bottom? Because Peter repented unto the Lord and Judas unto himself. The difference was as vast as that between Divine reference and self reference; as the difference between the Cross and the psychoanalytic couch. Judas recognized that he had betrayed "innocent blood," but he never wanted to be washed clean in it. Peter knew he had sinned and sought Redemption. Judas knew he had made a mistake and sought release—the first of the long army of escapists from the Cross. Divine pardon presupposes but never destroys human freedom. One wonders if Judas, as he stood beneath the tree that would bring him death, ever looked across the valley to the Tree that would have brought him life. On this difference of repenting unto the Lord and repenting unto self, as did Peter and Judas respectively, Paul would later on comment in these words:

Supernatural remorse leads to an abiding and salutary change of heart, whereas the world's remorse leads to death.
           II CORINTHIANS 7:10

Both lived in the same religious environment, heard the same words of the Word, were swept by the same winds of grace, and yet the internal reaction of each made the difference:

One man taken, one left, as they work together in the fields; one woman taken, one left, as they grind together at the mill.
           MATTHEW 24:40,41

Judas was the type who said, "What a fool I am"; Peter, "Oh, what a sinner." It is a paradox that we begin to be good only when we know we are evil. Judas had self-disgust which is a form of pride; Peter had not a regrettable experience, but a metanoia, a change of heart. The conversion of the mind is not necessarily the conversion of the will. Judas went to the confessional of his own paymaster; Peter to the Lord. Judas grieved for the consequences of his sin, as a single girl might sorrow over her pregnancy. Peter was sorry for the sin itself because he wounded Love. Guilt without hope in Christ, is despair and suicide. Guilt with hope in Christ, is mercy and joy. Judas took the money back to the temple priests. So is it always. When we give up Our Lord for any earthly thing, sooner or later it disgusts us; we no longer want it. Having loved the best, we can be satisfied with nothing less. Divinity is always betrayed out of all proportion to its due worth. And the tragedy is that he might have been St. Judas.

Peter and Judas illustrate how two called to the priesthood through the same spiritual experience of falling away from the Lord can end in a totally different way because of the response to or neglect of grace when the chips are down. Sometimes a reconciliation is sweeter than an unbroken friendship. Peter was always grateful for his grace. It shone in his Epistles. Each letter a man writes is characteristic of him. The Epistles of Paul to Timothy are notes of exhortation to be holy in his priesthood. The Epistles of John are a call to brotherhood. The Epistle of James is a plea for practical religion. What was the dominant note of the Epistles of Peter? It was the value of the pardon he had received, reminding us that our redemption was bought and paid for not "in earthly currency, silver or gold; it was paid in the precious Blood of Christ; no Lamb was ever so pure, so spotless a Victim" (I PETER 1:18,19).

## Causes Of The Priest's Fall And Resurrection

During a retreat, and often in the quiet hours of meditation, a priest grows discontent with his mediocrity, and wonders how he slipped into spiritual indifference. A study of the history of Peter shows that the decline can be due to a number of causes.

### 1. Neglect of Prayer

First in time and importance in the fall of Peter and in the fall of every priest is surely a neglect of prayer. Entering Gethsemane, Our Lord said: "Pray that you may not enter into temptation" (LUKE 22:40). While Our Blessed Lord was experiencing His agony in the garden, He who had no sin began to feel the penalty of sin, as if it were His own. He saw the betrayal of future Judases, the sins of heresy that would rend His Mystical Body, the militant atheism of the Communists, who (though they could not drive Him from the heavens) would drive His ambassadors from the earth. He saw the broken marriage vows, slanders, adulteries, apostasies, all the crimes that were thrust into His hands as if He Himself had committed them. While all these things were drawing the Blood from His Body, the Apostles were sleeping in the Garden. Men do not sleep when they are worried, but these slept.

Every soul can understand, at least dimly, the nature of the struggle that took place on the moonlit night in the Garden of Gethsemane. Every heart knows something about it. No one has ever come to the twenties—let alone the forties, the fifties, the sixties or the seventies of life—without reflecting on himself and the world round about him, and without knowing the tension that sin causes in the soul. Faults and follies do not efface themselves from the record of memory; sleeping tablets do not silence them; psychoanalysts cannot explain them away. While the sun of youth shines bright, it may blind the eye momentarily so that the outline of sin is obscure. But then comes a time of clarity—a sick bed, a sleepless night, the open sea, a moment of quiet, the innocence in the face of a child—when our sins, like spectres or phantoms, burn their unrelenting characters of fire upon our consciences. Their full seriousness may not have been realized in the moment of passion, but conscience bides its time. It will bear its stern uncompromising witness sometime, somewhere. It will force a dread upon the soul, a dread designed to make it cast itself back again to God. Such a soul experiences indescribable agonies and tortures, yet they are only a drop of the entire ocean of humanity's guilt which overwhelmed the Savior as if they were His own in the Garden.

While the apostles slept, the enemies plotted.

> Then He went back, and found them asleep; and He said to Peter, Simon, art thou sleeping? Hadst thou not strength to watch even for an hour?
> MARK 14:37

Our Lord came to the one whom He called a Rock, but He did not address him as Peter. He spoke to him in his human character, in the weakness of his flesh. "Simon," He said. Simon was in a deep sleep, and that was the first step in the fall of Peter. He neither watched nor did he pray. But it was not that night that Peter lost the battle. His defeat had been prepared in previous weeks. What is thought of today is done tomorrow. What we are at twenty we are apt to be at forty. The only difference is that the real characteristics have become more apparent. Spiritual slackness prepares the way for the wreck.

Our Blessed Lord chose His words to stress for Peter and the Church the double character of the priest—the spirit of the priest is of Christ, the flesh of the man.

> The spirit is willing enough, but the flesh is weak. MATTHEW 26:41

Peter and the other priests were placed in the world and trained to resist the forces of evil. If they were sheltered from evil, they would not need to be watchful. Faculties which are fully and frequently employed acquire the facility of the pianist's fingers. This is a law of nature. It applies equally in the spiritual world. Watchfulness against the forces of evil trains the spirit to resist. If salvation was completed by a single act, there would be no need of constant prayer. But danger is as long as life, and the Apostles and their successors find the strength to keep close to Him. One wonders if Peter did not recall the exact words Christ had used when years later he wrote:

> ... live wisely, and keep your senses awake to greet the hours of prayer. I PETER 4:7

St. Paul similarly insisted that watchfulness was a condition for keeping the Spirit of Christ against the inroads of the flesh:

> ... learn to live and move in the Spirit; then there is no danger of your giving way to the impulses of corrupt nature. The impulses of nature and the impulses of the Spirit are at war with one another; either is clean contrary to the other, and that is why you cannot do all that your will approves ... those who belong to Christ have crucified nature, with all its passions, all its impulses. GALATIANS 5:16-24

A priest's life spent so much in public must be fortified within with prayer and vigilance:

> Without Me you can do nothing. JOHN 17:19

The constant giving out of self needs replenishing from above. As the channel through which the waters of Life pass to the people, the priest must devote unceasing care and prayer to keep himself clean and holy. To recall St. Teresa of Avila, he who omits prayer needs no devil to cast him into hell; he casts himself into it. Peter slept when he was called to pray. That is the first step in the fall of a priest.

## 2. Substitution of Action for Prayer

Next in the spiritual decline of a priest comes the substitution of work for prayer. He now is too busy to pray; he has no time for meditation. He becomes so active that he loves the extraordinary. He immerses himself in endless visits, meetings, and conferences. Too busy to be on his knees, he is not too busy to swing swords, to blast out against public officials and bad politics. He does exactly what Peter did in the Garden, when Judas and the soldiers came to arrest Our Blessed Lord (JOHN 18:10,11):

> Then Simon Peter, who had a sword, drew it, and struck the high priest's servant, cutting off his right ear; Malchus was the name of the servant. Whereupon Jesus said to Peter, Put thy sword back into its sheath. Am I not to drink that cup which My Father himself has appointed for Me?

As a swordsman, Peter was an excellent fisherman. The best he could do, in his wild use of secular means, was to hack off the right ear of the High Priest's servant. There was still a lot of his old nature in Peter. He presumably intended to slay Malchus, but Divine Power prevented him. The last recorded miracle of Our Blessed Lord before His Resurrection was the healing of that ear (LUKE 22:51). It is possible that the healing of the wound was the reason Peter was not arrested.

Peter's action that night symbolizes all priests who avoid the obligations of their priesthood by being busy. Some lose themselves in a passion for buildings, others in organization, others in an endless round of banquets and speeches, committee meetings, drives. Such are the swords which take the place of prayer. Administration, long hours in offices, theatrical presentations, social evenings, parish feasts—they are the marks of prosperity that can kill the Spirit.

*In times of prosperity, the Church administers; but in times of adversity the Church shepherds.* A $2 million church is no sign of a $2 million faith, nor is a poor rectory the mark of a poor priesthood. Often it is not zeal for Christ which draws the sword of action but an empty and lonely soul. Boredom can beget ceaseless unreflective activity.

Aristotle says one vice is the enemy of spirituality, the vice of doing too much. When the Christ-spirit leaves, the flesh-spirit produces the "practical priest," the "priest of action." It is then labora, but no ora.

Pius XI had an extremely appropriate comment on this spirit.

> Attention must be called to the very great danger to which the priest exposes himself when, carried away by a false zeal, he neglects his own

personal sanctification in order to devote himself unreservedly to the external works of his ministry, however admirable these may be. ... It will make him run the risk of losing, if not Divine grace itself, at least the inspiration and unction of the Holy Spirit which gives such wonderful power and efficacy to the external works of the apostolate.

Pius XII restressed the danger of sword-swinging in place of prayer:

We cannot refrain from expressing our worry and anxiety to those who all too often are so caught up in a whirl of external activity that they neglect the primary duty of the priest, the sanctification of self. Those who rashly assert that salvation can be brought to men by what is rightly and properly called, the "heresy of action," must be called to a more correct judgment.

### 3. *Giving Up Mortification: Luke warmness*

After he gives up meditation and fills his day with "activism," the priest's next downward step is to give up mortification and become lukewarm.

> ... Peter followed Him at a long distance.         MATTHEW 26:58

At the Last Supper, Peter had promised everything; quickly he begins to give up everything. When Our Blessed Lord set His face toward Jerusalem, Peter and the others "followed Him with faint hearts" (MARK 10:32), dreading the prospect of the Cross. He felt, it is true, the tug of the Passion of Christ, but a reluctance to become irrevocably involved made him stay far behind. As a commentator of the ninth century wrote: "Peter could not have denied the Savior if he had stayed by His side." He would have stayed by His side, if he had not drawn his sword without orders, and if above all he had known how to watch and pray with the Savior. Every priest undergoes the same experience. Neglect of watching, prayer and mortification produces an inner uneasiness about being too close to the Lord.

When this happens, the priest's heart is no longer in his work. He celebrates Mass and says his office, but he rarely makes a visit to the Blessed Sacrament. He keeps the Lord at a distance. He mounts the pulpit to plead for the missions, but gives nothing out of his own pocket. He no longer assists at a Mass after he finishes his own. He loses the taste of spiritual things. Saintly priests annoy him. He observes the days of fasting and abstinence, but cuts a lot of corners. He whispers to his conscience: "Well, if I have not done all the good that I could, at least I did no harm."

Instead of contemplating the evil of which he has been guilty, he glories in the sins he avoids; he compares himself not with those who are better, but with those who are worse. He gives up spiritual reading, substitutes the Book of the Month for the Book of the Apocalypse. His sermons are unprepared. They are for the most part critical and complaining. All he achieves is to project his own mediocrity to others. His soul is empty. At most, it is confusedly aware that an ever increasing distance separates it from Our Lord. At night, when he awakens, the words of the Master ring in his ears:

> If any man has a mind to come My way, let him renounce self, and take up his cross, and follow Me. MATTHEW 16:24

Though Peter is following the Lord, he is actually walking toward a pit into which he will fall. He who does not advance in perfection, falls into imperfection. An untended garden becomes full of weeds. Things do not remain the same by being left alone. White fences do not stay white; they gradually become gray, then black. There are no plains in the spiritual life. We go up hill, or we go down. The moment we cease to row against the stream, the current carries us down the river.

What God said through Isaias of His people, He may also say of the priests who follow behind:

> This friend, that I love well, had a vineyard in a corner of his ground, all fruitfulness. He fenced it in, and cleared it of stones, and planted a choice vine there; built a tower too, in the middle, and set up a winepress in it, and it bore wild grapes instead.... I call upon you to give award between my vineyard and Me. What more could I have done for it? What say you of the wild grapes it bore, instead of the grapes I looked for? Let me tell you, then, what I mean to do to this vineyard of Mine. I mean to rob it of its hedge, so that all can plunder it, to break down its wall, so that it will be trodden under foot. I mean to make waste-land of it; no more pruning and digging; only briars and thorns will grow there, and I will forbid the clouds to water it. ISAIAS 5:1-7

The parable represents those who have consecrated themselves to the service of God. They are fenced in with sacerdotal graces, yet they end up neither hot nor cold, so that God would vomit them out of His mouth

(APOCALYPSE 3:16). God takes away the talent from the slothful servant and gives it to the diligent one (MATTHEW 25:29).

### 4. Satisfaction of Creature Wants, Emotions and Comforts

Peter first gave up prayer, then action, then mortification. When the moment of crisis comes, he is making himself comfortable by a fire, at first standing and then sitting.

> Peter followed at a long distance, right into the high priest's palace, and there sat down with the servants by the fire, to warm himself.
> MARK 14:54

What a spiritual biography! Peter was the last man who should have followed the Lord at a distance. His seniority and his position of leadership both carried additional responsibilities. But when a man has little spiritual satisfaction within, when the tide of his devotion has ebbed, he has to find some compensation for his inner loneliness. For Peter, this took the form of warming himself by a fire and of chatting with the servant girls. To compensate for internal poverty, one seeks to be rich on the outside. It was only after Adam and Eve had by sin lost the inner effulgence of grace that they became conscious of the fact that they were naked. They felt the need for clothes to cover their new-found shame; previously, their bodies had glowed with a mantle of charity woven by the fingers of God. It is almost universally true that excessive external display betrays an inner poverty and nakedness of soul.

To return to Simon Peter. It was the moment of crisis, and here he was making himself at home in an equivocal position. The Gospel narrative underscores the ironic contrasts. St. John (18:18) observes that it was cold, that Peter felt the need to warm himself by the fire. Peter by placing himself a distance from the Sun of Righteousness felt cold. His behavior was that which characterizes the bourgeois priest: comfortable, while others suffer; an armchair strategist on the missions, but himself doing nothing about them. Peter was now like the pastor who sits by his fire on Saturday while his curates hear confessions, instruct converts, take the sick calls. The warm glow of the fire in that courtyard was a "far better parish" to Simon than the garden of Gethsemane.

His love of luxury found him bad company. The warm fires of prosperity have overthrown many, who through want and troubles, had stood erect in grace. The outcome is that, withdrawn from the Lord, Simon encounters an occasion of sin. Lacking time for meditation, he yet has time for conversation. Though Jesus was at a distance, a girl was near. The lips of Peter which had but tasted the Eucharistic Banquet of Life already speak a lie. A short time ago, he was ready to die with Christ; now, without Him, he lacks the nerve to withstand a woman's curiosity.

Thou art the Christ, the Son of God,         JOHN 6:70

he then asserted. Now, juggling his theology, he protests like a coward:

I know nothing of the man.         MATTHEW 26:72

If Peter had stayed with Christ, no questioner could have wrung that shameful ambiguity from him. The subtlety of Satan creeps into the friendships of those who lack spirituality, causing them to hurt their friends more deeply than any enemy could. To sit by the fires of the ungodly may comfort the body, but it wrecks the Christ-principle within. Satan did not come to Peter "roaring like a lion" (I PETER 5:8), but as a frivolous girl indulging her curiosity. This was the moment in which the automatic connection between watching and praying was demonstrated in the life of Peter, as it is at some unanticipated moment in every life. The man who fails to watch, cannot expect an answer to prayer. Admittedly, God has the power to save whoever is falling, lest his bones be broken; but to ask for safety without watching is to "put the Lord thy God to the proof" (MATTHEW 4:7). God's special protection for His friends cannot be presumed upon when we have become indifferent to His friendship. Jonas chafed against God's word when he was told to go to Nineveh and preach penance; instead, he set his heart on Tarshish and found a ship standing ready to take him away from his mission (JONAS 1:3). Once the spirit of a priest grows cold, the enemies of Christ, the world, the flesh and the devil, quickly find a way to provide the "fire," the comfort and the company.

For every priest there is a lesson in the Gospel's observation that the priest who follows a long distance from Our Lord calls Him "a man." It is as if he said: "I was never meant for that kind of life; I never had a vocation." He similarly gets angry when anyone tells him that he is not Christlike. In him, as in Peter, the tendency is strong to revert to the Old Adam nature. One's mind conjures up Simon in his early days as a fisherman. One can almost hear the picturesque curses whenever his nets got snarled. While he lived in the intimate companionship of Our Blessed Lord, such words would not so much as occur to him; yet in a few hours he has a throwback. The curses pour from him, and this in the face of a young woman. Others have a better understanding of what the priest ought to do, than he himself has. The maid servant could tell

Peter he was supposed to be with the Galilean. Even those whose office is (like Martha's) to be busy with profane things, are often scandalized at the priest's failure to recognize that his office is to be with Christ.

The summons to be God's ambassador is no guarantee against weakness. Moses became arrogant when God chose him to lead His people, and he struck the rock to draw water from it (NUMBERS 20:7-12). David, the tenderest of all hearts, is betrayed into committing murder (II KINGS 11:14-27). Solomon, the wisest of all intellects, stoops to the folly of idolatry (III KINGS 11:4). Finally, when Peter had completed the triple denial, even nature protested. The first thing Our Lord did was to awaken Peter's memory, and He did it by the crowing of the cock. In that dark hour, when Peter had even forgotten to declare the Divinity of his Master, had forgotten his loyalty and his debtedness to the One Who called him to be the rock, one might have expected a lightning bolt, a thunderclap, to proclaim the enormity of the lapse. Christ settled for a sound Peter had heard a thousand times. A familiar sound, but with a new meaning, because it was the fulfillment of the Master's warning.

Nature is on God's side, not ours. It has

> in faith to Him ... fickleness to me,... traitorous trueness, and ... loyal deceit...
> Francis Thompson, The Hound of Heaven

The fall of the priest is completed by these steps: neglect of prayer, withdrawal to a distance from the Eucharistic Lord, dedication to a comfortable existence, negligence concerning occasions of sin; and finally, the substitution of a creature for the Christ.

## Chapter 11

## The Return to Divine Favor

Horrible as is this condition, it is not necessarily final. When Our Blessed Lord was led from the court, His face covered with spittle, He "turned and looked at Peter" (LUKE 22:61). The Master is bound, is insulted, is abandoned, is rejected. Yet He does not give up. He turns and looks at Peter. With boundless pity His eye seeks out the one who had just failed Him. He spoke no word. He just looked! But for Peter, what a refreshment of memory, what an awakening of love! Peter might deny the "man," but God would still love the man, Peter! The very fact that the Lord had to turn to look on Peter meant that Peter's back had been turned on the Lord. The wounded stag was seeking the thicket to bleed alone, but the Lord came to Peter's wounded heart to draw out the arrow.

And Peter went out, and wept bitterly.  LUKE 22:62

Peter was filled with repentance, as Judas in a few hours would be filled with remorse. Peter's sorrow was caused by the thought of sin itself or the wounding of the Person of God. Repentance is not concerned with consequences. This is what distinguishes it from remorse, which is inspired principally by fear of unpleasant consequences. The same mercy extended to the one who denied Him would be extended to those who would nail Him to the Cross, and to the penitent thief who would ask for forgiveness. Peter did not actually deny that Christ was the Son of God. He denied that he knew "the man," that he was one of His disciples. He did not abjure his faith. But he sinned. He failed the Master. And yet the Son of God chose Peter, who knew sin, rather than the beloved John as the Rock upon which to build His Church, that sinners and the weak might never have excuse to despair.

## THE LOVE OF CHRIST FOR HIS PRIESTS

> And the Lord turned, and looked at Peter....   LUKE 22:61

The incident probably occurred as Our Blessed Lord, after interrogation by Caiphas, was being led to the Sanhedrin. Our Divine Lord may even have heard Peter raise his well-known voice, have heard the oaths and curses assuring the bystanders that he did not know Jesus of Nazareth. Our Lord did not say: "I told you so." No burning words of condemnation passed His lips. Just one glance, a single look of wounded love. Such is the mercy of Our Lord when we are unfaithful and disloyal to Him! He seeks to win us back through added privilege and multiplied mercy! It is not only the fevered, the paralyzed and the lepers who know the tender compassion in the eyes of the Son Incarnate; it is above all, priests and sinners. It is not just the glance of Christ that brings repentance; it is also our response. The sun that shines so warmly both softens wax and hardens mud. The Divine Mercy calling the fallen hardens them to hell, or softens them to heaven.

In the synagogue at Caphamaum, Our Blessed Lord cast blazing eyes of anger on His baffled enemies as He wrought a miracle. With His Divine knowledge He knew that they were not willing to believe, would not be convinced were He to rise a thousand times from the dead. But Peter's attitude was different. One look of sorrowful reproach brought sorrow to his soul. The rich man who came to Our Lord was not yet prepared to go the whole way, though he was a sincere seeker after God. The Gospel tells us:

> Then Jesus fastened His eyes on him, and conceived a love for him.
> MARK 10:21

> The centurion recognized the Divine Majesty on the Cross and said: No doubt but this was the Son of God.   MARK 15:39

It is the same Divinity which was recalled to Peter when Jesus turned and looked at him. John, who was privileged to look so often on that dear Face, was haunted by It on the Isle of Patmos after the lapse of half a century. He spoke of how all the earth would wither away as Christ would come in judgment:

And now I saw a great throne, all white, and One sitting on it, at Whose glance earth and heaven vanished, and were found no more.
APOCALYPSE 20:11

That Face, too, would be the reward of all who would love Him and return to Him as Peter did:

... God's throne (which is the Lamb's throne) will be there, with his servants to worship Him, and to see his Face.... APOCALYPSE 22:3,4

Like Peter, every priest at one time or another gets out of step with Christ, follows behind, communes with worldly company and secular fires. Christ, nevertheless, treats him as He treated Peter. He constantly turns to look upon him. It was not Peter who thought of turning, but the Lord. Peter, because he was guilty, would by preference have looked anywhere else, but the Lord looked at him. This is the essential point for every follower of Christ to keep in mind when he sins—the Lord turns first.

No man understands wrong fully until he sees it in the light of the Face of Christ. He may feel mortified at the fool he made of himself, but he will sorrow only when he sees the Beloved crucified. The man who says, "I am so stupid" instead of "Lord, be merciful to me a sinner" is still far from rebirth.

What a lesson of tenderness is revealed by Our Lord's refusal to blast Peter! At such a moment, when one is teetering on the tightrope, a breath or a glance makes all the difference. It starts the return to God instead of plunging into the abyss of evil. As Christina G. Rossetti wrote:

O Jesu, gone so far apart
Only my heart can follow Thee,
That look which pierced St. Peter's heart
Turn now on me.

Thou who dost search me through and through
And mark the crooked ways I went,
Look on me, Lord, and make me too
Thy penitent.

One look at Divinity convinces us of sin. Peter the denier, under the eye of the Son of God, became at once Peter the penitent. That one look in which Divinity searches the soul, is the beginning of personal responsibility to God. We do not sin against abstractions or even against Commandments only; as persons, we sin against a Person. The awfulness of sin is not exhausted in the breaking of a Commandment; it embraces the re-crucifying of Christ. That is why the ultimate sorrow is related to the Crucifix, where each of us can read his autobiography. We see our pride in the Crown of Thorns; our lust and carnality in the nails; our forgetfulness of God in the pierced Feet, and our thievery in the riven Hands. Penitence is to hold ourselves up in God's pure and infinite Light and let Him shine our darkness away.

The difference between the sinner and saint is that one persists in sin, while the other weeps bitterly. The Greek word translated as "weeping" in the Gospel is one which implies a long and continued sorrow. Those who cannot find time to mourn for their sins also lack time to mend. The man gripped by remorse often takes to drink to dull his conscience. It is often not love of liquor, but hatred of something else, that makes a drunkard. The remorse of Judas led not to a striking of the breast in a Mea Culpa, but to the taking of a life. He had no heart to pray. Neither did he seek God's face to sue for mercy. But Peter sorrowed. He was humbled, not hardened.

Once the tears wash the eyes, the spiritual vision becomes clearer; that is why tears are often associated with the true understanding of sin. The tears in Peter's eyes were a rainbow of hope after a black storm. In them shone the entire spectrum of the radiant forgiveness of Christ's glance. Peter's memory of that life restoring glance was surely still in his mind when he wrote in his first Epistle:

> You had been like sheep going astray; now, you have been brought back to Him, your Shepherd, who keeps watch over your souls.
>
> I PETER 2:25

Christ still looks on us priests with sad but hope-filled eyes. He bids each of us, when the Simon is dominant, to resurrect our Peter vocation. No priest ever reaches a stage when "it is all up." David cried out in his misery and was heard. Peter, drowning after an act of rashness, was saved. When Thomas doubted, he was offered a pierced Heart to restore his faith. The Prodigal Son rose from swine and husks to a banquet in the Father's house.

Did priests but realize Infinite Love has need to communicate itself! One day a saintly soul prostrate before Jesus in the Tabernacle asked: "How dost Thou wish that I should call Thee?" And He replied: "Mercy." If we had never sinned, we never could call Jesus our Savior.

A religious accorded special revelations by the Sacred Heart declared that He spoke these words: "And now lastly I address Myself to My own consecrated ones, that they may make Me known to sinners and to the world. Many as yet are unable to understand what My true feelings are. They treat Me as One from Whom they live apart, know only slightly, and in Whom they have little confidence. Let them re-enkindle their faith and their love trustfully in My intimacy and love."

## ALL OUR PRIESTLY POWERS
## OVER SOULS DEPEND ON OUR LOVE OF OUR LORD

The next lesson Our Lord taught Peter was that love must constitute the basis of the pastoral office. It was the week after the Resurrection, and the Apostles were assembled by the Sea of Tiberias. Simon Peter, the established and accepted leader, said to Thomas, Nathaniel, James, John and two other disciples:

> I am going out fishing. JOHN 21:3

The word Peter used implied a progressive or habitually repeated action. Was Peter telling them that he was going permanently to his fishing business? It seems hard to imagine, and yet it is implied in the tense. In addition, Peter's character for all its good points, was vacillating and impetuous. He it was who had told Our Lord he would not deny Him, only to insist that he knew not the man. Leave your boats behind you, the Lord told Peter and the others, henceforth you will be fishers of men (LUKE 5:10). And here they are back at their old job.

On the Sea of Tiberias, night was the best time to fish. That night, nevertheless, they caught nothing. Work performed at the impulse of our own will, is futile. Then day broke and the morning light revealed the Risen Savior standing by the sea. No, they answered His question, they had caught nothing. Cast the net on the right side, He directed them; and there followed the catch of a multitude of fishes. Both Peter and John reacted characteristically.

As John was first to reach the empty tomb on Easter morn, so Peter was first to enter it; as John was first to believe that Christ was risen, so Peter was first to greet the Risen Christ; as John was first to see the Lord from the boat, so Peter was first to rush to the Lord, plunging into the sea in his enthusiasm.

Naked as he was in the boat, he cast a coat about him, forgot personal comfort, abandoned human companionship, and eagerly swam the hundred yards to the Master. John had the greater spiritual discernment, Peter the quicker action. It was John who leaned on the Master's breast the night of the Last Supper; he, too, was nearest the Cross, and to his care the Savior committed His mother; so now he was the first to recognize the Risen Savior on the shore. Once before, when Christ had walked on the waves toward the ship, Peter could not wait for the Master to come to him, but asked the Master bid him come upon the water. Now he swam to shore after girding himself out of reverence for his Savior.

The other six remained in the boat. When they came to shore, they saw fire, a fish laid on it, and some bread, which the compassionate Savior had prepared for them. The Son of God was preparing a meal for His poor fishermen; it must have reminded them of the bread and fishes He had multiplied when He had proclaimed Himself the Bread of Life. After they had dragged the net ashore and counted the one hundred and fifty-three fish they had caught, they were well convinced that it was the Lord. Nor did the symbolic significance escape them. Having called them to be fishers of men, He was offering a concrete anticipation of the size of the catch which would ultimately be drawn into the bark of Peter.

Christ had been pointed out by John the Baptist on the bank of the Jordan, at the start of His Public Life, as the "Lamb of God" (JOHN 1:29); now that He was about to leave this earth, He applied the same title to those who would believe in Him. He who had called Himself the Good Shepherd appointed others also to be shepherds. They had just ended the meal He had Himself prepared for them on the seashore. As earlier He had given the Eucharist after the supper, and the power to forgive sins after He had eaten with them; so now, after partaking of bread and fish, He turned to the one who had denied Him three times, and demanded a triple affirmation of love. The confession of love must precede the bestowing of authority, for authority without love is tyranny: "Simon, son of John, dost thou care for Me more than these others?" (JOHN 21:15).

One may properly wonder if the morning fire Our Lord had kindled reminded Peter of another fire some ten days before, when he denied the Master. Peter had denied by a fire; he was restored by a fire. Such is the scene of the conversation in which Christ commissions Peter to feed the lambs and the sheep.

### AUTHORITY INSEPARABLE FROM LOVE

Authority must never be without love. Love of Our Lord precedes any fruitful service in His Name. Such is the lesson which Christ once more inculcates as he reinstates Peter to the Apostolic office, from which he had fallen. Once again He addresses him as Simon, reminding him of the critical moments when Christ had first given him a new name and new authority (MATTHEW 16:17), and when He had warned him of his impending fall while promising restoration through His love (LUKE 22:31). Though authority in the Church is based on love, love in its turn is inseparable from obedience:

> If you have any love for Me, you must keep the commandments which I give you. JOHN 14:15

The Gospel account of Christ's triple question to Peter introduces a curious detail. The Greek text uses two different words, both of which are translated into English as "love." The first of these words is agapao, a word which implies a knowledge of the preciousness of the one who is loved. It is the word John uses to express God's love for fallen man, whom He so loved "that he gave his only-begotten Son, that those who believe in Him may not perish" (3:16). The other Greek word is phileo, indicating the response of the human spirit to anything that appears as pleasurable, a love implying some kind of friendship.

## LOVING AND LIKING

The first two times that Christ asks Peter to proclaim his love for Him, He uses the word agapao, whereas the third and final question contains the word phileo. But each time Peter in his answer uses the same word, the word phileo. In the New Testament, it is the less frequently used word to describe love. Agapao, implying an awakened and higher sense of value, occurs about 320 times; phileo, indicating a love of friendship and mutual attraction, only 45 times. To recreate the scene in the terms and form of a playwright might produce a result something like this:

Christ: Simon, son of John, do you love Me more than do these others, with a Divine, sacrificial, victim-like and self-surrendering love?

Peter: You know, Lord, that I love You with a deep, human, instinctive, personal affection, as my closest friend.

Christ: Simon, son of John, do you love Me more than do these others, with a divine, sacrificial, victim-like and self-surrendering love?

| | |
|---|---|
| Peter: | I have already told You, Master. You know that I love You with a deep, human, instinctive, personal affection, as my closest friend. |
| Christ: | Simon, son of John, do you love Me with a human, instinctive, deep, personal affection, as a very close friend? |
| Peter: | How often, Lord, must I repeat my answer? For the third time, I love You with the human, instinctive, deep, personal affection one has for one's closest friend. |

Peter's answer shows that he was hurt. He was grievously hurt. Yet the reason is not quite as simple as might appear on the surface. It was not just the thrice-repeated question that upset him. It was rather that the change from agapao to phileo indicated a scaling down of Our Lord's demands. He was no longer calling for the victim-kind of love for which He had first asked. It is as if Our Lord were putting His hands under that poor, weak, fragile love of Peter, just as He in fact starts with our poor, weak, human love as a beginning of a rich apostolate. The Lord asked for a love of devotion, and all He got was a love of emotion. But even that He does not reject. It is not enough, He says, but it is enough to start.

During the Public Life, when Our Blessed Lord had told Peter that he was a rock upon which He would build His Church, He prophesied also that He Himself would be crucified and would rise again. Peter then tempted Him away from the Cross. In reparation for that temptation which Our Lord called Satanic, He now notified Peter that He was not only commissioning Him with full authority to rule over His lambs and sheep, but that He was arranging for him yet another parallel with Himself, that Peter too would die upon the cross. "You will have a cross like that to which they nailed Me," He told Him in effect, "the cross you would have denied me and thus precluded My glory. Now you must learn what it really means to love. My love is a vestibule to death. Because I loved you, they killed Me; for your love of Me, they will kill you. I once said that the Good Shepherd gives His life for His sheep; now you are My shepherd in My place; you will receive the same reward for your labors as I have received—crossbeams, nails, and then ... life eternal."

> Believe me when I tell thee this;
> As a young man, thou wouldst gird
> thyself and walk where thou hadst the will to go,
> But when thou hast grown old,

> Thou wilt stretch out thy hands,
> And another shall gird thee, and carry thee
> where thou goest, not of thy own will. JOHN 21:18

Impulsive and self-willed in the days of his youth, Peter would in his old age glorify the Master by a death on the cross. From the day of Pentecost, the Spirit made Peter's decisions. He was led where he would not go. He had to leave the Holy City, where imprisonment and the sword awaited him. Next, his Divine Master directed him to Samaria, to the house of the Gentile, Cornelius; then to Rome, the new Babylon, where he was strengthened by the strangers of the Dispersion whom Paul had brought into the fold; finally, he was led to a cross to die a martyr's death on the hill of the Vatican. At his own request, he was crucified with his head downwards, deeming it unworthy to die like the Master. Inasmuch as he was the rock, it was fitting that he himself be laid in the earth as an impregnable foundation of the Church.

*The man who had tempted the Lord away from the Cross was the first apostle to embrace it himself.* His acceptance of the cross redounded to his Savior's glory more than all the zeal and impetuosity of his youth. When Peter did not yet understand that the cross was the means of redemption from sin, he offered his own death rather than that of the Master, asserting that even if all the others failed to defend Him, he would stand alone to protect Him. But after the illumination of Pentecost, he saw that it was the Cross of Calvary that gave meaning to the cross he would embrace. Toward the end of his life, when the cross was already in clear view ahead of him, Peter would write:

> I am assured, by what our Lord Jesus Christ has made known to me, that I must fold my tent before long. And I will see to it that, when I am gone, you shall always be able to remember what I have been saying. We were not crediting fables of man's invention, when we preached to you about the power of our Lord Jesus Christ, and about His coming; we had been eye-witnesses of His exaltation.
> II PETER 1:14-16

Humans seek the friendship of those who are above them in character and in power, but Our Lord condescends to ask our love. He will accept it even when it has little capacity for sacrifice and surrender. The trial of love is ultimately between the soul and Christ. When a priest is ordained, the bishop asks him searching questions; but the real examination is in the heart, and the interrogator is the ever-present and ever-living Savior. It is not recorded that Peter never again went fishing, but it is certain that all of his life he retained a five sense of the difference in his priesthood, between the joy of knowing the Lord and the sadness of falling away from Him.

Love alone can make easy the pastoral task of feeding lambs and sheep. Love it was that turned the seven years of Jacob's hard bondage for Rachel into so many pleasant days. Even the falls can be incorporated into sanctity. Peter is more glorious in heaven for his recovery, as Paul is more glorious for his renewed friendship for Mark after they quarrelled. The wrath of Moses, the lying of Abraham, the drunkenness of Noe, all are swept away in the great and final affirmation of love.

Our Lord often complains in the Scriptures. He expresses disappointment and surprise at the conduct of some of His followers. Yet, like Peter, He finds us on some shore, and with quick forgiveness asks us again to love.

As the physician feels his patient's pulse to judge his heart, so Our Lord tests the pulse of each priest's soul by his love. The test can sometimes be wounding, but that is because our sins have been wounds to Him. There is no mention of Our Lord having ever applied this test to anyone before His Passion and Death, of His having challenged an individual with the question if he loved Him. Now He acted with the assurance of one who has earned a claim on man's affection, a claim that the sinner's heart cannot resist.

After each affirmation of love, Our Blessed Lord committed Peter to apostolate and to service. These are the elements which keep love from degenerating into an indulgence of sentiment. He sent Mary Magdalen from the tomb to make an announcement to Peter, and He sent Peter from his confession to do the work of the Church. We may not separate ourselves from others even in the moment of the consciousness of our greatest self-distrust. The lesson is one for all priests: it was to Peter, in spite of his notorious betrayal, that Our Blessed Lord gave the keys of the Church.

Sympathy is the way to self-knowledge. Our own penitence deepens as we know our brother's sins. Every brother's fall reminds us of our need of vigilance. Nothing deepens our love for Christ like the larger knowledge of His grace which we gain as we see souls saved by Him. Peter could bear the better with the inadequacies of the flock, because of his recognition of himself as a sinful brother. St. Thomas Aquinas says that God sometimes permits people to sin in order to take them out of their pride, to awaken in them a sympathetic love for others.

The decision was and is a very personal one. There are no multitudes in the eyes of God. Just as He singled out from the crowd the woman who touched the hem of His garment (LUKE 8:43,44), so He singled out Peter. He had acted similarly before: "Adam; Where art thou?" (GENESIS 3:9); "Abraham, Abraham" (GENESIS 22:1); "Samuel, Samuel" (I KINGS 3:15); "Martha, Martha" (LUKE 10:41); "Saul, Saul" (ACTS 9:4); "Simon, Son of John" (JOHN 21:15).

## THREE FORMS OF LOVE

The measure of our priesthood is the level of our love. Love exists in three forms: unawakened, penitent, believing. The first stage includes very little love of Christ, because of an excessive love of the world; the second kind is not so much love, as "fear which has torment," because of sin; the third is the love that is "poured out in our hearts by the Holy Spirit, Whom we have received" (ROMANS 5:5). The unawakened man performs acts of obedience, but they are more apparent than real. The penitent's obedience is that of a slave. But in the true lover, obedience is filial. It produces prayer and holiness.

Rising above the multitudinous cares of the priest as pastor, his concern over schools, convents, finances, buildings and administration, the priest as another Christ must ultimately get back to the sublime truth that the one reality is the soul. For this does he sanctify himself. Pere Jean Baptiste Lacordaire, in Letters to Young Men, wrote:

> I am of your opinion about the mountains, the sea and the forest; they are the three great things in nature, and have many analogies, especially the sea and forest. I am as fond as yourself of them; but as old age creeps on, nature takes less hold upon us, and we feel the beauty of the saying of the Marquis de Vauvenargues, "Sooner or later, we enjoy only souls." This is why we can always love and be loved. Old age withers the body but to the soul that is not corrupted it gives a new youth. And the moment of death is that of the blossoming of our minds.

When love goes out of our heart, we hate the things we are obliged to do, or at least we cover up our deep feelings with the metallic ring of formalism. Our sermons become scoldings. Lost sheep become interruptions to our leisure. To minister at the altar of love with an unloving heart; to belong to a profession of self-sacrificing love, while seeking our own comfort; to offer but hollow words of love to suffering souls: these things bring their own punishment.

Even if one has not yet reached the level of love which permits performance of the duties of the apostolate without disturbing one's interior happiness, one can always follow the advice of St. Francis de Sales:

> If you cannot pray like a soul enjoying the gift of contemplation, you can at least make a spiritual reading and reflect on it; if not strong enough to fast, you may at least deprive yourself of a delicate morsel; if you cannot quit the world, you may at least guard against its spirit; if you cannot love God with a pure love, you may love Him at least out of gratitude; if you do not experience a lively sorrow for your sins, you can try to get it by asking it of God; you cannot bestow many alms, but you can give at least a drink of water; you cannot bear great insults, but you may bear at least a little reproach without murmuring; to be despised is beyond what you can endure, but you may bear with that little coldness manifested by your neighbor in his behavior toward you; the sacrifice of your life is not required of you, but you can put up with some inconvenience and preserve patience under some little trying circumstance.

Peter, restored, is close to a fire. That other fire at which he denied Christ is one the world made; but this fire Christ prepared. The enthusiasm, the effort, the passion lighted by the fires of the world leave but ashes and dust. Not so, however, when enkindled by Him Who came to cast fire upon the earth (LUKE 12:49).

## CHAPTER 12

## MELCHISEDECH AND BREAD

WHY are we called priests "in the fine of Melchisedech"? Why are we not priests in the line of Aaron, to whom the priesthood belonged in the Old Testament? The Epistle to the Hebrews (7:11) indicates the reason, namely, that the Levitical priesthood did not represent the perfection of the priesthood. "Now, there could be no need for a fresh priest to arise, accredited with Melchisedech's priesthood, not with Aaron's, if the Levitical priesthood had brought fulfilment." The reasons for the inadequacy of the Levitical priesthood were many.

1. The priesthood of Aaron was carnal, temporal, successive and perishing. The priesthood of Melchisedech, as symbolic of that of Christ, is eternal. The Levitical priests were personally unclean, in the liturgical sense of the word. They had to offer sacrifices for their sins, and death for each of them put an end to his ministrations.

But Melchisedech is eternal. This aspect of his priesthood is expressed in symbolic terms in the Bible:

> No name of father or mother, no pedigree, no date of birth or of death; there he stands, eternally, a priest, the true figure of the Son of God.         HEBREWS 7:3

The omission of any reference to Melchisedech's ancestry, birth or death, is the Holy Spirit's way of presenting him as the type of Our Lord.

Summarizing the difference between the two priesthoods, Scripture continues:

> Of those other priests there was a succession since death denied them permanence; whereas Jesus continues forever, and His Priestly

office is unchanging; that is why He can give eternal salvation to those who through Him make their way to God; He lives on still to make intercession on our behalf. HEBREWS 7:23-25

2. A second reason is that Our Lord combines within Himself both Kingship and Priesthood, and this was true also of Melchisedech.

Melchisedech, too, was there, the king of Salem. And he, priest as he was of the most high God ... GENESIS 14:18

Melchisedech was in his person king and priest, thereby foreshadowing the adorable Lord, in whom justice and peace would kiss each other (PSALM 84:10). Our Lord would not have peace without justice; hence He made "peace with them through His Blood, shed on the cross" (COLOSSIANS 1:20).

3. The "greatness" of Melchisedech was a foretelling of the greatness of Christ. Abraham acknowledged that Melchisedech was greater than he was, by paying him tribute:

To him, Abraham gave tithes of all he had won. GENESIS 14:20

This the Epistle to the HEBREWS (7:4-8) applies to Our Lord:

Consider how great a man was this, to whom the patriarch Abraham himself gave a tenth part of his chosen spoil. The descendants of Levi, when the priesthood is conferred on them, are allowed by the provisions of the law to take tithes from God's people, although these, like themselves, come from the privileged stock of Abraham; after all, they are their brothers; here is one who owns no common descent with them, taking tithes from Abraham himself. He blesses him, too, blesses the man to whom the promises have been made; and it is beyond all question that blessings are only given by what is greater in dignity to what is less. In the one case, the priests who receive tithe are only mortal men; in the other, it is a priest (so the record tells us) who lives on.

4. The priesthood of Melchisedech was sacramental and unbloody, not the offering of bullocks and goats.

And he, priest as he was of the most high God brought out bread and wine with him... GENESIS 14:18

Each day in Mass we mention the sacrifice of Melchisedech as sanctum sacrificium immaculatam hostiam. The sacrifice was a peaceful one, offered after Abraham had won the war against the four kings.

5. Our Lord Himself was of an ancestry distinct from that of the Levitical priesthood. He belonged to the tribe of Juda; not, like Aaron's sons, to the tribe of Levi. His line was different, not only because He is eternal, but also because, as the Epistle to the HEBREWS (7:14-18) insists, His temporal generation was different:

> Our Lord took His origin from Juda, that is certain, and Moses in speaking of this tribe, said nothing about priests. And something further becomes evident, when a fresh priest arises to fulfil the type of Melchisedech, appointed, not to obey the law, with its outward observances, but in the power of an unending life; (Thou art a priest in the line of Melchisedech, God says of him, forever).

The historical setting of the meeting between Abraham and Melchisedech is significant. All we know about Melchisedech is found in brief passages in GENESIS (14:18-20) and Psalm 109, and in the Epistle to the HEBREWS (5:6,10; 6:20; 7:17,21). Genesis reports that while Lot, Abraham's nephew, was living in Sodom, the city was attacked and taken by the armies of four powerful kings. It is the first war recorded in the Bible. In addition to capturing the king of Sodom, they seized Lot and his family. When Abraham learned of Lot's misadventure, he mustered a small army of 318 servants and gained a mighty victory. He not only recovered the spoils seized by the invaders, but he also freed Lot and his family.

Abraham had a right to everything gained by his victory. Would he avail himself of his right, ignoring the misfortune of others? Knowing that Abraham might have been tempted to have enriched himself materially, God sent help in the person of Melchisedech.

> Melchisedech, too, was there, the king of Salem. And he, priest as he was of the most high God, brought out bread and wine with him, and gave him this benediction, On Abram be the blessing of the most high God, Maker of heaven and earth, and blessed be that most high God, Whose protection has brought thy enemies into thy power.
> GENESIS 14:18-20

God won the victory for Abraham. The spoils therefore belonged not really to Abraham but to God, who in addition now promised Abraham an even greater reward. The help was accepted, and Abraham gave his tithe to the priest.

Later, when the king of Sodom came and told Abraham to keep the spoils for himself, Abraham was able to answer:

> By this hand, which I lift up to the Lord God, the Prince of heaven and earth, I will take nothing of thine, though it were but a thread from the wool or the strap of a shoe. Never shalt thou say, Abram got his wealth from me.     GENESIS 14:22,23

What noble words! He would keep nothing for himself. Because he had not sought wealth, as Solomon did not pray for it, he was given a special reward:

> Have no fear, Abram, I am to protect thee.     GENESIS 15:1

Thus does the heavenly High Priest bless those who do not seek the material spoils of earth.

We then are priests according to the line of Melchisedech. When the Levitical priesthood proved to be inadequate in the days of Heli and his sons (I KINGS 1:4,5; 2:12-17,22), God said:

> Afterwards, I will find Myself a priest that shall be a faithful interpreter of my mind and will.     I KINGS 2:35

The fulfillment is found in Christ, whose priests we are:

> So it is with Christ. He did not raise Himself to the dignity of the high priesthood; it was God that raised Him to it, when He said, Thou art My Son, I have begotten thee this day, and so, elsewhere, Thou art a priest for ever, in the line of Melchisedech.
>     HEBREWS 5:5,6

Since Melchisedech offered bread and wine, it is fitting to look for the Eucharistic Bread anticipated in the Old Testament.

## BREAD OF PRESENCE

God has always been present to His Church in a way different from His presence elsewhere. The Church of the Old Testament already enjoyed a prototype, show or symbol of the Eucharistic Presence. The ancient sanctuary contained two items of particular significance: the lampstand, and the bread of presence. St. John applies both to Christ, the Light of the World (JOHN 8:12) and the Bread of Life (JOHN 6).

## THE OLD TESTAMENT

The Epistle to the Hebrews (9:2) records that "there was an outer tabernacle, which contained the lampstand and the table and the loaves set out before God; sanctuary was the name given to this." The so-called table of the show-bread was important not so much for the table itself, as for the bread placed upon it. It was the Bread of Presence, literally "Bread of the Face." It was to this Bread of Presence that Christ referred in Matthew (12:4) as "the loaves set out there before the Lord." The bread was meant as a memorial placed continually in God's presence.

> The bread is to be a token-sacrifice to the Lord. LEVITICUS 24:7

Each Saturday a fresh supply of bread was substituted for the old, twelve loaves—one for each of the twelve tribes. All were thus represented, little Benjamin no less than royal Juda, Dan as well as the priestly Levi, and just as much for one tribe as for another. No part of God's family was forgotten. Each was fully represented, and they were always before Him.

> The table is to hold the loaves of bread which are to be set out continually in My Presence. EXODUS 25:30

The bread of the Old Testament was thus the presence of the people before the Lord, but the Bread of the New Testament is the Presence of the Lord before the people. In the Old Testament there was never a moment when they were out of His sight. Bread was a continuous reminder to Him of His covenant relation to them, and of His promises to them of a Savior and Redeemer. As the twelve tribes were made one in His Presence, so also, His ecclesia, His Church, so by "the one bread is made one body, though we are many in number; the same bread is shared by all" (I CORINTHIANS 10:17).

The Bread of Presence was before His Face; that is why it was called the continual bread.

> ... keep hallowed loaves set forth continually....
> II PARALIPOMENA 2:4

> ... the bread set forth there as always....
>
> NUMBERS 4:7

The bread was to be made of the finest flour and upon each row incense was placed to indicate that the offering was a sacrifice to the Lord.

> Put grains of fine incense upon them; the bread is to be a token sacrifice to the Lord.
>
> LEVITICUS 24:7

Thus was prefigured the union of the sacrament and sacrifice under the New Law.

Even a "sanctuary lamp" was provided—not that the Bread was the substance of the Body and Blood of Christ, but only a shadow, an anticipation.

> Never must the altar be empty of this perpetual fire.
>
> LEVITICUS 6:13

From that day to this, a lamp announces the Presence.

## The Holiness Of The Sanctuary

For the Christian who lives in the realm of grace, the demands of the holiness of God are not less demanding than they were for the Jew under the Old Testament. If those who rebelled in the desert did not escape judgment, much less shall we who are privileged to live in the fullness of revelation.

> Beware of excusing yourselves from listening to Him who is speaking to you. There was no escape for those others, who tried to excuse themselves when God uttered His warnings on earth; still less for us, if we turn away when He speaks from heaven.    HEBREWS 12:25

The Old Testament contains seven instances of sudden judgment in connection with the tabernacle or the temple, its liturgy, its worship, its vessels. Three of them had to do with the offering of incense, three with the Ark, and one with the candlestick.

Probably the first to die in the desert were Aaron's two sons who had just been ordained priests. God had sent down fire from heaven upon the altar of sacrifice and directed that it be always kept burning, like a sanctuary lamp before a tabernacle (LEVITICUS 9:23,24). What their sin was is uncertain, but it may have been drinking alcohol in forbidden circumstances (LEVITICUS 10:9), but in any case, they offered a strange fire. They may have lighted a fire themselves instead of taking it from the altar, and they may also have mixed a strange incense which was expressly forbidden (EXODUS 30:9,10): "whereupon the Lord sent down fire which devoured them and they died there in the Lord's presence" (LEVITICUS 10:2). To approach the tabernacle with the spirit of the world in our soul, instead of the spirit of Christ is to offer foreign fire. But whatever the sin of those Old Testament priests was, we are bidden to "worship God as He would have us worship Him, in awe and reverence; no doubt of it, our God is a consuming fire" (HEBREWS 12:28,29).

The Ark fell into the hands of the Philistines (I KINGS 4), because the Jews had used it as a magical charm to protect them in time of war. The Philistines put it in the Temple of Dagon, and the statue of the god fell prostrate before the Ark, as those who came to arrest Our Blessed Lord fell down at the mention of His Name (JOHN 18:6).

When the Philistines refused to acknowledge the power of God, great numbers of them died with the plague (I KINGS 5:6). As the Ark was a source of blessings to those who reverenced it, it was similarly a source of affliction to those who refused to recognize the power of God Who dwelt symbolically in it. The same is true of Christ.

> We are Christ's incense offered to God, making manifest both those who are achieving salvation and those who are on the road to ruin; as a deadly fume where it finds death, as a life-giving perfume where it finds life. Who can prove himself worthy of such a calling?
> II CORINTHIANS 2:15,16

Everywhere the Ark went, while it was in the hands of the Philistines, there went the punishment of God:

> No city was free from the fear of death, and God's heavy visitation; even those who survived had shameful sores to tend, and everywhere cries of anguish went up to heaven.                I KINGS 5:12

Though we see no such manifestations of this power when the Eucharist is profaned, may it not be that God is reserving His judgment for those who approach it without faith? Men may plead that they have eaten in His Presence and done wonderful works in His Name and cried "Lord, Lord," but He will say that He knows not such workers of iniquity (MATTHEW 7:21-23; LUKE 12:25-27).

The Philistines finally became penitent, returned the Ark, and offered tokens of reparation for their sins; but how much more mercy they would have obtained, if they had acknowledged God's Presence, not in terror, but in appeal to His mercy!

If God punished the Philistines so harshly for keeping the tabernacle, which was only a promise and prototype of the Eucharist, then what reverence should the Eucharist itself not awaken in those who have the reality and the substance! How terrible a thing it is to fall into the hands of the Living God! (HEBREWS 10:31) How feeble Nabuchodonosor seemed when he fed on grass (DANIEL 4:30)! What a contemptible "god" did Herod appear when worms were devouring his vitals (ACTS 12:21-23)! How Balthasar trembled with fear, his knees shaking at the sight of the handwriting on the wall (DANIEL 5:6)! How Felix fled from enlightenment when Paul reasoned with him about righteousness and judgment (ACTS 24:25)! Persons who are filled with slavish fear seek to banish what causes them terror, rather than part with the sin which alone makes God an object of dread. But to us has been given the power to call down the Lord on our altars! Our greater privileges should make us tremble at knowing how God punished those with fewer talents and less light.

Another Old Testament incident which helps the priest to see how much reverence God demands for His Sacrament is seen in the punishment that was given to the Bethsamites. They were happy to receive the Ark back from the Philistines, but they failed to show respect. Rather, manifesting an unlawful curiosity, they looked into it and were smitten by God (I KINGS 6:19).

Some things are too holy to be looked upon with curious eyes. Moses was not allowed to approach the burning bush to see why it was not consumed (EXODUS 3:5). The Old Testament had a very strict prohibition against any rude curiosity in relationship to sacred symbols. As Moses was told, "Do not come nearer" (EXODUS 3:5), so in relationship to the Ark, which was to be carried by Aaron and his sons: "None must pry into the secrets of the shrine while they are yet uncovered on pain of death" (NUMBERS 4:20).

For their sinful curiosity, "the Lord smote some of the Bethsamites themselves, for prying into the ark of the Lord" (I KINGS 6:19). The Bethsamites being Israelites and having Levites among them, knew the laws regarding the Sacred Ark and the reverence with which it should be treated. Probably the reason they pried into it was to see if the Philistines had put any gold into it, in addition to the gold offerings which they had placed in a separate coffer, when they brought it back. So doing, they broke the law which forbade the ordinary people even to approach the Ark, and directed the priest to cover it with a veil.

For irreverence to what was a mere figure of the Blessed Sacrament, the Philistines were afflicted with diseases, the Israelites visited with death. If the penalty seems to us severe, it is because our minds have fallen short of the reverence due to either what symbolizes His Presence, or what is the Presence Itself. After the disaster had fallen upon them,

> Who can stand his ground, the Bethsamites asked, before a God so Holy as this? I KINGS 6:20

After the Ark had been kept in the house of Abinadab for some time, his two sons, Oza and Ahio, were appointed as its drivers to prepare the way while the oxen were driven by Oza. They had reached the threshing floor of Nachon, when the oxen began to kick, thus tilting the Ark to one side. Oza put out his hand and caught hold of it. The act seemed a natural one in the circumstances, yet it was punished as a rash deed, it "provoked the Divine anger; the Lord smote him, and he died there beside the Ark" (II KINGS 6:7).

Such was the Lord's displeasure when any irreverence was shown to the Tabernacle. The Law was clear as to who might touch the Ark, and how it should be carried. It was not proper to put it in a wagon as had been done, nor was it to be touched by anyone except the priest:

> Then when Aaron and his sons have wrapped up the sanctuary and all its appurtenances ready for the march, the sons of Caath will enter and carry them away in their wrappings; they are not to touch the things of the sanctuary, on pain of death. NUMBERS 4:15

The Ark should have been carried by two staves, held by priests. Oza was not a priest and was accordingly not authorized to touch the holy thing. This violation of God's command may have been the fruit of an habitual irreverence induced by long familiarity with the Ark. God's action showed that no service was acceptable to Him unless regulated by strict adherence to His revealed Will. The utmost reverence was demanded of all who approached Him (LEVITICUS 10:3).

How strictly the Lord enjoins His priests:

> Keep yourselves unsullied, you that have the vessels of the Lord's worship in your charge. ISAIAS 52:11

The privilege of belonging to the Mystical Body of Christ implies both tremendous privileges and equal responsibilities.

Nation is none I have claimed for My own, save you; and guilt of yours is none that shall go unpunished.  AMOS 3:2

Such are the judgments falling upon men in connection with the tabernacle, or the temple, its worship, its holy vessels, or its priesthood. When all these are taken together, one trembles at the reverence God demands for the things that are His, and the punishment He metes out sometimes for the least infraction of what is dedicated to His service. The altar at which the priest stands is holy.

If the angels tremble, shall we not quake? But the Presence must not enkindle a fear born of sin or impiety, but a holy fear begotten of love for One Who dwells amongst us. As Leo XIII put it:

> Our Lord instituted It to call to mind the supreme Love whereby Our Redeemer poured forth all the treasures of His Heart, in order to remain with us until the end of time.

## THE REAL PRESENCE

It is a common experience to be stopped on the street by a stranger who asks: "Where does so and so live?" That same question through the centuries has been asked of those who believe in God:

Daily, I must listen to the taunt, Where is thy God now?  PSALM 41:4

To the one who is suffering, it may seem that God has vanished. But, in the calmer moments of the New Testament, His disciples one day asked Our Lord:

Where dost Thou live?  JOHN 1:38

John and Andrew had already heard Him speak; they had learned their theology, namely, that He is the "Lamb of God" (JOHN 1:36,37), and therefore, the Redeemer. There, bodily present, was the One for whom all the ages had breathlessly panted. They began to follow Our Lord, and He spoke the first words of His public Messianic life:

What would you have of Me?  JOHN 1:38

Man? Teacher? Savior? Esteem? Advancement? Power? What do each of us seek in Christ? Is it something He has, or is it He?

The response of the disciples was a simple question:

Where dost Thou live? JOHN 1:38

Where is His permanent Presence? Where His dwelling? We know His Power is in the mountains; His Wisdom in the laws of nature; His Love in gravitation pulling all things to a center. But this is not presence. These are but effects. But Body, Blood, Soul and Divinity—"Where dost Thou live?" We know the answer in theory. He dwells in the Eucharist.

But in practice, do we know it? Ah! that requires a special search, an extra effort, maybe an hour to find out. That is why in answer to their question, He answered:

Come and see. JOHN 1:39

The "come" is a visit; to "see" is to enjoy. The first words that fell from the lips of Him Who is the Bread of Life were an invitation to seek greater union with Him. John and Andrew called Him "Master" when they first saw Him, but now they were urged to discover that He was the "Lord." At the Last Supper, He was still "Master" to Judas, but to the others, He was "Lord."

From that day to this, first-hand knowledge of Him as Lord is given to priests who "come and see." Priests can follow, like John and Andrew. Eucharistic devotion is something added, something extra, something special in the understanding of Our Lord. One can know all the theology of the Lamb of God and Redemption, and still not walk that "extra" mile to know where He "dwells." To "come" demands leaving the rectory or the magazine; to "see" requires being in His Presence. But once before His tabernacle we can say with Job:

I have heard Thy Voice now; nay, more, I have had sight of Thee.
JOB 42:5

A newly ordained French priest received a visit from a strange priest of another nationality. The visitor being unkempt, he was given a poor room in the attic. The French priest lived to see that visitor canonized, as Don Bosco. On learning of the canonization, he reflected: "If I knew he was a saint, I would have given him a better room." What will be our thoughts on the day of judgment when we reflect on the thousands of times we passed our church or a chapel without even a quick prayer, a greeting? The innkeeper at Bethlehem did not "see" that it was He. The capitalists of the Gerasenes did not know it was He. The Samaritans, who refused to receive Him, did not know it was He.

Now as we ask the question: "Where dost Thou dwell?" He points to the tabernacle and says, "Come and see." We should do ill not to love Him when He brings Himself so close. John and Andrew set the example:

> They went and saw where He lived, and they stayed with Him all the rest of the day, from about the tenth hour onwards.     JOHN 1:39

The "went and saw" balanced the "come and see." But there was more: "and they stayed with Him." No priest who has ever risen from such an hour in His Presence will ever have any other words on his lips than those of Andrew:

> We have discovered the Messias.     JOHN 1:41

Immediately after that visit, Andrew brought his brother Peter to the Lord. The work of conversion is inseparably connected with long visits to Jesus in His dwelling.

## Chapter 13

## Judas and the First Crack in His Priesthood

WHERE does a spiritual decline begin? What is the first symptom of a train of sins? The traditionally listed enemies of spirituality are the world, the flesh, and the devil. But are not these secondary? Is there not first a detachment from something, before an attachment to anything, is possible? It is often said that Judas, the supreme example of the fallen apostle, was first corrupted through greed. The Gospel does not support this view. Greed could conceivably have been his intent when he accepted the call of Christ to follow Him. As it appeared in his life, it required a certain watchfulness to avoid detection. How he must have squirmed as Our Blessed Lord unfolded the parables of the vanity of wealth! Surely he realized that they applied to him.

Later, greed became bold. Judas protests the wastefulness of Mary for anointing the Feet of the Savior with costly ointment. Knowing the price of everything and the value of nothing, Judas calculated that the cost of the unguent would enable a man to live comfortably for a year. How disappointed must Judas have been when earlier he had heard Zaccheus of Jericho tell Our Lord:

> Here and now, Lord, I give half of what I have to the poor; and if I have wronged anyone in any way, I make restitution of it fourfold.
>
> LUKE 19:8

Judas must also have wondered why Matthew gave up a profitable post as collector of customs to follow the poverty of the Savior. Matthew may himself have been surprised that he was not made treasurer, because of his familiarity with monetary transactions. Love of money was present in Judas; this is obvious. It showed itself clearly when he saw the perfume broken over the Lord's Feet.

> What is the meaning of this waste?... It would have been possible to sell this at a great price, and give alms to the poor. MATTHEW 26:8,9

Mary obeyed the instinctive impulse of uncalculated love only to be charged for not having calculated. Lovers on earth concern themselves little about the usefulness of their gifts. True lovers of Christ do not measure their gifts. They break alabaster and give all. But to Judas, the cold-blooded spectator, it was useless waste. Avarice, indeed, can be one of the great sins of the priest, and perhaps the most insidious. It is a kind of "clean" sin, because it parades under the guise of prudence, of "caring for old age." Simon Magus, for example, very quickly got the idea that the laying on of hands was a good way to make money (ACTS 8:19). The good priest lives for his vocation; the avaricious priest lives on his vocation. When he attends a pastoral conference, he ignores every reference to the sanctification of the clergy, to moral and spiritual discipline, to visitation of the sick. But when the Bishop talks about salaries, stole fees, promotions, then he sits up and listens. He is always out to get a "better" parish, but for him "better" simply means more lucrative.

The words of the Lord to the contrary, the avaricious man believes that he can serve both God and Mammon. What Our Lord meant was that a man cannot divide his heart between God and money; and if he could, God wants no part of a divided heart. St. Paul said:

> You know well enough that wherever you give a slave's consent, you prove yourselves the slaves of that master; slaves of sin, marked out for death, or slaves of obedience, marked out for justification.
> ROMANS 6:16

It often happens that those who are fond of amassing wealth are sometimes sinless in other respects. They are celibates, they may even be meticulous about the external laws of the Church, but so were the Pharisees, "the Pharisees, who were fond of riches" (LUKE 16:14). It was to them that the Lord told the parable of the rich man and Lazarus (LUKE 16:19-31).

### WAS AVARICE THE BEGINNING OF THE FALL OF JUDAS?

But was avarice the cause of the fall of Judas? No! His fall began with lack of faith and trust in the Lord, which became evident when, at the time of the second Passover mentioned in St. John's Gospel, Jesus promised the Eucharist to the crowd that had followed Him to Capharnaum (JOHN 6). Peter believed and confessed his faith. But Jesus knew that not all of the Twelve were faithful:

> Have I not chosen all twelve of you? And one of you is a devil. He was speaking of Judas, son of Simon, the Iscariot, who was one of the twelve, and was to betray Him. JOHN 6:71,72

It was Judas's lack of faith that hardened his heart and confirmed him in his greed. A year later, again at Passover time, Our Lord reprimanded Judas for his money-madness. St. John opens his account of the tragedy of Calvary with the words: "Six days before the Paschal feast Jesus went to Bethany" (JOHN 12:1). There, in the house of Lazarus, Mary anointed Jesus. But he "who was to betray Him" (JOHN 12:4) protested that the money should have been given to the poor. By now it was clear that Judas "was a thief" (JOHN 12:6) and, at once reprimanding him and predicting His own death, Jesus answered,

> Let her alone; enough that she should keep it for the day when my body is prepared for burial. You have the poor among you always; I am not always among you. JOHN 12:7,8

Thus the story of Judas's fall is told in relation to the Pass-over. It was at a Passover that Our Lord first announced the Eucharist, and at another Passover He instituted it. The first rupture in the soul of Judas was when Our Lord said He would give man His Body and Blood as their food. The total collapse came the night of the Last Supper, when Our Blessed Lord fulfilled this promise. Here is unmistakable evidence that fidelity and holiness on the one hand, and betrayal and disloyalty on the other, are linked to the Eucharist, the Bread of Life. The first crack in the priesthood comes in our attitude to the Eucharist: the holiness with which we offer Mass, the sensitiveness of our devotion to the Blessed Sacrament.

The first mention in the Bible that Judas was a betrayer was not when he revealed his greed, but when Our Lord declared Himself the Bread of Life. On that occasion, Our Lord lost the support of three distinct types of follower; He lost the masses, because He refused to be a Bread King, giving the Eucharist instead of plenty; He lost various disciples who "walked no more in His company" (JOHN 6:67), because the Eucharist was to them a scandal; finally, He lost Judas.

Two who had been called by Christ to be priests are contrasted by St. John: Peter and Judas. When the wholesale desertions followed

Christ's announcement that He would give His Flesh for the Life of the world, Our Lord asked Peter if he, too, would leave. Peter answered:

> Lord, to whom should we go? Thy words are the words of eternal life; we have learned to believe, and are assured that Thou art the Christ, the Son of God. JOHN 6:69,70

The Heart of Our Lord now becomes sad because of what happened to His twelve. The number was symbolic, dating from the twelve patriarchs and the twelve tribes, and so often used with reference to the Apostles. (Was not each of the twelve Apostles from one of the twelve tribes?) There is, therefore, something tragic about the Divine complaint:

> Jesus answered them, Have I not chosen all twelve of you? And one of you is a devil. He was speaking of Judas son of Simon, the Iscariot, who was one of the twelve, and was to betray Him. JOHN 6:71,72

Avarice later! But now, long before the meal in Simon's house, long before his exchange with the Temple priests, Judas is first described as a betrayer, as Our Lord gives us His Flesh to eat and His Blood to drink. What did the thirty pieces of silver add to the selling of that Body and Blood? He had already denied it! He is yet a thief; then a traitor; later, an open ally of the enemy. He stole from the apostolic purse, developed a neurotic hatred both of money and of himself; finally, took his own life. But when did the fissure first show? When began the unseen collapse—so unseen that the Apostles at the Last Supper did not know of it? It began when he who was called to be a priest and victim, refused to accept the words of his Lord:

> As I live because of the Father, the living Father Who has sent Me, so he who eats Me will live, in his turn, because of Me. JOHN 6:58

The flesh! Certainly it explains certain aspects of priestly weakness. Worldliness! Love of stocks and bonds! Luxury! Alcohol! Mention any sin that comes to mind. These are the tails on the falling kites of the priesthood. But there was already a rent in the garment of holiness before these other forms of nakedness and shame appeared. Our Lord knows where all such overt and scandalous sins started. Maybe they started in a "fifteen minute Mass," a "one-minute thanksgiving," a flight from the night shirt to the alb, a failure to visit the Eucharistic Savior except "officially" when one "had" to celebrate Mass or conduct devotions. But somewhere, somehow, the man who is a priest because of the Eucharist, failed to be a Eucharistic priest. If a surgeon stayed away from human body and blood, would he not lose his proficiency? Is he not licensed precisely for body and blood? But we, who are not "licensed" but "ordained" for Body and Blood, how shall we retain our power, our holiness, our priestly skill, except by that lively faith in the Body and Blood of Christ?

## THE BETRAYAL AND THE PASSOVER

The Gospels seem to make a point about associating Judas with the Passover. Avarice, one of the effects of his failure to be Eucharistic, is first mentioned in this connection:

> Six days before the paschal feast, Jesus went to Bethany.
> JOHN 12:1

Such are the words with which the Beloved Disciple raises the curtain on the tragedy of Calvary. And who is first mentioned? Judas! As Mary, the sister of Lazarus, shows devotion to the Body and Blood of the Savior, anointing Him "for burial" (JOHN 12:7,8), so does Judas betray his greed and prepare to sell that Body and Blood.

The hypocrisy of Judas in expressing concern for the poor is stressed by Our Lord's identification of Himself that same week with the poor (MATTHEW 25:35). When Jesus reprimanded Judas and told him to "let her alone" (JOHN 12:7), the false apostle resolved to consummate the betrayal.

> And at that, one of the twelve, Judas who was called Iscariot, went to the chief priests and asked them, What will you pay me for handing Him over to you? Whereupon they laid down thirty pieces of silver, And he, from that time onwards, looked about for an opportunity to betray Him.
> MATTHEW 26:14-16

*The cross united not only Our Lord's friends but also His enemies.* The Saducees and Pharisees, Judas and the Sanhedrin, Rome and the Temple priests, Herod and Pilate—all those who had lesser enmities united in the greater hostility to Jesus, the Savior of the world. The Church, which is the continuing Christ, must always expect such hostile coalitions in time of crisis. Evil is hypersensitive to goodness. It detects a challenge to its existence, long before good men are awake to the signs of the times.

## Judas At The Last Supper

Now comes the Passover of Our Lord's Death when the true Lamb of God is sacrificed for us pilgrims to eternity. The twelve Apostles are gathered around Our Lord. Where did Judas sit at this first Mass? John was certainly on His Heart's side. Who was on the Lord's other side? Possibly Peter, though one detail suggests the contrary:

> Jesus had one disciple, whom He loved, who was now sitting with his head against Jesus' breast; to him, therefore, Simon Peter made a sign, and asked him, Who is it He means?  JOHN 13:23,24

If Peter was on the other side, he would hardly make a sign as here described.

Could Judas have been next to Our Lord? It is conceivable, for Our Lord makes many attempts to save those He has chosen. Matthew seems to suggest it, for how else could Christ have told Judas that He knew his intentions, while the others continued under the impression that he went out to help the poor (MATTHEW 26:22,25)? Betrayers and traitors rarely know they are discovered. If then, Judas was given that place as a sign of Divine Love, how, in his hardened heart, he must have thought: "If He knew what I am going to do, He would never have given me this place."

At this point Our Lord again referred to the Passover:

> I have longed and longed to share this Paschal meal with you before My Passion.  LUKE 22:15

Was Judas reminded of the other Passover when Our Lord had promised the Eucharist?

Also significant for Judas, though ignored by him, was the stress on humility at this solemn moment of the institution of the Eucharist. Our Lord insisted that in a certain sense, His apostles were kings. He did not deny their instinct for aristocracy, but He told them that theirs was to be the nobility of humility, the greatest becoming the least. To drive the lesson home, He reminded them of the position He occupied among them as Master and Lord of the table and yet free of every trace of superiority. Many times He repeated that He had come not to be served but to serve. To bear the burden of others and particularly their guilt was His reason for becoming the "Suffering Servant" foretold by Isaias (52:13-53:12). And not content with words, He reinforced them with example.

> And now, rising from supper, He laid His garments aside, took a towel, and put it about Him; and then He poured water into the basin, and began to wash the feet of His disciples, wiping them with the towel that girded Him.   JOHN 13:4

The minuteness of John's description is striking. It lists seven distinct actions: rising, laying His garments aside, taking a towel, putting it about Him, pouring water, washing the feet, wiping the feet with a towel. One can imagine an earthly king, just before he returns from a distant province, rendering a humble service to one of his subjects; but one would not say that he was doing it because he was about to return to his capital. Yet Our Blessed Lord is described as washing the disciples' feet because He is to go back to the Father. He had taught humility by precept: "He that humbles himself shall be exalted" (LUKE 14:11); by parable, as in the story of the Pharisee and the Publican; by example, as when He took a child in His arms; and now by condescension.

The scene was like a re-enactment of His Incarnation. Rising up from the Heavenly Banquet in intimate union of nature with the Father, He laid aside the garments of His glory, wrapped about His Divinity the towel of human nature, which He took from Mary; poured the laver of regeneration which is His Blood shed on the Cross to redeem men, and began washing the souls of His disciples and followers through the merits of His Death, Resurrection and Ascension. St. Paul expressed it beautifully:

> His Nature is, from the first, Divine, and yet He did not see, in the rank of Godhead, a prize to be coveted; He dispossessed Himself, and took the nature of a slave, fashioned in the likeness of men, and presenting Himself to us in human form; and then He lowered His own dignity, accepted an obedience which brought Him to death, death on a cross.   PHILIPPIANS 2:6-8

Once Peter's protests are stilled, the other disciples are motionless, lost in mute astonishment. When humility comes from the God-man as it does here, it is obvious that it will be through humility that men will go back to God. Each one would have withdrawn his feet out of the basin were it not for love which pervaded their hearts.

But Our Lord was still not willing to abandon Judas. Once more He tried to arouse him to a realization of what he planned.

> And you are clean now; only, not all of you.   JOHN 13:10

It was one thing to be selected as an apostle; it was another to be elected to salvation through observance of the corresponding obligations. But that the Apostles would realize that heresy or schisms or treachery in their ranks was not unexpected, Jesus cited Psalm 40 to show that it had been anticipated by the prophets:

> The man who shared My Bread has lifted his heel to trip Me up. I am telling you this now, before it happens, so that when it happens you may believe it was written of Me. JOHN 13:18,19

The reference was to David's sufferings at the hands of Achitophel, a disloyalty now identified as a prefigurement of what David's royal Son would suffer. The lowliest part of the body, the heel, was described in both instances as inflicting the wound. In Genesis (3:14) God told the serpent that the woman would crush him while he lay in ambush at her heels. It now seemed that the devil would have a momentary revenge, by using the heel to inflict a wound on the seed of the woman—the Lord. On another occasion Our Lord said:

> A man's enemies will be the people of his own house. MATTHEW 10:36

Only one who has suffered such betrayal from within the household can even faintly grasp the sadness of the Savior's soul that night. All the good example, counsel, companionship and inspiration are fruitless with those who will to do evil. One of the strongest expressions of sorrow expressed by Jesus now fell from His lips to describe His love of Judas and to lament the renegade apostle's free decision to sin.

> Jesus bore witness to the distress He felt in His Heart; Believe Me, He said, believe Me, one of you is to betray Me. JOHN 13:21

There were twelve questions in all. Ten of the apostles asked: "Is it I, Lord?"

> They were all full of sorrow, and began to say, one after another, Lord, is it I? MATTHEW 26:22

One, however, asked:

> Lord, who is it? JOHN 13:26

This was John himself. The twelfth had little choice but to continue his presence.

> Then Judas, he who was betraying Him, said openly, Master, is it I?
> MATTHEW 26:25

Notice that eleven called Him Lord; but Judas called Him Master. It is a perfect illustration of St. Paul's insistence that "it is only through the Holy Spirit that anyone can say, Jesus is the Lord" (I CORINTHIANS 12:3). Because the spirit that filled Judas was satanic, he called Him Master; the others called Him Lord, in full confession of Divinity.

Throughout the first part of the Passover meal, both Our Lord and Judas had been dipping their hands in the same dish of wine and fruit. The very fact that Our Lord chose bread as a symbol of the betrayal, might have reminded Judas of the Bread promised at Caphamaum. Humanly speaking, it would seem that Our Lord should have thundered out His denunciation of Judas, but rather in a last attempt to save him, He used the bread of fellowship.

> He answered, The man who has put his hand into the dish with Me will betray Me. The Son of Man goes on His way, as the scripture foretells of Him; But woe upon that man by whom the Son of Man is to be betrayed; better for that man if he had never been born.
> MATTHEW 26:23-25

In the presence of Divinity, who can be sure of his innocence? It was reasonable for every disciple to ask if it was he. Man is a mystery even to himself. He knows that within his heart there lie, coiled and dormant, serpents that at any moment can sting a neighbor, or even God, with their poison. None of them could be sure that he was not the traitor, even if none was conscious of a temptation to betray Him. Judas alone knew where he stood. Even though Our Lord revealed His knowledge of the treason, Judas remained fixed in his determination to do the evil. The revelation that the crime was uncovered and the evil stripped naked did not shame him into withdrawal.

Some recoil in horror when their sins are put bluntly before them. But though Judas saw his treachery described in all its deformity, he in effect declared in the language of Nietzsche: "Evil, be thou my good." Our Lord gave a sign to Judas. In answer to the question of the apostles ("Is it I?") He declared:

> It is the man to whom I give this piece of bread which I am dipping in the dish. Then He dipped the bread, and gave it to Judas the Son of Simon, the Iscariot. JOHN 13:26,27

That Judas committed his sin freely is evidenced by his subsequent remorse. So too was Christ free to make His betrayal the condition of His Cross. Evil men seem to run counter to the economy of God, to be an errant thread in the tapestry of life, but they all fit into the Divine Plan. If the wild wind roars from the black heavens, there is somewhere a sail to catch it and yoke it to the useful service of man.

When Our Lord said: "It is the man to whom I give this piece of bread which I am dipping in the dish," He was actually offering a gesture of friendship. The giving of the morsel seems to have been traditional among both Greeks and Semites. Socrates said that it was always a mark of favor to give a morsel to a table neighbor. Our Lord held open to Judas the opportunity to repent, as He later did once again in the Garden of Gethsemane. But though Our Lord held the door open, Judas would not enter. Rather would Satan enter in.

> The morsel once given, Satan entered into him; and Jesus said to him, Be quick on thy errand. JOHN 13:27

Satan possesses only willing victims. The marks of mercy and friendship extended by the Victim should have moved Judas to repentance. The bread must have burned his lips, as the thirty pieces of silver would later burn his hands. Only some minutes previously the Hands of the Son of God had washed the feet of Judas; now the same Divine Hands touch the lips of Judas with a morsel; in a few hours, the lips of Judas will kiss those of Our Lord in the final act of betrayal. The Divine Mediator, knowing all that would befall Him, directed Judas to open wider the curtain on the tragedy of Calvary. What Judas was to do, let him do quickly. The Lamb of God was ready for sacrifice.

The Divine Mercy did not identify the traitor, for Our Lord hid from the others the identity of the betrayer. The practice of the world which loves to spread scandals, even those which are untrue, is here reversed in the hiding of what is true. When they saw Judas leave, the others assumed that he went on a mission of charity.

> None of those who sat there could understand the drift of what He said; some of them thought, since Judas kept the common purse, that Jesus was saying to him, Go and buy what we need for the feast, or bidding him give some alms to the poor. JOHN 13:28

But Judas had gone out to sell, not to buy. He would minister not to the poor, but to the rich in charge of the temple treasury. Though Our Blessed Lord knew the evil intention of Judas, He still continued to behave kindly. He would bear the ignominy alone. In many instances, Jesus acted as though the effects of the deeds of others were unknown to Him. He knew that He would raise Lazarus from the dead, even when He wept. He knew who believed Him not, and who would betray Him, yet this did not harden His Sacred Heart. Judas rejected the last appeal, and thus despair remained in His heart.

Judas went out, "and it was night" (JOHN 13:30), an appropriate setting for a deed of darkness. It perhaps was a relief to be away from the Light of the World. Nature is in sympathy at times, at times in discord with our joys and sorrows. The sky is gloomy with clouds when there is melancholy within. Nature was suiting itself to the evil deeds of Judas. When he went out, he found not the fact of God's smiling sun but the Stygian blackness of night. It would also be night at midday when the Lord was crucified.

Judas is intelligible only in terms of the Body and Blood of Christ. Clawing at money was the effect, not the cause of a ruined priesthood.

## JUDAS AND THE PRIESTHOOD

1. Those who have been cradled in the sacred associations of the priesthood know best how to betray Our Lord. Judas knew where to find Our Lord after dark.

> Here there was a garden, into which He and His disciples went. Judas, His betrayer, knew the place well; Jesus and His disciples had often forgathered in it. JOHN 18:1,2

2. Divinity is so holy, that all betrayal must be prefaced by some mark of esteem or affection.

> It is none other, he told them, than the Man whom I shall greet with a kiss. MATTHEW 26:48

3. No bishop or priest knows the ultimate depth of spiritual sorrow and grief, until he has felt the hot blistering kiss of a brother in Christ who is a traitor.

4. A priest can always sell Our Lord, but no priest can buy Him.

Whereupon they laid down thirty pieces of silver.   MATTHEW 26:15

5. Any pleasure, profit or gain that one receives through rejecting the Eucharistic Lord proves so disgusting, that the beneficiary is impelled, like Judas, to throw it back in the face of those who gave it to us.

And now Judas, His betrayer, was full of remorse at seeing Him condemned, so that he brought back to the chief priests and elders their thirty pieces of silver; I have sinned, he told them, in betraying the Blood of an Innocent Man.   MATTHEW 27:34

Could not the money have been given to the poor? Judas never thought of that then.

6. Many psychoses and neuroses are due to an unrequited sense of guilt. The Lord would have pardoned Judas as He pardoned Peter, but Judas never asked for it.

When a man hates himself for what he has done and is without repentance to God, he will sometimes pound his breast as if to blot out a sin. There is a world of difference between pounding a breast in self-disgust, and pounding it with the mea culpa of one asking for pardon. Self-hatred can become so intense as to pound the life out of a man, leading him to suicide. Though death is a penalty of original sin and naturally feared by any normal person, some rush into its arms.

The conscience of Judas warned him before the sin. After the sin it gnawed, and the rending was such that he could not bear it. Down the valley of Cedron he went, that valley of so many ghostly associations. Jagged rocks and gnarled and stunted trees he chose as the proper place to empty himself of self. Everything around proclaimed his destiny and his end. Nothing was more revolting to his eyes than the gilded roof of the temple, for it reminded him of the Temple of God he had just sold. Every tree seemed the gibbet to which he had sentenced Innocent Blood. Every branch was an accusing finger. The very hill on which he stood overlooked Calvary, whereon the One he had sentenced to death would unite heaven and earth, a union he would now exert his final efforts to prevent. Throwing a rope over a limb of a tree, he hanged himself (MATTHEW 27:5).

The lesson is clear. We are Eucharistic priests. Watch a priest read Mass and you can tell how he treats souls in a confessional, how he ministers to the sick and poor, whether or not he is interested in making converts, whether he is more concerned about pleasing the Lord Bishop than the Lord God, how effective he is in instilling patience and resignation in those who suffer, whether he is an administrator or a shepherd, whether he loves the rich, or the rich and the poor, and whether he gives only money-sermons or Christ-words. The moral rot of the priesthood starts with a want of lively faith in the Divine Presence, and the sanctity of the priesthood starts there too.

## Chapter 14

## Why Make a Holy Hour?

WHAT good does a medical convention achieve if the doctors agree on the need for good health, but take no practical steps to implement their argument? So with a book on the priesthood. What concrete recommendations may be given to the priest to make him worthy of the supernal vocation to which he is called? One immediate and essential answer is the Holy Hour. But why make a Holy Hour?

1. Because it is time spent in the Presence of Our Lord Himself. If faith is alive, no further reason is needed.

2. Because in our busy life it takes considerable time to shake off the "noonday devils," the worldly cares which cling to our souls like dust. An hour with Our Lord follows the experience of the disciples on the road to Emmaus (LUKE 24:13-35). We begin by walking with Our Lord but our eyes are "held fast," so that we do not "recognize Him." Next, He converses with our soul, as we read the Scriptures. The third stage is one of sweet intimacy, as when "He sat down at table with them." The fourth stage is the full dawning of the mystery of the Eucharist. Our eyes are "opened" and we recognize Him. Finally we reach the point where we do not want to leave. The hour seemed so short. As we arise we ask:

> Were not our hearts burning within us when He spoke to us on the road, and when He made the Scriptures plain to us? LUKE 24:32

3. Because Our Lord asked for it.

> Had you no strength, then, to watch with Me even for an hour?
> MATTHEW 26:40

The word was addressed to Peter, but he is referred to as Simon. It is our Simon-nature which needs the hour. If the hour seems hard, it is because

> ... the spirit is willing enough, but the flesh is weak.   MARK 14:39

4. Because, as St. Thomas Aquinas tells us, the priest's power over the corpus mysticum follows from his power over the corpus physicum of Christ. It is because he consecrates the Body and Blood of Christ, that the priest can teach, govern and sanctify the members of the Church. Practically, this means that he walks into the confessional from the foot of the altar; that he mounts the pulpit after having enacted the mystery of redemption. Every sick call, every word of counsel in the parlor, every catechism lesson taught to children, every official act in the chancery, flows from the altar. All power resides there, and the more "short-cuts" we take from the tabernacle to our other priestly duties, the less spiritual strength we have for them.

> The Eucharist is the fons et caput of all the spiritual goods of the Church.   URBI ET ORBI, May 8, 1907

> It is from the Eucharist that all other Sacraments receive their efficacy.   Roman Catechism, Part II, Chapter 4, No. 47.

If all the sacraments, if all our preaching, confessing, administrating, and saving start with that Flame of Love, then how can we refuse to be sparked by it an hour a day?

5. Because the Holy Hour keeps a balance between the spiritual and the practical. Western philosophies tend to an activism in which God does nothing, and man everything; the Eastern philosophies tend to a quietism in which God does everything, and man nothing. The golden mean is Surgite postqtiam sederitis: action following rest; Martha walking with Mary; contemplata aliis tradere, in the words of St. Thomas. The Holy Hour unites the contemplative to the active life of the priest.

Thanks to the hour with Our Lord, our meditations and resolutions pass from the conscious to the subconscious and then become motives of action. A new spirit begins to pervade our sick calls, our sermons, our confessions. The change is effected by Our Lord Who fills our heart and works through our hands. A priest can give only what he possesses. To give Christ to others, one must possess Him.

6. Because revelations made by the Sacred Heart to saintly souls indicate that still unexplored depths of that Heart are reserved for

priests. There are veils of love behind which only the priest may penetrate, and from which he will emerge with an unction and power over souls far beyond his own strength.

The "house" of the priest is not the rectory. He is "at home" only where Christ is present. There alone he learns the secrets of love. To St. Margaret Mary, the Sacred Heart complained that so few priests answer His cry: "I am thirsty" (JOHN 19:28). His words to her were: "I have a burning thirst to be honored in the Blessed Sacrament, and I find hardly anyone who endeavors according to My desires to quench that thirst by making some returns to Me."

7. Because the Holy Hour will make us practice what we preach. It grieves the Sacred Heart to see a scandalous disparity between the high ideal of the priesthood and its poor realization.

> Here is an image, He said, of the kingdom of heaven; there was once a king, who held a marriage-feast for his son, and sent out his servants with a summons to all those whom he had invited to the wedding; but they would not come.  MATTHEW 22:2,3

It was written of Our Lord that He "set out to do and to teach"—facere et docere (ACTS 1:1). The priest who practices the Holy Hour will find that when he teaches, the people will say of him as of the Lord:

> All... were astonished at the gracious words which came from his mouth.  LUKE 4:22

8. Because the Holy Hour makes us obedient instruments of Divinity. In the Eucharist there is this double movement; first, of the priest to the Eucharistic Heart; and secondly, of the priest to the people. The priest who has given himself to the Heart of Our Blessed Lord, is known by Our Lord as "expendable" for His purposes. The priest becomes endowed with an extra power because of his suppleness in the hands of his Master. God gives some graces directly to souls, as a man gives alms to the poor man he happens to meet. But the Sacred Heart wishes great graces to be distributed to souls through the hands of His priests.

The effectiveness of priests has little or nothing to do with their natural endowments. A Eucharistic priest will be a better instrument of the Lord among souls than a learned one who loves Him less. One of the promises made to priests who love the Sacred Heart is: "I will give such priests the power of touching the most hardened hearts."

9. Because the Holy Hour helps us make reparation both for the sins of the world and for our own. When the Sacred Heart appeared to St.

Margaret Mary, it was His Heart, and not His Head, that was crowned with thorns. It was Love that was hurt. Black Masses, sacrilegious communions, scandals, militant atheism—who will make up for them? Who will be an Abraham for Sodom, a Mary for those who have no wine? The sins of the world are our sins, as if we had committed them. If they caused Our Lord a bloody sweat, to the point that He upbraided His disciples for failing to stay with Him an hour, shall we with Cain ask:

Is it for me to watch over my brother? GENESIS 4:9

The priest who asks what he can do about Communism knows that battles are won when his hands are lifted, like those of Moses, in prayer.

10. Because it will restore our lost spiritual vitality. Our hearts will be where our joys are. One reason why many fail to progress after many years in the priesthood, is that they shrink from casting the whole burden of their lives upon Our Lord. They fail to seek their joy in the union of their priesthood with the victimhood of Christ. They will sometimes remain stubborn, clinging to the things of sense, forgetful that the Eucharistic door is really not a door at all; it is not even a wall, for there we have the "breaking down the wall that was a barrier between us" (EPHESIANS 2:14).

The Sacred Heart promised through St. Margaret Mary to "make His priests like two-edged swords, which will make the holy fountain of penance spring up in them." Our lives at best are weak, perhaps broken like fragmented china. So we go to the Sacred Heart and ask ut congregate restaures, et restaurata conserves: that "Thou wouldst bring together and mend, mend and forever preserve, what now lies broken." We need to be cemented again by love into unity, and where can such love be found except in the Sacrament of unity?

11. Because the Holy Hour is the "Hour of Truth." Alone with Jesus, we there see ourselves, not as the people see us—always judging us to be better than we are—but as the Judge sees us. If we take praise seriously, nothing so deflates our pomposity as the realization of the helplessness to which the Lord of Heaven has reduced Himself, under the species of Bread. Our failings, our want of charity to other priests, our too hasty responses to those whose appearance offends us, our sugary kindness to the well dressed, our seeking out the rich, our avoiding the poor, our hurried Mass, our impatience in the confessional—all these the Eucharistic Lord draws out of our conscience.

Living in sin, grievous or venial, becomes intolerable for the priest who practices the Holy Hour. It is like having a doctor at hand to warn us of a growing cancer. Eventually, we are driven to ask the Divine

Physician to heal us. No sin is a hidden sin in meditation; no excuses are given. We take sin out of its lair and lay it before God. We always knew that God saw it; but in the Hour we see it. Our sins are placed before our eyes not as a human weakness, but as a recrucifying of Our Lord:

> Scrutinize me, O God, as Thou wilt, and read my heart; put me to the test, and examine my restless thoughts. See if on any false paths my heart is set, and Thyself lead me in the ways of old.
> PSALM 138:23,24

But there is no need to fear, because during the Hour, we enter into the private chambers of the Judge. We make friends with Him before the trial while making reparation for our sins.

12. Because it reduces our liability to temptation and weakness. Presenting ourselves before Our Lord in the Blessed Sacrament is like putting a tubercular patient in good air and sunlight. The virus of our sins cannot long exist in the face of the Light of the world.

> Always I can keep the Lord within sight; always He is at my right hand, to make me stand firm.
> PSALM 15:8

Our sinful impulses are prevented from arising through the barrier erected each day by the Hour. Our will becomes disposed to goodness with little conscious effort on our part. Satan, the roaring lion, was not permitted to put forth his hand to touch righteous Job, until he received permission (JOB 1:12). Certainly then will the Lord withhold serious fall from him who watches (I CORINTHIANS 10:13). With full confidence in his Eucharistic Lord, the priest will have a spiritual resiliency. He will bounce back quickly after a falling:

> Fall I, it is but to rise again, sit I in darkness, the Lord will be my light. The Lord's displeasure I must bear, I that have sinned against Him, till at last He admits my plea, and grants redress.
> MICHAEAS 7:8,9

The Lord will be favorable even to the weakest of us, if He finds us at His feet in adoration, disposing ourselves to receive Divine favors. No sooner had Saul of Tarsus, the persecutor, humbled himself before his Maker, than God sent a special messenger to his relief, telling him that "even now he is at his prayers" (ACTS 9:11). Even the priest who has fallen can expect reassurance, if he watches and prays.

> They shall increase, that hitherto had dwindled, be exalted, that once were brought low. JEREMIAS 30:19,20

13. Because the Holy Hour is a personal prayer. The Mass and the Breviary are official prayers. They belong to the Mystical Body of Christ. They do not belong to us personally. The priest who limits himself strictly to his official obligation and adoration, is like the union man who downs tools the moment the whistle blows. Love begins when duty finishes. It is a giving of the cloak when the coat is taken. It is walking the extra mile.

> Answer shall come ere cry for help is uttered, prayer find audience while it is yet on their lips. ISAIAS 65:24

Of course, we do not have to make a Holy Hour—and that is just the point. Love is never compelled, except in hell. There love has to submit to justice. To be forced to love would be a kind of hell. No man who loves a woman is obligated to give her an engagement ring; and no priest who loves the Sacred Heart ever has to give an engagement Hour.

"Would you, too, go away?" (JOHN 6:68) is weak love; "Art thou sleeping?" (MARK 14:37) is irresponsible love; "He had great possessions" (MATTHEW 19:22; MARK 10:22) is selfish love. But does the priest who loves His Lord have time for other activities before he performs acts of love "above and beyond the call of duty"? Does the patient love the physician who charges for every call, or does he begin to love when the physician says: "I just dropped by to see how you were"?

14. Meditation keeps us from seeking an external escape from our worries and miseries. When difficulties arise in the rectory, when nerves are made taut by false accusations, there is always a danger that we may look outwards, as the Israelites did, for release.

> From the Lord God, the Holy One of Israel, word was given you, Come back and keep still, and all shall be well with you; in quietness and in confidence lies your strength. But you would have none of it; To horse! you cried, We must flee! and flee you shall; We must ride swiftly, you said; but swifter still ride your pursuers. ISAIAS 30:15,16

No outward escape, neither pleasure, drink, friends or keeping busy, is an answer. The soul of a priest cannot "fly upon a horse"; he must take "wings" to a place where his "life is hidden away ... with Christ in God" (COLOSSIANS 3:3).

15. Finally, because the Holy Hour is necessary for the Church. No one can read the Old Testament without becoming conscious of the presence of God in history. How often did God use other nations to punish Israel for her sins! He made Assyria the "rod that executes My vengeance" (ISAIAS 10:5). The history of the world since the Incarnation is the Way of the Cross. The rise of nations and their fall remain related to the Kingdom of God. We cannot understand the mystery of God's government, for it is the "sealed book" of the Apocalypse. John wept when he saw it (APOCALYPSE 5:4). He could not understand why this moment of prosperity and that hour of adversity.

What we often forget is that all the judgments of God begin with the Church, as they began with Israel. Not politics, but theology is the key to the world. We bemoan the wickedness of men, but is not the Lord all the while looking at our own failures? Judgment begins with us:

> Make thy way, the Lord said to him, all through the city, from end to end of Jerusalem; and where thou findest men that weep and wail over the foul deeds done in it, mark their brows with a cross. To the others I heard Him say, Yours it is to traverse the city at his heels, and smite. Never let eye of yours melt with pity; old and young, man and maid, mother and child, all alike destroy till none is left, save only where you see the cross marked on them. And begin first with the temple itself. EZECHIEL 9:4-6

Amos gave the same lesson. The more unmerited the favors, he insisted, the greater the punishment:

> Nation is none I have claimed for my own, save you; and guilt of yours is none that shall go unpunished. AMOS 3:2

God speaks through Jeremias and says that punishment begins with the holy city, *in civitate mea.*

> Here am I beginning my work of vengeance with that city which is the shrine of My Name, and shall you be acquitted, you others, and go scot-free? That shall never be, says the Lord of hosts; to the sword if I appeal, it is for a whole world's punishment.
> JEREMIAS 25:29

Lest we think that we do not share responsibility for what comes upon the world in the New Testament, let Peter reaffirm the warning:

> The time is ripe for judgment to begin, and to begin with God's own household; and if our turn comes first, what will be its issue for those who refuse credence to God's message?
>
> I PETER 4:17

The Hand of God will strike first the Church, then the world. We who are the watchmen set on the walls, are the first to be judged. Jerusalem was destroyed only after Our Lord purged the Temple. Jacob's house felt the famine before the Egyptians did. The Jews were carried into captivity before the Assyrians fell to the Medes and Persians.

If then of dire things a sanctuario meo incipite, shall not we priests atone for the sins of the world, keep our priesthood holy for the sake of our country and the world, and be faithful? If judgment thus starts with the sanctuary, then so shall mercy. Thus can the world be saved. What a contribution could the 55,000 priests in the United States make to the peace of the world, if each spent an hour daily in the sanctuary! And how blessed for each would be the moment of death:

> Blessed is that servant who is found doing this when his Lord comes.
>
> LUKE 12:43

A priest ending his Holy Hour will say with John the Baptist:

> He must become more and more, I must become less and less.
>
> JOHN 3:30

The alleged superiority of being "in the chancery" or the alleged inferiority of being "only an assistant" dissolves before the tabernacle. What ultimate difference does it make if one is passed over for a "good" (rich) parish, or if the "second best" man in the diocese is made an officialis? Self-assertiveness gives way to Christ-assertiveness in the presence of the tabernacle. The priest who makes the Lord everything for an hour each morning is not seriously wounded by an episcopal "pass-over" when the promotion was logically his. The "littleness" of the Lord in the Eucharist makes "bigness" in the priest an absurdity.

Instead of being the "best man" in the nuptials of Christ and His Church, we sometimes act as if we sought to be the bridegroom—and that office the Lord will not surrender. In the Holy Hour, the priest learns to be concerned only with furthering the beauty of the Bride which is the Church, so that it may be presented with "no stain or wrinkle" (EPHESIANS 5:27) on the day of the Wedding of the Lamb.

To our parish, as Paul to the Corinthians, we say:

> I have betrothed you to Christ, so that no other but He should claim you, His bride without spot.     II CORINTHIANS 11:2

An inflexible law governs the influence of the priest on others: the more he is inflated, the less are the Lord and His Church glorified. Meditation on the "emptying" of the Savior in the Eucharist will keep him always conscious, that he is the moon receiving his light from the sun.

No Eucharistic bishop will ever say or even think: "I built twenty-one high schools, forty-three new parishes and six convents in nineteen years." He knows too well who provided the money—the people! He knows too well who gave the authority—the Church! He knows too well who supplied the help—his priests! Daily will he hear the Lord from the tabernacle whisper:

> After all, friend, who is it that gives thee this pre-eminence? What powers hast thou, that did not come to thee by gift? And if they came to thee by gift, why dost thou boast of them, as if there were no gift in question?     I CORINTHIANS 4:7

If the Lord had not given us a vocation, what would we be: insurance clerks, truck drivers, school teachers, doctors, farmers, waiters? The Lord did not choose any of us as the best. He picks "frail vessels." And as we gather together around the Eucharist and look at each other, we recognize in our hearts the truth of Paul's words:

> Consider, brethren, the circumstances of your own calling; not many of you are wise, in the world's fashion, not many powerful, not many well born.     I CORINTHIANS 1:26

We are not the best, otherwise the power of the Gospel would be in us, rather than in the Spirit. But where is this truth better learned than in the presence of the Mystery which seems bread, but is actually Emmanuel; so small that our hands can break it, so full of power that its breaking renews the Passion and Death of Christ? The decreased priest is the increased Christ. When the Eucharist is no more than a remote background to our lives, it is like having the sun low on the horizon behind us. We cast a shadow forward; and the lower the sun, the longer the shadow. If the Lord is far from us, scarcely visible, our own ego seems to grow important like our shadow, and with it our opinions and works take on the appearance of great substance. But this is an illusion. If, on the contrary, each day begins with the Eucharist before us as our rising sun, the shadow of the ego no longer hides our true face, and when the Sun of Justice reaches the meridian, no ego survives. Then the souls whom we tend, like the apostles at the Transfiguration, see "no one any more, but Jesus only with them" (MARK 9:7).

The sole requirement is the venture of faith, and the reward is the depths of intimacy for those who cultivate His friendship. To abide with Christ is spiritual fellowship, as He insisted on the solemn and sacred night of the Last Supper, the moment He chose to give us the Eucharist:

> You have only to live on in Me, and I will live on in you.   JOHN 15:4

He wants us in His dwelling:

> That you too, may be where I am.   JOHN 14:3

How far we miss the joys of our priesthood, when our only meetings with the Lord are "public audiences"—at Mass, devotions, stations of the Cross, whenever we have to be there. The Lord wants "private audiences." He wants a protracted audience, a full hour. John and Andrew stayed the entire day!

## Chapter 15

## How to Make the Holy Hour

If at all possible, the priest should make his daily Holy Hour before celebrating his Mass. Now that the Church's regulations on the pre-Eucharistic fast have been modified, he will be well advised to take a cup of coffee before he starts. The average American is physically, biologically, psychologically and neurologically unable to do anything worthwhile before he has a cup of coffee. And that goes for prayer, too. Even sisters in convents whose rules were written before electric percolators were developed, would do well to update their procedures. Let them have coffee before meditation.

Limit the saying of the Breviary to twenty minutes of the hour. The basic purpose of this hour is to meditate. Some spiritual writers recommend a mechanical division of the hour into four parts: thanksgiving, petition, adoration, reparation. This is unnecessarily artificial. An hour's conversation with a friend is not divided into four rigid segments or topics. The Holy Hour is not an official prayer; it is personal. Each priest, being a man, has a heart unlike any other in the world. This unique heart must make up the content of his prayer. God no more likes "circular letters" than we do. In addition to liturgical or official prayer, there must be the prayer of the heart. We constantly preach to others; in the Holy Hour we preach to ourselves.

Many books on meditation have a rigid format which is endurable in the seminary, but which the priest soon finds too dry for his purposes. The so-called "methods" of meditation are generally impractical and unsuited to our mentality. What they consist in is an analysis of a meditation which was already made, and which proved satisfactory for the one who made it. A child will run after a ball with grace and freedom of movement. But if he is told to narrate what he does every second, how he first lifts the right foot, then the left, all the spontaneity disappears. To base a meditation, first on the intellect, then on the will, and finally on the emotions, is to destroy intimacy. This is not what really happens. The intellect does not work first in meditation, then the will, then the imagination. The person meditates; all his faculties work together. To achieve this, the greatest possible freedom should be left to the individual:

> ... where the Lord's Spirit is, there is freedom.
> II CORINTHIANS 3:17

The best book for meditation is the Scripture. But since many of its depths need to be explained, a good spiritual commentary is valuable. Too often the Lord may have to repeat the complaint He voiced to His disciples:

> You do not understand the Scriptures or what is the Power of God.
> MATTHEW 22:29

Read the Scriptures, or a commentary, or any solid spiritual book, until a thought strikes you. Then close the book, and talk to Our Lord about it. But do not do all the talking. Listen also "Speak on, Lord, Thy servant is listening" (I KINGS 3:10) must not be: "Listen, Lord, Thy servant speaketh." We learn to speak through listening, and we grow in love of God through listening. Meditation is at least half listening:

> It is My turn to ask questions. JOB 40:2

When you are so fatigued and exhausted that you cannot pray, offer up your worthlessness. Does not a dog love to be near the master, even when the master gives him no evident sign of affection?

Allow no difficulty in making the Hour to be an excuse for giving it up. When making it is a pleasure, we can think of ourselves as priests; when it is an effort, we can remember that we are also victims. Then we become like Moses, who asked God to blot his name from the record, if this would win pardon for the people (EXODUS 32:31) and like Paul, who was willing to be accursed for his race (ROMANS 9:1-3). The very effort we put forth each day makes us masters of ourselves, and therefore, better servants of the Sacred Heart.

When tempted to give up the Hour, ask yourself which of these three excuses, which the Lord said (LUKE 9:57-62) would be ours, are keeping us back from total service: earthly desires, earthly love, or earthly grief.

## Sit Or Kneel?

Should one kneel, sit, stand or walk during the Holy Hour? Scripture records examples of each of these various attitudes. The publican who stood in the back of the Temple was accounted justified. St. Simplician, who succeeded St. Ambrose as Bishop of Milan, asked Augustine what was the proper attitude to pray, and why David did not kneel praying before the tabernacle. Augustine replied that one should adopt the bodily position best calculated to move the soul. Aristotle said that the soul by sitting becomes wise. St. Jerome's rule was that in praying and in meditating, the body should always take the position which seemed best for exciting the soul's internal devotion.

Sitting is sometimes associated with despair and weariness in Scripture. When Israel was brought into captivity, and Jerusalem left deserted:

> ... the prophet Jeremias sat down there and wept.
> 
> LAMENTATIONS 1:1

Elias, too, in his despair sat down under a juniper tree and "prayed to have done with life" (III KINGS 19:4). The exiles from Jerusalem are pictured in the Psalm

> We sat down by the streams of Babylon and wept there, remembering Sion.
> 
> PSALM 136:1

And when Moses was praying for victory against Amalec, his "arms grew weary; so they found him a stone to sit on and bade him be seated on it" (EXODUS 17:12).

On the other hand, Our Blessed Lord prayed in the Garden on His knees: "He fell upon his face in prayer" (MATTHEW 26:39). Stephen prayed in the same position: "Kneeling down, he cried, aloud, Lord, do not count this sin against them" (ACTS 7:59). After the miraculous draught of fishes: "Simon Peter fell down and caught Jesus by the knees; Leave me to myself, Lord, I am a sinner" (LUKE 5:8). St. Paul evidently prayed kneeling: "I fall on my knees to the Father of our Lord Jesus Christ" (EPHESIANS 3:14). The young man who came to Our Lord inquiring what he must do to receive eternal life "... knelt down before him" (MARK 10:17). Even when the soldiers mocked Our Blessed Lord, after beating Him over the head with a rod and spitting upon Him, they "bowed their knees in worship of Him" (MARK 15:19). The gesture of ridicule is an obvious mockery of a gesture of worship.

When Our Lord went into the Garden, He "knelt down to pray" (LUKE 22:41). When Peter raised Tabitha from the dead, he "went on his knees to pray" (ACTS 9:40). When Paul came to Ephesus, and quoted the only words spoken by Our Lord recorded in Scripture other than in the Gospels ("It is more blessed to give than to receive"), he "knelt down and prayed with them all" (ACTS 20:35,36). The Psalmist used a like expression: "Come in, then, fall we down in worship, bowing the knee before God who made us" (PSALM 94:6). The mother of the sons of Zebedee adopted the same position when seeking preferment for her two boys, "falling on her knees to make a request of Him" (MATTHEW 20:20).

The father who had the lunatic son came to Our Lord "and knelt before Him: Lord, he said, have pity on my son, who is a lunatic" (MATTHEW 17:14). The leper who came up to Our Blessed Lord in the synagogue in Galilee to be healed knelt at His feet and said, "If it be Thy Will, Thou hast power to make me clean" (MARK 1:40). The condition that the devil imposed upon Our Blessed Lord for giving Him all the kingdoms of the world was likewise that of kneeling: "If Thou wilt fall down before me and worship" (LUKE 4:7).

Peter, on the contrary, was standing when he warmed himself by the fire (JOHN 18:18,25).

The conclusion is obvious. It is best to kneel during the Hour, for it indicates humility, follows the example of Our Lord in the Garden, makes atonement for our failings, and is a polite gesture before the King of Kings.

## How Often?

Should the priest who hears the appeal of the suffering Savior to watch an Hour with Him, make the sacrifice once a week? No! It is too hard. What is done once a week is an interruption of our normal life. The temptation is to put it off until the end of the week, thereby running the risk of not doing it at all.

The weekly Holy Hour can never become a habit. Once a week is not a deep token of love. What mother is content to see her child once a week; what wife, her husband? Love is not intermittent. Medicines taken once a week can give little strength.

If the Holy Hour once a week is too difficult, how often should it be made? The answer is obvious. It should be made every day.

The Holy Hour made once a week is an interruption to the week. But made daily, its absence is an interruption. Furthermore, an act which becomes a habit by daily repetition, loses its difficulty. What at first was imperfectly performed, by habit becomes easier with each progressive stroke. If the Holy Hour is repeated daily at the same hour, we start it without premeditation; it becomes almost automatic. The daily Holy Hour becomes as easy as anything we do daily. It becomes not just a habit, but part of a priest's nature. As Aristotle wrote in his Rhetoric:

> That which has become habitual becomes, as it were, a part of our nature; habit is something like nature, for the difference between "often" and "always" is not great, and nature belongs to the idea of "always," habit to that of "often."

In the Old Testament the manna fell each day, not just weekly.

> But the Lord said to Moses, I mean to rain down bread upon you from heaven. It will be for the people to go out and gather enough for their needs, day by day; and so I shall have a test, whether they are ready to follow My orders or not. EXODUS 16:4

God promised to give them bread every day, but on the day before the Sabbath there fell a double supply, for none would fall on the Sabbath. This daily gathering was a test of love and obedience. The Lord always has a test: in the desert, as well as the Garden. The first parents were tested by the prohibition to eat the fruit of the tree of the knowledge of good and evil. The obedience of the Israelites was tested by the command, not to gather on ordinary days more than enough for that day. All life is a probation. The inference suggested is that under the new dispensation, a daily faith in the Eucharist by a Holy Hour is a proof of our faithfulness.

The manna taught a daily lesson of dependence on God, and it played an important part in the spiritual education of Israel. It came not by fits or in starts, but in a regular way. What the Lord gave daily, we can return daily.

The priest should think of the practice of the daily Holy Hour as something to continue for his whole life. The children of Israel ate the manna for forty years (EXODUS 16:35) until they came to the borders of the land of Chanaan. The forty years represent the pilgrimage of life.

It spiritually implies that every priest should daily gather heavenly manna for his soul.

The daily Holy Hour gives us wisdom. Daily adoration of the Eucharist was not only implied in the type or prefigurement of the manna, but also in the way wisdom is given to those who fulfill the indicated conditions. Our Lord said that those who did His Will would know His doctrine. This means that knowledge is necessary in the beginning in order to love, but that later love deepens knowledge. The Book of Proverbs, speaking of the wisdom that is older than this world, summons the soul to an early and a daily watching:

> Love Me, and thou shalt earn My Love; wait early at my doors, and thou shalt gain access to Me. PROVERBS 8:17

The mind of the priest who lives close to the tabernacle door gains a special illumination. The priest's mind and heart are best guided when they seek the Eucharistic Lord at dawn. The young priest too is strengthened who begins his watch at the tabernacle door in the first days of his priesthood.

Another passage of the Book of Proverbs describing the daily search for wisdom at the feet of the Lord, is frequently applied to the Blessed Mother:

> I was at His side, a master-workman, my delight increasing with each day, as I made play before Him all the while; made play in this world of dust, with the sons of Adam for my playfellows. PROVERBS 8:30-32

It is certainly worthy to note that this delight is described not as spasmodic or hebdomadal, but day by day. "Blessed are they who listen to Me, keep vigil, day by day, at My threshold, watching till I open My doors" (PROVERBS 8:34).

Daily exigencies demand a daily Holy Hour. The Lord's Prayer reminds us that yesterday's food does not nourish us today:

> Give us this day our daily bread. MATTHEW 6:11

Vitamins cannot be stored up. Spiritual energy has to be renewed; today's strength must come from the Lord today. Thus the monotony of life is broken, and there comes to the priest new power for each day's apostolate. The Holy Hour each day also destroys in the priest forebodings and worries about the future. Kneeling before the Eucharistic

Lord, he receives the rations for each day's march, worrying not at all about the morrow.

The Holy Hour should be a daily event because our crosses are daily, not weekly.

> If any man has a mind to come My way, let him renounce self, and take up his cross daily, and follow Me. LUKE 9:23

Our children, our missions, our debts, our ulcers, our pet peeves—none of them come in octaves. Their horizontal and vertical weavings form for us a daily cross. These daily crosses will sour us, sear our souls and make us bitter, unless we turn them into crucifixes; and how can that be done except by seeing them as coming from the Lord? That we can do only if we are with Him. The Holy Hour may be a sacrifice, but the Lord does not make the week the unit of sacrifice. He tells us our cross is daily.

One moment in which Our Lord exulted, was when He exclaimed in the midst of His disciples, that "the hour has come" (JOHN 17:1). The word "hour" He used only in relation to His Passion and Death. It was for that time, that hour, that the clock of time had been set in motion; it was for that hour, that the world was created, the Lamb slain, the dust of earth prepared. To it the patriarchs looked forward; to it we look backwards. Without it there would be no Mass, no absolution, no pardon. Will the true priest shrink from such an hour, willing to be a priest but not a victim? To offer, but not to be offered? To be a grain of incense but unready to be consumed in the fire? Rather must he each day take up his cross of watching saying with the Sacred Heart, "the hour has come."

Each day, while it is in his power to do so, because there will be a day and an hour that will not be his over which he will have no control, for

> ... that day and that hour you speak of, they are known to nobody, not even to the angels in heaven, MARK 13:32

It is not conceivable that a priest who has sanctified each day with its Hour will ever be rejected by the Judge. If Our Lord puts the day and the hour together to make it a symbol of judgment, then shall not we put the day and the hour together unto salvation, unto joy and unto love?

> Blessed is that servant who is found doing this when his Lord comes. LUKE 12:43

It may be objected, that an hour a day taken out of priestly work, means that much less good can be done. The very same objection was made to Paul's imprisonment. Yet from his prison St. Paul wrote to the Philippians to reassure them that, even if not actively preaching, he was doing good. Each priest in prayer can say as Paul in prison:

> I hasten to assure you, brethren, that my circumstances here have only had the effect of spreading the gospel further; so widely has my imprisonment become known, in Christ's honour, throughout the praetorium and to all the world beyond. PHILIPPIANS 1:12

All the things that were happening to him there, were furthering the Gospel. We all stand committed to Christ under a spiritual obligation to maintain a clear and decisive loyalty, not only for our own sake, but for that of all whom our steadfastness and watchfulness will strengthen. The daily Holy Hour is a limitation on time, but a limitation that is conquered by a superior spiritual good. By human standards nothing could be a greater waste than Paul in prison, just when Christianity was beginning to conquer the world. The same might be said of a pastor beginning a parish. Nothing could seem more wasteful than to sacrifice an hour for the Lord. But God's ways are different. The apparent reverse and discomfiture of man is turned into the triumph of truth. Mercies are garnered and resources found hidden by the priest who knocks on the tabernacle door.

Every pastor may properly ask if he should not give more attention to the tabernacle and the altar in his church, in order to emphasize the Real Presence. An altar which looks like a table and a tabernacle which looks like a box, help little to bring home to the viewer the Divine Presence. Would not the tabernacle perhaps be enriched by restoring the two cherubs prescribed under the law of Moses?

> Make a throne, too, of pure gold, two and a half cubits long, one and a half cubits broad, and two cherubs of pure beaten gold for the two ends of this throne, one to stand on either side of it; with their wings outspread to cover the throne, guardians of the shrine. They are to face one another across the throne. And this throne is to be the covering of the ark, and the ark's contents, the written law I mean to give thee. Thence will I issue my commands; from that throne of mercy, between the two cherubs that stand over the ark and its records, My Voice shall come to thee, whenever I send word through thee to the sons of Israel. EXODUS 25:17-22

The exact shape of the temple cherubim was kept secret by the Jews. The first century Jewish historian, Josephus, noted that "no one is able to state or conjecture of what form the cherubim were." The two wings of both cherubs were both so advanced in front of them and elevated, as to overshadow the top of the Ark of the Covenant. Their faces were bent toward one another, so that they both looked downward toward the Ark, as if watching over it. The Cherubs are spoken of as the seraphs of the Temple vision in ISAIAS (6:2), and also as the guardians of Paradise (GENESIS 3:24). Their wings were also a protecting shade for those who took refuge under them in Divine Mercy (PSALM 90:1-3). St. Peter said later that the angels loved to gaze and meditate upon the mystery of Redemption—an obvious reference to the position of the angels over the Ark of the Covenant.

> And now the angels can satisfy their eager gaze.     I PETER 1:12

The top of the Ark, sometimes called the Mercy Seat, was blood-stained, blood being sprinkled on it once a year. As a figure of the New Testament, the faces of the angels are therefore Christ-ward hovering over the cross and the Blood of Redemption.

The angel guarding the Garden of Delight to prevent the return of our first parents (GENESIS 3:24), now seems a counterpart of those placed to watch over the prototype of the Eucharist, except that the latter grasp no sword in their hands. Zacharias seems to tell us where the sword will be found, namely, in the Heart of the Shepherd Who offered His life for His sheep.

> What wounds be these in Thy Clasped Hands? Thus wounded was I, He shall answer, in the house of my friends. Up, sword, and attack this Shepherd of Mine ... says the Lord of hosts.
>                                           ZACHARIAS 13:6,7

The pastor's primary concern should be the tabernacle, not the rectory, not the ego, but the Lord, not his comfort, but God's glory. Wall to wall carpeting in a rectory goes poorly with an altar and tabernacle looking like a house on stilts. Should not the King have a better home than his representative? First things first, as David sang:

> Never will I come beneath the roof of my house, or climb up into the bed that is strewn for me; never shall these eyes have sleep, these eyelids close, until I have found the Lord a home, the great God of

Jacob a dwelling-place. ... Let thy priests go clad in the vesture of innocence, thy faithful people cry aloud with rejoicing.

PSALM 131:3-5,9

Some can be forgetful of the Eucharist, as Saul was unmindful of the ark. But David contrasted his own comfortable home with the poverty of the ark: "Here am I dwelling in a house all of cedar, while God's ark has nothing better than curtains of hide about it!" (II KINGS 7:2). David could not allow the Eternal God to dwell in an unfitting abode. The Lord rebukes those who build fine houses while neglecting His Temple:

Listen, the Lord said (to them through the prophet Aggaeus), is it not too early yet for you to have roofs over your heads, and My temple in ruins?... To your own houses you run helter-skelter, and My temple in ruins! That is why the skies are forbidden to rain on you.

AGGAEUS 1:4,9,10

But while we build churches worthy of the Eucharistic Lord, we will give 10 per cent of the cost to build humble homes for the same Lord in Africa and Asia. He who makes the daily Hour will think of this, for he knows that his parish must be a victimhood, as it is also a royal priesthood.

There will come moments when the Hour is difficult—most often on vacation, but sometimes in great distress. What then gives the priest courage? This may be a time of darkness, as when the Greeks had come to Our Lord saying, "We wish to see Jesus," probably because of the majesty and beauty of appearance which they revered so highly as followers of Apollo. But He pointed to His torn and battered Self on a hill, and then added that only through the Cross in their lives will there ever be beauty of soul in the newness of life.

He then paused for a moment as His soul was seized by a frightening apprehension of the Passion and being "made sin," of being betrayed, crucified, and abandoned. Out from the depths of His Sacred Heart welled these words:

And now My soul is distressed. What am I to say? I will say, Father, save Me from undergoing this hour of trial; And yet I have only reached this hour of trial that I might undergo it.    JOHN 12:27

These are almost the same words that He used later on in the Garden of Gethsemane—words that are inexplicable except for the fact that He was bearing the burden of the world's sins. It was only natural for Our

Blessed Lord to undergo a struggle inasmuch as He was a perfect man. But it was not the physical sufferings alone which troubled Him; He, like Stoics, philosophers, men and women of all ages, could have been calm in the face of great physical trials. But His distress was directed less to the pain, and more to the consciousness of the sins of the world which demanded these sufferings. The more He loved those for whom He was the ransom, the more His anguish would increase, as it is the faults of friends rather than enemies which most disturb hearts!

He certainly was not asking to be saved from the Cross, since He reprimanded His Apostles for trying to dissuade Him. Two opposites were united in Him, separated only in utterance: the desire for release, and submission to the Father's will. By laying bare His own soul, He told the Greeks self-sacrifice was not easy. They were not to be fanatics about wanting to die, for nature does not want to crucify itself; but on the other hand, they were not to turn their eyes from the Cross in cowardly dread. In His own case, now as always, the most sorrowful moods pass into the most blissful; there is never the Cross without the Resurrection; the "Hour" in which evil has mastery passes quickly into the "Day" where God is Victor.

And as at that moment, there came to Him a Voice from heaven, so there will come to the priest-victim a voice from the tabernacle.

## Chapter 16

## The Eucharist and the Body of the Priest

ONE effect of devotion to the Blessed Sacrament is a more lofty concept of the body. Much devotional literature is infected with a Jansenistic emphasis on the vileness of the body. It is represented as a "worm" and "the enemy of the soul," as if the soul could be saved without the body. Such contempt of the body forgets that man is a person, a composite of body and soul. In announcing the Eucharist, Our Blessed Lord spoke of it in relationship not only to the soul but also to the body which will share in the Resurrection.

> And He Who sent Me would have Me keep without loss, and raise up at the last day, all He has entrusted to Me. JOHN 6:39

Job, looking forward to the Resurrection while peering at his ulcerous sores, cried out:

> This at least I know, that One lives on Who will vindicate me, rising up from the dust when the last day comes. Once more my skin shall clothe me, and in my flesh shall I have sight of God. JOB 19:25

Similarly, the Lord speaks to Ezechiel:

> Will you doubt, then, the Lord's power, when I open your graves and revive you? EZECHIEL 37:13

This idea St. Paul developed at length (I CORINTHIANS 15:35-44), relating it to the Resurrection of Christ. The characteristics the body will assume will reflect those of the soul. If one pours a blue liquid into a glass, the glass looks blue. If one pours red into it, it looks red. If the soul is black within, the body will take on a like corruption. If the soul has a participation of the Divine Nature, the body will take on the radiance of Heaven. As Dante wrote in his Paradiso:

Glorious and sanctified flesh shall be put on us again, making our persons more pleasing through being all complete.

What was said of Our Blessed Lord as He came into the world should, therefore, be applicable to every priest.

Thou hast endowed Me instead with a body.   HEBREWS 10:6

What this means is that God would not be satisfied with the sacrifices of the Old Law (ISAIAS 1:11-17; JEREMIAS 7:21-23; OSEE 6:6), but that the Body which His Son took was to be the instrument of His divinity. It was thanks to the Body Mary gave Him that He could suffer. It was thanks to the same Body that Divinity walked this earth in the form of man:

In Christ the whole plenitude of Deity is embodied, and dwells in Him.   COLOSSIANS 2:9

In the wilderness, Satan appealed to the appetite of hunger after Our Lord had been fasting. But Our Lord made reparation for all such sins by offering His Body a Sacrifice on the Cross.

It may be asked why the emphasis in the Epistle to the Hebrews is placed upon the body which Our Lord took, and not upon the soul, as it is in ISAIAS (53:10). It was probably to stress the fact that the offering of Christ was to be by death, which required a body; and also to draw attention to the need to confirm the New Covenant by blood as well as the Old. Hence, Our Lord the night of the Last Supper changed the wine into Blood, calling it the Blood of the New Testament or Covenant; but the Blood could not be given without the Body.

Another reason may be to remind us that Christ's Human Nature (LUKE 1:35) did not constitute a distinct person, but pertained to the Second Person of the Blessed Trinity. The mystery of the Incarnation is that the Godhead dwelt in the Body; the mystery of Atonement is hidden in One offering of the Body of Christ; the mystery of sanctification is that the Holy Spirit dwells in and sanctifies the Body too.

Since the great High Priest stressed His Body as the source of sanctification for souls, then must not the priest who touches that Body of Christ in the Eucharist, see his own body incorporated in that same Eucharistic Lord?

This respect for the body will manifest itself in two ways: by purity of body, and by a spirit of sacrifice. For all Christians, but particularly for the priest who touches the Body of Christ, the obligation to be pure is clear:

> But your bodies are not meant for debauchery, they are meant for the Lord, and the Lord claims your bodies.
> I CORINTHIANS 6:13

> Have you never been told that your bodies belong to the Body of Christ?
> I CORINTHIANS 6:15

The body does not belong to the priest; he is only its trustee. He is obligated to use it according to the great High Priest's direction:

> You are no longer your own masters. A great price was paid to ransom you; glorify God by making your bodies the shrines of His Presence.
> I CORINTHIANS 6:19,20

It is not only the soul that is the Lord's; it is the body as well. Limb by limb, the body of the priest must be the same as that which the Son of God took, which for us was crucified, and which is now in glory at the right Hand of God. Once the priest actually sees it as the temple of God, he has to show it a greater respect. The way he dresses, how he presents himself to callers at the door, how he keeps his body disciplined, free from excesses of eating and drinking, these and all his relations to his body, are guided by a sense of what is proper to the temple which is God's. The body of the priest is the temple wall, his senses are its gate, his mind the nave, his heart the altar-priest and his soul the holy of holies.

There will even be a resulting pleasantness about the priest's face. Builders of medieval cathedrals spent much time on the doors to make them as worthy as possible. The face is the doorway of the soul, and it should not be a discredit to the temple. A dreary and sad look, peevishness and discontent, little befit those whose bodies are temples of the Holy Ghost and who touch the Body and Blood of Christ each morning at the altar. In the face will shine forth the Divine Presence.

## Purity

The purity of the priest is therefore spiritual before it is physical; it is theological, before it is physiological; it is Eucharistic, before it is hygienic. Purity is a reflection of faith; it is attitude before an act; a reverent inwardness, not a biological intactness.

Purity in the priest is not the result of something he "gives up"; it is reverence for mystery—and the mystery is creativeness. God has allowed creatures to share in His creation. Husband and wife prolong it by begetting fruit to their marriage, an incarnation of their mutual love. The ambassador of Christ is called to another kind of creativeness—he begets souls. He consecrates; he baptizes; he recreates souls in the confessional. In all these acts his body shares. Therefore, he has not surrendered certain functions of the body; he has transformed them, merged them into the Divine plan of redemption.

Consecrated virginity is the highest form of sacral or sacrificial love; it seeks nothing for itself, it seeks only the will of the Beloved. The world makes the mistake of assuming that virginity is opposed to love, as poverty is opposed to wealth. Rather, virginity is related to love, as a university education is related to a grammar-school education. Virginity is the mountain peak of love, as marriage is its hill. Simply because virginity is often associated with asceticism and penance, it is thought to mean only the giving up of something. The true picture is that asceticism is only the fence around the garden of virginity. A guard is always stationed around the crown jewels of England, not because England loves soldiers, but because it needs them to protect the jewels. So, the more precious the love, the greater the precautions to guard it. Since no love is more precious than that of the soul in love with God, the soul must ever be on the watch against lions who would overrun its green pastures. The grating in a Carmelite monastery is not to keep the sisters in, but to keep the world out.

As virginity is not the opposite of love, neither is it the opposite of generation. The Christian blessing on virginity did not abrogate the order of Genesis (1:22) to "increase and multiply," for virginity has its own generation. Mary's consecration of virginity was unique in that it resulted in a physical generation—the Word made Flesh. But it also set the pattern for spiritual generation, for she also begot the Christlike. In like manner, virgin love must not be barren. Rather must it say with Paul:

It was I that begot you in Jesus Christ...         I CORINTHIANS 4:15

When the woman in the crowd praised the Mother of Our Lord, He turned the praise to spiritual motherhood, and said that she who did the will of His Father in heaven was His mother. Relationship was here lifted from the level of the flesh, to the spirit. To beget a body is blessed; to save a soul, is more blessed, for such is the Father's Will. An idea thus can transform a vital function, not by condemning it to sterility, but by elevating it to a new fecundity of the Spirit. There would, therefore, seem to be implied in all virginity the necessity of apostleship and the begetting of souls for Christ. God, Who hated the man who buried his talent in the ground, will certainly despise those who pledge themselves to be in love with Him, and yet show no new life—converts or souls saved through contemplation.

## INSTRUCTING YOUTHS ON PURITY

In discussing with others the dignity of the body, the true priest will not limit himself to the routine repetition of the traditional prohibitions and the equal routine advice to imitate the Blessed Mother. The "don't" technique is that it makes the young wonder why their instinct of procreation should be so strong, if it has evil associated with it. On the other hand, the young wonder how the Blessed Mother is to be imitated. The ideal is so high and abstract as easily to seem impractical to the young.

As pure water is more than the absence of impurities, as a pure diamond is more than the absence of carbon, and as pure food is more than the absence of poison, so purity is more than the absence of voluptuousness. Because one defends the fortress against the enemy, it does not follow that the fortress itself contains no treasure.

Youth should be told by the priest, that every mystery contains two elements; one visible, the other invisible. For example, in Baptism, water is the visible element and the regenerating grace of the Christ is the invisible element. Sex is a mystery, too, because it has these two characteristics. Sex is something known to everyone, and yet it is something hidden from everyone. The known element is that everyone is either male or female. The invisible, hidden, mysterious element in sex is its capacity for creativeness, a sharing in some way of the creative power by which God made the world and all that is in it. As God's love is the creative principle of the universe, so God willed that the love of man and woman should be the creative principle of the family. This power of human beings to beget one made in their image and likeness partakes of God's creative power.

The young must be made to understand that the torch of life placed by God in their hands, must burn controlled unto the purpose and destiny set by reason and the God of reason. The mystery of creativeness which God put in them is surrounded with awe. A special reverence does envelop the power to be co-creators with God in the making of human life. It is this hidden element which in a special way belongs to God, as does the grace of God in the sacraments. Those who speak of sex alone concentrate on the physical or visible element, forgetting the spiritual or invisible mystery of creativeness. Humans in the sacraments supply the act, the bread, the water, and the words; God supplies the grace, the mystery. In the sacred act of creating life, man and woman supply the unity of the flesh; God supplies the soul and mystery. Such is the mystery of sex as the priest should explain it.

In youth, this awesomeness before the mystery manifests itself in a woman's timidity, which makes her shrink from a precocious or too ready surrender of her secret. In a man, the mystery is revealed in chivalry to women, which is something more than a mere sense of awe in the presence of the unknown. Because, too, of the reverence which envelops this mysterious power which came from God, mankind has always felt that it is to be used only by a special sanction from God and under certain relationships. That is why, traditionally, marriage has been associated with religious rites, to bear witness to the fact that the power of sex which comes from God, should have its use approved by God because it is destined to fulfill His creative designs.

Certain powers may properly be used only in certain relationships. What is lawful in one relationship is not lawful in another. A man can kill another man in a just war, but not in his private capacity as a citizen. A policeman can arrest someone as a duly appointed guardian of the law, but not otherwise. So, too, the "creativeness" of man and woman is lawful under certain relationships sanctioned by God, but not apart from that mysterious relationship called marriage.

Purity is now seen not as something negative, but positive. Purity is such a reverence for the mystery of creativeness, that it will suffer no schism between the use of the power to beget and its Divinely ordained purpose. The pure would no more think of isolating the capacity to share in God's creativeness, than they would think of using a knife for other than its humanly ordained purpose. Those things which God has joined together, the pure would never separate. Never would they use the material sign to dishonor the holy inner mystery, as they would not use the Bread of the altar, consecrated to God, to nourish the body alone.

Purity, then, is not mere physical intactness. The priest will tell the girl it is a firm resolve never to use the power until God sends her a husband. In the boy, it is a steadfast desire to wait upon God's will that he have a wife. In this sense true marriages are made in heaven; for when heaven makes them, body and soul do not pull in opposite directions. The physical aspect, known as sex, is not alienated from the invisible, mysterious aspect which is revealed only to the one willed by God to share in God's creativeness, in God's own time.

Youth will see that experience bears out the definition of purity as reverence for mystery. No one is scandalized at seeing people eat in public, or read in buses, or listen to music on the street, but they are shocked at dirty shows, foul books, or undue manifestations of affection in public. It is not because youths are prudes, nor because they are educated in Catholic schools, nor because they have not yet come under the "liberating" influence of a Freud, but because these things involve aspects of a mystery so deep, so personal, so incommunicable that they must not be vulgarized.

We like to see the American flag flying over a neighbor's head, but we do not want to see it under his feet. There is a mystery in that flag; it is more than cloth; it stands for the unseen, the spiritual, for love and devotion to country. The pure are shocked at the impure, because of the prostitution of the sacred; it makes the reverent, irreverent. The essence of obscenity is the turning of the inner mystery into a jest. Given a hidden presence of a God-gift in every person, as there is a hidden Divine Presence in the Bread of the altar, each person becomes a host. As one discerns the Bread of Angels under the sign of bread, so one discerns a soul and potential co-partnership with God's creativeness under a body. As the Catholic craves the embrace of Christ in the Sacrament because he first learned to love Him as a Person, so he reveres the body because he first learned to revere the soul. This is adoration in the first instance, and purity in the second.

In dealing with adults, the priest who has given his body to the Lord will explain to them the meaning of "two in one flesh." Not only in marriage, but outside marriage, every such act creates oneness and something that endures through eternity. There is no such thing as drinking the water and forgetting the glass:

> Am I to take what belongs to Christ and make it one with a harlot? God forbid. Or did you never hear that the man who unites himself to a harlot becomes one body with her? The two, we are told, will become one flesh. I CORINTHIANS 6:15,16

Each person possesses a gift which can be given only once, and received only once. In the unity of flesh he makes her a woman; she makes him a man. They may enjoy the gift many times, but once given, it can never be taken back, either in man or in woman. It is not just a physiological experience, but the unraveling of a mystery. As one can pass just once from ignorance to knowledge concerning a given fact or axiom, for example, the principle of contradiction, so one can pass just once from incompleteness to the full knowledge of self which the partner brings. Once that border line is crossed, neither belongs wholly to self. Their reciprocity has created dependence; the riddle has been solved, the mystery has been revealed; the dual have become a unity, either sanctioned by God or in defiance of His Will.

St. Paul also teaches a lesson the priest can communicate about the body.

> Any other sin a man commits, leaves the body untouched, but the fornicator is committing a crime against his own body.
> I CORINTHIANS 6:17,18

Drunkenness and gluttony are sins done in and by the body, are sins committed through abuse of the body; but they are still outside the body, that is, introduced from without. Fornication is the alienation of a body which is the Lord's and making it the body of someone else; it is the surrendering of the property of the Lord to another. It is a sin against a man's own body in his very nature.

After presenting to others the positive side of purity, then the ideal of the Blessed Mother becomes clear. She is the ideal love we see beyond all creature love, a love to which we instinctively turn when flesh-love fails. She is the ideal that God had in His Heart from all eternity—the Lady Whom He would call our Blessed "Mother." She is the one every man loves when he loves a woman—whether he knows it or not. She is what every woman wants to be, when she looks at herself. She is the woman every man marries in his ideal; she is hidden as an ideal in the discontent of every woman with the carnal aggressiveness of man; she is the secret desire every woman has to be honored and fostered. To know a woman in the hour of possession, a man must first have loved her in the exquisite hour of a dream. To be loved by man in the hour of possession, a woman must first want to be loved, fostered, and honored as an ideal. Beyond all human love is another love; that "other" is the image of the possible. It is that "possible" that each man and each woman loves when they love one another. That "possible" becomes real in the blueprint love of the One beloved of God before the world was made, and in that other love bringing Christ to us and us to Christ: Mary, the Immaculate Virgin, the Mother of God.

## The Priest's Body:
## A Living Sacrifice

The Eucharistic priest lives out Paul's words:

> I appeal to you by God's mercy to offer up your bodies as a living sacrifice, consecrated to God and worthy of His acceptance.
> ROMANS 12:1

St. Paul may have had in mind some of the sacrifices of the Old Law. The priest, having killed the animal, cut it open and took out all that was unclean. He then washed it, and consumed it on the altar with fire, before the Lord. Our great High Priest would have us wash externally from our guilt in His Blood, and then laying us open, would remove all that was corrupt within us by the washing and regeneration of the Holy Spirit, that we may be laid as holy sacrifices upon the altar and consumed before the Lord.

"Living" may be here understood as opposed to sensual lust which has its source in the body and against which the Apostle later complained (ROMANS 7:24). "Living" also may mean the continual sacrifice. The Greek word used in this text is the usual one for presenting sacrificial animals at the altar, but here our bodies are specified. The Jew had to present to God the body of an animal, the priest has to present his own body. Under the Law the animal was sacrificed; in the Mass, the priest is "sacrificed" and made a victim.

When the body is offered to God as a "reasonable sacrifice," the earth is trod not as a golf course, or a market, but as a temple. If our sole sentiment toward our great High Priest was a religious feeling not expressed in an appropriate form of sacrifice, our feelings would eventually die out. Expressing our priestly lives in sacrifice prevents piety from becoming emotional. Nothing gives so much power to the words of the priest in the pulpit, the classroom, or the home, as his self-denials. Nothing in this world is of value until offered or dedicated to a higher end. What is the worth of land, unless we do something with it? What is the worth of our body, unless it is spent for Christ?

The Sacrifice of the Mass which we offer is performed without any satisfaction to the senses. But when does it become sensible, tangible, lived-out, concrete? When the morning sacrifice is made visible in the living sacrifice of his body. Any excesses which dull the spirit and make it unfit to serve Him, any absorbing care about outward things which checks the growth of Christ in us, such things erect a barrier against the power of the priest to sanctify others ex opere operantis. There is no such thing as a "six o'clock Mass." The Mass is continuous—a "living sacrifice." What is mystically presented in the morning Mass must be bodily presented throughout the day.

Having died with Christ on the altar we continue the death in instructing converts, in burying the dead, in consoling the sick, in almsgiving for the Propagation of the Faith. No one will despise the sacrifices which the body ought to make, if the flame sacrifice is kindled at the Consecration.

The continuing sacrifice of the priest is of the heart and mind in thanksgiving (ROMANS 15:16; HEBREWS 13:15); the sacrifice of good deeds (HEBREWS 13:16); the sacrifice of broken hearts and contrite spirits (PSALM 50:17); the sacrifice of the whole man and the dedication of himself to God (I PETER 2:15; ROMANS 12:1; PHILIPPIANS 2:7).

That the motivation for our living sacrifice is the Eucharist is clear:

So it is the Lord's Death that you are heralding, whenever you eat this Bread and drink this Cup, until He comes.
I CORINTHIANS 11:26

The Eucharist is thus not only an incorporation to the Life of Christ, it is also an incorporation to His Death. Our Mass not only looks back to the first coming of Christ, but forward to His second coming. The Mass is also a mystical representation of the Death of Christ through the separate consecration of the Bread and Wine, typifying the separation of the Blood from the Body of Christ. This mystical and unbloody representation of the Death of Christ, commits us to the discipline and mortification of the body when we leave the altar. As Christ's Death was not a bare dying, but a death with high and glorious ends, so our re-enactment of it is not a mere historical recalling, but a practical living-out of the Cross. Without the prolongation of sacrifice there is only a speculative remembrance, such as one might have of a motion picture, but without a stirring up of mutual love and gratitude.

A decline in reverence in saying the Mass is going to be followed by a decline of sacrifice in the priestly activities of the day. The lazy priest will always work "hardest" to finish his Mass as quickly as possible. He does not want the trumpet call to sacrifice to be loud or too clear. But the saintly priest knows that wheat has to pass through a mill to become fit for the altar and grapes have to be crushed in the wine-press; so too must he be a victim, in order to offer worthily the sacrifice which proclaims and re-enacts the Death of Christ.

Monsignor Ronald Knox bids us reflect on our victimhood as we say in thanksgiving: "This is His Body which is being given for me; this is His Blood which is being shed for me—after all this lapse of time, He still comes to me in the posture of a Victim. And He wants to impress something of Himself on me; I am to be the wax, He the signet ring. Something, then, of the Victim He wants to see in me; does not the Imitation say it is up to every Christian to lead a dying life? Not for me, perhaps, to enter very deeply into the dispositions of my Crucified Savior, but to be rather more humble, when I am thwarted; rather more resigned, when things go wrong with me; rather less anxious to make a chart of my own spiritual progress, more ready to let Him do in me what He wants to do, without letting me know about it! If I could only die a little to the world, to my wishes, to myself; be patient and wait for His coming, content to herald His Death by dying with Him!"

Our struggle as priests then is not to become angelic and to live as if we had no body, but to become more Christ-like.

> This is my earnest longing and my hope ... that this body of mine will do Christ honour....  PHILIPPIANS 1:20

At the end of a busy day when fatigue sets in, because of all we did for Christ's sake, we can read in our body the traces of crucifixion: "We carry about continually in our bodies the dying state of Jesus, so that the living power of Jesus may be manifested in our bodies too" (II CORINTHIANS 4:10).

In the morning Mass we "announced the death of the Lord"; in parish, home, confessional and everywhere we prolonged it into exhaustion, knowing that such multiple "deaths" for others are the condition of the glorious resurrection of that same body. Some spiritual writers speak of the imitation of Christ as if it were only in the soul. St. Paul insists that the death of Christ is "manifested in our bodies." St. Paul uses two words for body, one is "sarks," which stands for man in his absence from God; the other is "soma," which stands for man in the solidarity of creation and made for God. The first is crucified for Christ's sake, the other is glorified for His sake. The "sarks" cannot inherit the Kingdom of God (I CORINTHIANS 15:50), but the "soma" can. Since the "body is for the Lord," then our body is not our own. The priest is not his own. "You are no longer your own masters. A great price was paid to ransom you; glorify God by making your bodies the shrines of His Presence" (I CORINTHIANS 6:19,20).

## Chapter 17

## The Priest and His Mother

EVERY priest has two mothers: one in the flesh, the other in the spirit. Much more is known about the former; much more has been written about the latter. There is no more rivalry between these two mothers than between the priest's earthly father and his heavenly Father. Often, one of the first acts of the mother of the flesh was to lay her son at the feet of the Blessed Mother, as did the author's mother, to symbolize the surrender of filiation. How many were the secret conferences between these two mothers in which the mother in the flesh begged the mother in Christ to have him one day hold a host and a chalice in his hands?

If it is true (as the Fathers say) that Mary conceived in her heart before she conceived in her womb, may not the same be said of the mothers of many priests? Some priests have been called at the eleventh hour, but many mothers may paraphrase the book of Proverbs and say: "The son was not as yet, and I conceived a priest." As God consulted with Mary to ask if she would give Him a human nature, so He often consults with the mother of a priest to ask her consent to the continuation of His priesthood. When the mother's dream is realized, what thoughts pass through the soul of her son, now a priest?

The priest, first, gives up the earthly love of a woman, as Mary gave up the earthly love of a man. His "I have no knowledge of woman" balances her "I have no knowledge of man" (LUKE 1:34). The expression in Scripture means carnal union, as in GENESIS 4:1 ("Adam had knowledge of his wife, Eve, and she conceived"). From the very beginning, the priest knows that love is simultaneously an affirmation and a negation. Every protestation of love is a limitation on every competing love. True love by its nature imposes restrictions. The married man imposes limitations on himself in respect to all women, but one. The priest admits of no exception, and he does so in the exercise of a perfect freedom. In the Incarnation, God established a beachhead in humanity, through the free choice of a woman; now Our Lord finds an extension of His priesthood in the free act of a priest. He waits upon our consent.

Our earthly mother willed in general to conceive, but when it would be realized was unforeseen and unpredictable. Not so the priest's surrender at ordination. His surrender is like Mary's. She willed her Son and she conceived. So the priest willed to be God's, and he can identify the day and the hour. The more he serves that surrender, the more he knows that only the Christ-fettered are free.

But a priest cannot live without love. The Blessed Mother knew there could be no conception without fire and passion. How could there be a son, since she had "no knowledge of man?" Heaven had the answer. Certainly, there would be fire and passion and love, but that fire and that love would be the Holy Spirit.

Neither can the priest live without love. If there is to be a generation of souls, and if he is to be a "father" begetting others in Christ, there must be love. That love is the same as Mary's; the File and Passion of the Holy Spirit overshadowing him. As in her, were united virginity and motherhood, so in the priest, there is to be the unity of virginity and fatherhood. This is not barrenness but fecundity, not the absence of love, but its ecstasy.

The next stage of the priest's love is service.

> So it is that the Son of Man did not come to have service done Him; He came to serve others ... MARK 10:45

As Mary's spiritual motherhood was not a privilege apart from humanity, so neither is the spiritual fatherhood of the priest. Nothing so provokes the service of others, as a sense of one's unworthiness when visited by the grace of God. Mary hastening over the hills in the Visitation, reveals how she, the handmaid of the Lord, became the handmaid of Elizabeth. She is now the example to the priest that the Christ within him must prompt dedication to "all those who are our friends in the common faith" (TITUS 3:15), and to all mankind. As Mary's visit sanctified John the Baptist, so the visit of the priest-victim will always sanctify souls.

Every sick call of the priest will be to him the mystery of the Visitation all over again. Carrying the Blessed Sacrament to his breast, in auto or on foot, makes him another Mary carrying the cloistered Christ within her pure body. No delays on sick calls, no tarrying while the family worries, but like Mary, the priest "hastens"—for nothing demands speed as much as the need of others. The more Christ-possessed the priest is, the more likely he is to hear from those who open the door to him who carries the Blessed Sacrament: "Why, as soon as ever the voice of thy greeting sounded in my ears" (LUKE 1:44), my heart leaped with joy. The holy priest inspires Magnificats in every visit to the sick, as the families of the parish say to him: "How have I deserved to be thus visited" (LUKE 1:43) by another Christ?

The priest has a deep love of Mary not only in his better moments, but even in his failings. He trusts in her intercession to combat his weakness. Then especially, he looks to her for special attention, knowing that the child who falls most often is apt to get most of the mother's kisses.

If ever the Simon-nature dominates him; if there come moments when, like Demas, he "has fallen in love with this present world" (II TIMOTHY 4:9); if he becomes known in the parish as a "golfer" or a "swell guy" or "one of the boys" rather than as a good priest, then he knows where he must go to help him find his Lord again. He must go to Mary. She, too, "lost" Christ. That physical loss was a symbol of the spiritual loss which the priest sustains in losing his first ardor. Mary's Heart is pierced with a sword at the loss of every alter Christus. But she also is in search of them. To have God and then lose Him is a greater loss than never to have Him. Mary and the weak priest suffer together, but in different ways. She felt the darkness of losing God, when the boy Jesus stayed on in Jerusalem unknown to her (LUKE 2:43). It was at this moment that Mary became the Refuge of Sinners. She understood what sin is; for she, a creature, experimentally lost the Creator. She lost the Child only in the mystical darkness of soul, while the priest, who falls, feels the moral blackness of an ungrateful heart. But Mary found the Child. To all bishops and priests through the ages, she gave the lesson that we are not to wait for the lost to come back; we must go in search of them. And her intercession will help in the most desperate cases, as we say with Augustine to her: "What all the other saints can do with your help, you alone can do without them."

At the Marriage Feast of Cana, Mary teaches the priest how much he belongs to the Church, and so little to himself. Up to this time and during the feast she is called "Jesus' mother" (JOHN 2:1,3). At its end, however, she becomes "woman" (JOHN 2:4). What happens here is like what happened when Christ was lost for three days. Mary had then said: "Thy father and I" (LUKE 2:48), and Our Lord immediately reminded her of His Heavenly Father, recalling the mystery of the Annunciation, and the fact that Joseph was only the putative father.

From that moment, Joseph disappears from Sacred Scripture; he is never seen again. At Cana, "Jesus' mother" asks for a manifestation of His Messianic role and Divinity; Our Lord tells her that the moment He works a miracle and begins His Public Life, He goes to His "Hour," the Cross. Once the "water blushes into wine" at the Divine look, she becomes "woman." As Joseph disappears at the Temple, so Mary as the Mother of Jesus, disappears to become the Mother of all whom He will redeem. She never speaks again in Sacred Scripture. She has spoken her last words, and what a beautiful valedictory they were:

Do whatever He tells you. JOHN 2:5

She now is the "universal Mother," the woman with the seed more numerous than the sands of the sea.

Through Mary's example and influence, there comes a moment in the priest's life when he realizes he does not belong to his family, his parish, his diocese, his country. He belongs to the missions and to the world; he belongs to humanity. The closer the priest gets to the mission of Christ, the more he loves every soul in the world. As Mary "mothered" all men at the Cross, so the priest "fathers" them. No bishop is consecrated for a diocese; he is consecrated for the world. He is assigned to a diocese only for jurisdictional reasons. The priest is not ordained for a diocese; he is ordained for souls. "He does not belong to our parish" is a valid jurisdictional reason for not handling a marriage case, but it is no valid reason for not considering the petitioner as a member of Christ, and therefore, entitled to the milk of human kindness. St. Thomas Aquinas tells us that Mary at the Annunciation spoke in the name of all humanity. At Cana she is given to humanity; at the foot of the Cross, she is confirmed as the mother of mankind.

Devotion to Mary keeps the priest from being the hireling, a hired servant with fixed hours, assigned duties, parish limits, and no lost sheep. There is no "on duty" for a priest. He is "on love" everywhere—on the golf course, in the airplane, in a restaurant, in a hospital. Nothing human is foreign to him. Every soul is either a potential convert, or a potential saint.

In the Passion, Mary teaches compassion to the priest. The saints least indulgent to themselves are the most indulgent to others. But the priest who leads an easy, unmortified life cannot speak the language of the affrighted. Self-raised above need, he cannot bend to console; or if he does, it is with condescension, not compassion. The good priest, on the contrary, sees Mary in the dust of human lives; she lives amidst terror, brain-washings, false accusations, libels, and all the other instruments of terror. The Immaculate is with the maculate, the sinless with the sinner. She bears neither rancor nor bitterness, but only pity, pity that they do not see or know how loving is that Love they are sending to death.

In her purity, Mary is on the mountaintop; in her compassion she is amidst curses, death cells, hangmen, executioners, and blood. A man may become so obsessed with his sinfulness as to refuse to cry to God for forgiveness, but he cannot shrink from invoking the intercession of God's Mother. If the good Holy Mother Mary, who deserved to be spared evil, could nevertheless, in the special Providence of her Son, have a cross, then how shall we, who deserve not to be ranked with her, expect to escape our meeting with a cross? "What have I done to deserve this?" is a cry of pride. What did Jesus do? What did Mary do? Let there be no complaint against God for sending a cross; let there only be wisdom enough to see that Mary is there making it lighter, making it sweeter, making it hers!

Every woe, every wound in the world is ours as a priest. So long as there is an innocent priest in a Siberian jail, I am in prison. So long as a missionary is without a roof over his head, I am homeless. Sharing with these there must be, if there is to be compassion. The priest will never sit and watch the world's enmity against Our Lord, knowing that Mary's co-operation was so real and active that she stood at the foot of the Cross. In every representation of the Crucifixion, the Magdalen is prostrate; she is almost always at the feet of Our Lord. But Mary is standing.

Finally, the death of the priest. Millions of times he has asked Mary to pray for him at the "hour of my death." It is to be hoped that he offered Mass to her once a week during his entire priesthood. Daily, he announced the death of the Lord in the Eucharist (I CORINTHIANS 11:26), and now he comes not to the end of his priesthood, for that never ends: "A priest forever in the line of Melchisedech" (PSALM 109:4; HEBREWS 5:6). But it is the end of probation. This is the one moment the priest looks most to Mary for her intercession. He sees the Crucifix before him and can hear once again His Lord saying to him, "This is thy mother" (JOHN 19:27). Death to those who are saved is infancy again, a second birth. That is why it is called natalitia or birthday in the liturgy. The world celebrates birthdays when men are born in the flesh; the Church, when souls are born in the Spirit.

But the priest knows that Mary is in labor, for he sees now all his failings in the white light of eternity. At Bethlehem, when she brought forth the High Priest there was no travail, but at the Cross she underwent the pangs of childbirth in becoming the woman or universal mother. The representative of her Divine Son now senses how much extra grief he caused her. But she will not surrender the burden, as she did not refuse John, who was indeed a poor exchange for Jesus.

Two words fall from the priest's lips repeatedly: "Jesus" and "Mary." He had always been a priest—now, at last, in death he is also a victim. Twice, the great High Priest had been a Victim, on entering the world, and on leaving it. Mary was at both altars, at Bethlehem and at Calvary. Mary was at the priest's altar on the day of ordination, too, and now she is with him at the hour of his death.

Mother of priests! Two loves were always in her life: the love of the Life of her Son, the love of the Death of her Son. The same two loves she bears to every priest. In the Incarnation she was the connecting link between Israel and Christ; at the Cross and Pentecost, she was the connecting link between Christ and His Church. Now she is the link between the priest-victim and the One who is always "making intercession for us in heaven."

Every priest at death wants to be laid in Mary's arms as was the Christ, Whose representative he is. As Mary said after the Crucifixion over her Son Who was laid in her arms: "This is my Body," so she will say at the death of every priest: "This is my body, my victim, my host. As I formed Jesus the Priest in my womb to be a Victim, so I helped Jesus, Sacerdos-Hostia, to grow in Thee."

Is it any wonder, then, that she is the Woman in every priest's life. No priest is his own. He belongs to the Mother of Jesus, once and always the Priest-Victim.

www.ingramcontent.com/pod-product-compliance
Lightning Source LLC
Chambersburg PA
CBHW020514080526
**44583CB00013B/593**